**lonely planet**

# Hong Kong

## Damian Harper
## Nicko Goncharoff

**Hong Kong**

**2nd edition**

**Published by**
**Lonely Planet Publications**
Head Office: PO Box 617, Hawthorn, Vic 3122, Australia
Branches: 150 Linden St, Oakland, CA 94607, USA
10a Spring Place, London NW5 3BH, UK
1 rue du Dahomey, 75011 Paris, France

**Printed by**
Colorcraft Ltd, Hong Kong

**Photographs by**

| | | |
|---|---|---|
| Glenn Beanland | Ted Carroll | Marie Cambon |
| Juliet Coombe/La Belle Aurore | Nicko Goncharoff | Hong Kong Dolphinwatch |
| Richard I'Anson | The Peninsula Hotel | Tony Wheeler |

Front cover: Neon reflections from Hong Kong's streetscape (Richard I'Anson)

**First Published**
September 1996

**This Edition**
August 1998

**Although the authors and publisher have tried to make the information as accurate as possible, they accept no responsibility for any loss, injury or inconvenience sustained by any person using this book.**

National Library of Australia Cataloguing in Publication Data

Harper, Damien.
Hong Kong.

2nd ed.
Includes index.
ISBN 0 86442 583 X.

1. Hong Kong (China) - Guidebooks. I. Title.

915.125045

text & maps © Lonely Planet 1998
photos © photographers as indicated 1998

## Damian Harper

After six years in the book trade (London, Paris and Dublin), Damian threw it in to study Chinese at London's School of Oriental and African Studies. He spent a year in Beijing as part of his course and there he met his Qingda-born wife, Dai Min. After graduating Damian fled England for Hong Kong and found temporary work with Sotheby's in the ceramics department. After working for a period as an editor and translator, Damian and his wife packed their bags and hit the road to help update the 6th edition of the *China* guide. He is a regular returnee to Hong Kong.

## Nicko Goncharoff

The author of the first edition of this guidebook, Nicko grew up in New York, found his true home while attending university in Colorado, and promptly left it upon graduating for a brief stint in Asia. He ended up staying for eight years, first living in Taiwan for nearly three years and then in Hong Kong. After writing for several magazines and a news wire service, Nicko joined the Lonely Planet team to work on the 5th edition of *China*. He now calls San Francisco his home, even if he's not there that often.

### From Damian

A host of people provided inspiration and invaluable help in the research and preparation of this book. First and foremost, hugs and kisses for my wife Dai Min for her unruffled good humour and patience. John Silver deserves special mention for his generosity. Katherine and Josephine Ratcliffe came up with all sorts of fine suggestions, and the use of a sterling camera. Peggy Yu came up trumps with much-needed material; cheers also to Gregor Prattley – the beer's on me when I make it to Japan. Thanks also to Toshihiro and Rie Mori, the BBC and all those I ran into who helped show the way and opened many doors.

### From the Publisher

This book was edited in Lonely Planet's Melbourne office by Richard Plunkett, with assistance from Justin Flynn and Peter Cruttenden. Leanne Peake coordinated the mapping, ably assisted by Chris Thomas. The design and layout was handled by design dynamo Glenn van der Knijff.

Katrina Browning, Miriam Cannell and Martin Hughes chipped in with the proofreading, and Isabelle Young cast an expert eye over the health section. Kerrie Williams helped out with the indexing. Thanks to Quentin Frayne for slaving away at the Chinese language sections, and to Charles Qin for assisting with the Chinese script at short notice. Trudi Canavan, Rachael Black and Mick Weldon provided the illustrations. Thanks to Michelle Glynn and Isabelle for doing a last-minute check of the maps, David Kemp for designing the cover and to Adam McCrow for the back-cover cartography.

### Warning & Request

Things change – prices go up, schedules change, good places go bad and bad places go bankrupt – nothing stays the same. So, if you find things better or worse, recently opened or long since closed, please tell us and help make the next edition of this guide even more accurate and useful.

We value all of the feedback we receive from travellers to Hong Kong. Julie Young coordinates a small team who read and acknowledge every letter, postcard and email, and ensure that every morsel of information finds its way to the appropriate authors, editors and publishers.

Everyone who writes to us will find their name in the next edition of the appropriate guide and will also receive a free subscription to our quarterly newsletter, *Planet Talk*. The very best contributions will be rewarded with a free Lonely Planet guide.

Excerpts from your correspondence may appear in new editions of this guide; in our newsletter, *Planet Talk*; or in updates on our Web site – so please let us know if you don't want your letter published.

## Thanks

Many thanks to the travellers who used the last edition of this guide and wrote to us with helpful hints, useful advice and interesting anecdotes. Your names follow:

Stephen Austin, N Boyer, Richard Brooks, Ward & Susan Browne, T Chaslain, John Davidson, EJ Deal, Rita Fan, Melissa Foo, Java Foxon, Caroline Gibson, Richard Graves, Rick Graves, Jane Hall, Daniel Hammond, DR Hood, Michelle House, MA Johnson, Andrew Jones, Tony Leung, Don McClellan, Tracey Merrie, Phillip Miller, Paul Murdock, Elja Narhi, Brian Nomi, Claude Payen, Signe Philip, Peter Rees, Kyla Reynolds, Anke Richmann, Andreas Rogall, Robert Schmitz, Lee Shackleford, Harry Shubart, Liz Storrar, Michelle Stoupe, Monica Thom, S Vriend, Janet Walker and Jennifer Whyte.

# Contents

*Dec. 22 to Jan. 3, 2002*
*Harbour Plaza 2187 8888*

# Introduction

Despite being thrown back into the arms of China, Hong Kong post-1997 is still that unique meeting place of east and west, of magic, charm and chatter that has fired the imaginations of travellers, traders, fortune-seekers, refugees and sailors for 150 years.

The final lowering of the Union Jack over Hong Kong was a moment the world had awaited with apprehension. The saga had reached a watershed of sorts; Hong Kong or 'Heung Gong' (literally 'Fragrant Harbour') had become the Hong Kong Special Administrative Region (Hong Kong SAR).

What has changed? Not the dynamism of this harbour city; Hong Kong is still aglow with vibrant self-appreciation. The financial heartland of Central on Hong Kong Island still glitters. The boundless energy of the Hong Kong people remains unsapped as they take the future in their stride. This energy translates into a barrage of sights, sounds and smells. The city streets surge with activity, crowds squeeze aboard trams that ferry them home while packed boats bounce over the waters of Victoria Harbour, leaving behind a backdrop of dazzling neon and intoxicating colour. The constant clatter of commerce hardly pauses, and all around can be heard the most garrulous tongue on earth: Cantonese. Those people on business come and go, occasionally sidling into wayside temples to cast prayers at the feet of the gods and divine the future.

Churches, temples and colonial buildings lie in the shadow of neighbouring skyscrapers. Busy thoroughfares yield to small alleys that lead to flourishing street markets. The early morning hours see the parks alive with the timeless and measured movements of *taijiquan* (tai chi) practitioners. And permeating all this hustle and bustle linger the fragrances of the city. The aromas of Cantonese cooking from countless kitchens hang over the streets, mixing with the scent of

Hong Kong circa 1860, building its future on maritime trade and a magnificent harbour.

dried fish and herbs while the perfumed smoke of incense beckons you into the hidden portal of a roadside shrine.

Hong Kong at night offers yet more. Lovers of good food will be spoilt for choice in the city's eclectic eateries. Hong Kong's bars offer everything from alternative to chic to the refined. And to see the early hours in, Hong Kong's nightclubs offer an energetic fusion of rhythms and moods.

If you want to escape the city, the Peak offers mist-wreathed walks along nature trails. And if you really want to visit an almost unspoiled Eden of lush green fields and banana trees, visit Lamma Island for an unexpected side to Hong Kong. The New Territories and other outlying islands also offer bracing walks among dramatic and spectacular countryside.

Now is the time to visit Hong Kong. Hotel prices and airfares have fallen considerably and there are some excellent deals out there. Good news for all of you who couldn't make it on the night of 30 June 1997.

# Facts about Hong Kong

## HISTORY

When Hong Kong was returned to China in 1997, it had existed as a British colony for 156 years – not a long history for what is today one of the world's great cities. But the shortness of that time line is part of Hong Kong's mystique. Stand amid the forest of skyscrapers in Central and try to imagine the 'barren island with hardly a house upon it' that British naval officers surveyed as they hoisted the Union Jack over the empire's newest addition in 1841. It is difficult to picture, for in its headlong dash toward ever-greater prosperity, Hong Kong has worked hard to bury its humble origins.

### Neglected Imperial Outpost

Clinging to the southern edge of Guangdong Province, the peninsula and islands that became Hong Kong counted only as a remote pocket in a neglected corner of the Qing Dynasty (1644-1911) empire. Inhabitants included scattered communities of farmers and fishermen as well as pirates, who hid from Qing authorities among the rocky islands that afforded easy access to the nearby Pearl River.

What society existed was dominated by just five Cantonese landowning families, or clans, each with its own walled villages and communal farmland. Other Chinese races included the Hakka, who were generally looked down upon by other Chinese, and the Tanka, who mostly lived on boats (taking their name from *tengga* or 'boat people' in Cantonese) and occupied an even lower social standing than the Hakka.

Though relatively isolated, the area saw a steady traffic of sampans, imperial war junks, pirate ships and cargo vessels headed to or from the Pearl River estuary. Some paused to anchor in the superb deep-water harbour at the tip of the Kowloon peninsula. By the early 19th century locals also began to see other, unfamiliar ships: the sleek, multi-masted schooners and brigs of the west.

### Western Trade & the Opium Wars

European ships were already a regular sight in the city of Guangzhou (then known as Canton), the one port through which China maintained contact with the outside world. For centuries it had played host to traders from South-East Asia, India and the Middle East. First contact with Western Europe came via the Portuguese who, in 1557, were given permission to set up base in nearby Macau. Britain, France and the Netherlands eventually followed. Their first overtures were haughtily rebuffed by the Chinese, who saw little profit in further trade with the 'Outer Barbarians', as all foreigners were classified. But Guangzhou finally opened to Europeans in 1685, and foreign traders were allowed to establish warehouses on the waterfront. There they sold textiles and manufactured goods, and bought tea and silk.

Trade grew, but since the Chinese were largely self-sufficient and disdained western manufactured goods, the balance was mostly in favour of China. This was not what the western merchants had in mind, and in the late 18th century they found a solution: opium. The British, having a virtually inexhaustible supply of the drug in India, developed the trade aggressively, and opium formed the basis of most their transactions with China by the start of the 19th century.

Alarmed by the soaring increase in opium addiction within his realm, Chinese Emperor Dao Guang decreed a ban on it in 1796. But in Guangzhou, 2400km away from Beijing, corrupt Chinese officials helped ensure that the trade continued, and fortunes were amassed on both sides. Imports of the drug jumped further after 1834, when the British East India Company lost its monopoly on China trade, and other British firms rushed in. All this was to change in 1839 with the arrival of Lin Zexu, a mandarin of unusual integrity with orders from Beijing to stamp out the opium trade. He succeeded in destroying 20,000 chests of opium, which led to Captain Charles Elliot, Britain's chief superintendent of trade, suspending all trade with China. In London, Foreign Secretary Lord Palmerston, egged on by prominent Scottish merchants in Guangzhou, William Jardine and James Matheson, ordered the navy in Guangzhou to force open the closed doors of Chinese trade.

The force arrived in June 1840, blockaded Guangzhou and then sailed north, occupying or blockading a number of ports and cities on the coast and the Yangtze River, ultimately threatening Beijing itself. The Chinese were forced to negotiate. Acting on his own authority, Captain Elliot demanded that a small, hilly island near the Pearl River estuary be ceded to the Brits 'in perpetuity'.

The place was familiar to British seamen, who had been using a waterfall on its southern shore as a source of fresh water, and knew the island as Hong Kong, after the Cantonese name for it, 'Heung Gong'. The name was usually interpreted as 'fragrant harbour' or 'incense port'. As Captain Elliot saw it, from here the British Empire and its merchants could conduct all their trade with China and establish a permanent outpost, under British sovereignty, in the Far East.

The Guangzhou merchants, members of the British Royal Navy and Lord Palmerston himself did not agree, however. A small barren island with nary a house on it was not the type of sweeping concession that a British victory was supposed to achieve. 'You have treated my instructions as if they were waste paper', Palmerston fumed at Elliot. British traders, in their newspaper the *Canton Press,* caustically observed that 'we now only require houses, inhabitants, and commerce to make this settlement one of the most valuable of our possessions'. Elliot was shunted off to the diplomatic backwaters of the USA, his foresight never to be acknowledged or rewarded.

On 26 January 1841 Commodore Gordon Bremmer led a contingent of naval men ashore and claimed Hong Kong Island for Queen and empire.

Sino-British tensions continued and the Chinese were forced to accept the Treaty of Nanking which, among other things, ceded Hong Kong to the British 'in perpetuity', this time officially. Hong Kong formally became a British possession on 26 June 1843, and its first governor, Sir Henry Pottinger, lost no time in declaring that the island would soon be awash in the riches of commerce. It would, but not in his lifetime.

The ending of the Second Anglo-Chinese War in 1860 gave the British another chance to expand their outpost. Along with other concessions, the Convention of Peking ceded to the British the Kowloon peninsula plus nearby Stonecutters Island.

Hong Kong made its last land grab in a moment of panic 40 years later when China was on the verge of being parcelled out into 'spheres of influence' by the western powers and Japan, all of which had sunk their claws into the country. The British army felt it needed more land to protect the colony, and in June 1898 the Second Convention of Peking presented Britain with what is now known as the New Territories. But instead of annexing the land outright, the British agreed to a 99 year lease, beginning 1 July 1898 and ending at midnight on 30 June 1997. Though those of the time probably gave it little thought, the countdown to British Hong Kong's expiration had begun.

### From Backwater to Boom Town

While merchants in Hong Kong prospered from the China trade, for decades the colony failed to live up to expectations. Fever and typhoons threatened life and property, and at first the colony attracted a fair number of criminals. However, by the end of the 19th century Hong Kong began to shape itself into a more substantial community. Gas and electrical power companies were set up, and ferries, electric trams and the Kowloon-Canton Railway finally provided a decent transport network. Nonetheless, in the years leading up to WWII, Hong Kong lived in the shadow of Shanghai, which had become the premier trade and financial centre of the Far East.

Though snubbed by its imperial masters, Hong Kong became a beacon for China's regular outflow of refugees. One of the earlier waves was sparked by the Chinese Revolution of 1911, which ousted the decaying Qing Dynasty and ushered in several decades of strife, rampaging warlords and mass starvation. Steady numbers continued to enter the colony during the 1920s and 1930s, but the stream became a flood after Japan invaded China in 1937: an estimated 750,000 mainland Chinese sought shelter in Hong Kong between 1937 and 1939.

But Hong Kong's British status only offered the refugees a temporary sanctuary. On 8 December 1941, in conjunction with its attack on US forces at Pearl Harbor, Japan's military swept down from Guangzhou into Hong Kong. After a week of fierce but futile resistance, the British forces surrendered, beginning nearly four years of Japanese occupation. Conditions were harsh, and in the later years Japan actually started deporting people from Hong Kong in a bid to ease a severe food shortage there.

Following the defeat and withdrawal of the Japanese, Hong Kong looked set to resume its sleepy routine. But events in China forced the colony in a new direction. The communist revolution in 1949 sent capitalist refugees pouring into Hong Kong. The following year Beijing sided with North Korea and went to war against the forces of the US and the United Nations. The subsequent embargo on all western trade with China threatened to strangle the colony economically. Hong Kong had to find another way to survive, and in doing so finally came into its own. On a paltry, war-torn foundation, foreign and Chinese businesses built an immense manufacturing and financial service centre that transformed Hong Kong into Asia's most vibrant city. A steady stream of refugees from China provided an enormous pool of cheap labour, and European, American and Asian investors provided the funds needed to employ it.

Working conditions in these early years of Hong Kong's industrial revolution were often Dickensian: 16-hour days, unsafe equipment, hideously low wages and child labour were all common. Refugee workers endured, and some even earned their way out of poverty and into prosperity. The Hong Kong government, after coming under international pressure, eventually began to set and enforce labour standards and the situation gradually improved.

By the end of the 1950s Hong Kong-made textiles, watches and basic electronics were finding their way into homes around the world. Though these products did not always carry a reputation for quality, the money they brought in started turning the colony into an unlikely economic powerhouse.

From 600,000 in 1945, Hong Kong's population soared to three million in 1960. Most of these new inhabitants had fled from Mao Zedong's communist China, which for some reason had not seen fit to reclaim Hong Kong militarily.

On the other hand, China was often quick to remind Hong Kong of its tenuous position. In 1962 it suddenly opened the border gates, allowing 70,000 people to flood into the colony in a matter of weeks. In 1967, at the height of the Cultural Revolution, Hong Kong again seemed doomed when riots inspired by the Red Guards rocked the colony. Several bombs were detonated. On 8 July 1967 a militia of 300 Chinese crossed the border with automatic rifles, killed five policemen and penetrated 3km into the New Territories before pulling back. Expatriates thought the end was near. Property values in Hong Kong fell sharply and panic spread through the business community. But Hong Kong's colonial masters held their ground and police gradually restored order, supported in most part by the locals.

As China went back into its shell, Hong Kong got on with the business of getting rich, which included improving the territory's infrastructure. In 1972, the cross-harbour tunnel opened, ending the reliance on ferry transport between Hong Kong Island and Kowloon. The next year, the first New Town was completed, paving the way towards better housing for Hong Kong's millions. By 1979 the colony even had its own subway with the opening of the first line of the Mass Transit Railway.

During the 1970s some of Hong Kong's Asian neighbours, including Taiwan, South Korea and Singapore, began to mimic the colony's success. Just as their cheap labour was threatening to undermine the competitive edge of Hong Kong manufacturers, China decided to emerge from nearly two decades of self-imposed isolation. Deng Xiaoping, who took control of China in the mayhem following Mao Zedong's death in 1976, opened up the country to tourism and foreign investment in 1978.

Deng's 'Open Door' policy, designed to pull China into the 20th century, revived Hong Kong's role as the gateway to its mysterious, gigantic northern neighbour. Hong Kong companies gradually began shifting their factories across the border, and foreign firms came in droves seeking out Hong Kong businesses for their China contacts and expertise. Investment in China grew and trade in Hong Kong skyrocketed as it became a transshipment point for China's exports, and later on, imports. Underpinning this boom was the drive to rake in profits ahead of 1997, when Hong Kong's unpredictable new master was due to take over.

### 'One Country, Two Systems'

Actually, few people gave much thought to Hong Kong's future until the early 1980s, when the British and Chinese governments started meeting to decide what would happen come 1997. In theory, Britain was legally bound only to hand back the New Territories. But with nearly half of Hong Kong's population living in those same New Territories, it would have been an awkward division.

More importantly, for Beijing, Hong Kong remained the last reminder of foreign imperialism on mother soil (Macau is a somewhat different story, having never been formally ceded to Portugal – it is due to return to Chinese rule in 1999). As China's economy and confidence grew, the British presence in Hong Kong became intolerable.

In December 1984 the British formally agreed to hand the entire colony back to China in 1997. The agreement, enshrined in a document known as the Sino-British Joint Declaration, theoretically allows Hong Kong to retain its present social, economic and legal systems for at least 50 years after 1997. The idea was to transform Hong Kong into a Special Administrative Region (SAR) of China upon the handover of sovereignty on 1 July 1997. Beijing's catch phrase for this is 'one country, two systems', whereby Hong Kong is allowed to stay capitalist after the handover, while across the border the Chinese continue with a system which they label socialist. Deng Xiaoping also called this *gangren zhi gang*, or 'Hong Kong people governing Hong Kong'.

As a follow-up to the Joint Declaration, in 1988 Beijing published the Basic Law for Hong Kong, a hefty document not unlike a constitution. The Basic Law permits the preservation of Hong Kong's legal system; guarantees the rights of property and ownership; gives residents the right to travel; permits Hong Kong to remain a free port and to continue independent membership of international organisations; and guarantees continuing employment after 1997 for Hong Kong's Chinese civil servants. The rights of assembly, free speech, association, correspondence, choice of occupation, academic research, religious belief and the right to strike are all included. The SAR should enjoy a high degree of autonomy except in foreign affairs and matters of defence.

Hong Kong's fledgling pro-democracy movement denounced the Joint Declaration as the new 'unequal treaty' and blasted Britain for selling out the best interests of Hong Kong's people in order to keep good economic relations with China. And like the treaty that gave Britain Hong Kong in 1841, local residents never had any say in these agreements – the negotiations were held entirely behind closed doors.

China insists that the Basic Law is the Hong Kong people's guarantee of the good life after 1997. Indeed, Chinese officials often bristle when Hong Kong politicians or journalists raise any doubts as to China's benevolent intentions. However, Beijing's actions have consistently given the people of Hong Kong good cause to worry.

## Business as Usual?

Post-handover Hong Kong appears on the surface to differ little from colonial times. The SAR has not banned any organisations, silenced any news media nor imposed itself unfairly on any individual, but despite the optimism that the peaceful transition of sovereignty seems to assure, many are looking at this stage as a period of preparation or evolution for the SAR. Scratching beneath the silvery surface, it is not hard to discover a potentially corrosive layer beneath.

An indication of where things could be headed was revealed by Tung Chee-hwa's professed admiration for Singapore. Many say that there has been a marked drift of power towards the Chief Executive during his current term. Tung Chee-hwa also lent his support to the Malaysian Prime Minister Mahathir Mohamad's call for the Universal Declaration of Human Rights to be revised to include 'Asian values'. 'Asian values' are generally considered to sanctify autocratic decision making and the subservience of the individual to the larger society (generally reflecting Confucian principles).

Hong Kong's first Chief Executive, Tung Chee-hwa

However, the biggest problem facing Hong Kong potentially comes from within Hong Kong itself. University campuses are almost devoid of political activism. Students are generally too obsessed with preparing for life ahead and the business of making money to worry about theoretical limits to their freedoms. Likewise, the media in Hong Kong has for many years been practising self-censorship to appease Beijing, resulting in increasingly banal newspaper coverage. Reporting is coming close to mirroring mainland Chinese journalism, with its principle of *baoxi bubaoyou* or 'report the good news, but not the bad'. Reading Hong Kong's English-language newspapers numbs your mind in a quite frightening way. The only real signs of life are in the frequent anti-American articles that hope for a pat on the head from Beijing.

The 1990 massacre in Tiananmen Square has been reinterpreted as an 'incident' in Hong Kong history textbooks, and the catastrophe of Mao Zedong's Great Leap Forward is no longer supported by including the figure of the tens of millions who died as a result. But it is not evident that these changes, nor the shifts in journalistic integrity, have occurred at Beijing's command. It appears that there is instead a tendency in the ex-colony to predict what Beijing *would* want.

If Hong Kong ever does stir and seek to test the limits to its freedoms, the SAR government has the, as yet untried, new Public Order and Societies Ordinance, which has the potential to restrict gatherings which constitute a threat to 'national security'. 'National security' is of course, highly subjective, and can include just about anything.

The Hong Kong people have not suffered much erosion of human freedoms since the takeover, but then they are a peaceful people who shun confrontation and just want to get on with the business of making money. There has been no real cause for confrontation so far, but the potential is still there. With the outward countenance of the Hong Kong SAR so subdued, perhaps one shouldn't forget the words of the expelled dissident Wang Bingzhang: 'China is like a boil. On the outside the skin is smooth but on the inside it's full of pus'. ■

Chief among these was the Tiananmen Square massacre of 4 June 1989, when Chinese troops used tanks and machine guns to break up pro-democracy demonstrations in Beijing. In Hong Kong, more than one million people attended rallies to protest the massacre in Beijing (one in six of the population). Confidence plummeted – the Hong Kong stock market fell 22% in one day, and

a lot of capital headed overseas. In the following weeks the Hong Kong government attempted to rebuild confidence, including the launch of a new HK$160 billion Airport & Port Project designed to shore up locals' faith in Hong Kong's future and lure back foreign investors.

But the signal had been sent. Hong Kong-based Chinese officials who had spoken out against the Tiananmen killings were yanked from their posts, or sought asylum in the USA and Europe. Those Hong Kongers with money and skills made a mad dash to emigrate to any country that would take them. Those that remained warned of a 'brain drain' that would cripple the economy.

Sino-British ties turned still worse with the arrival in 1992 of Chris Patten, Hong Kong's last British governor. A highly skilled politician, Patten immediately set out to give Hong Kong a last-minute democratic foundation; Patten wanted to be in the limelight and sought to politicise Hong Kong as much as possible before the return to China. He pushed through a series of legislative reforms which led to the direct election of both lawmakers and municipal officials.

Hong Kongers were by and large sceptical, with many wondering why Britain had chosen to wait until this late date to start experiments in democracy. China reached new peaks of rage, first levelling daily personal attacks on Patten, then threatening the post-1997 careers of any pro-democracy politicians or officials. When this didn't work, it targeted Hong Kong's economy. Negotiations on business contracts straddling 1997 suddenly dragged to a halt, and Beijing boycotted all talks on the new airport project, successfully scaring off foreign investors.

Sensing that it had alienated even its supporters in the colony, China backed off a bit, and in 1994 gave its blessing to the new airport (at Chek Lap Kok) and other Hong Kong business ventures. Its hostility toward direct elections remained, and China vowed to throw out all democratically elected legislators upon the return of sovereignty and replace them with a 'provisional legislature', which would serve until further elections were held under the new government. China's original concept of a 'through train', with the last British colonial legislature continuing to serve after the handover as the first legislature of the Hong Kong SAR, was scrapped.

On 31 August 1994, China adopted a resolution to terminate the terms of office of Hong Kong's three tiers of elected bodies (district boards, municipal councils and the legislature). The Provisional Legislative Council was later chosen by Beijing to prepare itself to replace the existing constitution of the Legislative Council; it operated from nearby Shenzhen, as it had no authority at all until the transferral of power. The Democratic Party in Hong Kong, who had 19 seats on the Legislative Council, were the strongest opposers of the 'illegality' of the new Provisional Legislative Council (*linshi lifahui*).

As for the executive branch of power, Beijing-led elections were held in 1996 for the position of Chief Executive, which was to replace the position of the governor under the British colonial regime. Predictably, the former shipping tycoon Tung Chee-hwa was chosen, elbowing everyone else out of the picture and preparing himself for power. He was, by and large, the acceptable face of China to Hong Kong, being largely affable, a speaker of Cantonese (although he was born in Shanghai) and English, and an expert businessman.

Despite the clamour from the Democrats that the Provisional Legislative Council was illegal, the panic as the 1997 handover drew near gave way to pragmatism. The feeling was that Hong Kong would have to make the most of the situation, pessimism would get it nowhere, and that optimism itself would generate stability and hope. The picture before the handover was rosy; the financial outlook was sunny and the economy strong. This paved the way for a smooth transferral of power and a gracious exit for the departing colonial power. China agreed to a low-key entry into Hong Kong, keeping the troops of the People's Liberation Army (PLA) off the streets (and desperately giving soldiers from northern provinces Cantonese lessons), and avoided coming down Nathan Rd in phalanxes of tanks. On the night of 30 June 1997, Chris Patten sailed away as the new rulers perused their domain. The handover celebrations had been watched by millions around the world; the now ex-governor wept and the Chinese President Jiang Zemin tried to restrain his ebullience.

## Tourism in Decline

Hong Kong needs an image makeover, many people say. With a 35% plunge in visitors in July 1998 compared to the same month in 1996 (the Japanese in particular have dropped away badly, a 68% drop in visitors over the two years), something is seriously wrong. The economic implications are huge – tourism earned HK$100 billion (US$12.8 billion) in 1996 and employs 12% of the workforce. Some say that Hong Kong has priced itself out of the market on the shopping and dining front; a contracting tourist market and greater competition should ensure fairer prices in future.

Some reasons for the deepening decline in tourism were very avoidable: Japanese newspapers revealed that Japanese and Korean tourists were being massively overcharged for hotel rooms. Some reports said they were paying more than three times what visitors from other countries were charged. Their entirely understandable response was to give Hong Kong a big miss. The simple moral of that is that it doesn't pay to rip off wealthy tourists, especially if you depend on them.

But a bigger problem is image. Hong Kong argues that all is the same as before, which in many ways is true. But the fact is that Hong Kong is not the same as before in one vital respect. It is no longer a British colony, and the 'colonial outpost' factor was a major selling point, especially since you could trundle up to the border with China and stare the red threat in the face. Many Japanese see Hong Kong as just another part of China now, and they don't visit China that much, or if they do, Hong Kong is now just one of a dozen cities they could visit. Hong Kong now offers a diminished mystique. The appeal is the same as ever for mainland Chinese, ironically, but that's a market that is difficult to tap.

Other changes have compounded the problem. Hong Kong cannot offer the bargains it once could, and its reputation as a shopping paradise is badly tarnished as retail prices have inexorably risen. The dining is still excellent, and this is one area that is flourishing – unfortunately the restaurants all depend to a large extent on the tourist dollar, so the two industries are intertwined.

Many answers wait in the wings. Turning the ex-governor's mansion into a museum of colonial history would be a great start. Devoting more attention to the arts and culture would guarantee Hong Kong's future role as a cultural capital of China.

Many say that more emphasis should be put on the outdoor attractions of the New Territories and the Outlying Islands, which would attract more young people put off by Hong Kong's strictly urban image. Lamma Island and Cheung Chau offer some excellent retreats that do much to give Hong Kong a different dimension; one of peace, quiet and pastoral walks. Backpackers should be made to feel more welcome by bringing guesthouse prices down to a level similar to those in Macau, but the current Hong Kong rents prohibit much price-cutting.

Whatever conclusions are drawn, Hong Kong will certainly see some changes as it rushes to deal with tourists in revolt. Despite the HK$100 million that the Chief Executive, Tung Chee-hwa, has thrown at the Hong Kong Tourist Association to find a solution, maybe the answer lies not in spending huge amounts of money on slick image and advertising, but instead a few simple changes could help reverse a serious decline. ∎

---

Initially, the new Hong Kong SAR started out on a good footing, and the hordes of photojournalists that had been propping up the bars of Central for weeks decided to screw on the lens cap and head home. There were no stories. Nothing untoward was happening; the world started to look elsewhere for news. The political storm that all awaited did not eventuate; China adopted a sensible hands-off policy that appears to be working well.

### A Shaky Beginning

However, political and social stability aside, Hong Kong became embroiled in the financial chaos that had besieged South-East Asia. The huge slump in the stock exchange in Hong Kong that occurred in January 1998, the collapse of Peregrine Investments and the rumours circulating about the imminent collapse of banks (like the Bank of Asia, which saw a run on deposit accounts by customers panicking over rumours that the bank was about to fold) created a mood of negativity and despair. One in five Hong Kong Chinese have invested in shares, and when share prices rapidly fell, there seemed to be no end to the anguish and uncertainty endured by the average family. The end of the first six months of Chinese rule was, economically speaking, disastrous, even though the events suffered had nothing to do with bad economic management or loss of confidence in Hong Kong, it was all part of regional economic uncertainty.

Tourism was also badly hit, with Japanese, Korean and Taiwanese and tourists from western countries staying away en masse. Many went instead to other Asian destinations where massive currency devaluations meant cheap holidays. The scare over avian flu (*qinliugan*) in Hong Kong, a potentially deadly form of flu that had leapt across the species barrier from birds, also kept tourists away. Masses of Taiwanese tourists cancelled their hugely reduced tickets from Cathay Pacific and other airlines because of the scare. The slump in tourism was particularly bad news for Hong Kong retailers, who depend to a large extent on foreign customers; if the industry does not improve, then many small businesses, restaurants and hotels will be out of business. The latter half of 1997 and early 1998 saw empty department stores and endless letters to the Hong Kong press about the plight of the local tourist industry. Also see the boxed text 'Tourism in Decline' on the previous page.

## GEOGRAPHY

With its magnificent harbour, steep peaks and surrounding islands, Hong Kong is one of the world's more geographically interesting cities. The territory's 1084 sq km is divided into four main areas – Hong Kong Island, Kowloon, the New Territories and the Outlying Islands.

Victoria Harbour is Hong Kong's centre of gravity, with most of the urban areas lining the northern or southern shores. Originally about one mile wide, the harbour is being squeezed by reclamation on both sides.

On the south side of the harbour lies Hong Kong Island, which covers 78 sq km, or just 7% of Hong Kong's land area. Most of the commercial and residential areas are on the north side of the island, including Central, the main business, banking and administrative district. The southern side of the island houses mostly wealthy residents and boasts some nice beaches. The two sides are separated by a backbone of steep hills, including Victoria Peak, Hong Kong's premier scenic viewpoint.

Kowloon is a peninsula on the north side of the harbour. The southern tip, Tsim Sha Tsui, is a major tourist area, and has seemingly endless blocks of shops and hotels. The areas further north and west are filled with residential and commercial towers and industrial zones that include some of the most cramped and dingy parts of Hong Kong. Boundary St, which cuts across the middle of the peninsula, marks where the British-Chinese border was before Britain snatched the rest of Kowloon along with the New Territories in 1898. Kowloon was named after a series of hills – the 'nine dragons' or *gau long* in Cantonese – that separate it from the New Territories. The name reflects the ancient Chinese belief that dragons inhabit mountains.

Sandwiched between Kowloon and the Chinese border, the New Territories occupy 980 sq km, or 91% of Hong Kong's land area. Originally Hong Kong's agricultural backyard, the New Territories now house nearly half of Hong Kong's population in the so-called New Towns, which are stark monuments to urban planning and function over form. But you can still find farms out here, as well as white sandy beaches and an impressive number of country parks.

The Outlying Islands incorporate all islands apart from Hong Kong Island. Officially, the Outlying Islands are part of the New Territories and make up about 20% of Hong Kong's total land area. There are 234 islands and while many are tiny rocks, the largest (Lantau Island) is nearly twice the size of Hong Kong Island. Previously, there were 235 islands until Stonecutters Island was absorbed by land reclamation off the western shore of the Kowloon peninsula. Some of the larger islands, including Lantau, Cheung Chau and Lamma, are well served by commuter ferries and offer both residents and visitors an escape from Hong Kong's blistering urban pace. They are also home to some excellent country parks. If you have the time,

RICHARD I'ANSON

TED CARROLL

RICHARD I'ANSON

Top: A panorama of Hong Kong Island's dazzling night show.
Bottom Left: The 'praying mantis' Bank of China Tower looms above its rivals in Central.
Bottom Right: The neon assault of the Nathan Rd shopping precinct in Tsim Sha Tsui.

Top Left: The stone guardian outside the Man Mo Temple, Sheung Wan.
Top Right: 'I'm in two minds about this one' – Kowloon Park sculpture.
Bottom: Studying the stock market? Or the horse-racing form guide? – Kowloon Park.

make a visit to at least one of the islands part of your itinerary.

## CLIMATE

Hong Kong is perched on the south-east coast of China just south of the tropic of Cancer, on much the same latitude as Hawaii or Calcutta. The climate is subtropical, but tends toward temperate for nearly half the year. This is because the huge land mass of Asia generates powerful blasts of frigid wind that blow from the north during winter. In summer, the seasonal wind reverses and blows from the south bringing hot, humid tropical air.

Late October to December usually sees sunny, dry weather with cool breezes, though for most of November it's still warm enough to go swimming. January and February are more cloudy and see occasional cold fronts. Temperatures can drop as low as 10°C in the New Territories, but snow and frost are quite rare. Not much rain falls, but when it does, it's usually a chilly, depressing drizzle that lasts for days. The mountains are often shrouded in mist, which can spoil visits to Victoria Peak and other scenic outlooks. Winter weather usually continues into March

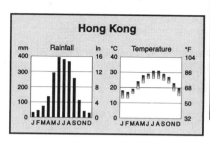

and often ends abruptly when the cold wind stops blowing. Even during winter, there are windless days when the weather becomes balmy.

March to April/May are usually pleasant months, as the scorching summer heat often doesn't arrive until June. But there's a higher chance of rain and humidity than in autumn.

Big thunderstorms become more frequent as June approaches. June tends to be the wettest month, with the beginning of the summer monsoon. On into July and temperatures usually hover between 26°C and 34°C through to the middle of September. Though there are occasional cool breezes off the sea, the heat is generally oppressive.

### Typhoons

Almost every year sees a typhoon bound for Hong Kong. Despite their awesome capacity for destruction, many residents welcome the odd tempest blowing into town with a clapping of hands, as it can guarantee them some time off work. But what exactly is a typhoon?

A typhoon is a violent tropical cyclone, a massive whirlpool of air currents often hundreds of kilometres wide. Feeding off moisture, tropical cyclones can only survive over warm oceans – once they hit land, they quickly die out. The 'eye' of the cyclone is generally tens of kilometres wide and consists of a column of descending air, sometimes completely calm in contrast to the surrounding vortex.

Cyclones can last for as long as a few weeks, but not all of them will mature into typhoons. Only about half of the cyclones in the South China Sea ever reach typhoon ferocity. The gradation of ferocity of tropical cyclones ascends as follows: Tropical Depression (up to 62km/h), Tropical Storm (63km/h to 87km/h), Severe Tropical Storm (88km/h to 117km/h) and Typhoon (118km/h or more).

Hong Kong is a small target, so the chances of a direct hit by a typhoon (ie a wind of typhoon intensity to pass within 100km of the city) is actually small. Only a dozen or so have struck in the past 50 years or so, despite the 15 or so gusting around in the vicinity every year. The No 10 signal goes up when this happens, as hurricane force winds are expected.

Some of the more destructive typhoons include Typhoon Wanda in 1962, which delivered hourly mean wind speeds of 133km/h and peak gusts of 259km/h. In 1983 Typhoon Ellen killed 22 and injured over 300, while insurance claims totalled over HK$300 million. Typhoon Brenda (1989) came heavily laden with rain and caused widespread flooding in the territory. ■

September brings a hint of cooler weather, but is also the month during which Hong Kong is most likely to be hit by typhoons, which can really mess with your travel plans. Typhoons vary in size from tropical storms to severe super-typhoons. If the typhoon passes by Hong Kong at a distance, it will bring a little rain and wind that might only last for half a day. If it scores a direct hit, the winds can be deadly and it may rain for days on end. You can't go outside for very long during a bad typhoon and most businesses shut down. When a typhoon becomes a possibility, warnings are broadcast continuously on TV and radio. You can also call the typhoon hotline (☎ 2835-1473).

### ECOLOGY & ENVIRONMENT

After nearly 150 years of ignoring the issue, in 1989 the Hong Kong government suddenly realised that Hong Kong was in danger of becoming a vast, densely populated cesspool. Hong Kong's 'laissez-faire' stance towards business and economic growth meant that few or no measures existed to control water, waste or air pollution.

The Environmental Protection Department was established to regulate the amount of pollution expelled into the environment. This is certainly needed to deal with the 14,240 tonnes of municipal waste and 29,000 tonnes of construction waste generated *each day* in Hong Kong. Most construction waste comes not from the erection of new buildings, but from the demolition of old ones. New landfills are being opened to absorb this enormous amount of trash and solid waste generated by Hong Kong's 6.4 million (and rising) inhabitants. An aggressive campaign is reminding locals not to treat roads, waterways and parks as rubbish bins, though not everyone gets the message (just look at the rubbish on the streets for starters). See page 219 for a list of Hong Kong environmental groups.

Victoria Harbour is in a pitiful state, still suffering from years of pollution and sewage being pumped into it. Factories, farms and restaurants in the New Territories are coming under the gun for dumping untreated waste

**Hong Kong's Vanishing Oyster Farms**

Once a tourist destination, the oyster farms of Lau Fau Shan are on the verge of clamming up once and for all. Lau Fau Shan, on the coast of Deep Water Bay, is the only part of Hong Kong suited to the cultivation of oysters, as salt water and fresh water mingle here to create the ideal habitat for the small bivalves.

But production has slumped, as 80% of all oysters consumed in Hong Kong now come from Shenzhen over the border, where production costs are lower. Another reason for this downsizing of the local oyster industry is that it's a tough job – the children of oyster farming families have left the shell-strewn shores of Lau Fau Shan and ventured to the bright lights of Hong Kong.

The finger is also pointed at pollution from factories in neighbouring Shenzhen. Toxic residues from farming are also to blame. In the 1970s oysters were regularly poached by thieves from across the border (some oyster farmers were even kidnapped and dragged off to China); but it all turned sour in 1979 when the oyster farms reported a 95% loss from disease. A further blow to the industry came when locally grown shellfish were associated with Hepatitis A and high cadmium levels. The amazing speed of growth in Shenzhen is bound to add to the demise of this once flourishing community of oyster farmers. ∎

into streams and the sea. Unfortunately, a great deal of damage has already been done: some New Territories streams are 'no better than open sewers', the government admits.

Hong Kong's pink dolphin population is under threat from chemical pollution, increased boat traffic and the destruction of much of the natural shoreline to make way for land reclamation schemes. The huge nature reserve and bird haven of Mai Po Marsh (see also the boxed text on page 20) is under threat from pig sewage flooding into Deep Bay, and now the increased pollution from Shenzhen raises the stakes against its survival. The bird sanctuaries in the wetlands around Mai Po of Tin Shui Wai, Kam Tin and Kwu Yung are under threat from government plans to build huge residential housing estates in the New Territories to satisfy the increasing demand for flats. Many of the birds have fled to Hong Kong to escape the manic industrial development in southern China. The oyster farms at Lau Fau Shan have been throttled by a mixture of pollution and competition from cheaper oyster cultivation across the border in China.

Air pollution is another serious problem. Smoke-belching factories, ceaseless construction and large numbers of diesel vehicles have made for dangerous levels of particulate matter and nitrogen dioxide. Cases of asthma and bronchial infections have soared in recent years, and doctors place the blame squarely on poor air quality. Travellers with respiratory conditions should take this into consideration. See the Health section in the Facts for the Visitor chapter for more details.

The government has also set up a monitoring system for swimming beaches, to check on the amount of disease-causing bacteria in the water. While this doesn't take into account floating trash or algae, it does give an idea of the type of health risk you face. For more information, refer to the Health section in the Facts for the Visitor chapter.

Not all of Hong Kong's land is ravaged by pollution. Around 40% of the territory's land area is protected by 21 country parks. Watershed protection was the major reason for making these areas off limits to development and private motor vehicles – all of Hong Kong's 17 reservoirs lie within the boundaries of the parks. Nevertheless, hikers, campers, bird-watchers and other nature-lovers all benefit. Most of the country parks are in the New Territories and the Outlying Islands, but even the higher mountainous slopes of Hong Kong Island are protected.

It remains to be seen whether China will continue to improve the fight against pollution in Hong Kong. However, there is little cause for optimism, considering China's appalling track record on environmental protection, and its insatiable desire to turn itself into an industrial wasteland.

## FLORA & FAUNA

Back in 1841, the British Foreign Secretary, Lord Palmerston, disparaged Hong Kong as a 'barren island with nary a house upon it'. While the lack of houses was nothing unusual, the barrenness certainly was. With abundant rainfall and a warm climate, the British might well have expected to find a dense jungle on the shores of southern China. Instead, they found Hong Kong nearly devoid of trees, a situation that persists today.

The simple reason for this is that Hong Kong's earlier inhabitants cut down all the trees. Massive land clearing by settlers started as long ago as the Song Dynasty (960-1279) and continued until the hills were stripped bare. With the forests removed, heavy summer showers quickly eroded Hong Kong's steep slopes, and the lack of topsoil prevented the forests from regenerating. However, remnants of the original forests can be found in steep ravines both on Hong Kong Island and in the New Territories, mostly within the boundaries of the country parks.

These days, most of the uninhabited regions of Hong Kong are open grasslands. Somewhat ironically, the only areas of Hong Kong that have seen any reforestation efforts are those inhabited by humans. The British were never happy about the lack of shade trees during the scorching summers, and thus planted quick-growing species around their colonial residences. The Chinese have also planted groves in an attempt to please the spirits of the deceased. Trees with commercial value like bamboo have been planted on a small scale in the agricultural regions of the New Territories. However, Hong Kong today has precious little to offer in the way of forests.

The loss of so much vegetation has also meant the loss of habitat for animals, and very few large creatures survive. But a walk in the New Territories or making a visit to one of the Outlying Islands will provide the eager entomologist or botanist with a splendid selection of insects and plant life. Huge butterflies the size of children's hands flutter about on Lamma Island, and equally large spiders hang suspended from webs in the trees. The butterflies really are quite beautiful and their size is extraordinary. Hong

Kong is home to more than 200 species of butterfly, many of which are unusually elegant and colourful. Dragonflies are plentiful and large moths also inhabit the territory, including giant silkworm moths, one type of which has a wingspan of more than 20cm!

Lamma Island, Cheung Chau, Lantau Island and the New Territories are thick with vegetation. Lamma has an amazing variety of plant life that even the most casual observer can appreciate. A walk at night on Lamma Island is accompanied by a host of scuttling noises coming from the undergrowth, and the croaking of frogs and toads. The dry racket of cicadas can be heard on the islands and the New Territories during summer.

Kowloon and the New Territories are home to quite a number of long-tailed macaques and rhesus monkeys. One monkey managed to make it to Kennedy Town on Hong Kong Island in early 1998 and was regularly spotted hanging from lampposts and traffic lights.

Weighing in at over 100kg are wild boars, found in some rural spots and regarded as pests because they dig up crops. Much more aesthetically pleasing, but rarely seen, are barking deer (also called muntjacs) and black-and-white quilled Chinese porcupines. The latter can be found even on the high slopes of Hong Kong Island. Small mammals thought to survive in the wild include ferret badgers, otters, masked palm civets, porcupines, shrews and bats. Wild monkeys can be found but are thought to be the descendants of escaped pets. Leopards and tigers were all but wiped out at the beginning of the 20th century. The last tiger seen in the New Territories was said to have been shot in 1915, though there are claims of sightings in later years. However, the Chinese leopard cat (weighing from only 2kg

## Mai Po Marsh

Beyond the bustling cityscapes of Hong Kong lies the New Territories, home to a fragile ecosystem of huge importance, the Mai Po Marsh nature reserve. Sitting on the edges of Deep Bay, Mai Po is a network of ponds and mudflats that attracts 70,000 water birds every winter. Together, Deep Bay and Mai Po form an essential stopping-off place for migratory birds.

Unfortunately Mai Po's future is uncertain. The water quality in Deep Bay is some of the worst around the coast of Hong Kong; the Environmental Protection Department has found that the levels of dissolved oxygen (DO) in the water have been declining since 1988. Levels of DO fell to zero on one occasion in summer 1996.

As a result, the numbers of crabs and mudskippers suffered a sharp drop in 1996, and it is these that the birds eat in winter. Although the number of birds that visited in the winter of 1996 did not show a decrease, anxious watchers are waiting for the knock-on effect to take place.

The pollution used to come from the vast amount of pig manure that was released into Deep Bay, but this has recently been curbed by a government ordinance which insists that pig slurry is treated before being flushed into the bay. This ordinance appears to be having an effect, but a potentially larger hazard has taken its place.

Deep Bay neighbours the city of Shenzhen in China, which is pumping out a rapidly increasing amount of sewage, 50% of which is untreated. The only real solution to this threat is for Shenzhen to build more sewage treatment facilities, but that will take time (especially as the city is expanding faster than its infrastructure can manage). Luckily for the beleaguered Mai Po, 1997 saw one of the wettest years on record, and the large volume of rain water has flushed out and diluted many of the pollutants. The number of crabs and mudskippers has increased, but this could just be a temporary improvement in the ecology.

If the lower links of the food chain are seriously imperilled, then the 270 or more species of bird that depend on Mai Po could disappear, as well as mammals such as leopard cats and otters.

In September 1995, Mai Po and inner Deep Water Bay were declared a 'wetland of international importance'. The Mai Po nature reserve can be visited by contacting the Worldwide Fund for Nature (WWF) (☎ 2526-4473), who conduct tours of the area on Sunday and public holidays. The WWF has taken more than 40,000 visitors to the area. ■

to 5kg) is still found in remote parts of the territory. A massive Burmese python was caught slithering around on Lantau Island in 1997.

An interesting creature is the Chinese pangolin, a scaly mammal that resembles an armadillo. When attacked, it rolls itself up into an unappetising ball. Unfortunately, its existence is threatened because the Chinese regard its flesh to be a tonic medicine and an aphrodisiac.

There are more than 250 species of bird to be found in Hong Kong, in large part due to the establishment of the Mai Po Marsh conservation site. Encompassing 380 hectares of mudflats, shrimp ponds and dwarf mangroves, the marshes are a safe haven for both resident and migratory birds, and not a bad place for bird-watchers either. It attracts an estimated 70,000 water birds every winter. Roughly 300 species of bird have been spotted in the area.

Hong Kong's waters are rich in sea life, sharks included. Popular beaches have shark nets to keep them out. The territory is also visited by four species of whale, and 11 species of dolphin.

## GOVERNMENT & POLITICS

The Hong Kong Special Administrative Region (SAR) is a unique phenomenon within China, or for that matter, anywhere else in the world (although Macau will have a similar political system after 20 December 1999). The treaties and accords accompanying the Joint Declaration have guaranteed a high degree of autonomy for Hong Kong, allowing it to retain its capitalist system for 50 years from 30 June 1997.

Hong Kong is not politically democratic, nor has it ever been. Democratic elements exist within its political structure, but this is by no means across the board, and it is highly unlikely that democracy will develop any further. Business rather than politics have always governed Hong Kong, and its people are largely apolitical. Political power is said by many to be drifting more towards the business sector. The last British governor tried hard to politicise Hong Kong, but with limited success.

The executive branch of power is led by the Chief Executive (a position currently occupied by Shanghai-born business tycoon, Tung Chee-hwa), who is supported by an Executive Council, which advises on policy matters. The Chief Secretary of the administration is responsible to the Chief Executive for the formulation of government policies and their implementation. The Chief Executive is further supported by a Financial Secretary, responsible for the fiscal and economic policies of the government. The Secretary for Justice is responsible for drafting all legislation.

The legislature makes and debates laws, controls public expenditure and checks the power (supposedly) of the administration. Hong Kong's current Legislative Council replaced LEGCO, 18 of whose 60 members were directly elected in a system arranged by the last governor, Chris Patten.

The judiciary administers justice and interprets the law as enacted by the legislature. It is independent from the executive and the legislature. The Court of Final Appeal now has the power of final adjudication, rather than the Judicial Committee of the Privy Council in London.

Next in line is the Urban Council, which is in charge of the day-to-day running of services in Hong Kong Island and Kowloon, including street cleaning, garbage collection, food hygiene, hawkers' licences, public recreation and the like. In the New Territories, the Regional Council has much the same functions as the Urban Council.

On the next rung down are the District Boards, of which there are 18, set up in 1982 to give Hong Kong residents a degree of control over their local area. The boards consist of government officials and elected representatives from the district.

Politically, things have gone surprisingly smoothly, but there are subtle changes afoot. Many say that Hong Kong has become far more executive-led and that power is drifting into the hands of Tung Chee-hwa. Martin Lee, the leader of the Democratic Party, has described this process as 'the beginning of the Singapore-isation of Hong Kong'. Important legislation is being shoved through the legislature, a body which people are worried is quickly becoming a rubber-stamping office. Legislation was quickly passed to change to the system for legislative elections held in May 1998; this system has dramatically reduced the franchise, and business constituencies now have much greater influence. Many say that the shift towards the executive means that it will be able to make decisions that will be immune from the law. Furthermore, the civil service and the bureaucracy is becoming less open and accountable (openness was strongly fostered by Patten), with a corresponding fear that the corruption that dogged it in the past will return. However, the Independent Commission Against Corruption (ICAC) maintains that it will continue to exercise its right to probe all levels in its pursuit of fairness and the application of the law. The ICAC has apparently seen no weakening in its influence, but it's early days yet.

The new political hegemony is apparently working OK. But Beijing has not been tested in any way; it has, indeed, given Hong Kong the autonomy it needs to flourish, but that is the easy part. Beijing knows that it is safer to separate itself from Hong Kong as much as possible. As long as Hong Kong carries on making money and making little noise, it is thought that Beijing will be content to leave things alone. It is generally felt, however, that if there was any large-scale dissent, Beijing would have to react. Some predict that a slow and gradual erosion of rights and legal safeguards in Hong Kong could well provoke such a reaction.

It has been noted that the policing of demonstrations has become more authoritarian, with larger numbers of police present. This has been generally interpreted as a desire for law and order at all costs; Hong Kong has one of the highest ratios of police to citizens in the world, with 427 for every 100,000 people. It will be interesting to see whether the annual vigil, held in Victoria Park, to commemorate the Tiananmen Square massa-cre will be permitted to take place in the future; the 1997 event saw a larger than average turnout.

## ECONOMY

This is Hong Kong's heart and soul. Where other societies find identity in their cultural history, political system or revolutionary ingenuity, Hong Kong looks to its robust economy. It's as simple as that. For proof, pick up any newspaper, walk through any neighbourhood or eavesdrop on a lunchtime conversation. Making money, and making a lot of it, is what it's all about.

Despite the economic catastrophe at the end of 1997 that severely cracked optimism in Pacific Rim countries, Hong Kong is still a capitalist's dream: free enterprise and free trade, very low taxes, a hard-working labour force, a world-class seaport and airport facilities, excellent telecommunications and a new government that has retained the hands-off approach to private business that was the hallmark of its predecessor.

Hong Kong's push forward really began when it shifted away from manufacturing and toward services, as a response to the opening up of China and its cheaper labour market. Most producers moved their factories over the border and some large service firms, such as Hongkong Telecom, even moved back-room administrative operations north to Guangdong Province.

China's roaring economic growth helped spark a boom in Hong Kong service industries like shipping, telecommunications, banking and insurance. Service industries, including import and export trade, employ more than 75% of Hong Kong's workforce and make up nearly 80% of its GDP.

Much of this growth in the services sector is underpinned by trade, which has expanded 37-fold over the past two decades. As an entrepôt for the flood of goods into and out of China, Hong Kong has become the world's 8th largest trading entity. The total annual value of visible trade (which excludes trade in services) had risen to more than US$180 billion by 1998. Domestic exports, or products made and sent out from Hong

Kong, only amount to around 20% of total exports, reflecting the shrinking number of domestic factories. The bulk of goods sent out from Hong Kong are re-exports: semi-finished and finished goods imported into the territory for additional processing or simply for transshipment, which are then exported to their final destination overseas. Hong Kong still has one of the freest economies in the world, as well as one of the most competitive.

Being almost entirely dependent on imported resources to meet the needs of its 6.4 million inhabitants, Hong Kong is also a prodigious importer. In fact imports usually outweigh exports, meaning the territory habitually posts a trade deficit. However this is usually offset by Hong Kong's robust exports of business, finance and trade-related services, which yield a sustained surplus in so-called 'invisible trade'.

Not surprisingly, China has become Hong Kong's largest trading partner, supplying the territory with around 33% of its total imports, and taking about 33% of its re-exports. Exports to mainland China equal approximately 33% of all trade between Hong Kong and the world; exports to the USA equal about 22%. Japan, Germany, the UK, Taiwan and Singapore are also large export markets. Hong Kong's container port and airport are the busiest in the world for cargo.

This steady stream of trade and business has allowed Hong Kong to maintain average GDP growth of around 5% during the 1990s. While enviable, such healthy growth in Hong Kong's situation of limited land and resources has kept consumer price inflation persistently high, with an annual rise in the cost of living of about 7%. Property prices and rents have been astronomically high. Recently, however, property prices have dropped considerably, reacting to the overall downturn in the economy, and many middle-class home owners have found that their properties are worth far less than what they paid for them; rising interest rates have added to the pressure on many of these mortgage holders.

Traditionally, labour has been scarce in Hong Kong, and for years the unemployment rate was locked between 1.5% and 2%. Workers from the Philippines (and increasingly from China) are brought in to help meet demand for manual labour, such as domestic help and construction.

Hong Kong can rightfully claim to be one of Asia's most important financial centres, along with Tokyo. Of the world's top 100 banks, 85 have operations in Hong Kong. The territory's stock market, once ridiculed as no more than an upmarket casino, complete with shady dealers, now ranks among the world's top 10 in terms of market capitalisation. Its foreign exchange market is one of the world's largest. In 1995 Hong Kong's banks and deposit-taking institutions held around US$600 billion in external assets, about 8% of the world total.

In line with this image, the Hong Kong government keeps its own finances in good order, in a way that most western developed countries can only dream about. Personal income tax is a flat 15%, and the corporate profits tax is capped at 16.5%.

China has become the number one investor in town, having pumped billions of US dollars into the local economy during the 1990s. Chinese firms have become major players in the property and financial markets, and long-time Hong Kong blue chip firms, such as Hongkong Telecom and Swire Pacific, now count companies from the mainland among their key shareholders. They also have invested heavily in key infrastructure projects related to the huge Chek Lap Kok airport programme. Obviously someone in Beijing is expecting Hong Kong to stay profitable for quite some time yet.

Hong Kong has reciprocated this investment by itself pouring HK$774 billion (US$100 billion) into mainland China. Most of this goes directly into Guangdong Province, which shares many cultural and linguistic ties with Hong Kong.

## POPULATION & PEOPLE

Hong Kong's population is roughly 6.4 million, making it one of the most densely populated places in the world. The overall density of the population works out to about 5800 people per sq km, but this figure is deceiving since there is a wide variation from area to area. The urban areas of Hong Kong Island and Kowloon pack in over 25,000 people per sq km, compared with only 2860 in the rural New Territories.

About 98% of Hong Kong's population is ethnic Chinese, most of whom are Cantonese, who have their origins in Guangdong Province. About 60% were born in the territory. About 33% of the population lives in Kowloon, 22% on Hong Kong Island, and 45% in the New Territories, with around 2% of the latter living in the Outlying Islands.

If any groups can truly claim to belong to Hong Kong, they are the Tanka, the nomadic boat people who have fished the local waters for centuries, and the Hakka, who farmed the New Territories long before Charles Elliot thought about running the Union Jack up a flagpole. The Hakka are a distinct group which emigrated from northern to southern China centuries ago to flee persecution. Hakka means 'guest'. Hakka women can be

recognised in the New Territories by their distinctive spliced-bamboo hats with wide brims and black-cloth fringes. The Hakka dialect is different from Cantonese, although the two languages share many similarities.

Hong Kong has a large expat community which numbered 146,400 at the time of the handover in July 1997. Of this number, the three largest communities were as follows: 146,400 were Filipinos, 40,900 were Americans and 34,300 were Indonesians. Some of the remainder are half or quarter Chinese, but Beijing has indicated that citizenship can only be endowed on those Hong Kongers of pure 'Chinese descent'. In other words, race is the deciding factor, not place of birth. This poses a problem for other nationalities, such as Hong Kong's long-standing Indian residents, rendered stateless in 1997. Even if they're allowed to stay, many doubt China will allow them to travel freely outside Hong Kong. Large numbers of British people left before 1 April 1998, when the visa-free period expired. After that, if they want to stay in Hong Kong and work, they will need to possess a work visa. In order to acquire one,

## Cantonese Pride

The Cantonese of Hong Kong are a plucky lot, and display an ethnic chauvinism rarely encountered in the rest of China. They consider themselves to be perfect exemplars of what it means to be Chinese, despite being colonised and exposed to barbarian ways for 150 years. The northern Chinese call the southern Chinese 'southern barbarians', while southern Chinese call those who hail from the north of China 'northern barbarians'; *gwailos* (foreigners, especially of European descent) take note; barbarianism is obviously relative.

The Cantonese dialect is also considered by the *Heunggongyan*, as the Hong Kong Cantonese calls themselves, to be the true Chinese language. This notion flabbergasts the northern Chinese, who speak Mandarin and look upon Cantonese as an uncivilised aberration. In fact, the Cantonese have a point, as it is argued that the language is closer to that spoken in earlier ages in China. Poetry from the Tang Dynasty (618-907) tends to rhyme better when read aloud in Cantonese than in Mandarin. It also keeps a fair number of classical Chinese expressions in its daily vocabulary, while Mandarin has shorn itself of many of these. It is common to meet Cantonese who claim that modern Mandarin (called Putonghua) is not truly Chinese, but an invention.

Chinese people from northern China are not considered to have reached the cultural heights that the Hong Kong Cantonese have. By the same token, Chinese from other parts of China are almost universally suspicious of the Cantonese and slag them off.

Gwailos are treated ambivalently, because they represent modernity, style and prosperity while at the same time being barbaric. The dividing line between gwailos and Chinese blurs in the case of Chinese people who have lived in western countries. Indians (*a cha*) living in Hong Kong are almost universally looked down upon by the Hong Kong Chinese, even though they are respected for their diligence and facility with languages, including the infamously tricky Cantonese dialect. ■

the company employing them will have to prove that the job they perform cannot be done by a local. As a consequence, a large number of unskilled and semiskilled workers are set to leave permanently. English pubs and bars are finding it difficult to recruit western staff, because it is argued that the job could be adequately performed by a local person.

Many argue that this exodus will gradually erode the standards of service once enjoyed by Hong Kong. A case in point was the maintenance of the shark nets on Hong Kong's beaches that was given to a Chinese company in 1997; the company that won the contract failed to perform adequate daily checks, resulting in a compromise of safety for swimmers. The contract was apparently offered to the company as it made the lowest bid, and because it was operated by Chinese; the job has now gone to a company hiring western divers (at greater cost). If this trend continues, many see a drop in standards as inevitable.

## ARTS

Mention art in relation to Hong Kong, and the term 'cultural desert' will likely soon grace the conversation. It's not an altogether fair description, and is usually uttered by jaded residents who have lost the energy to look for what's out there. Granted, in a city where some people proudly declare that making money is the most important thing in life, the arts tend to take a back seat. But there's still a good deal on offer, especially in the performing arts. There are both philharmonic and Chinese orchestras, Chinese and modern dance troupes, a ballet company, several theatre groups and numerous art schools and organisations. Government funds also allow local venues to bring in top international performers. Hong Kong also hosts international art and folk festivals annually, which showcase both local and overseas artists and works.

On a more grassroots level, local street opera troupes occasionally pop up around the city to lay siege to neighbourhoods for several days with their armoury of clashing cymbals, gongs and high-pitched warbling. Both local and mainland Chinese opera troupes can also sometimes be seen in more formal venues.

Despite being next door to China and its venerable 5000-year-old cultural heritage, Hong Kong comes up a bit short on visual arts. At one time it was scorned for having the worst museums in the British Empire. It has tried to make amends, and now there are 16 museums of various types throughout the territory, though some would be hard pressed to justify their existence. Of the 16, only five can really be considered art museums. Along with a few galleries here and there (see the Shopping chapter for more details of art galleries in Hong Kong), there are enough paintings and sculpture (and even a few ceramics and bronzes) to keep one interested, but to savour the true genius of Chinese art you must head to either Beijing or Taipei.

Some exquisite works do make their way to Hong Kong, but mostly en route to the auction block. Art auctions are big business in Hong Kong, and both Christie's and Sotheby's do a brisk trade, selling to buyers from Japan, Taiwan and Singapore (often via telephone). The auction previews give one the opportunity to see all the pieces coming up for auction (see under Arts, Crafts & Antiques in the Shopping chapter for further information on Sotheby's and Christie's).

### Architecture

Architecture enthusiasts will find Hong Kong Island's Central district fascinating. A whole medley of modern buildings have gone up since the 1980s that make Central and Wan Chai a mecca of the modern and postmodern. The Bank of China Tower, the Hongkong and Shanghai Bank Building, Citibank Plaza, the Lippo Centre, Exchange Square, Central Plaza, the Entertainment Building and the Centre (the tallest building in Hong Kong, at 99 Queen's Rd, Central) are all impressive and very photogenic. The recently completed extension to the Hong Kong Convention and Exhibition Centre makes for fascinating viewing (inside and out) and also offers great views of both sides of Victoria Harbour. Kowloon does not have any really tall buildings, but this may change as there used to be height restrictions for the safety of planes landing at Kai Tak airport.

Unfortunately, progress has been made at the expense of history. A look through any coffee-table book of old Hong Kong will show what used to be, before the ball and chain. Over the years Hong Kong has played host to scores of Chinese temples, walled villages, Qing Dynasty forts, Victorian mansions and Edwardian hotels. But few structures have survived Hong Kong's ceaseless cycle of destruction and rebuilding.

About the only examples of pre-colonial Chinese architecture left in urban Hong Kong are temples: the Tin Hau temples in Tin Hau (near Causeway Bay), Shau Kei Wan and Aberdeen date from the mid-1800s. Government-run museums in Chai Wan and Tsuen Wan have preserved a few buildings left over from villages that predate the arrival of the British. But for anything more substantial, one has to go to the New Territories or the Outlying Islands, where walled villages, fortresses and 18th century temples can be found.

Colonial architecture is also in fairly short supply. Most of what is left can be found on Hong Kong Island, including the Legislative Council building (formerly the Supreme Court) in Central, the old police station in Stanley and an old sanatorium near Caine Lane in Sheung Wan. The Hong Kong Antiquities & Monuments Office (☎ 2721-2326), itself housed in a 1900 British schoolhouse on 136 Nathan Rd in Kowloon, has information and occasional exhibits on current preservation efforts.

## Chinese Opera

For nearly a thousand years, Chinese opera has given voice to the moral dilemmas, folk legends and romantic aspirations of China's people. With its garish costumes, shrill singing, sharp percussion and martial arts displays, Chinese opera may seem a world away from its western counterpart. But the themes are pretty much the same: mortal heroes battle overwhelmingly powerful foes; legendary spirits defend the world against evil; lovers seek escape from domineering and disapproving parents.

For those used to western music, Chinese opera performances may take some getting used to. Both male and female performers sing in an almost reedy falsetto designed to pierce through crowd noise, and the instrumental accompaniment often takes the form of drumming, gonging and other non-melodic punctuation. And even with today's 'shortened' performances, an average opera lasts around three hours. But even if you don't fall in love with it, Chinese opera is worth seeing at least once, to appreciate an art form that has remained in many ways unchanged for thousands of years.

There are three types of Chinese opera performed in Hong Kong. Top of the line among Chinese culture buffs is reckoned to be the Beijing variety, a highly refined style which uses almost no scenery but a variety of traditional props. This is usually where you can find the acrobatics and swordplay. The Cantonese variety is more 'music hall', usually with a 'boy meets girl' theme, and often incorporating modern and foreign references. The most traditional is Chiu Chow, now the least performed of the three. It is staged almost as it was in the Ming Dynasty, with stories from Chiu Chow legends and folklore. The Chiu Chow or Chaozhou are an ethnic group from the easternmost region of Guangdong Province.

Operas are usually categorised as 'civil' or 'martial': the latter may be more interesting to newcomers, as they are full of 'battles' that give the actors a chance to demonstrate their martial arts skills.

Much of the meaning in a Chinese opera can be derived from costumes, props and body language, so a little homework beforehand may make things easier to understand and enjoy. An excellent introduction to the mysterious world of Chinese opera is offered by Chen Kaige's wonderful film, *Farewell My Concubine*, starring Gong Li and Zhang Guoying. The Hong Kong Tourist Association (HKTA) offers a handout entitled *Hong*

*Kong's Musical Heritage – Chinese Opera* that gives a good summary of the origins, symbols and workings of performances.

Since the handover you have the added opportunity to watch Chinese revolutionary opera classics like *The White-Haired Girl* and *Taking Tiger Mountain by Strategy*, which will have radical left-wing lecturers and academics on the edges of their seats.

## Dance

There are three professional dance companies in Hong Kong. The Hong Kong Dance Company focuses on Chinese traditional and folk dances as well as full-length dance dramas based on local and Chinese themes. The City Contemporary Dance Company stages modern dance performances that include new commissions and past works, often choreographed by locals. Both companies frequently work with artists from China, and sometimes with those from other Asian countries.

Hong Kong also has its very own ballet company. Founded in 1979, the Hong Kong Ballet regularly performs both classical and modern pieces, and tours overseas each year.

One Chinese tradition that still lives on in Hong Kong is that of the lion dance. A group of dancers/martial artists takes position under an elaborately painted costume of a mythical Chinese lion. To the accompaniment of blazing firecrackers and banging cymbals, the lion leaps its way around the crowd, giving the dancers a chance to demonstrate their acrobatic prowess. Lion dances are now most commonly seen at the openings of new businesses or buildings. The Urban and Regional councils, along with the Hong Kong Chinese Martial Arts Association, also usually sponsor an annual lion dance tournament in December.

## Film

Though foreign movies are always popular with local audiences, Hong Kong itself has an incredibly vibrant film industry. Despite its small size, the territory now produces around 600 films per year, second only to India. In addition to their home market, most of these films are targeted at countries throughout Asia and sometimes further afield.

While profitable, Hong Kong films are saddled with a reputation for churning out mindless action, nonsense comedies and sickening romances. In many cases this is well earned. Popular actors and actresses will sometimes work on several films simultaneously, as do film crews, with the result that quality suffers. Films that do well at the box office invariably spawn a slew of imitations, so that moviegoers will face a glut of movies about unbeatable gamblers or double-fisted gunmen, for example. The international success of the (admittedly better than average) film *Rumble in the Bronx*, starring the legendary Jackie Chan, gives an idea of what to expect.

But in recent years some productions have helped the Hong Kong film industry earn a bit more respect by focusing on society and individuals rather than kung fu fights and bimbos. In particular, the success of *Farewell My Concubine* (a story about a Chinese opera troupe) at the 1993 Cannes Film Festival helped open eyes around the world to Hong Kong's potential. Directed by mainland Chinese director Chen Kaige, the film was a joint project between Chinese and Hong Kong producers. These joint ventures are the kind of films to look out for: China's influence seems to bring new cultural and creative depth to the productions. A classic film about Hong Kong is the 1994 film *Chungking Express*, a haunting series of stories of love and obsessions unfold to a bewitching soundtrack.

The annual Hong Kong International Film Festival, started in 1976, brings in hundreds of films from around the world, and is now billed as one of the world's major noncompetitive film festivals.

## Music

Hong Kong's music scene is dominated by 'Canto-pop', basically a synergy of Cantonese lyrics with western pop music. There is an entire constellation of local stars that, while perhaps known in Asia, are all but unheard of in the west. Some are movie stars who like the idea of cutting a record, while others are genuine musicians and songwriters. The latter tend to turn out more original compositions, often blending western rock or pop with traditional Chinese melodies or rhythms. Many younger Hong Kongers pay homage to their favourite stars by crooning their tunes at karaoke bars, which are by far Hong Kong's most popular music venues.

However, classical music is also alive and well in Hong Kong. The city boasts a Chinese orchestra, as well as a philharmonic, sinfonietta and chamber orchestra. Overseas performers of world repute frequently make it to Hong Kong, sometimes even giving performances in the New Territories as well as the city centre. The number of foreign performances soars during the Hong Kong Arts Festival, held in February/March every year.

Jazz, rock and other forms of modern music are hit or miss. The lack of decent venues often discourages major international acts from passing through and the local music scene is still underdeveloped. With all the karaoke and Canto-pop, local musicians have a tough time generating enough support. The bright spots in the bleak landscape are the Jazz Club, which books top musicians year after year, and the Fringe Club, which encourages the development of local music and organises an annual arts and music event, the Festival Fringe. See the Entertainment chapter for more details.

### Theatre

Probably because of Hong Kong's colonial history, nearly all theatre is western in form, if not content. But most productions are staged in Cantonese, and a large number are new plays by Hong Kong writers. The plays often provide an insightful and sometimes humorous look at contemporary Hong Kong life. In a way, Hong Kong may be home to the most progressive theatre in contemporary Chinese culture. It is certainly more interesting than China, where the state still ensures productions are bland and politically correct.

More conservative is the Hong Kong Repertory Theatre, which tends toward larger scale productions of both original works on Chinese themes or translated western plays. Actors in many of the local companies are graduates of the Hong Kong Academy for Performing Arts, which also stages some interesting student shows, most of which are Cantonese versions of well-known western plays.

English-language theatre in Hong Kong is mostly the domain of expatriate amateurs. Plays are more often than not scripted by local writers. The Hong Kong Cultural Centre and the Hong Kong Academy for Performing Arts also host foreign productions, spanning everything from grandiose western musicals such as *Les Misérables* to spartan Japanese *kyogen* plays (refer to the Performing Arts section of the Entertainment chapter for details).

### Painting & Sculpture

Painting in Hong Kong falls into three broad categories: modern local, classical Chinese and western. Paintings by local Hong Kong artists often echo their angst-filled counterparts in the west. Styles and techniques tend to differ of course, as Hong Kong painters often seek new ways to blend east and west. There are also locals who are dedicated to preserving such classical Chinese disciplines as calligraphy and landscape (*sansui*) painting. Many of these have spent years studying in China, and their work tends to reflect current trends in classical painting there. While Hong Kong does not have a great deal of home-grown western-style art, exhibits from abroad are regularly on display at the Hong Kong Museum of Art in Tsim Sha Tsui. There are many art galleries in Hong Kong which stage exhibitions of local and western pieces; see the Shopping chapter for further information.

Most of Hong Kong's sculpture seems to be located in public places; by and large it seems to be modern in inspiration, being more cerebral than aesthetically inspiring – you will have to search hard to find classical lines. The deep pockets of Hong Kong's land developers have allowed them to adorn their flagship properties with some prestigious pieces. So in front of Central's Exchange Square, one can find Henry Moore's large bronze *Oval with Points,* and *Taiji* by Taiwanese artist Zhu Ming. Facing the eastern side of the Jardine House is *Double Oval,* also by Henry Moore. Inside the Chater Rd entrance of the Mandarin Oriental Hotel are two copper reliefs by noted Chinese artist Cheung Yee. More of Cheung's work can be found on the walls of the nearby Prince's Building and the Landmark shopping mall. Across the harbour in Tsim Sha Tsui, near the Hong Kong Cultural Centre, stands *The Flying Frenchman* by Cezar, a gift from a French company. This unusual piece was not all that well received by the local media, but people have learned to live with it.

The Salisbury Garden, east of the Cultural Centre, contains a number of large sculptures by local sculptors. There are some more pieces by younger Hong Kong artists at Kowloon Park's Sculpture Walk, some of which may leave viewers scratching their heads.

## SOCIETY & CONDUCT
### Traditional Culture

While Hong Kong is very westernised, many old Chinese traditions persist. Whether people still believe in all of them, or are in some cases just going through the motions, is hard to say. The British colonial government largely tried to keep its nose out of Chinese culture. Even polygamy was legally sanctioned for the Chinese community until 1971. The extent that traditions have survived, perished or been watered down has been mainly determined by Hong Kongers themselves.

**Superstitions** Southern Chinese culture embraces a wealth of guidelines on controlling the amount of good or bad luck in one's life. Many of these ideas live on in Hong Kong in varying degrees. Despite what tourist pamphlets and coffee-table books may tell you, not everyone believes in all these superstitions. But there are certain ones that still affect people's daily lives.

One of the most prevalent is the belief in the power of numbers. In Cantonese, which has several tones but a limited number of consonant-vowel combinations, many words share the same pronunciation: the difference is marked by the tone the word carries. This gives rise to numerous homonyms. The number three sounds similar to 'life', nine like 'eternity' and the ever-popular number eight like 'prosperity.' Lowest on the list is four, which has the same pronunciation as the word for 'death'.

Thus companies or home buyers will shell out extra money for an address that contains one or more number eights. Each year the Hong Kong government draws in millions of dollars for charity by auctioning off automobile licence plates which feature lucky numbers: the bidding always reaches ridiculous heights. Dates and prices are affected too. The Bank of China Tower was opened on 8 August 1988 – a rare union of the prosperous numbers. Couples rush to be married if there's an eight in the date – August is a busy month! Many restaurants will offer set dinners for HK$88. And of course gamblers at the horse-racing track will lean toward the luckier numbers, though the more sophisticated punters have long gone over to the machinations of random theory. A few buildings around the city are missing their 4th or 14th floors, but overall people seem able to live with the number four, despite its ominous overtones. In fact, there is a Rolls-Royce owned by a Chinese driver that you might see on the streets of Hong Kong that has the vehicle registration number '4'.

Some foods are also luckier than others. On birthdays, celebrants may eat noodles, as the long strands symbolise longevity. Sea moss, which in Cantonese has the same sound as 'prosperity' is always an auspicious ingredient. Peach juice is believed to be a life-giving elixir, while garlic and ginger can protect babies against evil.

As the god of longevity rides on the back of the deer, parts of this animal are often used

## Chinese Medicine

Hong Kong offers a good opportunity to try Chinese medicine. Chinese doctors and pharmacies are easy to find, and some speak English. Some cures may work for you, but it's generally best to keep your experiments limited to minor health problems. And make sure the doctor you see clearly understands what you're saying; using the wrong remedy may leave you sicker than you were to begin with.

Chinese herbalists claim to have all sorts of treatments for stomach aches, headaches, colds, flu and sore throats as well as long-term problems like asthma. While some of these remedies may be effective, it seems to vary from person to person. What they can do for more serious illnesses like cancer and heart disease is far less certain. For potentially life-threatening conditions such as chest pains or appendicitis, it's best to see a doctor of the modern (western) tradition.

Most herbal medicines are fairly safe, and produce few side effects. However there have been a few cases in recent years where people have died from taking too much of a certain herb, or using it under the wrong conditions. Notable among these is *chan su*, a brown rock-like substance that includes dried toad secretions and steroids found in teas made from the oleander shrub and the foxglove. Used in some aphrodisiacs, the herb sparked irregular heartbeats and eventually fatal heart attacks in four men in the USA in 1995. Other herbs to steer clear of are: *encommiae ulmoide* (which, depending on the dosage, can raise or lower blood pressure) and arsenite (which is given in external doses of less than 0.03g to treat asthma – take it internally and it will kill you). These are the exception rather than the rule, and chances of this type of problem are low.

A small number of Chinese medicines make use of parts of endangered animals, such as rhinoceros horn. As expensive as rhino horn is, it's likely that herbalists are using false advertising by slipping in water buffalo horn instead. Nonetheless, why take a chance on hastening the extinction of a species in order to cure a cold? Make sure you check what's in the herbal concoction you're about to buy.

A good place to purchase herbal medicines is Yue Hwa Chinese Products Emporium at the north-west corner of Nathan and Jordan Rds, just above Jordan MTR station in Yau Ma Tei (Map 4). In Sheung Wan, try the Eu-Yan Sang Pharmacy, on Queen's Rd Central, just west of Peel St (Map 6). Before buying anything, explain your condition to a Chinese chemist and ask for a recommendation. They consider this part of their job.

You can also try acupuncture in Hong Kong. Getting stuck with needles might not sound pleasant, but if done properly it doesn't hurt. And it can be surprisingly effective. Often it depends on the skill of the acupuncturist and the condition being treated. While acupuncture itself is probably harmless, one should not forget that AIDS and hepatitis B can be spread easily by contaminated needles. In western countries, the use of disposable acupuncture needles has become routine, but this is not necessarily the case in Hong Kong.

The following organisations could also be worth checking: Chinese Acupuncture Association (☎ 2545-7640), ground floor, 3 Aberdeen St, Central; and the International Acupuncture Society (☎ 2771-1066), Room 1113A, 11th floor, Champion Building, 301-309 Nathan Rd, Yau Ma Tei. ∎

in Chinese medicine to cure ailments and prolong life. Similarly, the long life of the tortoise can be absorbed through a soup made from it. The carp, which can live for up to 40 years, is among the most prized possessions in a wealthy household's fish pond.

**Chinese Zodiac** Astrology has a long history in China and is integrated with religious beliefs. As in the western astrological system, there are 12 zodiac signs. However, unlike the western system, your sign is based on the year rather than the month in which you were born. Still, this is a simplification.

The exact day and time of birth are also carefully considered in charting the precise astrological path.

If you want to know your sign in the Chinese zodiac, look up your year of birth in the chart on the next page. However, it's a little more complicated than this because Chinese astrology goes by the lunar calendar. The Chinese Lunar New Year usually falls in late January or early February, so the first month will be included in the year before.

It is said that the animal year chart originated when Buddha commanded all the beasts of the earth to assemble before him. The names of the years were established

| Chinese Zodiac | | | | | | | |
|---|---|---|---|---|---|---|---|
| Rat | 1924 | 1936 | 1948 | 1960 | 1972 | 1984 | 1996 |
| Ox/Cow | 1925 | 1937 | 1949 | 1961 | 1973 | 1985 | 1997 |
| Tiger | 1926 | 1938 | 1950 | 1962 | 1974 | 1986 | 1998 |
| Rabbit | 1927 | 1939 | 1951 | 1963 | 1975 | 1987 | 1999 |
| Dragon | 1928 | 1940 | 1952 | 1964 | 1976 | 1988 | 2000 |
| Snake | 1929 | 1941 | 1953 | 1965 | 1977 | 1989 | 2001 |
| Horse | 1930 | 1942 | 1954 | 1966 | 1978 | 1990 | 2002 |
| Goat | 1931 | 1943 | 1955 | 1967 | 1979 | 1991 | 2003 |
| Monkey | 1932 | 1944 | 1956 | 1968 | 1980 | 1992 | 2004 |
| Rooster | 1933 | 1945 | 1957 | 1969 | 1981 | 1993 | 2005 |
| Dog | 1934 | 1946 | 1958 | 1970 | 1982 | 1994 | 2006 |
| Pig | 1935 | 1947 | 1959 | 1971 | 1983 | 1995 | 2007 |

according to the first 12 animals' order of arrival. There is no cat year; apparently the rat tricked the cat into arriving late.

Being born or married in a particular year is believed to determine one's fortune. In this era of modern birth-control techniques, Chinese parents will often carefully manipulate the birth times of their children. The year of the dragon sees the biggest jump in the birth rate, closely followed by the year of the tiger.

Traditionally, the Chinese calculate age differently to most other cultures. Believing that life begins at the moment of conception, Chinese would consider a baby already one year old when it leaves the mother's womb. So older people or those from rural communities may quote you an age that is actually one year older than that according to the western calendar.

The Chinese zodiac also plays a key role in almanacs, which people will consult to choose auspicious dates for weddings, household moves, business openings and so on. These guides even advise when to cut one's hair or to sweep: one wouldn't want to brush one's good luck away due to ill timing!

**Five Elements** The ancient theory of the five elements (*nghang*) is also important in determining your character. According to the Chinese, the year you were born in belongs to one of the five elements: wood, water, fire, earth or metal. These elements in turn are part of a cycle of creation and destruction whereby wood creates fire, fire creates earth (ash), earth creates metal (ore), metal creates water (through condensation on, say, a sheet of metal) and water creates wood (through growth); conversely, earth destroys water (by damming it), water destroys fire, fire destroys metal (melting), metal destroys wood (axe), and wood destroys earth (by breaking it up with roots). If you are born in a metal year, it might be bad news to marry someone who is born in a wood year. But not necessarily, for each element is subdivided into 12 more degrees, so you can be of a very weak metal and marry someone of a strong wood nature, and get on fine! Many Chinese couples determine which is the best year to have a child so that it will harmonise with their elemental signs.

**Fortune-Telling** If you're of a mind to have your destiny laid out for you, you'll not be short of choices in Hong Kong. You can go to a temple and consult the gods and spirits, have your palm or face read, or consult an almanac.

Probably the most popular method of divination in Hong Kong is using the 'fortune sticks'. The altar of a temple, whether Buddhist or Taoist, is usually flanked by stacks of the wooden sticks (*chim*), which are housed in bamboo canisters. The routine is to ask the spirits or gods a question and shake the canister until one stick falls out. Each stick bears a numeral, which corresponds to a printed slip of paper in a set held by the temple keeper. That slip of paper should be taken to the temple's fortune-teller, who can interpret its particular meaning for you. The fortune-teller will also study your face and ask your date and time of birth. Kowloon's Wong Tai Sin Temple is one of the best places to get your fortune told. It's usually also easy to find fortune-tellers at the Tin Hau temples in Wan Chai and Yau Ma Tei.

If you are just seeking a simple 'yes' or 'no' to a question, and wish to bypass the fortune-teller, you may turn to two clam-shaped pieces of wood called *bui* (which means 'shell' in Cantonese). The way they fall when thrown in the air in front of the altar indicates the gods' answer to your query. One side of each piece of wood is *yeung*, or male/positive; the other side is *yam*, which is female/negative. If both pieces land with the same side up, the answer is negative. But if they land with different sides up, it indicates a balance of yam (yin) and yueng (yang), and denotes a positive answer.

Palm-readers usually examine both the lines and features of the hand. Palms are thought to be emotional – their lines change in tune with one's life, and can reveal the past and what the future may hold, depending on what actions one takes. Readings for men are taken from the left palm, those for women from the right.

To augment their study, palmists will examine one's facial features: there are 48 recognised eye patterns which reveal character and fortune, and eight basic facial shapes. Clues are also provided by the shape of your ears, nose, mouth, lips and eyebrows. For example, people with small earlobes are considered less likely to become wealthy. As with the fortune-stick seers, you will also probably be asked to provide the date and time of your birth. Palmists can be found near street markets, including Temple St in Yau Ma Tei, their trade identified by palm charts on large signs or cards. The longer the line of people waiting, the better chance that the palmist has a good reputation.

Other fortune tellers resort to the mysterious *Yikging* (or *Jauyi*), better known in the west as the *Book of Changes* or *I Ching*. The

---

**Colour & Custom**

There's more to a colour than meets the eye, at least for the Chinese. White is the colour of death, and mourners at traditional Chinese funerals will often wear white cloaks, sometimes with a black ribbon. Black on white is traditionally associated with funerals, and if you ever see a large circular flower board in black and white, it denotes someone's passing. It used to be that sending a white sheet of paper with black writing on it was a bad omen, but in these days of word processors and laser-jet printers, that belief has gone by the wayside.

Red is a far happier colour, symbolising prosperity. In traditional Chinese weddings the bride would wear red, though today the red gown is usually reserved for the wedding reception; tuxedos and white wedding dresses are the norm in Hong Kong. Restaurants, temples and other places where people congregate are often decked out in red. However, it is not considered good form to write notes, letters or sign one's name in red ink. Hong Kongers don't seem too clear on why this is, but Taiwanese say that it implies the writer lacks intelligence.

Yellow, which was always the colour of the emperor, was believed to repel evil spirits, which is why temple fortune papers are printed on yellow paper. Black also supposedly stands for treachery, but this idea wilted under the forces of fashion – black clothing was all the rage among stylish young women in Hong Kong during the 1990s. ∎

---

process of reading the hexagrams of the Yikging (*Yijing* in Mandarin) lies in a process called *bukgwa*.

Some Chinese families turn to almanacs for do-it-yourself fortune-telling. Based on the Chinese zodiac, these volumes identify the good and bad aspects for each day of the year, enabling the reader to pick dates for special occasions. The books also give instructions for more thorough self-help fortune-telling. Computer software exists these days for rapid determining of one's future.

**Fung Shui** The Chinese term *fung shui* literally means 'wind-water', and it always pops up in any mention of Chinese traditions in Hong Kong. As a result it's become fairly clichéd, but that doesn't diminish its role in life and business in the territory.

Fung shui (geomancy) aims to balance the elements of nature to produce a harmonious, prosperous environment. It's based on classical Chinese writings, has been in practice since the 12th century AD, and continues to play a role in the design and construction of buildings, highways, parks, tunnels and grave sites, among other things. Not everyone believes in fung shui, but at the same time, few dare flout its dictates. To do so may invite business failure, ill health or a decline in family fortunes.

Before construction or renovation begins, fung shui experts (geomancers) are called in. The Hongkong and Shanghai Bank Building, the Bank of China Tower and Citibank Plaza are just some of the towering monuments to modernity that have taken fung shui into account in their design. The two lions that guard the entrance to the Hongkong and Shanghai Bank Building were positioned at the precise place and time dictated auspicious by a respected geomancer. This way they would be sure to protect the bank (and its depositors) against water-borne spirits in Victoria Harbour. The former governor's residence was considered by many to have been located and designed by someone well-versed in the laws of fung shui. It was protected at the back by a wall of trees and the winding road that led up to it confused any bad spirits. Unfortunately, the malign fung shui of the Bank of China Tower loomed over the building and abnegated any benign influence that it might previously have enjoyed. When building its new headquarters, Hang Seng Bank had to tear down a newly constructed walkway over Connaught Rd when a geomancer pronounced it ill-positioned. The walkway was rebuilt a few metres to the right, at a cost of several million Hong Kong dollars.

To guard against evil spirits, who can only move in straight lines, doors to the outside will sometimes be positioned at an angle. For similar reasons, sofas or beds cannot face doorways. Ideally, homes and businesses should have a view of calm water, as this allows one to see their good fortune floating on calm seas. In the absence of a sea view, which commands an exorbitant price in land-scarce Hong Kong, a properly positioned indoor fishtank will do. Corporate heads are not supposed to have offices that face west: otherwise their company profits will go the same direction as the setting sun. If a business runs into bad times, a geomancer may be called in to search for any evil spirits lurking about. If the bad luck persists, a Taoist priest may have to come and perform an exorcism. Houses often have small fung shui objects placed strategically around the rooms. It is common to see two little dragons coiled up on the floor opposite the door, or two small golden lions looking out of the windows.

Trees can house spirits, so some villages and temples in the New Territories still have fung shui groves to provide a place for the good spirits to live. Attempts to cut down fung shui groves to construct new buildings or public works have sometimes led to massive protests and even violent confrontations – the solution may be a large cash payment to the village to 'placate the spirits'. Even then, it's a delicate situation and the help of a professional geomancer will undoubtedly be required to avoid trouble.

In the rural areas, and sometimes in the city, you may come across little octagonal mirrors on doorways or windows. That's fung shui at work again: the mirrors are designed to reflect away any evil demons trying to slip indoors. The octagonal mirrors are in the shape of the *baatgwa*, an eight-sided arrangement of the eight trigrams of the *Yikging* (*Book of Changes*), and often have the trigrams marked out as well.

**Taijiquan** Formerly spelled *taichichuan*, this form of slow motion shadow-boxing has been popular in China for centuries. It is basically a form of exercise, but it's also a martial art. In Cantonese it is known as *taigikkuen*.

*Taijiquan* (literally 'fist of the supreme ultimate') is very popular among old people and also with young women who believe it will help keep their bodies looking good. The movements are supposed to develop the breathing muscles, promote digestion and improve muscle tone. It seems to work: there are some pretty sprightly old men and women to be found practising out there. In fact, some of the harder schools (like the Chen school) are exhausting and extremely painful to perform.

Experts in taijiquan can also use it for the art's deepest purpose, as a martial art. The art emphasises softness and takes its inspiration from the Taoist classic, the *Daode Jing* (the classic text of the Way and its Power) by the sage Laozi. Aikido is a similar martial art, although Aikido does not practise slow forms and is essentially a grappling art (with wrist locks) while taijiquan is basically a striking art (with punches and kicks).

According to tradition, taijiquan is best performed at dawn, most commonly in parks or gardens. The most popular park for taijiquan is Victoria Park in Causeway Bay. Other popular venues include the Zoological & Botanical Gardens in Central, and Kowloon Park in Tsim Sha Tsui (see the Things to See & Do chapter for details on courses in taijiquan and other martial arts).

### Appearance & Conduct

**Public Etiquette** Hong Kong is an international city in many ways, and there are few things travellers can do that will really faze locals. It may be good to keep in mind though that Hong Kong is no longer a great place to bargain. In many places where prices are clearly marked, such as department or chain stores, trying to talk the price below what's listed will only result in a frustrated salesperson. The rip-off camera and electronic shops of Tsim Sha Tsui are another matter: they expect bargaining, and often mark their prices up so tourists will start negotiating from a higher price level.

Sometimes Hong Kong salespeople can be rude and annoying without you having done anything. This is really a no-win situation, as they obviously don't care much about your patronage. The best thing to do is try some other place, which is pretty easy to do in this retail-crazed city.

If you visit someone's home, it's best to bring a gift of some kind. Fruit or chocolates will do, and alcohol such as brandy or whisky is usually OK too. Even if the host doesn't drink, sooner or later he or she will have guests that do. If for some reason you should think of giving a clock as a present, think again. To more traditional Chinese the clock symbolises mortality, so giving one is akin to a harbinger of death, not the most cheery of gifts.

The Chinese are on the whole quite casual when it comes to table manners, but there are some rules that should be observed when eating. For details see the 'Food Etiquette' boxed text in the Places to Eat chapter.

Fashion is taken quite seriously in Hong Kong, but at the same time you can go to most restaurants and hotels in casual dress. Sadly, even The Peninsula allows high-tea drinkers to wear jeans and tennis shoes, though some other hotels, notably the Mandarin Oriental, enforce a stricter dress code. This relaxed attitude does not extend to the business world, where dark suit and tie and conservative skirt and blouse rule supreme.

If you go to the beach, keep in mind that in Hong Kong, as in most Asian societies, nude or topless sunbathing is considered rude and offensive.

One last point. Hong Kong is a frightfully expensive place. Hotel rooms can easily cost HK$2500 per night, a beer at a bar HK$50. If you make or have any Hong Kong friends, try and spare them endless complaints about how much everything costs. They're already well aware of it.

**The Group** When it comes to leisure, the more the merrier. In general Hong Kongers love to hit the shopping malls, movies or hiking trails in large groups. Despite the infiltration of many western ways into Hong Kong society, the idea of solo recreation is almost as alien here as in China and Taiwan. It's not surprising on a country hiking trail to run across 20 to 30 Hong Kongers raising a ruckus, screaming at each other via walkie-talkies and seemingly ignoring the nature around them. It's the same scene while eating, drinking or singing – having a large group ensures a festive atmosphere. This doesn't mean that you won't find single hikers, or someone enjoying a good book at a café. Every city has its loners. And of course, the group mentality stops short at romance: a stroll along the Tsim Sha Tsui promenade at night will show that double-dating is not in style.

**Face** Much is made of the 'mysterious' Oriental concept of face, which is roughly equivalent to status or respect. Sinologists, writers and other observers love to point to the lengths which Chinese people will go to 'gain face'. Truth be told, this hardly sets the Chinese apart from other cultures. Westerners and other Asians have also been known to purchase ridiculously expensive clothing, jewellery or cars for the sake of impressing those around them. It is true that getting into a loud argument with, for instance, a shopkeeper in front of a crowd will probably get you nowhere: he or she will do their best not to knuckle under and lose face. But again, this is hardly an attitude that is unique to the Chinese, or Asia for that matter. If you want to help people gain face, treat them with respect and show consideration for their culture.

**Money** As any speaker of Cantonese can tell you, most conversations you hear on the bus, subway or street are about prices, incomes, rents and debts. And while Hong Kong people are more discreet than their compatriots in China, occasionally they will shock foreign visitors by asking point-blank about salaries, costs and other financial affairs that many westerners consider conversational taboo.

Actually it's not all that surprising. Hong Kong has long been a haven for refugees from China, and for many, memories of poverty and chaos are just one generation away. Making money is the best way to protect oneself and one's family against any future misfortune. This is worth keeping in

mind if a Hong Konger matter-of-factly tells you that the prime goal of life is to make money. In the context of Hong Kong, this is an honourable goal.

Of course it's not just about refugees and saving for the future. Hong Kong is without a doubt one of the world's most materialistic societies. The city has a stunning number of luxury retail stores and shopping malls, and don't think they survive on tourist dollars alone. One of the main reasons to make money is in order to buy things which show other people how much money you make. This attitude can extend to relationships: 'no flat, no car, no mobile phone – no chance' Hong Kong women have been heard to say of prospective suitors.

Not everyone buys into it: many of Hong Kong's young songwriters and playwrights often take aim against this love of money in their work. For now however, their voice remains in the minority.

### RELIGION

Buddhism and Taoism are the dominant religions in Hong Kong, though Confucianism, ancestor worship and ancient animist beliefs have also been incorporated into the milieu. The number of active Buddhists is estimated at 650,000 to 700,000. This figure probably also includes a good number of Taoists.

On a daily level the Chinese are much less concerned with the high-minded philosophies and asceticism of Buddha, Confucius or Laozi than they are with the pursuit of worldly success, the appeasement of the dead and the spirits, and the seeking of hidden knowledge about the future.

It can be difficult to distinguish the lines between religion, superstition and traditional practices such as fung shui. All three come into play when trying to influence the course of luck and fortune. Gods have to be appeased, bad spirits blown away and sleeping dragons soothed to keep luck on your side.

Visits to temples are usually made to ask the gods' blessings for specific issues: a relative's health, family prosperity, the success of a business, even a lucky day at the horse-racing track! Fung shui and the Chinese zodiac also play key roles in choosing dates for funerals, and sites for graves and ancestral shrines.

Hong Kong has approximately 600 temples, monasteries and shrines, most of which are Buddhist or Taoist. Of Hong Kong's hundreds of temples, more than 40 are public ones maintained by the Chinese Temples Committee, which gets its income from donations by worshippers. Temples are usually dedicated to one or two deities whose images can be found in the main hall. Side halls house images of subsidiary gods. Since Buddhism and Taoism are both accepted as traditional Chinese religions, deities from both are often honoured within the same temple. The majority of temples are tiny but there are some enormous ones such as the Po Lin Monastery on Lantau Island, the Temple of Ten Thousand Buddhas at Sha Tin and Wong Tai Sin in Kowloon.

Aside from the Chinese religions, there are several other faiths represented in Hong Kong's cosmopolitan population. There are about 500,000 Christians, about 51% of whom are Protestant and 49% are Catholic. Due to the zeal of lay Christians and missionaries, the number of independent Protestant churches has steadily risen since the 1970s, and now includes around 950 congregations.

The Catholic Church established its first mission in Hong Kong in 1841, when the British took possession. The present bishop, John Baptist Cheng-chung Wu, was made a cardinal in 1988. The majority of services at the 62 parishes are conducted in Cantonese, though a few churches provide services in English.

Hong Kong is also home to around 50,000 Muslims. More than half are Chinese, the rest either locally born non-Chinese or hailing from Pakistan, India, Malaysia, Indonesia, the Middle East or Africa. Four principal mosques are used daily for prayers. The oldest is the Jamia Mosque on Shelley St, in the Mid-Levels, which was established in the late 19th century and rebuilt in 1915. Over in Kowloon, stands the Kowloon Mosque and Islamic Centre, a white marble structure that has become somewhat of a Tsim Sha Tsui landmark. There are also around 12,000 Hindus in Hong Kong, as well as smaller Sikh and Jewish communities.

### Religious Services

The following places either offer services or will tell you when and where they are held. Check the *Yellow Pages* for a more comprehensive list of Hong Kong churches and other places of worship.

*Anglican* – St John's Cathedral (☎ 2523-4157), 4-8 Garden Rd, Central

*Baha'i* – (☎ 2367-6407), Flat C-6, 11th floor, Hankow Centre, Middle Rd, Tsim Sha Tsui

*Catholic* – St Joseph's (☎ 2552-3992), 37 Garden Rd, Central

*Christian Scientist* – (☎ 2524-2701), 31 MacDonnell Rd, Central

*Hindu* – (☎ 2572-5284), Wong Nai Chung Rd, Happy Valley

*Jewish* – Synagogue Ohel Leah (☎ 2801-5440), 70 Robinson Rd, Mid-Levels

*Methodist* – (☎ 2575-7817), 271 Queen's Rd East, Wan Chai

*Mormon* – Church of the Latter Day Saints (☎ 2559-3325), 7 Castle Rd, Mid-Levels

*Muslim* – Islamic Union (☎ 2575-2218), 40 Oi Kwan Rd, Wan Chai

*Quaker* – Society of Friends (☎ 2697-7283), 3rd floor, Conference Room, Mariners Club, Middle Rd, Tsim Sha Tsui

*Sikh* – (☎ 2574-9837), 371 Queen's Rd East, Wan Chai

# Facts for the Visitor

## WHEN TO GO

In terms of weather, October-November and April-May are probably the best times to visit. Temperatures are moderate, and there's a good chance of clear skies and sun. May through to September tends to see a lot of rain, and from June to August the sweltering heat and humidity make for rather sweaty sightseeing. For more details, see the Climate section in the Facts about Hong Kong chapter.

Under normal conditions, Hong Kong hotels have two high seasons: September to January, and March to June. During this time rates go up, and rooms are often hard to find. Airfares to Hong Kong are also usually higher around these times. This was generally the golden rule until the handover, but the subsequent slump in tourism brought fierce competition among airlines and hotels. Cuts of up to 50% in hotel room prices and huge discounts in airfares greeted travellers in late 1997 (see the Getting There & Away and Places to Stay chapters for more information).

Travel in and out of Hong Kong can be difficult during Chinese New Year, which falls around late January/early February. Planes are usually full, and the border with China becomes a living hell as millions (yes, millions) of locals flood to the mainland to visit relatives. On the other hand, the crowds that can make Hong Kong a tiring place to visit are absent during this time, and more and more shops and restaurants only close for one day during the holiday, instead of the traditional three to seven day break.

If you're planning to leave Hong Kong for the UK or the USA in August, book your flight early. You will be competing for seats with tens of thousands of Hong Kong students, most going to universities abroad.

## ORIENTATION

Surprisingly, a good deal of Hong Kong's 1084 sq km is comprised of mountains, sparsely inhabited islands and country parks. The city itself is crammed into a relatively small area centred around Victoria Harbour. Hong Kong Island lies to the south, the Kowloon peninsula to the north. The urban area basically runs from the north side of Hong Kong Island to the Kowloon Hills, which mark the effective border between the peninsula and the New Territories.

Urban Hong Kong is divided into numerous districts. The main business, banking and administrative district is Central, on Hong Kong Island directly across from Tsim Sha Tsui, which lies at the tip of the Kowloon peninsula. Going west from Central will take you through the districts of Sheung Wan and Kennedy Town, which have some of Hong Kong's oldest residential neighbourhoods.

To the east of Central lies Admiralty, which is basically a group of commercial and government office blocks, and then Wan Chai, home to scores of little family-run shops, some good restaurants, pubs, clubs and a small strip of seedy hostess bars. Next along is Causeway Bay, one of Hong Kong's major shopping and entertainment areas, and home to many Japanese department stores. Nestled behind Wan Chai and Causeway Bay, at the foot of the hills, is Happy Valley, an upmarket residential area as well as the site of one of Hong Kong's two horse-racing tracks. East of Causeway Bay you will find the districts of Tin Hau, North Point, Tai Koo, Shau Kei Wan and Chai Wan where the mix becomes more residential/industrial. Towering above it all is the Peak, the exclusive residential district that has been home to Hong Kong's upper crust since the territory was founded.

On the Kowloon side, Tsim Sha Tsui, and the districts of Jordan and Yau Ma Tei to the north, are home to the bulk of Hong Kong's hotels and retail shops. Tsim Sha Tsui also boasts numerous restaurants, bars and clubs. Mong Kok, north of Yau Ma Tei, is another major shopping area, though mostly for locals as opposed to tourists. The eastern side of the peninsula, which includes districts like Hung Hom, Ho Man Tin and To Kwa Wan, is mainly residential or industrial. One exception is Tsim Sha Tsui East, where you will find a few hotels, shopping plazas, office blocks and nightclubs.

Most of these districts are relatively compact, making Hong Kong a great place to explore on foot. Sheung Wan and Wan Chai on Hong Kong Island, and Yau Ma Tei and Mong Kok in Kowloon, all offer good possibilities for strolling around and checking out the local lifestyle. The Peak not only has spectacular views of Hong Kong, but a series of tree-lined walkways and trails as well. And if your feet get tired, Hong Kong's outstanding public transport network will help get you to your destination quickly and, for the most part, comfortably.

## MAPS

Good maps are easy to get in Hong Kong. The Hong Kong Tourist Association (HKTA) hands out free copies of its *Official Hong Kong Map* booklet at its offices at Kai Tak and Chek Lap Kok airports, the Star Ferry Terminal in Tsim Sha Tsui and Jardine House in Central. Maps are divided by district, have both English and Chinese script, list hotels and shopping centres and are easy to read. Similar maps can be found at the back of *The Official Hong Kong Guide* and *Hong Kong Now!*, both of which are put out by the HKTA, and are usually available in hotels as well as HKTA offices.

A series of free maps is put out by The Map Company (☎ 2537-7605). In addition to an overall *Map of Hong Kong* there are separate maps of the main centres, but they are not very detailed. These maps can usually be found at hotels, some bars and Oliver's Super Sandwiches shops. If you can't locate one, call the company.

If you're looking for greater detail, topographical accuracy and excellent colour reproduction, it's worth investing in the *Hong Kong Guidebook*, published by Universal Publications and regularly updated. Although it's HK$60, it's worth it for its

sheer quality and legibility. Compiled in both English and Chinese, is also includes such useful information as bus routes, timetables and hotel lists. The 1998 version comes with a Public Transport Boarding Guide which is bursting with information, but many of the destinations are written only in Chinese. It is available from most bookstores. The *Hong Kong Official Guide Map* (put out by the government) has both overall and district maps and is available from most bookstores. Other maps worth looking out for include the *Hong Kong Touring Map* (HK$18) and the *Detailed City Map of Hong Kong Island* (HK$22), both published by Universal Publications, and the *Hong Kong* map (HK$55) published by Berndston & Berndston, an all-weather map sealed in plastic.

The government also sells a series of countryside maps that are extremely useful if you plan to go hiking in the hills. These are available at the Government Publications Office (☎ 2537-1910) in the Government Office Building, Queensway Government Offices, 88 Queensway, Admiralty (Map 5). The office is open from 9 am to 4 pm daily, and 9 am to 1 pm on Saturday. Those of you who are seriously into maps can try the Map Publications Centre (☎ 2848-2480), 14th floor, Murray Building, Garden Rd, Central (near the Peak Tram Terminus); there is another office on the Kowloon side at 382 Nathan Rd, Yau Ma Tei. Universal Publications puts out a series of waterproof maps of the New Territories and Outlying Islands that are more reasonably priced (HK$22) and wonderfully detailed; look out for them.

Unfortunately there are no good bus maps for the city. Your best option here may be Universal Publications' *Hong Kong Guidebook* mentioned earlier. The Hong Kong Transport Department also publishes a hefty tome entitled *Public Transport in Hong Kong – A Guide to Services*. For HK$40 you get a comprehensive rundown of every bus, minibus, ferry and rail route in the territory – quite a bit more info than you need unless you're planning a long-term stay. The book is sold at the Government Publications Office.

## TOURIST OFFICES

The HKTA is a government-sponsored organisation dedicated to promoting Hong Kong tourism and dealing with any inquiries visitors may have. It has several local offices and telephone inquiries lines, and produces reams of useful pamphlets and publications. It also runs an extensive network of overseas offices.

### Information Centres

The HKTA runs three information centres with helpful staff to answer questions. They also provide maps and a wide variety of literature on sights, hotels, food, local customs, tours and so on. Though mostly free, some of their publications must be purchased. You will find the centres at:

Chek Lap Kok airport – opening hours not fixed at time of writing (information is provided for arriving passengers only)

Shop 8, Basement, Jardine House, 1 Connaught Place, Central – open from 9 am to 6 pm weekdays, 9 am to 1 pm Saturday

Star Ferry Terminal, Tsim Sha Tsui – open from 8 am to 6 pm weekdays, 9 am to 5 pm weekends and holidays

The HKTA also has an extensive collection of editorial features that give more detailed information on various aspects of Hong Kong life and Chinese culture. The information centres should have a master list, but you may have to wait for the features to be mailed or faxed to you from the head office, where they are stocked. Alternatively, you can go in person to HKTA's head office (☎ 2807-6543; Web site www.hkta.org), on the 10th floor, Citicorp Centre, 18 Whitfield Rd, North Point.

HKTA also have an office in Beijing (☎ (86-10) 6465-1603), C211A Office Building, Beijing Lufthansa Centre, No 50 Liangmaqiao Rd, Chaoyang District, Beijing 100016

### Telephone & Fax Services

The HKTA runs a hotline (☎ 2807-6177) to handle tourist queries. Multilingual staff are on hand from 8 am to 6 pm from Monday to Friday, or from 9 am to 5 pm on weekends and holidays.

If you have access to a fax, you can take advantage of the HKTA fax information service. The data available includes HKTA member hotels, restaurants, places to shop, questions concerning visas and so on. To do this, if your fax machine has a handset, pick it up first and dial 90060-771-128; if the machine has no handset, set it to polling mode before dialling. After you connect you'll receive a list of available topics and the appropriate fax numbers to call to receive the data. You can call this service from abroad and there is no additional charge beyond what you pay for an international phone connection. If calling from within Hong Kong, the local phone company tacks on a charge of HK$2 per minute between 8 am and 9 pm, reduced to HK$1 at all other times.

### Overseas Offices

The offices of the HKTA abroad include the following:

Australia
    (☎ (02) 9283 3083) Level 4, Hong Kong House, 80 Druitt St, Sydney, NSW 2000
Canada
    (☎ (416) 366-2389) 3rd floor, Hong Kong Trade Centre, Temperance St, Toronto, Ontario M5H 1Y6
France
    (☎ 01 47 20 39 54) Escalier C, 8th floor, 53 Rue François 1er, 75008, Paris
Germany
    (☎ (069) 9 59 12 90) Humboldt Strasse 94, D60318 Frankfurt am Main
Italy
    (☎ (06) 68 80 13 36) c/o Sergat Italia Srl, Casella Postale 620, 00100 Roma Centro, Italy
Japan
    (☎ (03) 5219-8288) 2nd floor, Kokusai Building, 3-1-1 Marunouchi, Chiyoda-ku, Tokyo 100
    (☎ (06) 299-9240) 8th floor, Osaka Saitama Building, 3-5-13 Awaji-machi, Chuo-ku, Osaka 541
Korea
    (☎ (822) 778 4403) c/o Glocom Korea, Suite 1005, Paiknam Building, 188-3 Eulchiro 1-ka, Chung-Gu, Seoul
New Zealand
    (☎ (09) 575 2707) PO Box 2120, Auckland

Singapore
  (☎ (65) 336 5800) 9 Temasek Blvd, 34-03 Suntec Tower Two, Singapore 038989
South Africa
  (☎ (011) 339 4865) c/o Development Promotions Pty Ltd, PO Box 9874, Johannesburg 2000
Spain
  (☎ (93) 414 1794) c/o Sergat Espana SL, Pau Casals 4, 08021 Barcelona
Taiwan
  (☎ (02) 581 2967) 9th floor, 18 Chang'an E Rd, Section 1, Taipei
UK
  (☎ (0171) 930 4775) 4th/5th floors, 125 Pall Mall, London, SW1Y 5EA
USA
  (☎ (630) 575-2828) Suite 200, 610 Enterprise Dr, Oak Brook, IL 60521
  (☎ (212) 869-5008) 5th floor, 590 Fifth Ave, New York, NY 10036-4706
  (☎ (310) 208-4582) Suite 1220, 10940 Wilshire Blvd, Los Angeles, CA 90024-3915

## DOCUMENTS

### Visas

**Tourist Visas** Most visitors to Hong Kong still don't need a visa. The exception is for blacklisted countries, many of which (ironically) have or had communist regimes: Hong Kong has always made it difficult for nationals from such countries to enter its borders, and despite the return of Hong Kong to the communist motherland of China, this tradition paradoxically continues. Nationals that always require visas to travel to Hong Kong include those from China, Afghanistan, Cambodia, Romania, Vietnam and Cuba.

Most of the rules remain the same as they were before the handover. What the future situation will be is difficult to guess, for the visa issue will reflect the political situation in Hong Kong and the whims of those in power. For the foreseeable future, however, things will remain much the same.

The only real changes affect British travellers. Currently, British citizens who hold UK passports can stay for up to six months without a visa. This can be extended. Citizens of Commonwealth countries (including British Dependent Territories citizens, British Overseas citizens, British subjects and British protected persons) do not require a visa for a stay of up to three months. There

is a British Citizens Unit on the 6th floor of Immigration Tower in Wan Chai, if you have any queries. Citizens of most western European countries are also permitted to stay for three months without a visa. Americans, Japanese, South Africans and Germans (and the majority of Latin American countries) do not require visas for a visit of one month or less.

Officially, visitors have to show that they have adequate funds for their stay and that they have an onward ticket or a return ticket to their own country. In practice, this rule is seldom enforced, except in the case when a visa is required. Visitors from the following countries *must* have a visa: Afghanistan, Albania, Bulgaria, Cambodia, China, CIS (former USSR), Costa Rican provisional passport holders, Cuba, Czech Republic, Hungary, Iran, Iraq, Laos, Lebanon, Libya, Mongolia, Myanmar (Burma), North Korea, Panamanian special passport holders, Romania, Slovakia, Somalia, Sudan, Syria, Taiwan, Tonga, Vatican service passports, Vietnam, Yemen, Yugoslavia and all stateless persons. If you do need a visa, apply to the nearest Chinese consulate.

Visitors are not permitted to take up employment, establish any business or enrol as students. If you want to engage in employment, education or residence you must have a work visa beforehand. It is very hard to change your visa status *after* arrival in Hong Kong. Anyone wishing to stay longer than the visa free period must apply for a visa before travelling to Hong Kong. Also be aware that all the above is just a guide and that (although it is very unlikely) immigration authorities have the right to refuse permission to enter Hong Kong.

**Work Visas** You will need a company on your side to get a work visa for Hong Kong. The Hong Kong Immigration Department requires proof that you have been offered employment, usually in the form of a contract. The prospective employer is also obliged to show that the work you plan to do cannot be performed by a local. Usually, visitors must leave Hong Kong in order to obtain a work permit, returning only when it is ready. Exceptions are made however, especially if the company explains that it urgently needs to fill a position. Work visas are generally granted for between one and three years. Extensions should be applied for a month before the visa expires.

Overseas, applications for work visas can be made at any Chinese consulate. For more information in Hong Kong, contact the Hong Kong Immigration Department, 2nd floor, Immigration Tower (Map 7), 7 Gloucester Rd, Wan Chai (☎ 2824-6111; fax 2877-7711; email enquiry@immd.gcn.gov.hk; Web site www.info.gov.hk/immd/).

**Visa Extensions** Visa extensions are not usually granted unless there are special circumstances such as a cancelled flight, illness, registration in a legitimate course of study, marriage to a local and so on. If you should accidentally overstay your visa, upon leaving you will likely be detained at immigration, asked to fill out an extension form and then cough up HK$150 for the service fee. The extension only allows you to leave the territory legally: it doesn't entitle you to a longer stay.

One way to get a de facto extension is to leave Hong Kong for a few days in Macau or China. Upon returning you will get another month or three months, depending on your nationality. It's probably not a good idea to try this too many times: immigration officers are wise to this scam.

For further information about extensions, contact the Immigration Department.

### Identity Cards

Anyone staying in Hong Kong for more than three months is required to have a Hong Kong Identity Card. If you wish to register for an identity card, phone the 24 hour telephone appointment service on ☎ 2598-0888 or go to the identity card issuing office on the 24th floor of the Immigration Tower in Wan Chai; take your passport. These are obtained at the Immigration Department. In any event, all visitors and residents are supposed to carry identification at all times in Hong Kong. It doesn't need to be a passport –

anything with a photo on it will do. This is because the immigration authorities do frequent spot checks to catch illegal workers and those who overstay their visas.

If you're planning a prolonged stay in Hong Kong and are using your passport as ID, it's wise to register it with your consulate – this makes the replacement process much simpler in case it gets lost.

Those doing business in Hong Kong should be aware that Hong Kong Chinese consider business cards as standard protocol and hand them out whenever they can. You should do the same – preferably with your company name and your name and address in Chinese on the reverse. These can be made up very cheaply in Hong Kong; about HK$300 should buy you about two hundred cards. Business card printing shops can be found in many places, and Sheung Wan is a good place to start.

### Travel Insurance

A travel insurance policy covering health, property theft, flight cancellations and so on is always a good idea. Though basic medical treatment is reasonably priced in Hong Kong, more involved procedures can get quite expensive, so it's probably best to opt for a policy that covers higher expenses. Travel insurance needs to be purchased in advance: you can't get it in Hong Kong unless you can furnish proof of local residence, and even then the insurance is only valid for travel outside the territory. Consult your travel agent or local insurance agent for information on policies.

Hopefully you won't need medical care, but do keep in mind that any health insurance policy you have at home is probably not valid outside your country for long periods of time. The usual procedure with health insurance is that you pay in cash first for services rendered and then later present the receipts to the insurance company for reimbursement after you return home. Other policies stipulate that you call collect to a centre in your home country, where an immediate assessment of your problem is made.

### Driver's Licence

If you're planning on renting or borrowing a car in Hong Kong, an overseas licence will do: it's not necessary to furnish an international driver's licence, though it can't hurt to have one in case you're journeying beyond Hong Kong. Most rental car agencies also require at least one credit card. If you're planning to stay long-term, you must turn in your own licence for a Hong Kong one within 12 months. For details, check with the Transport Department Licensing Division (☎ 2804-2600 24 hour hotline) which has four licensing offices spread throughout the territory. There is a licence issuing office on the 3rd floor of the United Centre, 95 Queensway, Wan Chai. From June 1997, a 10 year licence costs HK$900.

### Health Certificates

Hong Kong is a good place to get vaccinations for onward destinations in Asia. For this reason, as well as in case you need medical treatment, it's not a bad idea to bring an International Health Certificate, which carries a record of any vaccinations you've had, and any other salient health details. These can also be issued in Hong Kong for travel in other countries.

### Hostelling International Card

Hong Kong's seven hostels require guests to be members of the International Youth Hostels Federation, so it would be wise to organise this at home. Some hostels will let you stay subject to a HK$30 nightly surcharge, known as a 'welcome stamp'. Six welcome stamps would be the equivalent of an IYHF membership, which is valid for 12 months and costs HK$180. For more information, contact the Hong Kong Youth Hostels Association (☎ 2788-1638), Room 225-226, Block 19, Shek Kip Mei Estate, Kowloon.

### Student Cards

Student cards will get you small breaks on admission fees to museums and sights in Hong Kong, but very few guesthouses will give you a discount – a notable exception is the STB Hostel (☎ 2710-9199) in Mong Kok.

An International Student Identity Card (ISIC) entitles the holder to a number of discounts on airfares, trains, museums etc. To get this card, inquire at your home campus. These can also be issued by the Hong Kong Student Travel Bureau.

### Photocopies

It's a good idea to have photocopies of vital documents in a separate place from your wallet, handbag or money belt. These would include copies of passport data pages, birth certificate, employment documents, education qualifications and a list of travellers cheque serial numbers. You may even consider putting an emergency cash stash in with these items. For complete peace of mind, leave a set with someone back home as well.

### CONSULATES

Below are some of the diplomatic missions in Hong Kong. There's a complete list in the *Yellow Pages for Consumers*. It's best to call and check on opening times – some of those consular officials take pretty long lunch breaks. Some countries are represented by honorary consuls, who are typically business people employed in commercial firms: it is advisable to phone beforehand to find out if they're available.

Although Hong Kong is now part of China, there is still a Chinese consulate in Hong Kong.

Australia
    (☎ 2827-8881) 23rd & 24th floors, Harbour Centre, 25 Harbour Rd, Wan Chai
Canada
    (☎ 2847-7420) 11th-14th floors, Tower One, Exchange Square, 8 Connaught Place, Central
China
    (☎ 2827-9569) Visa Office of the People's Republic of China, 5th floor, Lower Block, 26 Harbour Rd, Wan Chai
France
    (☎ 2529-4351) 26th floor, Tower Two, Admiralty Centre, 18 Harcourt Rd, Admiralty
Germany
    (☎ 2529-8855) 21st floor, United Centre, 95 Queensway, Admiralty

India
(☎ 2528-4028) 16th floor, United Centre, 95 Queensway, Central
Indonesia
(☎ 2890-4421) 127-129 Leighton Rd, Causeway Bay
Ireland
(☎ 2826-2798) 22nd floor, Prince's Building, 10 Chater Rd, Central
Japan
(☎ 2522-1184) 46th floor, Tower One, Exchange Square, 8 Connaught Place, Central
Korea (South)
(☎ 2529-4141) 5th floor, Far East Finance Centre, 16 Harcourt Rd, Central
Malaysia
(☎ 2527-0921) 24th floor, Malaysia Building, 50 Gloucester Rd, Wan Chai
Myanmar (Burma)
(☎ 2827-7929) Room 2421-2425, 24th floor, Sun Hung Kai Centre, 30 Harbour Rd, Wan Chai
Netherlands
(☎ 2522-5127) 3rd floor, China Building, 29 Queen's Rd, Central
New Zealand
(☎ 2877-4488) Room 2705, Jardine House, Connaught Rd, Central
Philippines
(☎ 2866-8738) Room 602, 6th floor, United Centre, 95 Queensway, Admiralty
Singapore
(☎ 2527-2212) Room 901, Tower One, Admiralty Centre, 18 Harcourt Rd, Admiralty
Taiwan
(☎ 2525-8315) Chung Hwa Travel Service, 4th floor, Lippo Centre, 89 Queensway, Central
Thailand
(☎ 2521-6481) 8th floor, Fairmont House, 8 Cotton Tree Dr, Central
UK
(☎ 2901-3000) 1 Supreme Court Rd, Central
USA
(☎ 2523-9011) 26 Garden Rd, Central
Vietnam
(☎ 2591-4510) 15th floor, Great Smart Tower, 230 Wan Chai Rd, Wan Chai

## CUSTOMS

Even though Hong Kong is a duty-free port, there are still items on which duty is charged. In particular, there are high import taxes on cigarettes and alcohol. The duty-free allowance for visitors is 200 cigarettes (or 50 cigars or 250g of tobacco) and one litre of alcohol. Apart from these limits there are no other import tax worries, so you can bring in reasonable quantities of almost anything without paying taxes or obtaining permits.

Fireworks are illegal to bring into Hong Kong. Hong Kongers returning from Macau and China are often vigorously searched for this reason, especially at the time of the Chinese New Year. Firearms are strictly controlled and special permits are needed to import one.

Penalties for illegal drug importation are severe, including long jail terms and steep fines. It makes no difference whether it's heroin, opium or marijuana – the law makes no distinction.

## MONEY
### Currency

The local currency is the Hong Kong dollar, which is divided into 100 cents.

Bills come in denominations of HK$20 (grey), HK$50 (blue), HK$100 (red), HK$500 (brown) and HK$1000 (yellow). Coins are issued in denominations of 10 cents, 20 cents, 50 cents, HK$1, HK$2, HK$5 and HK$10.

Interestingly, Hong Kong currency is issued by three local banks, rather than by the government as in most other economies. The Hongkong and Shanghai Bank (often shortened to Hongkong Bank) and Standard Chartered Bank have long been Hong Kong's two designated note issuers. Though the bills issued by each share the same colours, their design is different. In May 1994 the Bank of China became the third note-issuing bank. In a further bow to 1997, the two British banks stopped issuing notes carrying references to the British monarchy, switching to designs that are more palatable to the Chinese government.

By the end of 1997, approximately one quarter of the 4.5 billion coins issued in Hong Kong had already left for the mainland, or been taken away by souvenir hunters; of the remaining 3.3 billion in local circulation, about 800 million were minted in the colonial era! Coins with the Queen's head were in fact still quite plentiful at the time of writing, especially the small 10 and 20 cents pieces, even though there was an overall shortage of small denomination coins. New coins are stamped with the new symbol of Hong Kong, the bauhinia flower. Watch out for fake H$1000 and HK$500 notes; in 1997 the market was swamped with forgeries, prompting many retailers to refuse to accept them. Most of these are manufactured in Taiwan or on the mainland.

### Exchange Rates

Since 1983, the Hong Kong dollar has been pegged to the US dollar at a rate of US$1 to HK$7.80, though it is allowed to fluctuate within a narrow range around this level. This move was aimed at deterring rampant speculation in the currency that had been threatening the local economy. The 'peg', as it's called, frequently comes under attack by analysts, as it limits Hong Kong's fiscal policy options. At the moment the Hong Kong dollar generally moves against other currencies in line with the US dollar; if the peg goes, then wild fluctuations will occur as the Hong Kong dollar devalues.

The following exchange rates were current at the time of writing:

| Australia | A$1 | = | HK$5.30 |
| Canada | C$1 | = | HK$5.32 |
| China | Y1 | = | HK$0.93 |
| France | FFr1 | = | HK$1.27 |
| Germany | DM1 | = | HK$4.26 |
| Japan | ¥100 | = | HK$6.13 |
| Malaysia | R1 | = | HK$1.91 |
| New Zealand | NZ$1 | = | HK$4.46 |
| Philippines | P1 | = | HK$0.19 |
| Singapore | S$1 | = | HK$4.55 |
| Switzerland | SFr1 | = | HK$5.24 |
| Taiwan | NT$1 | = | HK$0.24 |
| Thailand | B1 | = | HK$0.16 |
| UK | £1 | = | HK$12.71 |
| USA | US$1 | = | HK$7.73 |

### Changing Money

There are few places on earth where it's easier to change money than Hong Kong. Most banks have foreign exchange counters, and tourist areas are also littered with moneychanging shops. Banks and moneychangers can exchange all major trading currencies and many minor ones as well. Due to Hong Kong's lack of exchange controls, there is no foreign currency black market.

**Cash** Banks generally offer the best rates, the moneychanging counters at the airport the worst.

However some banks charge a commission (unless you are an account holder, in which case it's free). Hongkong Bank, Hang Seng Bank and Standard Chartered Bank all levy fees of HK$50 for each transaction. If you're changing several hundred US dollars or more you'll be given a better rate, which makes up for the fee. Hong Kong is saturated with the branches of all three banks, so you should have little trouble finding one.

Your best bet is probably Dao Heng Bank, which not only gives a slightly better rate than most other banks, but also does not charge a commission. One of Dao Heng's most convenient locations for visitors is its foreign exchange counter on the main floor of Towers One and Two, Exchange Square, 8 Connaught Rd, Central.

Licensed moneychangers, such as Thomas Cook and Chequepoint, are abundant in tourist areas like Tsim Sha Tsui. Their chief advantage is that they stay open on Sunday, holidays and late into the evening when banks are closed. They claim to charge no commission, but give lousy exchange rates equivalent to a 5% commission instead. These rates are clearly posted, though if you're changing several hundred US dollars or more you should be able to bargain for a better rate. Before the actual exchange is made, the moneychanger is required by law to give you a form to sign clearly showing the amount, exchange rate and any service charges. Of the moneychangers, the ones operating at Chungking Mansions on Nathan Rd in Tsim Sha Tsui usually offer the best rates.

Bank hours are from 9 am to 4 pm Monday to Friday, and from 9 am to noon or 1 pm on Saturday. Try to avoid changing money at hotels, which offer rates that are only marginally better than the usurious airport moneychangers.

**Travellers Cheques** Nearly all banks will cash travellers cheques, and all charge a fee, often irrespective of whether you are an account holder or not. Again, the best deal is probably Dao Heng Bank, which charges a flat rate of HK$20. Hongkong Bank charges 0.375% of the total amount, while Standard Chartered tacks on a HK$50 commission. Hang Seng charges HK$60 per encashment. Licensed moneychangers don't levy a commission, but sometimes give a slightly lower rate for travellers cheques, though this can improve if you change a significant sum.

Hong Kong is a good place to buy travellers cheques. Generally the fee is 1% of the total value of cheques purchased (generally for a minimum HK$50 worth of cheques).

### International Transfers

As one of Asia's leading financial centres, Hong Kong is a great place to arrange international money transfers.

The larger banks, including Hongkong Bank and Standard Chartered, can easily handle bank drafts and telegraphic transfers. Fees for these services usually range from HK$100 to HK$150. Hongkong Bank's international transfer desk (☎ 2748-3322) is on the 3rd floor of the main branch, 1 Queen's Rd, Central. Standard Chartered Bank's main branch is next door. When arranging a transfer, be sure to get the Hong Kong bank's address and routing number.

### ATM Cards

There are two major ATM networks in Hong Kong. Hongkong Bank and Hang Seng Bank operate one which accepts a fairly large number of international ATM systems, such as Plus and Cirrus, as well as Visa credit and debit cards. The Jetco network, used by Standard Chartered and a host of smaller Hong Kong banks, accepts Cirrus ATM cards and MasterCard credit and debit cards. The ATM systems accepted are displayed above the ATM machines. Payment is in Hong Kong dollars only. Midland Bank customers can use their ATM cards with Hongkong Bank machines to draw from their account in the UK, as Midland is part of Hongkong Bank.

Using an ATM or debit card is one of the cheapest ways to get money from overseas, as the only fees levied are those by your home bank for ATM withdrawals.

If you're staying long-term, or if you are moving there, then obtaining a Hongkong Bank ETC ATM card will give you access to the Hang Seng Bank as well as the Hongkong Bank ATM system (which has over 800 machines). See the maps at the back of this guide for some of the Hongkong Bank ATMs around the city and islands (it's worth bearing in mind that most of the Outlying Islands have ATMs, so you don't have to travel there loaded with money). Again, if you are staying long-term, Hongkong Bank issues a card called Mondex which you can use when shopping; money is automatically transferred from your bank account.

### Credit Cards

Credit cards are widely accepted in Hong Kong, especially since some of the industry heavies launched massive marketing campaigns several years ago to convert the locals. Many restaurants and all but the smallest shops take credit cards, though some tack on a 3% to 5% surcharge. Check first. The most commonly accepted credit cards include American Express, Diners Club, JCB, MasterCard and Visa. The main offices are:

American Express International Inc – (☎ 2885-9366) 20th floor, Somerset House, Tai Koo Place, 979 Kings Rd, Tai Koo

Diners Club International – (☎ 2860-1888) 42nd floor, Hopewell Centre, 183 Queen's Rd East, Wan Chai

JCB International (Asia) – (☎ 2366-7203; Japanese language ☎ 2366-7211) Room 509, Hong Kong Pacific Centre, 28 Hankow Rd, Tsim Sha Tsui

MasterCard International – (☎ 2598-8038) Suite 1401-4, Dah Sing Financial Centre, 108 Gloucester Rd, Wan Chai

Visa International – (☎ 2523-8152) Lippo Tower, Tamar St, Admiralty

### Costs

Hong Kong is one of Asia's most expensive cities both to visit and live in. Travellers'

**FACTS FOR THE VISITOR**

wallets are usually hit hardest by accommodation, eating out and entertainment.

Still, there are options for the budget traveller. A room at a hostel or guesthouse will cost between HK$65 and HK$350 per night. Breakfast at a hole-in-the-wall Chinese place or an Oliver's Super Sandwiches shop will run from HK$25 to HK$35, lunch in a noodle shop or fast-food restaurant HK$30 to HK$50. For dinner, if you have tired of noodle shops, keep an eye out for set dinner deals: sometimes you can get an appetiser, main course, dessert and coffee for around HK$100. Add in another HK$200 for transport and extras like snacks, drinks and admission fees and you've got a daily budget of HK$450 to $HK750. Those on a tight budget could probably cut this back to HK$250 to HK$350, though this would make for a spartan stay indeed. The truly spartan could, theoretically, spend the night on a dorm bed and just have three meals at McDonald's, travel by tram and ferry and only spend about HK$130 a day.

If you have more to spend, it's easily done. A double room at a mid-range hotel costs around HK$650 to HK$1200 per night, and HK$1300 to HK$2500 or more at one of the higher-end places. Don't forget however, that many hotels offer good deals if business is slack – ask if they have any special offers.

Meals, once you leave the budget places behind, can also be quite expensive. Lunch at an average restaurant in Central or Tsim Sha Tsui will usually cost from HK$150 to HK$250 per person, and dinner from HK$300 to HK$500 or higher.

One of the easiest ways to empty your wallet is to visit Hong Kong's bars. Prices for beer and cocktails are on a par with those in Tokyo. A beer usually costs from HK$30 to HK$50, and cocktails slightly more. One way around these prices is to target happy hours, usually held between 4 and 8 pm (although times vary), when prices are generally halved, or you get two drinks for the price of one. Cigarettes are reasonably cheap, if you avoid buying them in bars. Beer is very cheap if bought in supermarkets, especially the lesser-known brands.

Public transport in Hong Kong is generally quite affordable. The trams and the Star Ferry, at HK$1.60 and HK$1.70 respectively, are bargains. At the other end of the spectrum, the subway, or MTR, is relatively pricey: a single ride can cost anywhere from HK$4 to HK$13. For your money however, you get a clean, fast ride. Taxis are not unreasonably priced.

### Tipping & Bargaining

Tipping is somewhat haphazard in Hong Kong. In restaurants, locals often only leave several Hong Kong dollars in coins. Many restaurants levy a 10% service charge, though whether this money ever gets to the waiter is doubtful. If you appreciated the service you received, it doesn't hurt to leave a little more; at least the person who served you will (probably) receive the money. Always check your bill carefully – with so much money awash in Hong Kong, restaurants often overcharge.

There is no need to tip taxi drivers unless, again, you feel they were particularly nice or helpful. Bellhops at hotels do expect a tip; HK$10 to HK$20 should do. If you use the porters at the airport, HK$2 to HK$3 per bag is the general rule.

Tipping in bars is pretty much up to you. Naturally if you expect to be sitting on that bar stool for any length of time, it might be a good idea to get the bartender on your side with a little cash persuasion. Many bars have a policy of forcing you to sit down and then a waiter will serve you, expecting a tip. If you don't want this, just order the drink yourself and sit at a table.

Bargaining is expected in Hong Kong's tourist districts, but less so elsewhere. Trying to bargain something down to say, half the original price, may be counter-productive. If the shop allows it, it probably means the prices were far too high to begin with. If the shop is that dishonest (and many are, particularly in the Tsim Sha Tsui tourist ghetto), the staff will probably find other ways to cheat you, like selling electronics with missing components, or a second-hand camera instead of a new one. Many of these rip-off shops don't post prices on their goods. In an honest shop, you shouldn't be able to bargain more than a 10% discount, if they'll bargain at all. Bargaining is definitely out in department stores and garment chain stores, such as Giordano or U2, but you can certainly try at jewellery stores for that Rolex you always wanted (see the Shopping chapter for more information).

### Taxes
There is no sales tax in Hong Kong, which has contributed to the city's (diminishing) reputation as a shopping paradise. About the only tax which visitors are likely to run into is a 5% tax on hotel rates. Hotels add this to their own 10% service charge, making for a total surcharge of 15%.

### DOING BUSINESS
There is probably no city in Asia that makes doing business more convenient than Hong Kong. The city has excellent transport and communications infrastructure and abundant business services. A great many local businesses are used to dealing with foreigners, which lowers the risk of any cultural misunderstandings.

The Hong Kong government does its best to help overseas firms and executives link up with local suppliers or investment partners, and sweetens the pot by keeping both personal and corporate income taxes low (flat rates of 15% and 16.5% respectively).

The territory's legal system, modelled after that of the UK, gives ample recourse to the law, which has made Hong Kong a better investment environment than most other Asian countries. The Basic Law (China's guarantee that things will stay the same) stipulates that Hong Kong will keep its own laws, based on the British Common Law system (with an independent judiciary and a final Court of Appeal based in Hong Kong). So far, things have gone according to plan, but it would be rash to predict anything other that a collective hope that all will continue as before. There is little doubt that China can learn a significant amount about effective legal practices from maintaining the current system. China's own legal system has proven to be of little help to foreign investors embroiled in disputes with Chinese partners.

In general, however, it has remained easy to do business and make money in Hong Kong. China itself has tens of billions of US dollars invested in the territory's property and equity markets, a reassuring sign for the future. Mainland Chinese firms are flooding into Hong Kong, which may make it easier to find business partners in China with experience in the international arena. And the change in government will hopefully not affect the efficiency of Hong Kong's business service industry, which is noted for getting things done on time with a minimum of hassle.

### Trade & Business Organisations
**Government Organisations** The largest and most visible of these is the Hong Kong Trade Development Council (TDC), which for 30 years has been promoting Hong Kong as a trading and manufacturing partner for foreign businesses. The TDC has myriad facilities to ease the way for foreign firms involving themselves in trade in Hong Kong. The facilities in its top-notch office include its TDC Business Library (☎ 2584-4333), which attracts over 10,000 visitors a year to a veritable database of business contacts, trade and investment opportunities. Also on hand are more than 70 CD-ROMs for access to essential world trade information (you can also use the Internet for free although you have to pay for printing, HK$3 per page). The TDC phone-fax service provides a list of 100,000 Hong Kong manufacturers and more – just phone (☎ 2584-4188) and information will be sent to you by fax (although there is a charge per record so have your credit card handy). The TDC also sponsors or takes part in numerous trade fairs each year (the Convention & Exhibition Centre was hugely expanded in 1997) and publishes a wealth of literature on Hong Kong markets and products. HK Enterprise Internet is TDC's electronically published magazine, posted on the TDC home page (Web site www.tdc.org.hk).

In Hong Kong you can find the TDC head office (Map 7; ☎ 2584-4333) on the 38th floor, Office Tower, Convention Plaza, 1 Harbour Rd, Wan Chai. The council also has more than 50 representative offices in numerous countries.

The Hong Kong Industry Department offers information and assistance to overseas investors at its One-Stop Unit (☎ 2737-2434), 14th floor, Ocean Centre, 5 Canton Rd, Tsim Sha Tsui.

Another source for trade information, statistics, government regulations and product certification is the Hong Kong Trade Department (☎ 2392-2922), Trade Department Tower, 700 Nathan Rd, Mong Kok.

**Chambers of Commerce**  Hong Kong is well served by both local and overseas chambers. The largest among the locals is the Hong Kong General Chamber of Commerce (☎ 2529-9229), 22nd floor, United Centre, 95 Queensway, Admiralty. It has more than 4000 members and boasts 10 offices throughout the territory. In addition to its various member services, the chamber offers a host of services for foreign executives and firms such as translation, serviced offices, secretarial help and printing.

The Chinese General Chamber of Commerce (☎ 2525-6385; email cgcc@cgcc.org.hk; Web site www.cgcc.org.hk), more oriented towards local firms, is authorised to issue Certificates of Hong Kong origin for trade purposes. Its address is 7th floor, Chinese General Chamber of Commerce Building, 24-25 Connaught Rd, Central. So is the Chinese Manufacturers' Association of Hong Kong (☎ 2545-6166), which also operates testing laboratories for product certification. It can be found on the 3rd floor, CMA Building, 64-66 Connaught Rd, Central.

The American Chamber of Commerce (☎ 2526-0165; fax 2537-1682; email amcham@amcham.org.hk) can be found on the 19th floor of the Bank of America Tower (Map 6), 12 Harcourt Rd, Central. For a complete listing of local and overseas chambers check the *Yellow Pages for Businesses*.

**Business Services**
There are literally hundreds of companies offering services for either visiting executives or small firms that need to contract out various tasks. It pays to check around and compare not only prices but the extent of services offered. Below are brief descriptions and addresses of some business service firms. Complete listings can be found in either *Yellow Pages for Businesses* or the *Business White Pages Telephone Directory*. With the exception of banking, the Hong Kong General Chamber of Commerce (see the previous section) also offers many services for visiting business people.

The two major banks for business and traders are the Hongkong and Shanghai Bank (☎ 2822-1111) at 1 Queen's Rd Central in Central, and Hang Seng Bank (☎ 2825-5111) at 83 Des Voeux Rd, Central. Both offer extensive corporate services and trade financing. For business with China, you may have to go through the Bank of China (☎ 2826-6888) at 1 Garden Rd, Central, though service at one of the Hong Kong banks is likely to be better.

Other organisations that could be useful to those on business are the Hong Kong Consumer Council (☎ 2304-1234), 191 Java Rd, North Point; the Employers' Federation of Hong Kong (☎ 2528-0536), 1001 East Town Building, 41 Lockhart Rd, Wan Chai; and the Hong Kong Industrial Technology Centre Corporation (☎ 2788-5400), 78 Tat Chee Ave, Kowloon.

In Hong Kong, secretarial services often include accounting, so check carefully to see what you might be paying for. Another alternative is to rent a serviced office, where secretarial services are generally provided. The further from Central, the less expensive these services get, though they are all pretty pricey.

For printing, Tappan Printing (☎ 2561-0101) has a good reputation for high quality, large-scale printing work, and is a favourite of many Hong Kong magazine publishers. For smaller printing jobs, Alphagraphics (☎ 2525-5568) has English-speaking staff, and handles desktop publishing, copying, binding, and so on.

TED CARROLL

TED CARROLL

Three views at different times of the day of Hong Kong Island's financial and administrative hub. The districts of Central, Sheung Wan and Admiralty contain some of the world's highest prices for real estate, as well as some of the most ambitious modern architecture.

Top: Kowloon Park, formerly the site of a barracks and now a vital breathing space.
Bottom Left: Top of the line – The Peninsula Hotel, Tsim Sha Tsui.
Bottom Right: Riding the cable car between the two halves of Ocean Park near Aberdeen.

There are many translation and interpreting companies to choose from, though it might be wise to request a sample, as some agencies can't always deliver the flawless translations they invariably promise. International firms in Hong Kong that offer simultaneous interpreting in a wide range of languages include KERN (Hong Kong) (☎ 2850-4455); there are many small and independent Hong Kong translation centres of varying standards; these include Multilingual Translation Services (☎ 2581-9099) and Polyglot Translations (☎ 2851-7232). One reliable business is Language Line (☎ 2511-2677), 163 Hennessy Rd, Wan Chai, which offers editorial, interpretation and translation services. The Hong Kong General Chamber of Commerce (☎ 2529-9229) offers a decent, and reasonably fast, translation service.

For translations into European languages, try one of the many cultural centres (for more details, see the Cultural Centres section later in this chapter).

## POST & COMMUNICATIONS
### Post

Hong Kong's postal system is generally excellent – letters are sometimes delivered the same day they are sent! Postage rates are on a par with most developed countries. Mailboxes and post offices are clearly marked in English. Unfortunately mailboxes are few and far between – you may end up holding on to your mail until you reach a post office. The English spoken at post offices in Hong Kong is generally very good.

On the Hong Kong Island side, the General Post Office (GPO) is on your right as you alight from the Star Ferry in Central (Map 6). If there are long lines there, you can try the post office at the government offices west of Exchange Square along the elevated walkway. On the Kowloon side, one of the most convenient post offices is at 10 Middle Rd, east of Nathan Rd in Tsim Sha Tsui (Map 5). Another good post office (and less crowded) is in the basement of the Albion Plaza, 2-6 Granville Rd, just off Nathan Rd, Tsim Sha Tsui. All post offices are open Monday to Saturday from 8 am to 6 pm, and are closed on Sunday and public holidays.

**Airmail** The Hong Kong postal service divides the world into two zones. Zone 1 is China, Japan, Taiwan, South Korea, India, Indonesia and South-East Asia generally. Rates for letters and postcards are HK$2.10 (Zone 1) and HK$2.60 (Zone 2) for the first 10g; and HK$1.10 and HK$1.20 respectively for each additional 10g. Aerograms are HK$2.10 for both zones.

**Parcels** Parcel and surface mail service is also divided into two zones, but not the same as for airmail. Zone 1 is China, Macau and Taiwan. Zone 2 is all other countries. Rates vary widely depending on the destination. Parcels shipped by surface mail take about six to 10 weeks to reach the US or UK, but cost about half as much as airmail. Post offices also sell cardboard boxes, allowing you to pack and send on the spot.

**Speedpost** Rates for the postal service's international express mail facility varies widely according to destination, but there is little relation to actual distance. For example, a 250g Speedpost letter to Australia costs HK$85 but to China it's HK$90 and to Singapore HK$65! The main factors seem to be the availability of air transport and efficiency of mail handling at the destination country. Speedpost is usually at least twice as fast as regular airmail, and is usually cheaper than using private express mail companies such as DHL or Federal Express.

**Courier Services** Private companies offering rapid document and small parcel service (32kg limit) include DHL (☎ 2765-8111), Federal Express (☎ 2730-3333), and TNT Express (☎ 2331-2663). All three companies have numerous collection points, so call for the one nearest you; many MTR stations have DHL offices, including Central, Admiralty and Causeway Bay. DHL offers 24 hour collection.

For larger items, you will need the services of a freight forwarder. Foremost in this market is United Parcel Service (UPS) at the World Finance Centre in Canton Rd, Tsim Sha Tsui. UPS also offers a small parcel courier service (☎ 2735-3535).

**Receiving Mail** There are poste restante services at the GPO and other large post offices. Mail will generally be held for two months. Address an envelope c/o Poste Restante, GPO Hong Kong, and it will go to the Hong Kong Island side. If you want letters to go to the Kowloon side, they should be addressed c/o Poste Restante, Tsim Sha Tsui Post Office, 10 Middle Rd, Tsim Sha Tsui.

**Telephone**
Hongkong Telecom, a joint venture more than 58% owned by Britain's Cable & Wireless, enjoyed for decades a total monopoly on phone services (but not pagers). Since 1994 other companies (Hutchison Communications, New T&T and New World) have been permitted into the local market, but the lucrative long-distance monopoly will continue until the year 2006. However this has been eaten into by competitors offering long-distance calls, after buying international access from Hongkong Telecom. Hongkong Telecom in general offers good service, and long-distance rates, while no bargain, are among the lowest in Asia.

All calls made within Hong Kong are local calls and therefore free, except for public pay phones which cost HK$1 per local call with no extra charges for chatting a long time. The pay phones normally accept HK$2 coins but do *not* give change, though you can make a second call by pressing the 'FC' (Follow-on Call) button before hanging up.

There are free public phones in the arrival area of the airport. You can find public pay phones in the airport, ferry terminals, post offices and hotel lobbies. On the street they are annoyingly rare, and usually positioned in the busiest and noisiest areas. However, many shops have phones placed outside on the street which you can use and a large number of Wellcome and Park n' Shop supermarkets have free phones that customers can use.

**Mobile Phones**
Mobile phones are everywhere in Hong Kong. I think I even saw a baby in a pram with one once – everyone just took it in their stride without a second look. Mobile phones partly explain why everyone bumps into each other while walking down the street in Hong Kong. The only answer is to buy one and walk in a perfectly straight line down the pavement while jabbering into it and staring into the middle distance. In fact, if you want to get somewhere quick, just charge down the street with this lump of plastic next to your ear and the masses will part like the Red Sea.

Despite still having a lingering element of chic, on the whole mobile phones (*dageda*) have become part of life, and not having a mobile phone creates a similar reaction to not wearing trousers. Excuses will get you nowhere – Hong Kong Chinese assume you must be deaf if you don't have one. The smaller the better as well, reversing the usual male preoccupation with size – 'Yeah, but look at mine; small or what?'. The best are the midget numbers that look like you're talking into a pack of 10 cigarettes, which apparently some people accidentally do by mistake (very uncool).

Scares that mobile phones might cause brain cancer have not been convincingly buried, but headaches are a definitive side-effect. Like when the person you are sitting next to in the cinema starts hunting for their phone, which is amusingly programmed to play *Jingle Bells* repeatedly, in a pitch approaching ultrasound.

**Damian Harper**

If you decide to stay long-term in Hong Kong, residential line rental is HK$67 per month, plus HK$13 for a basic push-button telephone. The installation fee is HK$530. For more information, call ☎ 2888-2888. Other useful numbers include Hutchison Telecom (☎ 2807-9011), New World Telephone (☎ 2138-2200), and New T&T (☎ 2112-1121).

**International Calls** If you want to phone overseas, it's cheapest to use an IDD (International Direct Dial) telephone. You can place an IDD call from most phone boxes, but you'll need a stack of HK$5 coins handy if your call is going to be anything but very brief. An alternative is to buy a phonecard, which come in denominations of HK$50, HK$100 or HK$250. You can find phonecards in shops, at all 7-Eleven stores or at a Hongkong Telecom office. Phones that take the cards can be frustratingly scarce: you can find them at some 7-Elevens, Hongkong Telecom Service Centres and occasionally among groups of public phones.

ElephantTalk phonecards and Hongkong Telecom Hello phonecards are also widely available; the difference between these phonecards and the ones above is that you can use any phone to call from, and just punch in a PIN code which identifies your card and the credit remaining. They come in HK$100, HK$200 and HK$300 denominations. Hello phonecards can be picked up at Hongkong Telecom service centres; ElephantTalk cards can be picked up cheaply from some of the guesthouses in Chungking Mansions who typically sell them at a reduced rate (eg HK$80 for a HK$100 card).

To make an IDD call from Hong Kong, dial 001, then the country code, area code and number. If you're using someone else's phone and you want to know how much the call will cost, dial 003 instead of 001 and the operator will call back to report the cost.

If you go to Hongkong Telecom, there are various options for overseas phone calls: operator-connected calls (paid in advance with a minimum of three minutes); IDD which you dial yourself after paying a deposit (the unused portion of your deposit is refunded); reverse charges (which requires a small deposit – refundable if the charge is accepted or if the call doesn't get through); or simply buying a phonecard. You can place international calls at any of the following Hongkong Telecom Service Centres (listed more-or-less in order of convenience for travellers):

*Hong Kong Island*
Shop 116, Prince's Building, Chater Rd, Central (Map 6)
290-292 Hennessy Rd, Wan Chai – open from 10 am to 8 pm Monday to Saturday, closed public holidays

2nd floor, Jusco Department Store, Kornhill Plaza North, 1 Kornhill Rd, Quarry Bay – open from 10 am to 7 pm daily, including public holidays
*Kowloon*
Hermes House, 10 Middle Rd, Tsim Sha Tsui (Map 5) – open 24 hours, including public holidays
Shop 43f, ground floor, Ma Tau Wai Rd, Hung Hom – open from 9 am to 7 pm Monday to Saturday and public holidays
*New Territories*
Shop 303-313, ground floor, Castle Peak Rd, Tsuen Wan, – open from 9 am to 7 pm Monday to Saturday, closed public holidays
Shop 31b-e, level 3, Sha Tin Centre, Sha Tin – open from 9 am to 7 pm Monday to Saturday, noon to 6 pm Sunday and public holidays

Another option is to make use of the home direct service, which takes you straight through to a local operator in the country dialled. You can then make a reverse charge (collect) call or a credit card call with a telephone credit card valid in that country. Home direct dialling codes for some countries are listed in the table below. Some places, including Kai Tak and Chek Lap Kok airports, some hotels and shopping centres, have home direct phones where you simply press a button labelled USA, UK, Canada, or

### International Dialling Codes

| Country | Direct Dial | Home Direct |
|---|---|---|
| Australia | 001-61 | 800-0061 |
| Canada | 001-1 | 800-1100 |
| France | 001-33 | 800-0033 |
| Germany | 001-49 | 800-0049 |
| Indonesia | 001-62 | 800-0062 |
| Italy | 001-39 | 800-0039 |
| Japan | 001-81 | 800-0181 |
| Korea | 001-82 | 800-0082 |
| Malaysia | 001-60 | 800-0060 |
| Netherlands | 001-31 | 800-0031 |
| New Zealand | 001-64 | 800-0064 |
| Singapore | 001-65 | 800-0065 |
| Spain | 001-34 | 800-0034 |
| Sweden | 001-46 | 800-0046 |
| Taiwan | 001-886 | 800-0886 |
| Thailand | 001-66 | 800-0066 |
| UK | 001-44 | 800-0044 |
| USA | 001-1 | 800-1111* |

*\* Through AT&T; you can also dial 800-1121 (MCI) or 800-1877 (Sprint), and for Hawaii you can dial 800-1188*

wherever, to be put through to your home operator. For details call ☎ 013. You may want to check whether your home telephone company supports home direct services before leaving for Hong Kong.

To phone Hong Kong from overseas, use your country's international dialling code plus Hong Kong's country code – 852 – followed by the local eight digit number.

For those who make frequent calls, joining a call-back service to take advantage of the cheaper phone rates of other countries may make sense (although things to look out for include hidden costs and long delays in connection). Companies that can provide this service include Primecall (☎ (800) 698-1232), Global Access (☎ 2651-8466) and Master-call International (☎ 2722-6118).

**Useful Phone Numbers & Prefixes** If you're wanting to call cities or regions in mainland China, your best bet is to ring ☎ 012 (China dialling assistance) or ☎ 013 (international dialling assistance). Following is a list of useful numbers.

| | |
|---|---|
| Ambulance, Fire & Police | ☎ 999 |
| Credit Card Calls | ☎ 011 |
| Crime Reports & Police Matters | ☎ 2527-7177 |
| Cyclone (Typhoon) Warning | ☎ 2835-1473 |
| Inquiries | |
| Directory Inquiries | ☎ 1081 |
| Fax Directory | ☎ 10014 |
| Free Ambulance Service (St John's) | |
| Hong Kong Island | ☎ 2576-6555 |
| Kowloon | ☎ 2713-5555 |
| New Territories | ☎ 2639-2555 |
| Information hotlines | |
| general | ☎ 1000 |
| business | ☎ 1028 |
| Reverse Billing | ☎ 010 |
| Taxi Complaints | ☎ 2527-7177 |
| Time & Weather | ☎ 18501 |

**Telephone Directories** Currently the line-up includes the *Yellow Pages for Consumers* (three volumes, all bilingual), the *Yellow Pages for Businesses* (one volume, English only), the *Business White Pages Telephone Directory* (one volume each in English and Chinese), the *Residential Directories* (three

volumes, all bilingual) and the *Hong Kong Fax Directory* (one volume, English or Chinese). The *Yellow Pages* are available over the Internet (Web site www.hkt.com/directory). If you're staying for any length of time in Hong Kong, you should at least pick up the *Yellow Pages for Businesses* and the *Yellow Pages for Consumers*. These are available through Hongkong Telecom shops or at one of their service centres; call ☎ 1000 for more details.

**Mobile Phones & Pagers** Hong Kong boasts the world's highest per capita usage of cellular phones and pagers. These things have become an integral part of Hong Kong urban life. Generally, you cannot rent cellular phones in Hong Kong, but you can certainly buy one. Hongkong Telecom can rent you a mobile phone as well as sell you one.

Pagers can be rented from a wide variety of sources. Hongkong Telecom charges a fairly low monthly fee, but tacks on usage fees and a large deposit. Other companies that rent and sell pagers include ABC Communications (☎ 2710-0333), Hutchison Paging (☎ 2838-4667) and Star Paging (☎ 2771-1111).

**Fax, Email & Internet**
Hongkong Telecom offers fax services at its service centres. Rates per page range from HK$15 (Hong Kong) to HK$45 (Europe), depending on the destination country. You can also receive faxes for HK$10 per page. Most hotels and even many youth hostels allow their guests to send and receive faxes. The surcharge for sending is usually 10% above cost, and receiving is normally HK$10 per page. If dialling your own fax for an overseas transmission, use the international prefix 002 (for a data line) rather than 001 (for a voice line).

For those who want or need to stay in touch via electronic mail, Hong Kong is a good place to log on. There are more than 80 Internet service providers in Hong Kong; CompuServe (☎ 3002-8332) and America Online (☎ 2519-9040), two of the world's largest online services, both have nodes in Hong Kong. Members should check with their respective services in advance to find out the telephone numbers for the nodes, as these can change from time to time.

If you want to dial direct to overseas online services, you can try Datapak – Hongkong Telecom's packet switching network. Hongkong Telecom's Internet access service is call Netvigator – for more details call ☎ 2888-1278. Other ISPs are ABC Net (☎ 2710-0363), Asia Online (☎ 2837-8888) and Hong Kong Star Internet (☎ 2781-6552).

Star Internet also has an office next to World Wide House on Des Voeux Rd, Central (Map 6) where you can use the Internet for free, although the terminals are usually occupied by anxious stock market watchers. Other places you can use the Internet for free include the Trade Development Council Business Library (☎ 2584-4333) and the British Council Library (☎ 2913-5125) – although you cannot use email.

If you're staying in Hong Kong for an extended period, you may want to look into Hong Kong Internet & Gateway Services (☎ 2527-4888; email aaron@hk.net), which charges an initial fee of HK$100, and a monthly subscription rate of HK$100. The online fee is HK$18 per hour; you get issued with a roaming number so you can access your email at local rates from abroad.

If your hotel doesn't have email facilities, don't despair. Kublai's Cyberdiner is at hand on the 3rd floor, One Capital Place, 18 Luard Rd, Wan Chai (☎ 2529-9117); Kublai's is not just a great Mongolian barbecue eatery, but you can also sit down with a coffee, get an email address and get chatting online. The service is free, and the Cyberdiner is open from noon to 11 pm.

Xyberia cybercafé (☎ 2984-1008; fax 2984-7618; email sahr@xyberia.com) is on hand for those who want to surf the net, espresso in hand. You'll have to take the ferry to find it, however, as it's at Shop C, Sea View Building, 1 Ngan Wan Rd, Mui Wo, Lantau (the first Internet café on any of the Outlying Islands).

## BOOKS

Hong Kong's British heritage has left it with a number of well-stocked English-language bookstores. Whether you're looking for books about the territory, literature, paperback fiction or textbooks, you stand a good chance of finding it in Hong Kong. Unfortunately books in Hong Kong are very expensive. For information on specific bookshops, look under Bookshops & Stationery in the Shopping chapter.

Most books are published in different editions by different publishers in different countries. As a result, a book might be a hardcover rarity in one country while it's readily available in paperback elsewhere. Your local bookstore or library can advise you on the availability of the following recommendations.

### Lonely Planet

If you're interested in the New Territories or the Outlying Islands, Lonely Planet's *Hong Kong, Macau & Guangzhou* can show you where to go. Lonely Planet also publishes several guides to the region, such as *North-East Asia on a shoestring*, *South-East Asia on a shoestring*, *South-West China* and *China*. There is also a *Cantonese phrasebook*.

### Culture & Society

For a rundown on the customs, manners and etiquette of the Cantonese people of Hong Kong, try *Cantonese Culture* by Ingram & Ng. Anthony Lawrence, a former BBC correspondent and resident of Hong Kong for nearly 40 years, takes a fairly upbeat look at Hong Kong attitudes and superstitions in *The Fragrant Chinese*. Along the same lines, *Games Hong Kong People Play* is a lighthearted examination of Hong Kong habits, morals and chicanery. In *Letters from Hong Kong*, Isabel Taylor Escoba gives a biting yet humorous view of Hong Kong through the eyes of a resident Filipino.

Very academic, but a great read nonetheless is *Hong Kong: the Anthropology of a Chinese Metropolis*. Grant Evans delves into the world of temples, fung shui and street language in a vivid attempt to bring the social and cultural world of the Hong Kong Chinese alive.

*City of Darkness – Life in the Kowloon Walled City* by Girard & Lambot uses photos and text to tell the story of the now-demolished tenement fortress in Kowloon that was off limits to the Hong Kong authorities.

Most bookshops have bundles of photographic and colour books on Hong Kong that make for good presents. There are many available, although a great number are dated, especially those concerning Hong Kong's magnificent architecture. The Trade Development Council Business Library (see the earlier Trade & Business Organisations section) has a large number of books devoted to Hong Kong's modern buildings.

## History

Hong Kong's colourful history makes for good reading. One of the best ways to tour it is through Jan Morris' *Hong Kong – Epilogue to an Empire*. The book is written with flair and moves seamlessly between past and present to find what made Hong Kong so unique among British colonial possessions. The last edition was published in 1997.

*The Last Governor* is a large and compelling study of Chris Patten, the ex-governor of the territory, and tackles the hefty subject of the last British administration of Hong Kong.

Long considered the definitive history of the territory, *A History of Hong Kong* by GB Endacott is a detailed but very dry account of Hong Kong's progress, researched largely from official documents. The second edition dates from 1974, and thus lacks any account of the last two tumultuous decades. The foregoing is not to be confused with *A History of Hong Kong* by Frank Welsh. This monumental hardback is more recent and, while still thorough, makes for easier reading than Endacott's work. Form Asia, which has numerous books on Hong Kong, takes an interesting look at the territory's structural past in *Building Hong Kong – A History of the City through its Architecture*.

Maurice Collin's *Foreign Mud* tells the sordid story of the Anglo-Chinese opium wars. *The Potent Poppy* by Michael Robson is a more updated version of the same story, in coffee-table format with colour photos. *The Taipans – Hong Kong's Merchant Princes* tells the story of the English and Scottish merchants who profited from the opium wars and founded the trading houses that would dominate Hong Kong's business world for the next century.

A rare and extremely detailed look at Hong Kong between world wars can be had in *Hong Kong Under Imperial Rule 1911-1941* (East Asian Historical Monographs, 1987) by Norman Miners. WWII buffs may be interested in *The Lasting Honour – The Fall of Hong Kong, 1941*, in which Oliver Lindsay takes a professional look at the failed defence of Hong Kong against the Japanese Imperial Army.

## Business

There is no shortage of guides to doing business in Hong Kong, though none of them will likely be able to tell you where the profits lie. *Establishing a Company in Hong Kong* by Stephen Terry walks you through the bureaucratic steps needed to set up shop in the territory. Basic facts on Hong Kong's government, markets, residential and business services and establishing a company are laid out in *Setting Up in Hong Kong* by Fiona Campbell. *Establishing an Office in Hong Kong* is a regularly updated reference work that, despite being primarily for Americans, is full of up-to-date, useful information. For a look at local business etiquette, try *Hong Kong Business: The Portable Encyclopedia for Doing Business with Hong Kong*, which also has sections on taxation, the economy and financial institutions, among others.

## Language

If you're interested in tackling one the world's most difficult languages (as the Cantonese are proud to proclaim), *Cantonese – A Complete Course for Beginners* promises to have you chatting comfortably with locals after 26 lessons. Easier said than done, but perhaps worth a try. If you really want to take the bull by the horns, tackle Sidney Lau's unparalleled achievement, his six-volume Cantonese course, from *Elementary Cantonese* to *Advanced Cantonese*. Although dated, the language used is colloquial and the lessons are exhaustive in their use of exercises. Sidney Lau is also the author of the excellent, but hulking *Cantonese-English Dictionary*. Lonely Planet publishes a *Cantonese phrasebook* that should see you through any excursions out to the night market, or the New Territories. For a simple list of phrases and a pronunciation guide, you could try *Instant Cantonese* by Bill Loh & Nick Theobold.

### Fiction

Unfortunately Hong Kong does not seem to have inspired many good novelists, but there are a few good tales worth reading.

The most famous of these must be Richard Mason's *The World of Suzie Wong*. Written in 1957, this delightful tale of a British painter who falls in love with a Hong Kong prostitute still makes an excellent read. It was made into a film starring William Holden and Nancy Kwan in 1960.

Paul Theroux's *Kowloon Tong* is a great read that portrays end-of-the-line expats in Hong Kong in 1996, on the eve of the June 1997 handover.

Spy-thriller author John Le Carre's *The Honourable Schoolboy* is set against the backdrop of early 1970s Hong Kong and Indochina, and is considered one of his better works.

James Clavell, who made his reputation writing about Japanese samurai in *Shogun*, has produced two entertaining Hong Kong novels. *Tai-Pan* is a racy historical fiction of Hong Kong's early merchant days. The protagonists' descendants then appear in the epic-length *Noble House* which is set in the 1960s and 1970s. Also set in Hong Kong and China are Robert Elegant's *Dynasty* and *Mandarin*, though these don't read as well as Clavell's offerings.

For historical accuracy, sharp humour and a rip-roaring read, pick up a copy of George MacDonald Frasier's *Flashman and the Dragon*. Though most of the story takes place in China, Flashman – the most decorated, womanising, bullying, witty poltroon of Victorian England – gets a fine start in Hong Kong that gives a good perspective on English attitudes during the opium wars. *An Insular Possession* by Timothy Mo is a very well-written novel set in pre-colonial Hong Kong. *Getting to Lamma* by Jane Alexander is a fictional adventure that ends up on the wonderful island of Lamma.

### Guides

There are some good books available for those who want to delve deeper into Hong Kong. *The Hong Kong Leisure Guide* gives brief descriptions, addresses, phone numbers and other vital statistics for all sorts of leisure and recreational activities in the territory, from batik to mahjong to parachuting. It's well worth picking up if you plan to stay in Hong Kong for a prolonged period. For a guide to Hong Kong's mid-range and expensive restaurants, you can try *Hong Kong's Best Restaurants*, which is published annually by *Hong Kong Tatler Magazine*. Better still is the annual restaurant guide put out by *HK Magazine*, which includes cheaper places and is a lot more fun to read.

Though it has a bit of an American slant, *Living in Hong Kong* is regularly updated and has loads of useful information for anyone planning to move to Hong Kong.

If you have a lot of time on your hands and want to learn about country hikes in detail, try Stella L Thrower's *Hong Kong Country Parks*, which is published by the Hong Kong government and is available at the Government Publications Office.

### NEWSPAPERS & MAGAZINES

Hong Kong has long been a bastion of media freedom in Asia. This will almost certainly change, as China has little patience for any media criticism. Some Hong Kong newspaper publishers and television stations have already started exercising self-censorship to avoid ruffling feathers in Beijing. The situation has not had as great an impact as one might think. Most journalism in Hong Kong focuses on economics, business and finance,

## Mad Dogs & Chinamen

Hitting the streets with a snarl in March 1996, *Mad Dog Daily* is a vehemently anti-communist Cantonese paper that really gets up the noses of those wandering the corridors of power in Beijing. Published by an ex-professor in the Department of Current Affairs at Zhuhai University, Huang Yumin, *Mad Dog Daily* is deliberately confrontational – the name and the logo of a vociferous bulldog points to its role as a watchdog for Hong Kong.

*Mad Dog Daily* felt it was time to turn the tide against the growing tendency towards self-censorship that typifies both the English and Chinese language press. Newspapers are becoming more and more of the Chinese mainland *baoxi bubaoyou* (report the good news, not the bad) attitude as typified by *Renmin Ribao* (*People's Daily*). *Mad Dog Daily* wants to push all the wrong buttons in Beijing, and it's not afraid of being put down – the only way it can be closed down is if some pretty draconian laws are put into effect. Huang Yumin has said 'I am only too happy to provide a test case'. Beijing must be more than keen to slip a sedative overdose in this particular dog's dinner, but their hands are tied. With the rest of the world watching, maybe a mad dog truly is man's best friend.

Other papers and periodicals on Beijing's 'We are not in the least bit amused' blacklist include: *Cheng Ming, Ming Pao, Apple Daily, Next, Hong Kong Economic Journal, Front-Line Magazine* and *Open Magazine*, among others. ■

and hence can usually skirt sensitive issues. But not always. In 1994 a Hong Kong reporter working in Beijing was jailed for 12 years after he wrote a story on interest rates and central bank gold sales, which China (after the fact) deemed state secrets. And in January 1996, China announced new controls on foreign wire services disseminating economic and financial news in China, Hong Kong, Macau and (arrogantly enough) Taiwan.

For the time being, the media in Hong Kong continues to struggle with new realities. There are two local English-language newspapers: the *South China Morning Post* and the *Hong Kong Standard*. The *South China Morning Post* (HK$7), also known as the 'Pro China Morning Post', is the most widely read, but is in fact read by more Hong Kong Chinese than expats. It's the world's most profitable newspaper, due to classified advertisement sales. The *Hong Kong Standard* (HK$6) generally does a better job of being more rigorous in its reporting, although the market niche is definitely there for some gutsy journalism. Both papers are also available on the Internet: *Hong Kong Standard*, www.hkstandard.com; *South China Morning Post*, www.scmp.com.

Three international newspapers produce Asian editions which are printed in Hong Kong. These are the *Asian Wall Street Journal, USA Today* and the *International Herald Tribune. Asia Times* is a relative newcomer to the market. Overseas newspapers are flown in on a regular basis, but they are expensive. You can find them on sale in bookshops that sell magazines and papers. Hong Kong also has its share of news magazines, including *Asiaweek, Far Eastern Economic Review* and *Asian Business* and a slew of Asian-focused business magazines. *Time, Newsweek* and *The Economist* are all available. On the leisure side, *Hong Kong Tatler* and *Home Journal* are for those interested in local lifestyle.

All this is a drop in the bucket compared with the Chinese print media. There are nearly 50 Chinese newspapers in Hong Kong, giving the city the world's highest per capita ratio of newspapers. Most of these cover general news, although there are five or six devoted solely to finance, and more than 12 reporting solely on horse-racing! Some have colourful names: the *Mad Dog Daily* hit the streets in 1996 (see the boxed text 'Mad Dogs and Chinamen' above).

If you want to see what's happening in Hong Kong entertainment and nightlife, pick up a copy of the excellent *HK Magazine*. It's on the ball with local gossip and behind-the-scenes stories, all dished up in fine writing that's like a breath of fresh air after the mostly stale alternatives. It's published weekly and is available free in bars, some restaurants, Oliver's Super Sandwiches shops, and hotels. In addition to music, cinema and performing arts listings, it carries lively articles on current trends in the city, reviews of restaurants and bars, and a classifieds section that makes for pretty interesting reading. Also worth checking out is *bc Magazine*, a monthly guide to Hong Kong's entertainment and partying scene. One of its most useful features is its complete listing of bars and clubs. It is also free and can usually be found alongside *HK Magazine*. If you're staying on the Outlying Islands, look out for *The Islands' Orbital*, a free newspaper dealing with the more bohemian aspects of island culture.

The HKTA has several free information publications, including the monthly *Official Hong Kong Guide* and the weekly *Hong Kong Now!* which has listings of cultural events. These are available at HKTA information centres, hotels and shopping malls.

## RADIO & TV

Government-funded Radio Television Hong Kong operates three English-language radio stations. Radio 3 (AM 567 kHz) has a mix of news, documentaries and entertainment; Radio 4 (FM 97.6 to 98.9 mHz) offers classical music in a bilingual format; and Radio 6 (AM 675 kHz) relays the BBC World Service. Commercial Radio's Quote 864 (AM 864 kHz) is a music station with mainly English-language music. Another private operator, Metro Broadcast, operates Hit Radio (FM 99.7 mHz) which plays pop music for younger people, and FM Select (FM 104 mHz), aimed at listeners age 25 and up. The English-language newspapers publish a daily guide to radio programmes.

Hong Kong's terrestrial TV channels are run by two companies: Television Broadcasts (TVB) and Asia Television Ltd (ATV). Each company operates one English-language and one Cantonese-language channel, making a total of four stations in Hong Kong. The two English channels are TVB Pearl (channel 3) and ATV World (channel 4), the Cantonese channels TVB Jade (channel 1) and ATV Home (channel 2). The programme schedule is listed every day in the English-language newspapers. Both Pearl and World regularly repeat films and generally have an unimaginative menu of programmes.

Hong Kong's own satellite television station Star TV (☎ 2621-8888) has a total of five channels, is available at most hotels and is free for anyone who owns a satellite dish (about 500,000 people). Star broadcasts across Asia, and can even be seen in China, though only its sports, music and Chinese drama channels are generally allowed. English-language channels have begun to be cut back to make space for more Mandarin broadcasts. Other regional broadcasters based in Hong Kong include NBC, TBS and sports channel ESPN.

As if this city-state needed more, Wharf Cable (☎ 2112-6868) entered the scene in 1993. Started up by the local conglomerate Wharf Holdings, the station currently offers 20 channels and has plans to expand this to 39 channels.

## PHOTOGRAPHY & VIDEO

With all the tourists, photographers and photojournalists in this city, it's easy getting cameras, film and supplies. The best place to go for equipment and accessories is Stanley St in Central. See the Cameras & Film section of the Shopping chapter for more information.

If you are bringing along a camcorder or the like, bear in mind that Hong Kong uses the PAL standard. If you use NTSC or SECAM you may want to bring some extra cartridges, though you should be able to find some in Hong Kong.

There's few problems taking photos in Hong Kong, and you're unlikely to find a gloved hand over your lens. Politically sensitive photo opportunities are few and far between, because of the unobtrusive PLA presence and the general business-as-usual feel of post-1997 Hong Kong. Those with a keen sense of photography will find a treasure chest of opportunities in Hong Kong.

FACTS FOR THE VISITOR

However, when walking about, think before you take photos. Places like pawn shops and mahjong parlours want to keep low profiles: aiming your camera at them could invite an angry response. Many older Chinese people strongly object to having their picture taken, so be considerate. If you're headed up to the Peak to catch stunning views of Hong Kong on film, the late afternoon is the best time to go, when the sun is shining down on the city.

## TIME
Hong Kong Standard Time is eight hours ahead of Greenwich Mean Time (GMT). Thus when it is midday in Hong Kong, it is 8 pm the previous day in Los Angeles; 11 pm the previous day in New York; 4 am in London; midday in Singapore; and 2 pm in Melbourne. Hong Kong does not have day-light-saving time.

## ELECTRICITY
The standard is 220V, 50 Hz (cycles per second) AC. Electrical shops in Hong Kong and elsewhere sell handy pocket-sized transformers which will step down the electricity to 110V, but most mini-transformers are only rated for 50 watts.

Hong Kong's system of plugs and sockets is a nightmare. Some electric outlets are designed to accommodate three round pins, others are wired for three square pins of the British design and others still for two-pin plugs! Not surprisingly, inexpensive plug adaptors are widely available in Hong Kong supermarkets, though this is not much comfort when you find you can't plug in your coffee machine in the morning. Don't forget that adaptors are *not* transformers. If you ignore this warning and plug a 110V appliance into a 220V outlet, it will be sparks and fireworks.

## LAUNDRY
Laundry services are pretty easy to find in Hong Kong, with the exception of the business district of Central. Most hotels, and even the cheap youth hostels, have a laundry service. Prices at private laundromats are normally about HK$28 for 3kg, HK$7 for

each additional kilo. If it's less than 3kg, you still pay the same, so you might want to throw in your clothes together with a friend's.

Dry-cleaners are easy to spot as well, and some laundromats offer dry-cleaning as well. Dry-cleaning a shirt costs around HK$15, a skirt HK$30 and trousers from HK$35 to HK$40.

## WEIGHTS & MEASURES
The international metric system is in official use in Hong Kong. In practice, traditional Chinese weights and measures are still common.

If you want to shop in the local markets, become familiar with Chinese units of weight. Things are sold by the *leung*, which is equivalent to 37.8g, or *gan*, where one gan is about 600g. There are 16 leung to the gan.

Gold is sold by the *tael* which is exactly the same as a leung, and you will find many banks selling gold in Hong Kong: the tael price is displayed right alongside the international ounce price.

## HEALTH
Looking after one's health in Hong Kong should pose few problems. While not such a healthy place to live in the longer term, there are only a few issues that visitors need be aware of. Access to health care is convenient, standards are generally high and English-speaking doctors abound. Medical costs are a bit lower than in many developed countries, especially the USA.

No special vaccinations are required for Hong Kong. However, it would be wise to consider both hepatitis A and B, tetanus and influenza (during winter). A hepatitis B vaccination is particularly sensible, as it's very common in Hong Kong (see later in this section). Hong Kong is also a good place to get vaccinations for onward travel to other countries in Asia. For these, try a public hospital if you don't mind a longer wait, or a private hospital or doctors' office if you can afford it. The number of reported AIDS cases is comparatively low in Hong Kong; safe sex should of course still be observed.

While Hong Kong's public hospitals provide low-cost care to residents, visitors and other non-Hong Kong taxpayers are usually asked to pay more (there is no National Health Service in Hong Kong); many Hong Kong residents are also covered by the company they work for. Thus it is advisable to take out some travel insurance – see the Documents section earlier in this chapter.

You can buy almost any medication across the counter in Hong Kong or get it by prescription. It would be a good idea to take along details of any specialist prescriptions

---

### Everyday Health

Normal body temperature is 37°C or 98.6°F; more than 2°C (4°F) higher indicates a high fever. The normal adult pulse rate is 60 to 100 per minute (children 80 to 100, babies 100 to 140). As a general rule the pulse increases about 20 beats per minute for each °C (2°F) rise in fever.

Respiration (breathing) rate is also an indicator of illness. Count the number of breaths per minute: between 12 and 20 is normal for adults and older children (up to 30 for younger children, 40 for babies). People with a high fever or serious respiratory illness breathe more quickly than normal. More than 40 shallow breaths a minute may be an indication of pneumonia. ■

---

you may need. Many pharmacies just hand over the medication whether you have a prescription or not!

If you wear glasses, bring a spare pair of glasses and your prescription. Be warned that frames in Hong Kong are usually extremely expensive. *Optical 88* and *The Optical Shop* are two of the best known chains in Hong Kong.

Oral contraceptives are widely available, though it is still preferable to bring your own supply. Condoms are easy to find as well. It is best to buy a western brand, as the local and Japanese brands are not known for their reliability.

### Medical Problems

**Air & Water Pollution** Hong Kong's air quality is abysmal. You will notice how women in Hong Kong walk around with their hands over their mouths. On the streets, one is often bombarded with smells that defy description. In January 1996, only six months after setting up a monitoring index, the government issued a day-long health alert warning people with respiratory ailments or heart conditions to stay indoors. The cause is the large number of diesel vehicles, factory emissions and the endless construction which kicks up clouds of dirt and concrete dust. People with asthma may

---

### Medical Kit Check List

Consider taking a basic medical kit including:

☐ **Aspirin** or paracetamol (acetaminophen in the USA) – for pain or fever.

☐ **Antihistamine** (such as Benadryl) – useful as a decongestant for colds and allergies, to ease the itch from insect bites or stings, and to help prevent motion sickness. Antihistamines may cause sedation and interact with alcohol so care should be taken when using them; take one you know and have used before, if possible.

☐ **Antibiotics** – useful if you're travelling well off the beaten track, but they must be prescribed; carry the prescription with you.

☐ **Loperamide** (eg Imodium) or Lomotil for diarrhoea; prochlorperazine (eg Stemetil) or metaclopramide (eg Maxalon) for nausea and vomiting.

☐ **Rehydration mixture** – for treatment of severe diarrhoea; particularly important for travelling with children.

☐ **Antiseptic** such as povidone-iodine (eg Betadine) – for cuts and grazes.

☐ **Multivitamins** – especially for long trips when dietary vitamin intake may be inadequate.

☐ **Calamine lotion** or **aluminium sulphate spray** (eg Stingose) – to ease irritation from bites or stings.

☐ **Bandages** and Band-Aids.

☐ **Scissors, tweezers** and a **thermometer** (note that mercury thermometers are prohibited by airlines).

☐ **Cold and flu tablets** and **throat lozenges** – pseudoephedrine hydrochloride (Sudafed) may be useful if flying with a cold to avoid ear damage.

☐ **Insect repellent, sunscreen, lip balm** and **chap stick**.

find it difficult to breath and easy to contract chest infections, and should have plenty of medication on hand. It may also be wise to start using an asthma suppressant several weeks before arriving in Hong Kong.

Water pollution is also bad, and it's getting worse. The government has set up a system to monitor the quality of water at Hong Kong's beaches. The index is based on the amount of disease-causing bacteria present in the water, which indicates levels of faecal pollution. Water quality is divided into categories of good, fair, poor and very poor. Water ratings of Hong Kong's beaches are usually published in the local newspapers, especially during warmer months. Take note that most local beaches fall well below World Health Organization standards for swimming.

**Drinking Water & Food** The Hong Kong government says it's perfectly safe to drink the tap water. This said, many residents boil it anyway. Hong Kong's old plumbing means that bacteria may lurk in corroded pits in the pipes themselves. It may be a good idea to follow the locals and either boil your drinking water or buy mineral water. If you go hiking in the countryside do not drink from any stream or pond – it is likely contaminated by fertiliser, cow dung or waste chemicals.

If self-catering, be extra careful in the preparation of foods, and wash vegetables very carefully, as many vegetables bought from street markets have been imported from Guangdong, where they are often fertilised with human manure. Fresh seafood should be cooked thoroughly (at 100°C for five minutes) and never eaten raw.

Eating in Hong Kong restaurants is by and large safe; cases of upset stomach and diarrhoea do occur, but not too often. Street markets are also generally OK (but see the warning above about fresh vegetables); be more cautious of the street stalls selling steamed or fried dumplings – these have been known to pass on some nasty stomach bugs. Waterside restaurants sometimes have the disturbing habit of using harbour water

---

**Nutrition**

If your food is poor or limited in availability, if you're travelling hard and fast and therefore missing meals, or if you simply lose your appetite, you can soon start to lose weight and place your health at risk.

Make sure that your diet is well balanced. Cooked eggs, beans, lentils and nuts are all safe ways to get protein. Fruit you can peel (bananas, oranges or mandarins for example) is usually safe (melons can harbour bacteria in their flesh and are best avoided) and a good source of vitamins. Try to eat plenty of grains (including rice) and bread. Remember that although food is generally safer if it is cooked well, overcooked food loses much of its nutritional value. If your diet isn't well balanced or if your food intake is insufficient, it's a good idea to take vitamin and iron pills.

In hot climates make sure that you drink enough – don't rely on feeling thirsty to indicate when you should drink. Not needing to urinate or passing small amounts of very dark yellow urine are danger signs. Always carry a water bottle with you on long trips. Excessive sweating can lead to loss of salt and therefore muscle cramping. Salt tablets are not a good idea as a preventative, but in places where salt is not used much adding salt to food can help. ■

---

to fill their fish storage tanks. The government is cracking down on this, but you might want to try and check all the same.

If you're hungering for shellfish, make sure it comes from somewhere other than Hong Kong waters: local clams and oysters are tasty but can be risky too. Prawns, lobsters and other sea creatures are OK.

**Hepatitis** Though Hong Kong is not nearly as bad as China, or even Taiwan for that matter, it is still possible to catch hepatitis here, and more than 1500 cases are reported annually. About 10% of the population are carriers of hepatitis B. Many probably contracted it in China. Still, it's not a bad idea to get vaccinations for both hepatitis A and B before you leave home. There is a combined hepatitis A and B vaccination, Twinrix. Three injections are required over a period of six months. Hepatitis B is spread through contact with the blood and bodily fluids of an infected person. In other words, it can be transmitted sexually and through dirty needles used in acupuncture, tattooing and by drug addicts.

Poor hygienic conditions in restaurants are a common cause of hepatitis A, so try and avoid any place that looks really filthy. Unwashed fresh vegetables and shellfish are the usual culprits, along with dirty plates and utensils. Be vigilant – epidemics of the disease do occur in Hong Kong, with a major one in 1992 infecting 3500 people.

**Tuberculosis** The infection rate for TB is surprisingly high in Hong Kong – more than 7000 cases are reported annually (resulting in about 400 deaths). The problem is that the TB virus is spread in the air, and with Hong Kong having such a dense population, it is easily spread. While there is no reason to be unduly alarmed, if you're travelling with children it might be wise to have them vaccinated. These days, nearly all children born in Hong Kong are immunised at birth, but not so in many other countries. For adults, a skin test before and after travelling to Hong Kong, to determine whether exposure has occurred, is recommended.

### Medical Assistance

Every hospital in Hong Kong has a number of English-speaking doctors and staff, and most private doctors speak English as well. Dental care is available, but fees are quite high; it's best to visit a private dentist – many are trained abroad and speak excellent English. Public hospitals charge low fees, but Hong Kong residents pay less than foreign visitors. Private doctors' fees are often higher, so it pays to make some inquiries first; if you have a friend living in Hong Kong, get a recommendation or contact the Association of American Doctors in Hong Kong (☎ 2523-2123), who can provide you with a list of capable doctors.

Most pharmacies in Hong Kong are open from 9 am to 6 pm, with some until 8 pm. Watson's has branches all over Hong Kong and can supply most pharmaceutical needs.

Public hospitals, all of which have 24-hour casualty wards, include:

Princess Margaret Hospital (☎ 2990-1111), Lai Chi Kok, Kowloon
Prince of Wales Hospital (☎ 2636-2211), Sha Tin, New Territories
Queen Elizabeth Hospital (☎ 2958-8888), Yau Ma Tei
Queen Mary Hospital (☎ 2855-4111), Pok Fu Lam, Hong Kong Island

There are some excellent private hospitals in Hong Kong, but their prices reflect the fact that they must operate at a profit. Some of these include:

Baptist Hospital (☎ 2337-4141), Kowloon Tong, Kowloon
Canossa Hospital (☎ 2522-2181), 1 Old Peak Rd, Mid-Levels
Hong Kong Adventist Hospital (☎ 2574-6211), 40 Stubbs Rd, Wan Chai
Hong Kong Central Hospital (☎ 2522-3141), Central
Matilda & War Memorial Hospital (☎ 2849-0111), 41 Mt Kellet Rd, The Peak
St Paul's Hospital (☎ 2890-6008), Causeway Bay

### Emergencies, Counselling & Organisations

In the event of a medical emergency dial ☎ 999: operators speak English. St John's offers a free ambulance service on Hong Kong Island (☎ 2576-6555), Kowloon (☎ 2713-5555) and the New Territories (☎ 2639-2555). Some people find life in Hong Kong difficult to adapt to, especially long-term residents. There are a few places who can help: phone St John's Counselling Service (☎ 2525-7207) or the Community Advice Bureau (☎ 2815-5444). Other useful help lines and organisations include:

| | |
|---|---|
| AIDS Concern Help Line | ☎ 2898-4422 |
| Alcoholics Anonymous | ☎ 2522-5665 |
| Drug Abuse Hotline | ☎ 2366-8822 |
| HIV Information and Drop-In Centre | ☎ 2523-0531 |
| Narcotics Anonymous | ☎ 2813-7343 |
| Rape Hotline | ☎ 2572-2222 |
| Samaritans | ☎ 2896-0000 |

### TOILETS

Though it could definitely do with more, Hong Kong does have a network of public toilets. Some areas of the city are better than others: Central has five or six, while Tsim

Sha Tsui has a paltry two. In general Hong Kong Island seems better equipped on this front. Most public parks have public toilets. Others are seemingly placed at random.

Facilities are relatively clean, considering the use they get. Toilets come in both sit-down and squat versions. There is no fee for using them, and all are marked with English signs.

## WOMEN TRAVELLERS

Hong Kong is by and large a safe city for women travellers, but there are still a few things to be aware of. Female travellers staying in guesthouses or other budget accommodation are sometimes approached by pleasant-mannered men offering them modelling or escort work. Don't accept these offers. These guys are basically assistant pimps whose task is to dig up women for nightclubs or brothels. Most of these rackets are run by Triads (Hong Kong's equivalent of the Mafia), who are not people to mess with. Chungking Mansions seems to be a popular hunting ground for these characters.

Groping and other forms of sexual harassment are not too common, but do occur, especially on crowded buses and subways. Rape is also relatively rare, and local women regularly walk alone at night. But it still does take place, and some victims have reported that local police and hospital staff can be less than sympathetic. However, as long as you avoid darkened alleys and secluded parks, or travel in pairs, there should be few problems. A useful phone number is the Rape Hotline (☎ 2572-2222).

## GAY & LESBIAN TRAVELLERS

While Hong Kong is more enlightened than many other Asian cities, homosexuality is still anathema to many Hong Kong Chinese. However, the situation has improved considerably over the last few years, and the burgeoning gay scene in Hong Kong is far more ostentatious than it was. The lesbian scene in Hong Kong is still pretty much under wraps, however. *HK Magazine* sometimes has information on clubs, events and associations that may be of interest. Details

of the flourishing gay bar scene are described in the Entertainment chapter. The age of consent is 21.

## DISABLED TRAVELLERS

Hong Kong has made a few scattered attempts to make urban areas more accessible to disabled people. Some buildings and walkways have ramps, some restaurants have special rest rooms and some subway stations have lifts for those who can't negotiate stairs or escalators.

The Hong Kong Transport Department puts out a free publication called *Guide to Public Transport Services in Hong Kong for Disabled Persons*, which gives a complete rundown of facilities on buses, subways, trains, ferries and so on. It also gives telephone numbers for the various transport operators and other services aimed at assisting disabled travellers. The booklet is available at some MTR subway stations and from the Transport Department (☎ 2829-5258), 41st floor, Immigration Tower (Map 7), 7 Gloucester Rd, Wan Chai.

The Hong Kong Federation of Handicapped People (☎ 2759-6412) may be able to help visitors with disabilities, though they are set up to deal mostly with local companies and individuals.

## HONG KONG FOR CHILDREN

Hong Kong may not seem a great place to take the kids. After all, who wants to pound the pavement with their parents in search of bargains in Tsim Sha Tsui? Fortunately there's a lot more to Hong Kong than shopping, including a number of places that should be fun for kids and any adults they drag along.

Ocean Park, near Aberdeen on the south side of Hong Kong Island, has a number of hair-raising rides, as well as dolphin and whale shows and a really cool aquarium that includes a walkway through a shark tank. Adjacent to Ocean Park is Water World, a seasonal water amusement park with pools, giant slides and the like. On the other side of Ocean Park lies Middle Kingdom, a somewhat cheesy simulation of ancient China.

Back on the other side of Hong Kong, in Central, Hong Kong Park has a great aviary and, nearby, a fine playground. Opposite the park, across Garden Rd, the Hong Kong Zoological & Botanical Gardens has a well-stocked zoo and plenty of space for kids to run around and work off some nervous energy. Also nearby is the Peak Tram – the ride alone is fine entertainment, but once on top there are plenty of trails and walkways to explore. Also at the top is the Peak Tower which houses a number of modern adventure rides and shows. Kids also might get a kick out of the gaudy statues and figurines that cover the Tiger Balm Gardens, which are located near Causeway Bay.

Over on Kowloon, the first stop for kids is the Hong Kong Space Museum in Tsim Sha Tsui, which has all sorts of spacecraft models, sky shows and Omnimax movies. The Hong Kong Science Museum in Tsim Sha Tsui East is also worth a visit and has lots of hands-on exhibits to shore up flagging attention spans.

Kowloon Park has a complex of indoor and outdoor swimming pools that seems built just for kids. The park is also home to the Hong Kong Museum of History, which has life-size models of an old Chinese fishing boat and 19th century Hong Kong streets.

If you don't mind making the trip out to the New Territories, the Hong Kong Railway Museum has a pretty good collection of locomotives, carriages and other rolling stock on outdoor display, some of which can be entered. For information on this and all the above attractions, see the Things to See & Do chapter.

Of course Hong Kong also has plenty of beaches and country parks for more outdoor-minded youngsters and adults. A ferry ride out to one of the Outlying Islands, with their beaches, hiking trails and fishing villages, is fabulous for a fun day's outing. Refer to the Excursions chapter for details.

## LIBRARIES

Hong Kong has a fairly extensive system of public libraries. The most useful for travellers is the main library (☎ 2921-2555) at City Hall, High Block, Central, just east of the Star Ferry Terminal (Map 6). With a passport and a HK$130 deposit, foreign visitors can get a temporary library card allowing them to take out books (it has an extensive collection of books in English). There is also a good reference library. The library is open Monday to Thursday from 10 am to 7 pm, Fridays from 10 am to 9 pm, Saturday from 10 am to 5 pm and Sunday from 10 am to 1 pm. It is closed on public holidays.

For locations of other libraries, call the City Hall main library: their English-speaking staff should be able to help you. The American Library (☎ 2523-9011), in the American Consulate, 26 Garden Rd, Central, has good research facilities and is open on weekdays from 10 am to 6 pm. For those on business, the Trade Development Council Business Library (☎ 2584-4333) is well stocked with relevant books and CD-ROMs; you can find it on the 38th floor, Office Tower, Convention Plaza, 1 Harbour Rd, Wan Chai; it's open Monday to Friday from 9 am to 6 pm and Saturday from 9 am to 1 pm.

Various cultural centres, including the Alliance Française, British Council and Goethe Institut, maintain libraries as well. See the Cultural Centres section following.

## CULTURAL CENTRES

Several countries have set up centres in Hong Kong to promote understanding of their culture and society. All of them offer language courses, and most show films or host seminars. A few also have libraries.

The largest of these centres is the British Council (☎ 2913-5125), which has moved to new offices at 3 Supreme Court Rd, Admiralty (Map 6). Its main role is to provide English-language classes and give access to British expertise in science and technology, but it also sponsors cultural programmes and has a library which can be used for free (although you can only take books, CDs and videos out if you are a member of the library). The library also offers free Internet access. This is the place if you want to leaf through recent papers and magazines from the UK.

The Alliance Française (☎ 2527-7825), 2nd floor, 123 Hennessy Rd, Wan Chai (Map 7), also has a library and offers a wide range of cultural activities. Dante Alighieri (☎ 2573-0343), at 704 Trinity House, 165-171 Wan Chai Rd, Wan Chai, is the Italian cultural society and offers language courses and other subjects. Also on hand is a video and book library.

If you're looking for German books, films or just the chance to meet a fellow German speaker, try the Goethe Institut (☎ 2802-0088) on the 14th floor, Hong Kong Arts Centre, 2 Harbour Rd, Wan Chai (Map 7).

La Sociedad Hispanica de Hong Kong (☎ 2407-8800) offers classes in Spanish language and culture and organises Spanish dinners, video evenings and so on. The address is GPO Box 11751, Hong Kong.

## DANGERS & ANNOYANCES

Hong Kong is a safe city to visit, but it does have some annoying aspects that you must learn to deal with, such as constant crowds or incessant noise. Even if you are a smoker you may find the air in Hong Kong's bars a bit rich for your lungs. A few restaurants have non-smoking areas, but the general rule in most places is 'join the cloud'.

### Rudeness

Next to shopping, one of the things Hong Kong is best known for is the rudeness of its people. This is in part because most visitors deal with people in the tourist trade rather than ordinary Hong Kong residents. It's fairly common for visitors to encounter sullen salespeople who pretend you don't exist or pushy ones who hurl abuse if you don't buy the product you asked to look at.

Truth be told, rudeness doesn't end in the tourist ghettos. On the street you may find people elbowing you out of their way, refusing to step aside or blatantly jumping in front of you to steal the cab you just flagged down. Hong Kong phone manners must rate among the worst on earth: it's common to have someone on the other end hang up on you in mid-query. One notable exception, however,

is queuing up, which most people seem to respect (unlike the rest of China).

This doesn't mean every visitor will encounter such appalling behaviour. Like anywhere, some people in Hong Kong are charming, generous and helpful. Staff in clothing stores such as Giordano or in large department stores can make shopping a pleasure. Ask a person directions, and he or she may end up showing you the whole way. It's just that Hong Kong seems to have more than its fair share of impolite individuals. Some can be mollified by a show of patience and politeness. Others are impossible. If you have the misfortune to encounter any of the latter, it's best just to laugh it off and leave them to their miserable lives.

### Shopping Rip-Offs

Most Hong Kong shops are honest and give you what you pay for. However, in some areas, notably Tsim Sha Tsui and Causeway Bay, there are shopkeepers who won't blink at selling you shoddy or used equipment at ridiculous prices. The most frequent offenders are the electronics and camera shops that don't put prices on any of their goods.

You may be able to avoid these types by looking for the logo of the Hong Kong Tourist Association, which is a red Chinese junk sailing against a white background. HKTA member shops are officially required to meet a series of ethical and operating standards. Unfortunately there are some member stores which are still pretty shady. Appliance chain stores such as Fortress or department stores are generally reliable.

For more details on potential rip-off tactics and how to avoid them, see the Shopping chapter.

### Theft

Despite its obvious prosperity and low unemployment rate, Hong Kong is not free of riff-raff who choose crime as their occupation. While violent crime mostly stays within the local gangster community, theft is more common, and unfortunately tourists are prime targets.

The biggest worry for travellers is probably pickpockets, who favour crowded buses, subways, ferries and shopping districts. The problem has been reduced by undercover police who specialise in catching pickpockets, but it's still a problem, so keep your cash secured in a moneybelt or inside zippered pockets.

Bag-snatchers also do well in Hong Kong. A few unfortunate souls have had their luggage nicked this way right in the airport when they wandered off for a minute to use the toilets or change money. The same principle applies in restaurants and pubs – if your bag doesn't accompany you to the toilet, don't expect to find it when you return.

If you're staying in budget accommodation, keep a close eye on your belongings, as theft occurs in these places too. Sadly, the culprit could well be a fellow traveller, some of whom arrive in Hong Kong totally broke with no prospects for employment, nor any self-respect.

Hong Kong continues to fight a persistent drug abuse problem. It is estimated that there are more than 40,000 drug addicts in the territory, with heroin as the drug of choice. Again for travellers this means being careful with your valuables. It is generally safe to walk around at night, but it's best to stick to well-lit areas. Tourist districts like Tsim Sha Tsui are heavily patrolled by the police and there is little danger of violent crime, though theft can occur anywhere.

If you get robbed or pickpocketed, you can obtain a loss report for insurance purposes at the Central District Police Station, 10 Hollywood Rd (at Pottinger St) in Central (Map 6). There are English-speaking staff here.

## LEGAL MATTERS

Unless you do something stupid like steal from a fellow traveller, it's pretty hard to run afoul of the law in Hong Kong. Two exceptions are drug use and drunk driving. Penalties for illegal drug use are severe, ranging from deportation to long jail terms. While other countries draw a line between marijuana and more addictive substances like cocaine and heroin, Hong Kong is equally serious about all of them. Police sometimes do spot checks of bars in the Lan Kwai Fong area in Central, looking for people either using or peddling marijuana, hashish or heroin. Hong Kong's finest also sometimes pay a visit to passengers disembarking the ferry at Lamma Island, home to the territory's erstwhile expat slacker community. Don't forget that although Hong Kong possesses a more benign legal system than over the electrified fence to the north, Hong Kong is now under Chinese rule, and in China they routinely shoot people for drug-running (and send the family of the deceased a bill for the cost of the bullet). Just a thought.

Drunk driving has long been overlooked in Hong Kong, but police are starting to crack down. Patrol cars are being equipped with breathalysers and penalties stiffened. In any case, Hong Kong's outstanding public transport system means there is no real excuse to drink and drive.

If you run into legal trouble and don't have the funds to hire a lawyer, the Legal Aid Department (☎ 2537-7677) provides both residents and nonresidents with representation, subject to a means and merits test.

## BUSINESS HOURS

Office hours are weekdays from 9 am to 5 or 6 pm, and on Saturday from 9 am to noon (business employees wear jeans on Saturday, irrespective of rank or affluence). Lunch hour is from 1 to 2 pm and many offices simply shut down and lock the door at this time. Banks are open weekdays from 9 am to 4.30 pm and do not close for lunch. On Saturday they are only open from 9 am to 12.30 pm.

Many Hong Kong companies still run on a 5½ day working week, but this concept is beginning to fall out of favour. Some companies use the promise of a five day week in their 'help wanted' advertisements to lure new employees.

Stores and restaurants that cater to the tourist trade keep longer hours, but almost nothing opens before 9 am. Even tourist-related businesses shut down by 9 or 10 pm, and many will close for major holidays, especially Chinese New Year.

Restaurants generally open from 11.30 am to 2.30 pm for lunch and 6 to 11 pm for dinner. Of course there are many exceptions to this rule. Some pubs keep the kitchen open until 1 am and Chinese noodle shops often run from early in the morning until the wee hours. Bars generally open at noon or 6 pm and close anywhere between 2 and 6 am.

## PUBLIC HOLIDAYS

Western and Chinese culture combine to create an interesting mix of holidays. Trying to determine the exact date of the Chinese holidays is a bit tricky since there are two calendars in use in Hong Kong – the Gregorian calendar and the Chinese lunar calendar. As the two calendars do not correspond exactly, an extra month is added to the lunar calendar once every 30 months. The result is that the Lunar New Year, the most important Chinese holiday, can fall anywhere between 21 January and 28 February on the Gregorian calendar.

Lunar New Year, more widely referred to as Chinese New Year, can be a bad time to fly in or out of Hong Kong, as most flights are booked solid. For four days the border with China becomes a riot zone as millions of Hong Kongers flock to their relatives on the mainland. On the other hand, Hong Kong basically shuts down for three days during this holiday, so it should be easy to find a hotel room. Although shops, supermarkets and restaurants used to shut for three days to a week, many now only take one day off, making Chinese New Year a more practical time to visit Hong Kong.

Though not as bad as Chinese New Year, Ching Ming (Tomb-Sweeping Day) is another public holiday, held in early April. Public transport is extremely crowded and the border crossing into China once again becomes a nightmare. The Easter holiday is often close to Ching Ming Festival, and is locally known as the 'foreigner's Ching Ming'. Christmas is the other big holiday time for locals, so again booking flights can be a bit difficult.

The return of Hong Kong to China has seen a shake-up of the public holiday system. Gone is the revelry usually seen on the Queen's birthday, instead Hong Kong grinds to a halt and has a long lie in on 1 October, National Day (establishment of the People's Republic of China); the day after National Day also merits a vacation. SAR Establishment Day is held on the anniversary of the handover of Hong Kong to China, warranting a break from work. The eviction of Japanese forces from Hong Kong at the end of WWII by allied forces (after Nagasaki and Hiroshima were blitzed) has now become Sino-Japanese War Victory Day. The rewriting of history has sadly begun in earnest.

Public holidays are as follows:

*New Year* – the first weekday in January

*Chinese New Year* – three days; in late January or February

*Easter* – three days; from Good Friday to Easter Sunday

*Ching Ming (Tomb-Sweeping Day) Festival* – one day; usually during the first week in April

*Tuen Ng (Dragon Boat) Festival* – one day; in late May, early June

*SAR Establishment Day* – 30 June; celebrates the resumption of sovereignty over Hong Kong by China

*Sino-Japanese War Victory Day* – held on a Monday in mid to late August; preceding Saturday is also a public holiday

*Mid-Autumn (Moon) Festival* – one day; in September or October

*National Day* – 1 & 2 October, celebrates the establishment of the People's Republic of China

*Chung Yeung Festival* – one day; in October

*Christmas & Boxing Day* – 25 & 26 December

## FESTIVALS

Many Chinese festivals go back hundreds or thousands of years, their true origins often lost in the mists of time. The reasons for each festival vary and you will generally find there are a couple of tales to choose from. The HKTA's free leaflet *Chinese Festivals: Dates* will tell you the exact dates that festivals are celebrated that year. There are a good number of them held between January and October, so if you visit during that time you stand a good chance of catching one.

## January to June

*Chinese New Year* This festival is a family one, with little for the visitor to see except a fireworks display on New Year's Eve. To start the New Year properly can determine one's fortune for the entire year. Therefore, houses are cleaned, debts paid off and feuds, no matter how bitter, are ended – even if it's only for the day. The New Year is usually held in late January of February.

*Yuen Siu (Lantern Festival)* In some ways this festival is more interesting than the Chinese New Year. At the end of the New Year celebrations, lanterns in traditional designs are lit in homes, restaurants and temples. Out in the residential areas, you'll see people carrying colourful lanterns through the streets.

*Ching Ming (Tomb-Sweeping Day)* Ching Ming is a time for visiting graves, traditionally to ask ancestral spirits if they are satisfied with their descendants. Graves are cleaned and food and wine left for the spirits, while incense and paper money are burned for the dead. The festival is held in early April.

*Tin Hau Festival* This is one of Hong Kong's most colourful occasions as Tin Hau, patroness of fishing people, is one of the territory's most popular goddesses. Junks on the water are decorated with flags and sail in long rows to Tin Hau's temples to pray for clear skies and good catches. The festival is held in April or May.

A young participant in traditional costume at Cheung Chau's Bun Festival.

*Cheung Chau Bun Festival* One of Hong Kong's most lively occasions, this Taoist festival on the island of Cheung Chau takes its name from its huge bun towers – bamboo scaffolding covered with edible buns. If you go to Cheung Chau a week or so before the festival you'll see these huge bamboo towers being built in the courtyard of the colourful Pak Tai Temple. In times past, hundreds of people would scramble up the bun towers to fetch one of the holy buns for good luck. The third day of the festival (a Sunday) is the most interesting due to a procession with floats, stilt walkers and people dressed as legendary characters. Most fascinating are the 'floating children' who are carried through the streets on poles, as if floating over the crowd. Accommodation in Cheung Chau is heavily booked at this time and the ferries out there are always packed. The bun festival is held over four days in May.

*Birthday of Lord Buddha* Also known as the Bathing of Lord Buddha, this festival is rather more sedate than Taoist holidays. The Buddha's statue is taken from monasteries and temples and ceremoniously bathed in water scented with sandalwood and herbs. Later the water is drunk by the faithful, who believe it has great curative powers.

*Tuen Ng (Dragon Boat) Festival* This one is a lot of fun despite the fact that it commemorates the sad tale of Qu Yuan, a 3rd century BC poet-statesman who hurled himself into a river in Hunan Province to protest against the corrupt government. Onlookers raced to the scene in their boats to save him but were too late. People throw dumplings into the water to keep the hungry fish away from his body. The festival is held in June.

## July to December

*Birthday of Lu Pan, Master Builder* A master architect, magician, engineer, inventor and designer, Lu Pan is worshipped by anyone connected with the building trade. The celebration occurs around mid to late July. The Lu Pan temple in Kennedy Town at the top of Li·Po Lung Path comes colourfully alive at this time.

*Ghost Month* On the first day of the seventh moon (late August or early September), the gates of hell are opened and 'hungry ghosts' – the spirits of those who were unloved, forgotten by family or suffered a violent death – are free for two weeks to walk the earth. On the 14th day, called the Yue Lan Festival, hungry ghosts receive offerings of food from the living before returning down below. Paper cars, paper houses and paper money are burnt, and these goodies become the property of the ghosts.

*Mid-Autumn (Moon) Festival* This festival recalls an uprising against the Mongols in the 14th century when plans for the revolution were passed around in cakes. Moon cakes are still eaten and there are many varieties. Everyone heads for the hilltops, where they light special lanterns and watch the moon rise. For young couples, it's a romantic holiday – a time to be together and gaze at the moon.

*Cheung Yeung Festival* This low-key holiday commemorates the story of an Eastern Han Dynasty man who, on the advice of a soothsayer, took his family away to a high place to avoid a pending disaster. The man returned a day later to find every living thing in his village had been destroyed. Many people head to the high spots again to remember. The festival is usually held in October.

## WORK

It used to be the case that British citizens, British passport holders and registered British subjects did not need work visas. That's all history now. Everyone who wants to work in Hong Kong now has to first obtain a work visa. All those Brits who were allowed to work without a visa in Hong Kong had until 1 April 1998 to furnish sponsorship from the companies they were working for (to prove that they were really needed and the job could not be done by a local Chinese person); if they couldn't they were out – this led to a huge exodus. More and more unskilled and semi-skilled jobs are going to local and mainland Chinese, so it is harder for foreigners to find this kind of work.

Ironically, it has been even harder for mainland Chinese to come to Hong Kong to work (legally) after 30 June 1997 than it was *before* the handover (the last thing China wanted was hundreds of thousands of Chinese rushing for the much higher salaries and standards of living).

Foreign nationals must get an employment visa from the Hong Kong Immigration Department before arrival. This is not easy to arrange – you need a job skill which cannot easily be performed by a local, and your employer must be willing to sponsor you. For more details see the Documents section earlier in this chapter.

Under-the-table employment is possible to obtain, but there are stiff penalties for employers who hire foreigners illegally (the penalties are routinely advertised on TV as a

### The Taxman Cometh

With a flat basic salary tax rate of 15%, the Hong Kong SAR is for many a tax paradise. Interest on your bank account is not taxed, nor are those bags of money made on the stock market or other forms of capital gains (unless they are your primary source of income). The feel-good tax factor further improves with the absence of sales tax and value-added tax.

Your first HK$100,000 is tax-free (more if you're married) and you won't get taxed until your second year anyway. However, because tax is not deducted from your monthly pay, but arrives in the form of a tax bill, it can be quite a shock to see how much you owe when it comes. Many make a break for the border at this point; you won't be stopped leaving Hong Kong, but you'll be asked to fork out up front if you try and return (with a fine tacked on). So if you're going to spend a while in the ex-colony, it's advisable to put a portion of your monthly salary into a high interest deposit account so the moolah is there when it's needed.

If you're being sent to Hong Kong on an employment package, it's important to make sure the wording of your contract is in your favour. As many expats have housing partially or fully provided, you will want to know whether this is taxable or not. If you have a housing allowance, it is assumed that this is arranged in the form of money given to you, and thus it is a taxable sum. But if your employer rebates the rent you pay, or somehow 'gives' you the accommodation, then you will pay less tax. It is worth discussing this with your employer, as it is often just a question of wording. Employers can also come up with a holiday allowance which offers tax deductions for taking a vacation! In fact, with enough patience and ingenuity, you can make your employer pick up the tab for most of your expenses (eg phone and electricity bills), which means you don't get taxed on those either. Many employers also offer medical schemes, which is important as Hong Kong is not a welfare state.

If you're planning to move to Hong Kong, discuss these matters with your employer and see how far they are willing to go or make an appointment with a tax expert who will illuminate you on what potential savings you could make. ■

reminder). These rules are vigorously enforced against employers who hire labourers from China, because of the justifiable fear of a wave of illegal immigrants. Despite the rules, plenty of westerners do find temporary illegal work in Hong Kong, but there are considerable risks.

### Finding a Job

Many travellers drop into Hong Kong looking for short-term work to top up cash reserves before heading off to other destinations in Asia. Some wind up staying much longer than anticipated. Success in finding work depends largely on what skills you have. Those with professional backgrounds in such fields as engineering, computer programming and finance will have less trouble. If you don't have a career background, finding work is possible though more difficult, and high wages may elude you.

The job market in Hong Kong is adapting to the new realities of the post-handover period. The situation is far from stable, and it is impossible to predict future trends, but one consequence of all the uncertainty before the handover was that many skilled and talented Chinese people fled Hong Kong. This opened up professional positions, in certain companies, to foreigners with the necessary skills. This however does not apply to all companies, and some big names are only taking on those of Chinese descent, while sidelining foreigners. Also, large numbers of the Hong Kong Chinese who fled have returned or are returning, at ease with the generally optimistic situation.

Overall though, the Hong Kong employment market is still energetic, dynamic and diverse. It's worth bearing in mind that job loyalty is a dirty word in Hong Kong – some residents change jobs four times a year. The quest is always for that higher salary (if you want to know why, look at the size of the mortgages) and employees are regularly enticed away from positions. This creates a swiftly changing job market, with bundles of choice; just look at the jobs section of the *South China Morning Post* on a Saturday for an idea of the range and volume of available jobs (that is just the tip of the iceberg as well). It's worth bearing in mind, however, that for every job there are a large number of people angling for the same position.

Many of the professional Hong Kong Chinese who made the permanent move away from the ex-colony took with them their excellent English language skills. This, coupled with an increasing emphasis on the use of Mandarin (in business and in the classroom), has led to a swift decline in the level of spoken English. All this is creating job opportunities for foreigners – the list is endless: racecourse commentators, English teachers, financial editors, magazine editors, TV and radio presenters, tour guides and bar staff are just a few of the positions that require native English-language staff. Those with English-language teaching training (eg TEFL) will find a bountiful market for their skills. At the time of writing, the Hong Kong Department of Education was advertising for native teachers of English (with school experience) to move to Hong Kong, enticed by the prospect of HK$15,000 a month housing allowance and a basic salary in excess of HK$25,000 (the average salary in Hong Kong is about HK$12,000 a month). This led to an outcry from local teachers who do not receive a housing allowance. If you don't have teaching qualifications, you can still contact schools for they may have conversational classes, or you can advertise yourself as a tutor of conversational English; you can expect to earn at least HK$200 an hour doing this (many Hong Kong Chinese have their company pay for extra English lessons).

For professional jobs, registering with Hong Kong personnel agencies or headhunters is important. Drake (☎ 2848-9288) is a popular employment agency that often advertises – it's worth getting on their list. You can always check classified ads in the local newspapers. The Saturday edition of the *South China Morning Post*, or the Friday edition of the *Hong Kong Standard* are particularly helpful. *Recruit*, a vast job hunters magazine is available (free) after 5 pm on Friday and Monday in MTR stations. *HK Magazine* also has a jobs section that is useful. If you are hired locally, you will not come in for the 'expatriate package', which includes a generous housing allowance (among other incentives); you can only earn that if you are posted from abroad, as part of relocation expenses.

For more temporary work the best course is probably going door-to-door and asking. A good place to start looking is in bars and western restaurants in Lan Kwai Fong, Wan Chai, Tsim Sha Tsui and Lamma Island. Besides finding opportunities for waiting and bar work, people in *gwailo* bars and restaurants may have tips on English-teaching, modelling jobs, secretarial work and so on. As in most places, who you know can count for more than what you know.

Living expenses in Hong Kong are quite high, especially rent, so be sure to reach an agreement on salary before you begin any job. In general, unskilled foreign labourers can negotiate salaries from HK$50 to HK$80 per hour. Your nationality makes a difference – unfair as it might seem, Filipinos and Thais earn considerably less than westerners for doing the same work.

Modelling is another possibility for both men and women. You can find modelling companies and agencies listed in the *Yellow Pages for Businesses*, but again, contacts are vital. If you are a repository of terrific martial arts techniques, have a great sense of humour, possess appalling acting skills and a love of adventure then look out for parts as the baddie *gwailo* in Hong Kong's frenetic cinema industry. On a less glamorous note, sandwich selling companies in Central and Wan Chai regularly advertise in newspapers and magazines for people to distribute sandwiches during the busy lunch hour.

# Getting There & Away

## AIR

Things used to be pretty predictable when it came to judging prices for flights to Hong Kong. At the time of writing however, everything was up in the air, so to speak. Major airlines were teaming up with hotels to offer amazing bargains to lure tourists back to the ex-colony. It is impossible to predict whether the current spate of price-slashing and deal-making can continue, but it is a safe bet to assume that prices will remain low and appealing. If Hong Kong's tourism slump continues, prices can only get lower. The following prices listed should be taken with a pinch of salt, therefore, and you should check out the market thoroughly for the best deal.

### The USA & Canada

Direct flights to Hong Kong from the west coast take around 13 hours nonstop. Flying from the east coast will require at least one stopover, which usually stretches the flight to a mind-numbing 20 hours. Jet lag hits hard after these flights, considering a time difference of between 12 and 15 hours.

Standard fares vary dramatically depending on the season and on the state of the tourist market. Often the cheapest fares lurk in the Chinatown areas of major cities – check the travel agents listings in the papers and go for the Chinese-sounding ones. In San Francisco for example, shop around in the Clay St and Waverly Place area for cheap Chinese bucket shops. Tickets are usually valid for one year from the date of issue, though some are only good for six months. Note that one-way tickets are often priced at 60% to 75% of the return fare – not good value.

If you're heading to Hong Kong during the low season, carriers like Asiana, Korean Air or China Airlines can get you there from San Francisco or Los Angeles for less than US$600, not including tax. Canadian Airlines offer a similarly priced flight via Vancouver. Most of these flights make a stop in the carrier's home country: Asiana and Korean Air take you through Seoul, China Airlines through Taipei. This is not always such a bad thing, as it's usually easy to arrange a stopover for little or no extra charge.

Flights from New York start at around US$750 return during the low season, and US$1000 during the high season. Asiana, Korean Air or China Airlines are among the cheapest, though you will be facing two stops; the first is usually Anchorage, the second Seoul or Taipei. United Airlines and Northwest Airlines offer one-stop flights via Tokyo, though travel times often work out the same.

For current low fares, check the Sunday travel sections of newspapers like the *New York Times* and the *Los Angeles Times*. Council Travel and STA Travel are two travel agencies specialising in budget deals. Both have branches across the USA and Canada. On the west coast, a good travel agency to try is Overseas Tours (☎ (800) 222-5292), 475 El Camino Real, Room 206, Millbrae, CA 94030. A good place for low-cost fares from the east coast is Amerasia Travel & Tours (☎ (212) 227-9224), Suite 401, 198 Canal St, New York, NY, 10013. Both seem to be quite reliable, and can arrange mail-order purchases using a credit card.

Fares from Canada are similar to those from the USA. Fares from Vancouver can often match those of San Francisco, though eastern cities such as Toronto or Montreal tend to cost more than flying from New York. Travel Cuts offers cheap return and one-way fares to Hong Kong, and has offices in a number of Canadian cities including Vancouver, Edmonton, Toronto and Ottawa.

If you're thinking of heading to the USA or Canada from Hong Kong, return fares start at around HK$5520 to New York on Air China. A return ticket to Toronto will cost about HK$4400, and to Vancouver, about HK$4100. Prices may be lower during October/November and May/June. One-way

## Air Travel Glossary

**Apex** Apex, or 'advance purchase excursion' is a discounted ticket which must be paid for in advance. There are penalties if you wish to change it.

**Baggage Allowance** This will be written on your ticket: usually one 20kg item to go in the hold, plus one item of hand luggage.
**Bucket Shop** An unbonded travel agency specialising in discounted airline tickets.
**Bumped** Just because you have a confirmed seat doesn't mean you're going to get on the plane – see Overbooking.

**Cancellation Penalties** If you have to cancel or change an Apex ticket there are often heavy penalties involved. Insurance can sometimes be taken out against these penalties. Some airlines impose penalties on regular tickets as well, particularly against 'no-show' passengers.
**Check-In** Airlines ask you to check in a certain time ahead of the flight departure (usually 1½ hours on international flights). If you fail to check in on time and the flight is overbooked, the airline can cancel your booking and give your seat to somebody else.
**Confirmation** Having a ticket written out with the flight and date you want doesn't mean you have a seat until the agent has checked with the airline that your status is 'OK' or confirmed. Meanwhile you could just be 'on request'.

**Discounted Tickets** There are two types of discounted fares – officially discounted (see Promotional Fares) and unofficially discounted. The lowest prices often impose drawbacks like flying with unpopular airlines, inconvenient schedules, or unpleasant routes and connections. A discounted ticket can save you other things than money – you may be able to pay Apex prices without the associated Apex advance booking and other requirements. Discounted tickets only exist where there is fierce competition.

**Full Fares** Airlines traditionally offer 1st class (coded F), business class (coded J) and economy class (coded Y) tickets. These days there are so many promotional and discounted fares available from the regular economy class that few passengers pay full economy fare.

**Lost Tickets** If you lose your airline ticket an airline will usually treat it like a travellers' cheque and, after inquiries, issue you with another one. Legally, however, an airline is entitled to treat it like cash and if you lose it then it's gone forever. Take good care of your tickets.

**No-Shows** No-shows are passengers who fail to show up for their flight, sometimes due to unexpected delays or disasters, sometimes due to simply forgetting, sometimes because they made more than one booking and didn't bother to cancel the one they didn't want. Full-fare passengers who fail to turn up are sometimes entitled to travel on a later flight. The rest of us are penalised (see Cancellation Penalties).

**On Request** An unconfirmed booking for a flight, see Confirmation.

---

flights are generally priced at 55% to 60% of return airfares.

### Europe

Flight times between Europe and Hong Kong vary widely depending on the route taken. The most common and direct route is via the Middle East. The advent of the 747-400 and Airbus 340 has resulted in more nonstop flights to Hong Kong from Amsterdam, Frankfurt, London and Paris. However, many flights make at least one stop, often in Dubai or Bangkok. Flight times range anywhere from 14 hours for direct flights from London to 20 hours or more for cut-rate excursions on cash-hungry eastern European or Middle Eastern carriers.

At the time of writing, ticket prices were still in a state of flux. Prior to the handover, you could fly economy return for around UK£500 on tickets valid for 14 days to six months. Virgin Atlantic, British Airways and Cathay Pacific would occasionally thrash out a brief price war and then things would return to normal. In January/February 1998, it was possible to fly return to Hong Kong and stay for three nights at a decent mid-range hotel all for around UK£420.

**Open Jaws** A return ticket where you fly out to one place but return from another. If available this can save you backtracking to your arrival point.

**Overbooking** Airlines hate to fly empty seats and since every flight has some passengers who fail to show up (see No-Shows) airlines often book more passengers than they have seats. Usually the excess passengers balance those who fail to show up but occasionally somebody gets bumped. If this happens, guess who it is most likely to be? The passengers who check in late.

**Promotional Fares** Officially discounted fares like Apex fares which are available from travel agents or direct from the airline.

**Reconfirmation** At least 72 hours prior to departure time of an onward or return flight you must contact the airline and 'reconfirm' that you intend to be on the flight. If you don't do this the airline can delete your name from the passenger list and you could lose your seat. You don't have to reconfirm if your stopover is less than 72 hours. It doesn't hurt to reconfirm more than once. A few airlines don't require reconfirmation, others absolutely insist on it.

**Restrictions** Discounted tickets often have various restrictions on them – advance purchase is the most usual one (see Apex). Others are restrictions on the minimum and maximum period you must be away, such as a minimum of 14 days or a maximum of one year. See Cancellation Penalties.

**Standby** A discounted ticket where you only fly if there is a seat free at the last moment. Standby fares are usually only available on domestic routes.

**Tickets Out** An entry requirement for many countries is that you have an onward or return ticket, in other words, a ticket out of the country. If you're not sure what you intend to do next, the easiest solution is to buy the cheapest onward ticket to a neighbouring country or a ticket from a reliable airline which can later be refunded if you do not use it.

**Transferred Tickets** Airline tickets cannot be transferred from one person to another. Travellers sometimes try to sell the return half of their ticket, but officials can ask you to prove that you are the person named on the ticket. This is unlikely to happen on domestic flights, on an international flight tickets may be compared with passports.

**Travel Agencies** Travel agencies vary widely and you should ensure you use one that suits your needs. Some simply handle tours while full-service agencies handle everything from tours and tickets to car rental and hotel bookings. A good one will do all these things and can save you a lot of money but if all you want is a ticket at the lowest possible price, then you really need an agency specialising in discounted tickets. A discount ticket agency, however, may not be useful for other things, like hotel bookings.

**Travel Periods** Some officially discounted fares, Apex fares in particular, vary with the time of year. There is often a low (off-peak) season and a high (peak) season. Sometimes there's an intermediate or shoulder season as well. At peak times, when everyone wants to fly, not only will the officially discounted fares be higher but so will unofficially discounted fares or there may simply be no discounted tickets available. Usually the fare depends on your outward flight – if you depart in the high season and return in the low season, you pay the high-season fare. ∎

Good deals from London or Manchester can be had with British Airways, Air France, Alitalia, Gulf Air, Malaysia Airlines, KLM-Royal Dutch Airlines, Singapore Airlines and Thai Airways International. These airlines often do not charge extra if passengers want to stopover en route, and some offer stopover packages which encourage it. Just remember that in general, the cheaper the airfare the more inconvenient the route. Gulf Air and Singapore Airlines are among the airlines that offer the best value for money in terms of comfort (even though flights go via Dubai and Singapore, respectively).

It's a good idea to ask around in Europe's Chinatowns for the best deals, as the bargains are usually hammered·out by the Chinese community who are regular fliers (especially at the Chinese New Year). In London some of these outlets apparently will only sell to Chinese people, but Reliance in Little Newport St is a good bet, as is Samtung Travel (☎ (0171) 437 6888), 12 Newport Place. Even before all the price-slashing started, you could still pick up return tickets for around UK£450.

London in general is an excellent place to scout out other good deals. STA Travel

(☎ (0171) 361 6262) at 74 Old Brompton Rd, London SW7, Trailfinders (☎ (0171) 938 3444) at 46 Earls Court Rd, London W8 7RG, and Travel Bug (☎ (0171) 835 2000, (0161) 721 4000) all offer good prices on return flights to Hong Kong and can also put together interesting round-the-world (RTW) routes that include Hong Kong. The London entertainment weekly *Time Out* and the various free papers carry ads for discount travel agencies, but beware of prices that seem too good to be true; they are often shady deals. Make sure you get the tickets before you hand over the cash.

In continental Europe, Amsterdam, Brussels and Antwerp are good places for buying discount air tickets. The cheapest prices are usually on a par with those in London.

At the time of writing, Singapore Airlines was offering return tickets to London for HK$3450 (via Singapore), though this price is usually more like HK$6000. Virgin Atlantic and British Airways were offering return tickets for HK$4480 for a six month return; prices are generally much higher. One-way flights generally cost half that of return tickets.

### Australia & New Zealand

Depending on your departure point from Australia, the flight to Hong Kong takes between eight and 12 hours. Although this is still a fairly long flight, there is only a two hour time change between Sydney and Hong Kong, so jet lag is not a worry.

Ticket prices are generally expensive, and the cheapest tickets to purchase are APEX tickets, which have set return dates. The published fares on Qantas and Cathay Pacific usually cost A$1359 return but are often discounted to around A$1200. Fares on Ansett are around A$950 to A$1100 return. You can also usually get free stopovers in either Singapore, Bangkok or Kuala Lumpur if you fly with Singapore Airlines, Thai Airways International or Malaysia Airlines.

The weekend travel sections of papers like Melbourne's *The Age* or the *Sydney Morning Herald* are good sources of travel information. STA Travel and the Flight Centre are

good places to look for discount tickets. Both have offices all over Australia.

Auckland to Hong Kong is served mainly by Air New Zealand and Cathay Pacific. Fares are similar to those for Australia, and start at around NZ$1129 return.

If you've a mind to escape Hong Kong's urban frenzy for Australia's beaches, a two-month return ticket will normally cost you HK$8000 on Qantas (roughly the same as Ansett), but at the time of writing Qantas had two-week returns for HK$3800. Philippine Airlines return tickets are good value at HK$5100. Ninety day return fares to Auckland are HK$6620 on Singapore Airlines. One-way tickets are priced at around 75% of the return airfare.

### Asia

Hong Kong is the air transport hub linking the northern and southern parts of Asia, which makes it a great access point for almost anywhere in the region. On routes that see heavy competition, such as Hong Kong-Bangkok and Hong Kong-Taipei it's easier to find good prices. However travel to and from Tokyo and Singapore remains expensive despite an increase in the number of carriers serving both cities. Philippine Airlines usually offers the cheapest flights within Asia, as long as you don't mind flying via Manila.

**China** There are no bargain fares into China. The Chinese government sets the prices, and all the domestic airlines toe the line, as does Dragonair, a joint venture between Cathay Pacific and China's CAAC with an extensive network in China. Flights can be difficult to book due to the enormous volume of business travellers and Asian tourists, so plan ahead if possible. As an example, some return fares are: Guangzhou HK$1020, Kunming HK$3150, Beijing HK$4680, Chengdu HK$4570 and Shanghai HK$3310. One-way fares are exactly half the return price.

**Japan** There is no shortage of flights to and from Japan, just a lack of affordable ones.

The cheapest flights start at around ¥750,000 return on United Airlines or Northwest Airlines. Japan Airlines and All Nippon Airways usually charge ¥760,000 to ¥775,000. Prices out of Hong Kong are around HK$4000 return, but at the time of writing you could pick up a return ticket to Tokyo on United Airlines for HK$2920. The flight from Tokyo to Hong Kong takes about five hours.

**Singapore** The three hour flight to Singapore can cost anywhere from HK$2020 for a 30 day return on Cathay Pacific to HK$3000 for a 30 day return on United Airlines (daily flights). At the time of writing, Qantas was offering flights from Hong Kong for HK$2550. Prices out of Singapore are about the same. In Singapore try Airmaster Travel, 46 Bencoolen St and check in the *Straits Times* for agents.

**South Korea** South Korea's Asiana Airlines usually has the cheapest flights between Hong Kong and Seoul at around HK$2800 for a 14 day return. Cathay Pacific is considerably more expensive at HK$3600 for a 17 day return ticket, but at the time of writing Cathay had a promotion for two people to go for HK$3100 each. Ticket prices out of Seoul are usually higher than from Hong Kong. It's roughly five hours flying time between the two cities. In Seoul, you could try Top Air Travel Co (☎ 82-2-736-5111; fax 82-2-725-3687), at Suite 301 Sunil Building, 231 Insadong, Chongro-ku.

**Taiwan** There are something like 15 flights a day between Taiwan and Hong Kong, with many of the seats taken by Taiwanese businessmen shuttling to and from China (they have to go via Hong Kong). This frequency will definitely drop off if direct flights between China and Taiwan open up, which has been in the planning stage for some time. The cheapest way to get to Taipei from Hong Kong is on Japan Asia, who have daily flights to Taipei for HK$1390 return. Daily flights on either Cathay Pacific or China Airlines will cost you HK$2650 return (minimum stay three days). Similar flights

out of Taipei cost around NT$10,000 return, though there are cheaper deals available. Flying time is about 1½ hours.

**Thailand** The Hong Kong-Bangkok route offers some of the best deals in Asia. Cheap tickets abound, with return flights to Bangkok on Gulf Air costing HK$1800 and HK$1900 on Qantas. At the time of writing you could pick up a return to Bangkok for HK$1500 on Cathay Pacific. The flight takes three hours. Prices out of Bangkok are about the same; try the travel agents on Khao San Rd for the cheapest fares.

**Other Asian Centres** There are regular flights between Hong Kong and other major Asian cities including Jakarta, Kuala Lumpur, Manila, New Delhi and Ho Chi Minh City (Saigon).

### Other Regions
There are also flights between Hong Kong and Russia (Moscow, HK$7550 return), the Middle East (Dubai, HK$7000 return), Africa (Johannesburg, HK$9000 return) and South America (Rio de Janeiro, HK$13,000 return).

### Round-the-World Tickets
Round-the-world (RTW) fares are put together by two or more airlines and allow you to make a circuit of the world using their combined routes. A typical RTW ticket is valid for one year, allows unlimited stopovers along the way and costs about UK£1200 or US$2000. One example that includes Hong Kong would be a British Airways/United Airlines combination flying London-New York-Los Angeles-Sydney-Hong Kong-London. There are a great many options involving different combinations of airlines and routes. Generally, routes which stay north of the equator are a little cheaper than routes that include destinations like Australia or South America. Most packages require you to keep moving in the same direction.

Enterprising travel agents put together their own RTW fares at much lower prices than the joint airline deals but, of course, the cheapest fares will involve unpopular airlines and less popular routes.

### Airline Offices

Following is a list of major airline offices in Hong Kong. Where applicable, reservation and reconfirmation telephone numbers (Res) are followed by flight information numbers (Info).

Aeroflot
(☎ Res 2845-4232; Info 2769-8126) Room 22, New Henry House, 10 Ice House St, Central

Air Canada
(☎ 2522-1001) New Henry House, 10 Ice House St, Central

Air France
(☎ Res 2524-8145; Info 2769-6662) 21st floor, Alexandra House, 7 Des Voeux Rd, Central

Air India
(☎ Res 2522-1176; Info 2769-6558) 42nd floor, Gloucester Tower, 11 Pedder St, Central

Air New Zealand
(☎ Res 2524-9041; Info 2769-8571) 1601 Fairmont House, 8 Cotton Tree Dr, Central

Alitalia
(☎ Res 2543-6998; Info 2769-6448) 806 Vicwood Plaza, 199 Des Voeux Rd, Central

All Nippon Airways
(☎ Res 2810-7100; Info 2769-8609) Room 2512, Pacific Place Two, 88 Queensway, Admiralty

American Airlines
(☎ 2826-9269) Room 1738, Swire House, 9 Connaught Rd, Central

Asiana Airlines
(☎ Res 2523-8585; Info 2769-7782) 34th floor, Gloucester Tower, 11 Pedder St, Central

British Airways
(☎ Res 2868-0303; Info 2868-0768) 30th floor, Alexandra House, 20 Chater Rd, Central

CAAC
(☎ 2840-1199) ground floor, 17 Queen's Rd, Central
(☎ 2739-0022) ground floor, Mirador Arcade, 54-64B Nathan Rd, Tsim Sha Tsui
(☎ 2398-2683) room 906, 9th floor, Argyle Centre, 688 Leighton Rd, Mong Kok

Canadian Airlines International
(☎ 2868-3123; Info 2769-7113) Room 1702, Swire House, 9 Connaught Rd, Central

Cathay Pacific Airways
(☎ Res 2747-1888; Info 2747-1234) ground floor, Swire House, 9 Connaught Rd, Central

Shop 53, New World Shopping Centre, Tsim Sha Tsui

China Airlines (Taiwan)
(☎ Res 2868-2299; Info 2769-8361) 3rd floor, St George's Building, 2 Ice House St, Central

Dragonair
(☎ Res 2590-1188; Info 2769-7728) 22nd floor, Devon House, Tai Koo Place, Quarry Bay

Garuda Indonesia
(☎ Res 2840-0000; Info 2769-6689) 7th floor, Henley Building, 5 Queen's Rd Central

Japan Airlines
(☎ Res 2523-0081; Info 2769-6524) 20th floor, Gloucester Tower, 11 Pedder St, Central
Harbour View Holiday Inn, Mody Rd, Tsim Sha Tsui East

KLM-Royal Dutch Airlines
(☎ 2808-2111) Room 2201, 22nd floor, World Trade Centre, 280 Gloucester Rd, Causeway Bay

Korean Air
(☎ Res 2368-6221; Info 2769-7511) ground floor, St George's Building, 2 Ice House St, Central
ground floor, Tsim Sha Tsui Centre, 77 Mody Rd, Tsim Sha Tsui East

Lufthansa Airlines
(☎ Res 2868-2313; Info 2769-6560) Room 1109-1110, Wing Shan Tower, 173 Des Voeux Rd, Central

Malaysian Airlines
(☎ Res 2521-8181; Info 2769-6038) 23rd floor, Central Tower, 28 Queen's Rd, Central

Northwest Airlines
(☎ 2810-4288) 29th floor, Alexandra House, 7 Des Voeux Rd, Central

Philippine Airlines
(☎ Res 2369-4521; Info 2769-6253) Room 6, ground floor, East Ocean Centre, 98 Granville Rd, Tsim Sha Tsui East

Qantas Airways
(☎ Res 2842-1438; Info 2842-1400) Room 1422/1443, Swire House, 11 Chater Rd, Central

Scandinavian Airlines
(☎ Res 2865-1370; Info 2769-7017) Room 1401, Harcourt House, 39 Gloucester Rd, Wan Chai

Singapore Airlines
(☎ Res 2520-2233; Info 2769-6387) 17th floor, United Centre, 95 Queensway, Admiralty

Swissair
(☎ 2529-3670) 8th floor, Tower II, Admiralty Centre, 18 Harcourt Rd, Admiralty

Thai Airways International
(☎ Res 2529-5601; Info 2769-6038) 24th floor, United Centre, 95 Queensway, Admiralty
Shop 124. 1st floor, World Wide Plaza, Des Voeux Rd & Pedder St, Central

United Airlines
(☎ Res 2810-4888; Info 2769-7279) 29th floor, Gloucester Tower, 11 Pedder St, Central

Vietnam Airlines
(☎ 2810-6680) Room 1206, Peregrine Tower, Lippo Centre, 89 Queensway, Admiralty
Virgin Atlantic
(☎ 2532-6060) 27th floor, Kinwick Centre, 32 Hollywood Rd, Central

## Arriving in Hong Kong

The days of daredevil landings at Hong Kong's Kai Tak airport will be over when the new airport at Chek Lap Kok opens in July 1998. Despite the mixed feelings surrounding its demise, the breathtaking descents over Kowloon were never really worth the backwardness and inefficiency that was Kai Tak. The airport's single runway was one of the world's busiest, with aircraft movements separated by only several minutes during peak times of the day. This, coupled with airport's small size, meant long lines at immigration and customs.

All of this has changed with the opening of the new HK$156.4 billion airport at Chek Lap Kok, a huge patch of reclaimed land to the north of Lantau Island. The passenger terminal will consist of eight levels, 120 shops (including moneychanging desks and banks) and 288 check-in counters, dwarfing Kai Tak.

The HK$156.4 billion budget also included the building of one of the world's largest suspension bridges capable of supporting both road and rail transport (the 2.2km Tsing Ma Bridge, linking the islands of Tsing Yi and Ma Wan); the construction of several huge new highways (including the 12.5km North Lantau Expressway); a monumental harbour reclamation project to provide land for the 2km (six lane) Western Harbour Crossing, connecting Sai Ying Pun (Sheung Wan) and West Kowloon; and the construction of the airport railway tunnel, which has been laid on the seabed of Victoria Harbour.

The 34km airport railway, still being built at the time of writing, will connect Chek Lap Kok with Hong Kong Island, with stops at Kowloon, Tai Kok Tsui, Lai King and Tsing Yi. All told, it will take just 23 minutes to get to Hong Kong Island by rail; the service will run from 6 am to 1 am every day. Another rail link will connect Tung Chung, the New Town just to the south of the airport on Lantau Island, with Hong Kong Island, taking trains to Tung Chung via Kowloon, Olympic, Lai King and Tsing Yi.

The airport was originally due to open to coincide with the handover of Hong Kong to China, but a series of delays pushed the opening back until early July 1998.

The new airport's expanded facilities will almost certainly cut down waiting times at immigration, baggage claim and check-in. A second runway at Chek Lap Kok is due to open in October 1998. The airport is predicted to be able to handle 40 aircraft movements in one hour at maximum capacity, and the terminal will be a state-of-the-art world of moving walkways, conveying you past a tempting backdrop of facilities and shops. (For those who find huge civil engineering feats irresistible, then check out the information on the Airport Core Programme Exhibition Centre in the Things to See & Do chapter.)

After landing, look out for the Hong Kong Tourist Association's information centre, where you can supply yourself with maps and heaps of information on transport, dining, sights and a host of other subjects concerning Hong Kong. They are all free and worth taking, although you can end up overloaded!

Also a must is a visit to the Hong Kong Hotels Association. If you're looking for mid-range or top-end hotel accommodation and you're not booked in anywhere yet, this is the place to try. Staff here can often get a 50% discount on a hotel's walk-in rates. The association represents a huge number of hotels in Hong Kong and stocks all their brochures, so you can take your time working out which best suits your needs, or which offers the best deal. The office does not handle hostels, guesthouses or other budget accommodation.

If you need money, try and change as little as possible at the airport moneychangers; their rates are the worst in town. If you have an ATM card you might want to try the machines in the arrival hall, which support global networks including Plus and Cirrus, and dispense Hong Kong dollars.

For information on getting from the airport into town, see the following Getting Around chapter.

### Leaving Hong Kong

If you want to keep your seat, make sure to reconfirm your onward or return ticket at least 72 hours before your flight. If you don't there's a good chance you'll get bumped from your flight. The heavy volume of traffic through Hong Kong means there's almost always someone else who wants your seat.

If you are flying with either Cathay Pacific or United Airlines you can take advantage of their city check-in services, which allow you to check your bags and receive your boarding pass in advance. This is also a good way to get that window or aisle seat you've been hoping for. With United Airlines, you must go to its office (see the Airline Offices section earlier) in Central with your passport and you will be issued a boarding pass. Cathay Pacific allows you to check in either the day before or the same day if it's at least three hours before departure. On Hong Kong Island their city check-in is at the Pacific Place Mall in Queensway, Admiralty, and at China Hong Kong City in Tsim Sha Tsui. You can also collect your boarding pass from the office of Northwest Airlines, if you are flying with them. Dragonair offers a phone check-in facility for their club members, and Malaysia Airlines offers the same service to their 1st and business class passengers. It's best to call ahead and check.

Chek Lap Kok airport levies a departure tax of HK$100 (provisionally) per person, so be sure to have at least this much Hong Kong currency on hand when you check in; don't blow all your money and end up with HK$5 on you as you sprint for your plane. Charges for overweight checked baggage are also high, so check with your carrier about weight limits before you go on a major shopping spree. Officials were extremely strict about this at Kai Tak airport, and bags were crushed mercilessly into a frame representing the

maximum size permissible. Chek Lap Kok could well be as thorough.

Flight boardings and departures were not announced in Kai Tak; at the time of writing it is unsure whether this tradition will continue, so if you find yourself waiting in the departure hall, keep an eye on your boarding gate to make sure they're not leaving without you.

### TRAIN
### China

The only way in and out of Hong Kong by land is through China. The most convenient mode of land transport is the Kowloon-Guangzhou high-speed express train (some go via Changping), which covers the 182km route in approximately two hours. There is also one departure daily to Zhaoqing via Foshan. There is also a direct rail link now between Kowloon and Beijing and Shanghai. Trains to Beijing (via Guangzhou, Changsha, Wuchang and Zhengzhou) leave on alternate days, take 30 hours and cost HK$706 (hard sleeper), HK$934 (soft sleeper) and HK$1191 (deluxe soft sleeper). Trains to Shanghai (via Guangzhou and Hangzhou) also leave on alternate days, take 29 hours and cost HK$627 (hard sleeper), HK$825 (soft sleeper) and HK$1039 (deluxe soft sleeper).

From Hong Kong you catch trains at the Kowloon-Canton Railway (KCR) terminus in Hung Hom, Kowloon (Map 5). As the immigration formalities must be completed before boarding, passengers are requested to arrive at Hung Hom station 45 minutes before boarding the train. To get to the station from Tsim Sha Tsui by public transport, take the 5C bus from the Star Ferry Terminal, the 8A bus from nearby on Salisbury Rd or the No 8 green minibus from Middle Rd.

Timetables change, but current departure times for the high-speed train from Hong Kong to Guangzhou are 8.35 am, 9.25 am, 11.35 am and 12.55 pm. In the other direction, they leave from Guangzhou for Hong Kong at 8.40 and 10 am, 3.15 and 5.45 pm. At Guangzhou railway station, trains leave from the eastern end of the terminal, not from the main station building. The train to Zhaoqing leaves Kowloon at 3.35 pm.

In Hong Kong, tickets can be booked up to seven days in advance at China Travel Service (CTS – China's government-owned travel agency; see the address list at the end of this section) or the KCR terminus in Hung Hom. Passengers who buy tickets over the phone (☎ 2947-7888) are required to collect them at least one hour before the train departs from the Hung Hom KCR terminus. Tickets can also be bought at the Mong Kok, Kowloon Tong and Sha Tin station's ticket offices. Return tickets will not be issued within five days of departure. The gate closes 20 minutes before the train departs, so get there in good time. Some travel agents can handle these bookings as well.

Second class one-way tickets for the high-speed express trains to Guangzhou are HK$220 (child HK$110); 1st class costs HK$250. Prices can increase across the board by HK$40 during 'high season' (meaning whenever Guangzhou hosts a major trade fair or during public holidays). CTS does not accept credit cards, so bring cash or go through a travel agent. There is also a luggage consignment charge from Hung Hom to Guangzhou of HK$4.90 per 5kg.

A cheaper but less convenient option is to take the KCR commuter railway to the station at Lo Wu, cross through immigration into the Chinese border city of Shenzhen and catch a local train to Guangzhou. There are around 20 trains to and from Guangzhou daily, and the ride takes between 2½ and three hours. Hard seats (the Chinese equivalent of 2nd class) cost anywhere from HK$92 to HK$112 depending on the type of train. Soft seats (1st class) cost between HK$103 and HK$118.

If you're thinking of heading into China from Hong Kong, CTS can help book onward train connections from Guangzhou. This is worth looking into, as buying a ticket in Guangzhou (for say, Beijing or Chengdu) can be a nightmare of long lines, pickpockets and frustration. CTS can also buy tickets for you between larger destinations in China,

outside of Guangzhou (for example, from Shanghai to Beijing), but not for less travelled routes (but ask just in case).

CTS offices in Hong Kong are open from 9 am to 5 pm weekdays and 9 am to 1 pm Saturday. Only the Tsim Sha Tsui and Mong Kok offices are open from 9 am to 1 pm Sunday. Locations include:

Head Office – (☎ 2853-3888) 2nd floor, 78-83 Connaught Rd, Central
Central – (☎ 2521-7163) Mezzanine, China Travel Building, 77 Queen's Rd
Mong Kok – (☎ 2789-5970) 2nd floor, 62-72 Sai Yee St
North Point – (☎ 2565-8610) ground floor, 196-202 Java Rd
Tsim Sha Tsui – (☎ 2315-7188) 1st floor, Alpha House, 27-33 Nathan Rd
Wan Chai – (☎ 2832-3866) ground floor, Southern Centre, 138 Hennessy Rd

### Europe

From Europe, you can reach Hong Kong by rail, though most travellers following this route also tour China. Don't take this rail journey just to save money – a direct flight from Europe to Hong Kong works out to be about the same price or less. The idea is to get a good, long look at Russia, Mongolia and China along the way.

It's a long haul. The most commonly taken routes are from Western Europe to Moscow, then on to Beijing via the Trans-Manchurian or Trans-Mongolian railways. From Beijing there are through trains to Kowloon every other day (see the previous section). The minimum time needed for the whole journey (one way) is roughly 10 days, though most travellers spend some time in China.

In Hong Kong, tickets for the Beijing to Moscow journey can be booked at Moonsky Star (☎ 2723-1376; fax 2723-6653; email 100267.2570@compuserve.com), 4th floor, block E, Flat 6E, Chungking Mansions, Tsim Sha Tsui. Staff there are helpful and can also help with visas and tailor your ticket to include stops en route. Although Moonsky has an office in Beijing, arranging trips through China and Russia can be very difficult, so make allowances if the staff have trouble getting you exactly what you want. You can also try Time Travel (☎ 2366-6222; fax 2739-5413) in the same building, on the 16th floor, block A, Chungking Mansions, 36 Nathan Rd, Tsim Sha Tsui.

A popular book about the journey is the *Trans-Siberian Handbook* by Bryn Thomas.

### China Visas

These can be arranged by CTS and most travel agents; many guesthouses and hotels can also arrange visas, for a small fee. If you want to save a little money and don't mind spending the time to do it yourself, you can go to the Visa Office of the People's Republic of China (☎ 2827-9569), 5th floor, Lower Block, 26 Harbour Rd, Wan Chai (Map 7). At the time of writing, visas processed in two days cost HK$180, in a single day (express) HK$430. US passport holders are charged HK$340 and HK$590 respectively for the service, China's response to a 1994 increase in US visa fees. You must supply two photos, which can be taken at the visa office for HK$35.

### BUS

Several transport companies in Hong Kong offer bus services to Guangzhou, Shenzhen, and several other destinations in Guangdong Province. The most reliable of these is Citybus, which also operates a domestic bus network in Hong Kong. There are five buses daily to Guangzhou, leaving from Citybus stations at China Hong Kong City in Tsim Sha Tsui and Sha Tin City One in the New Territories. Tickets are HK$180 one way. Buses from Guangzhou to Hong Kong also depart from major hotels, two popular ones being the Garden Hotel and the Victory Hotel in Guangzhou. Citybus also runs eight buses daily to Shenzhen, including two departures from the Island Shangri-La Hotel in Admiralty. Tickets are HK$65 weekdays, HK$85 weekends. Information and credit-card bookings are handled by Citybus (☎ 2736-3888), CTS (☎ 2853-3888) and MTR Travel Services Centre (☎ 2922-4800). The latter also has offices in MTR stations at Admiralty, Causeway Bay, Mong Kok, Tsim Sha Tsui, Tai Koo and Tsuen Wan.

CTS runs frequent buses to Guangzhou and Shenzhen, leaving approximately hourly from Wan Chai, Hung Hom, Mong Kok and Tsuen Wan. The adult single fare to Guangzhou is HK$185; child HK$135 (discounts available if there are three or more of you). For more information call ☎ 2764-9803. There are numerous other small bus companies that run regular coaches to Guangzhou. A single ticket with Chenda Yongan Travel Company (☎ 2336-1111) is HK$150.

If you take the bus, don't forget to get your visa first! For details, see under China Visas in the earlier Train section.

### BOAT

Like buses and trains, most boats leaving Hong Kong are bound for China. The only exceptions are the luxury cruise ships which sometimes pass through the territory on their worldwide journeys.

From China Hong Kong City you can board daily jet catamarans and hovercraft to destinations in neighbouring Guangdong Province, including Shenzhen, Nanhai, Huizhou, Zhuhai and Guangzhou. Tickets for the hovercraft to Guangzhou (over two hours) are HK$190 and for the jet catamaran (three hours) HK$183. Departures are from the China Hong Kong City terminal in Tsim Sha Tsui. Boats to Guangzhou aren't much faster or convenient than trains or buses, but do let you take in some nice river scenery. Turbo Cat (☎ 2851-1700) has two sailings daily to East River Guangzhou (the Guangzhou Economic Zone), departing at 7.15 am and 1.30 pm; tickets are HK$250 from Kowloon and HK$225 from Guangzhou, the journey takes two hours.

The Hong Kong & Yaumatei Ferry Company (☎ 2525-1108) has two morning and two evening boats to Shekou in Shenzhen; tickets are HK$110 from Hong Kong and HK$90 from Shekou. Departures are from the China ferry terminal in Tsim Sha Tsui.

The terminal at China Hong Kong City also has daily morning jet boats to Wuzhou (10 hours, HK$410) in Guangxi Province,

Transportation in Hong Kong and Macau. Get set for the ride of your life (top left); a Hong Kong city tram provides fine views at a leisurely pace (top right); the Macau pedicab (middle left) is outlasting the man-powered rickshaws of Hong Kong, where there are only a few still in use; and (bottom) the Star Ferry line is a tourist attraction all of its own.

TED CARROLL

RICHARD I'ANSON

RICHARD I'ANSON

GLENN BEANLAND

Top: Hong Kong's economic success has given it one of Asia's most modern skylines.
Middle Left: Harbour views abound from these multi-storey apartments in Aberdeen.
Bottom: Compact apartments in Aberdeen (left) and a distinctive apartment block in Repulse
Bay – the hole is a concession to the laws of fung shui or geomancy (right).

from where you can link up with buses to Guilin, Yangshuo and Nanning. If you have time, you can even take a ship up the eastern coast of China to Xiamen or Shanghai. There are usually only four to five departures monthly for each destination. There are also three to four ships a month to Haikou, Hainan Island. For information on getting to Macau by sea, see the Macau section in the Excursions chapter.

Sailing times and ticket prices are subject to frequent change. For the latest information as well as bookings you can either go to the ticket windows at China Hong Kong City in Tsim Sha Tsui (Map 5) or contact CTS (see the Train section earlier in this chapter for details).

## TRAVEL AGENTS

Hong Kong is a great place to arrange onward travel in Asia, or to almost anywhere for that matter. A look through the travel pages of Hong Kong's Sunday English-language newspapers will show that there are dozens of travel agents specialising in the discount ticket business. Sometimes you can get a great deal through these outfits, but it pays to be cautious. Some of the 'bucket shops', as the budget operators are called, promise one thing but deliver another. At worst they may even take your money, close up shop and disappear. One way to tell is to see if they are listed in the telephone book, since fly-by-night operators don't stay around long enough to get listed.

Hong Kong does have a number of excellent, reliable travel agents to choose from. If they can't get you the ticket price you saw in the paper, it probably means it never existed.

One of the best places to go is Phoenix Services (☎ 2722-7378), Room A, 7th floor, Milton Mansion, 96 Nathan Rd, Tsim Sha Tsui. Staff are friendly, patient and work hard to get you the best price possible. While they handle bookings for anywhere, their speciality is Vietnam. Another outfit that gets good reviews is Traveller Services (☎ 2375-2222), Room 1012, Silvercord Tower 1, 30 Canton Rd, Tsim Sha Tsui. In the same neighbourhood is Shoestring Travel (☎ 2723-

2306), Flat A, 4th floor, Alpha House, 27-33 Nathan Rd, Tsim Sha Tsui.

Many travellers still use the Hong Kong Student Travel Bureau (☎ 2730-3269), Room 835, 8th floor, Star House, Tsim Sha Tsui. If you hold an ISIC card you can get a discount. They have several branch offices: Argyle Centre (☎ 2390-0421), Room 1812, 688 Nathan Rd, Mong Kok; and Room 608 (☎ 2833-9909), Hang Lung Centre, Patterson St, Causeway Bay.

If you need a ticket quickly, Hong Kong Four Seas Tours Ltd (☎ 2722-6112) has branches all over the place. Prices usually aren't as low as the discount operations listed above, but you'll almost always get the seat you need and they will deliver your ticket to you.

When going for the cheapest possible fares, remember that the number of such seats may be limited, and there are often severe restrictions. With the cheapest tickets, you often have to pay the travel agent first and then pick up the ticket at the airport – just make sure you understand any of the limitations involved.

## WARNING

This chapter is particularly vulnerable to change – prices for international travel are volatile, routes are introduced and cancelled, schedules change, special deals come and ago, and rules and visa requirements are amended. Airlines and governments seem to take a perverse pleasure in making price structures and regulations as complicated as possible. You should check directly with the airline or travel agent to make sure you understand how a fare (and the ticket you may buy) works. In addition, the travel industry is highly competitive and there are many lurks and perks; the downturn in tourism after the handover was particularly effective in slashing prices and instigating excellent deals. The upshot of this is that you should contact as many airlines and travel agents as possible before you part with your cash. The details provided in this chapter should be treated as pointers and are not a substitute for careful, up-to-date research.

# Getting Around

Hong Kong boasts one of the world's best public transport systems. Even out in the New Territories there are very few places that aren't served by buses. Within the urban areas transport options are as diverse as they are efficient; you can travel by minibus, tram, subway train, ferry, hovercraft, double-decker bus, taxi – take your pick. There is a wide variance in fares between the different modes, but in general it doesn't cost much to get around. Interestingly, most services are run by private companies, which make money doing it. It's enough to make a western city planner blush.

## TO/FROM THE AIRPORT
### Airport Railway
When the airport railway opens in mid-1998, regular departures will ferry passengers from Chek Lap Kok to Central on Hong Kong Island in approximately 23 minutes. The airport railway consists of two lines, but the one of most use to travellers will be the Airport Express, with departures initially every eight minutes, dropping to every four and a half minutes once fully operational. The other line is a local service for the Tung Chung New Town near Chek Lap Kok.

The Airport Express stops at Tsing Yi, West Kowloon and Central. The train promises to be a comfortable ride, with seat-back TV sets. An in-town check-in service exist whereby you can check in your luggage on Hong Kong Island and Kowloon, leaving you free to go shopping while your bags are forwarded to their final destination. Information screens at Airport Express stations allow you to check on the status of your flight. A one-way ticket is expected to cost around HK$100.

Prices have not yet been announced. The other line is the Tung Chung line, which will run from Tung Chung New Town via Tsing Yi, Lai King, Olympic, and Kowloon to Central. Trains on the latter are not as hi-tech as the Airport Express, and the service is more for local passengers than international arrivals.

### Airbus
Hong Kong Island and Kowloon are connected to the airport by airbus. The most useful routes for travellers are the A11 and the A21, which will take you to most of the major hotel and guesthouse areas.

The buses are air-conditioned and have plenty of room for luggage. English and Chinese announcements notify passengers of hotels serviced at each stop. No change is given on the buses although change is available at the airport bus service centre. Routes are as follows:

A11 – Sheung Wan, Central, Admiralty, Wan Chai, Causeway Bay (HK$40); buses leave every 12 minutes

A12 – Sheung Wan, Central, Admiralty, Wan Chai, Causeway Bay, Tin Hau, Fortress Hill, North Point, Quarry Bay, Tai Koo, Sai Wan Ho (HK$45); buses leave every 15 minutes

A21 – Mong Kok, Yau Ma Tei, Jordan, Tsim Sha Tsui, and Kowloon KCR station (HK$33); buses leave every 10 minutes

A22 – Jordan, Hung Hom, To Kwa Wan, Kowloon Bay, Ngau Tau Kok, Kwun Tong, Lam Tin (HK$39); buses leave every 15 minutes

A31 – Tsing Yi, Kwai Chung, Tsuen Wan (HK$17); buses leave every 15 minutes

A41 – Tsing Yi, Sha Tin (HK$20); buses leave every 20 minutes

### Taxi
Taking a taxi is the only other public transport option for the airport. The taxi stand is just outside the airport exit. Getting a taxi from Chek Lap Kok airport is expensive, as it's so far from town. A taxi to Central will probably cost you more than HK$150; this price includes HK$45 for the use of the Western Harbour Tunnel, (HK$30 one-way); the calculation covers the driver's return to the Kowloon side. To go to Kowloon from the airport will cost at least HK$100. There is a luggage fee of HK$5 per bag, though not

all drivers insist on this. For more information on fares, see the Taxi section later on in this chapter.

## TRAIN
### Mass Transit Railway (MTR)

One of the world's most modern subway systems, the MTR is clean, fast and safe. Though it costs a bit more than most other forms of public transport, it is the quickest way to most urban destinations. Trains run every two to four minutes from 6 am to 1 am daily on three lines (see Map 14). Fares range from HK$4 to HK$13. A fourth line is due to open to coincide with the July 1998 opening of the new airport at Chek Lap Kok which will speed visitors to Central, via western Kowloon.

For short hauls, the MTR is not great value. If you want to cross the harbour from Tsim Sha Tsui to Central, the MTR is about five times the price of the Star Ferry with none of the views, and only marginally faster. But if your destination is further away, say North Point or Tsuen Wan, the MTR is considerably faster than a ferry or a bus and about the same price. The MTR also connects with the Kowloon-Guangzhou express train at Kowloon Tong station. Also, it's air-conditioned, which is nice in summer. If possible it's best to skirt rush hours; 7.30 to 9.30 am and 5 to 7 pm. Some 2.4 million people use the MTR every day, most of them at these times. Joining the crowd is no fun.

Riding the MTR is dead easy – just follow the signs. Everything is automated, from the ticket vending machines to the turnstiles. Ticket machines take HK$5, HK$2, HK$1 and 50c pieces and give change; a handful of machines take HK$20 notes. There are change machines that accept coins only – notes must be changed at the ticket offices or Hang Seng Bank offices located in the stations. Once you pass through the turnstiles, you also only have 90 minutes to complete the journey before the ticket becomes void.

The MTR uses 'smart tickets', which have a magnetic coding strip on the back. When you pass through the turnstile, the card is encoded with the station identification and time. At the other end, the exit turnstile reads where you came from, the time and how much you paid, and lets you through if all is in order. Don't worry if you underpaid by punching the wrong button on the ticket machine, you can pay the difference at the other end.

You can't buy return tickets, but you can purchase an Octopus card if you are going to do quite a bit of travelling during your stay in Hong Kong. This rather clever device allows you to travel on the MTR, the KCR East Rail, KCR Light Rail (including KCR Light Rail shuttle bus), most of the KMB and Citybus cross-harbour routes and all Outlying Island and New Town routes of the Hong Kong & Yaumatei Ferry Company. This gives you access to six different modes of transport in Hong Kong on one card – all you do is touch the fare-deducting processors at stations with the microchip-loaded Octopus card.

Octopus cards can be bought from ticket offices or customer service centres in MTR stations, KCR East Rail, KCR Light Rail and certain piers of the Hong Kong & Yaumatei Ferry Company. The cards cost HK$150 for adults and HK$70 for children and senior citizens (a refundable deposit of HK$50 is included in the price). Octopus cards are reloadable to pump up your credit, just go to one of the machines or ticket offices located in all stations (you can add value to the figure of HK$1000). The card has a maximum negative value of HK$35 which is recovered the next time you reload it (hence the deposit). There may well be a tourist Octopus in the future. If you have any queries, call the Octopus hotline on ☎ 2993-8880.

Avoid the MTR 'tourist ticket' which costs HK$25 but is only good for HK$20 worth of travel. For your extra HK$5 you get to keep the ticket as a second-rate souvenir.

Children aged two or under can travel free and there are special child/student tickets (for children aged three to 11). Passengers aged 12 or over can only use the student tickets if they are carrying a Hong Kong Student Identity Card – an ISIC card is not acceptable.

Smoking, eating and drinking are not permitted in MTR stations or on trains, and violators are subject to heavy fines if caught. You are not supposed to carry large objects (like bicycles) aboard trains either, though backpacks and suitcases are OK.

Unfortunately there are no toilets in the stations. If you leave something on the train, you might be able to reclaim your goods at the lost property office at Admiralty station between 11 am and 6.45 pm, Monday to Saturday. For other queries, call the passenger information hotline (☎ 2750-0170).

### Kowloon-Canton Railway (KCR)

This is a single-line commuter railway running from Kowloon to the border with mainland China at Lo Wu. The KCR is a quick way to get up to the New Territories, and the ride offers some nice views as well.

The KCR is cheap, with a 30 minute ride to Sheung Shui costing just HK$9 (HK$18 1st class), although the trip to the border at Lo Wu costs HK$33 (HK$66 1st class). Trains run about every five to 10 minutes, except during rush hours, when the interval falls to every three minutes. Kids under three travel for free, with a reduced fare for three to 12-year-olds. A new double-decker high speed train runs from Hong Hom to Lo Wu in 15 minutes; tickets cost HK$66.

You can change from the MTR to the KCR at Kowloon Tong station. The southernmost station on the line at Hung Hom is easily reached from Tsim Sha Tsui by taking green minibus No 8 from Middle Rd. You can use your Octopus card (see the previous Mass Transit Railway section for information on Octopus) on the KCR, and you can ride all the way up to Lo Wu if you plan to travel around mainland China (see the Getting There & Away chapter for more details). The KCR customer services hotline is ☎ 2602-7799.

### Light Rail Transit (LRT)

This is rather like a modern air-con version of the tram. The LRT runs on the road surface and stops at designated stations. However,

it's much faster than the tram, at times reaching a maximum speed of 70km/h.

Most visitors don't ever set foot on the LRT, as it only runs in the western New Territories, connecting the city of Tuen Mun with Yuen Long. There are plans to connect it with the MTR and KCR networks.

There are five LRT lines connecting various small suburbs. The system operates from 5.30 am to 12.30 am Monday to Saturday, and from 6 am to midnight on Sunday and holidays. The LRT terminus in Tuen Mun is at the hovercraft pier, from where you can catch a ferry to Central. Fares on the LRT are HK$4 to HK$5.80 for adults and tickets are purchased from vending machines (change is available from change booths). Octopus cards can be used on the LRT (see the Mass Transit Railway section earlier for more information on Octopus). The system of fare collection is unique for Hong Kong – there are no gates or turnstiles and customers are 'trusted' to pay. However, that 'trust' is enforced by occasional police spot checks with fines for those who haven't purchased a ticket (HK$290 plus possible prosecution).

### BUS

The extensive bus and minibus system offers a bewildering number of routes that will take you nearly anywhere you want to go in Hong Kong. You are most likely to use the buses to explore the south side of Hong Kong Island and the New Territories. The north side of Hong Kong Island and most of Kowloon are well served by the MTR.

### Ordinary Bus

Most buses are of the double-decker variety, which is great for visitors. A front seat on the upper deck beats any tour bus for views. A fair number of buses now have air-conditioning, which can be a lifesaver in summer. However, temperatures are set so low you may find your extremities turning blue, especially at the autumn/winter junction when they are still blasting out frigid air. Air-con buses generally cost about 40% more than their non air-con counterparts.

Fares range from HK$2.50 to HK$30. Payment is made into a fare box upon entry, so have plenty of change handy as no change is given, which is infuriating. Otherwise invest in an Octopus card (see the earlier Mass Transit Railway section for information on Octopus) that you can use on the majority of KMB and Citybus cross-harbour routes. There are no ticket collectors. To alight, push the bell strip or button just before your stop.

Most buses run from around 6 am to midnight, though some routes close as early as 7 pm. There are a few night buses that ply the roads between midnight and 6 am, but not on routes that visitors will generally use except for the cross-harbour buses (see the following section).

Buses are run by three private operators. China Motor Bus (CMB) has most of the routes on Hong Kong Island, which is unfortunate, as its service is generally miserable. It will probably to lose its franchise in late 1998 due to an appalling track record and extensive lists of complaints; the lines it operates will be put up for tender. Far better is Citybus, which managed to win some CMB routes in the early 1990s and has since expanded. The majority of Citybuses are plush air-con coaches, and drivers tend to be a bit more sedate than their CMB counterparts; unfortunately all bus drivers drive like maniacs and crashes are not infrequent. Kowloon and the New Territories are served by Kowloon Motor Bus (KMB). CMB buses are blue and white, Citybuses yellow and KMB buses red and cream.

In Central, the most important bus terminal is on the ground floor right under Exchange Square. From here you can catch buses to Aberdeen, Repulse Bay, Stanley and other destinations on the south side of Hong Kong Island. In Kowloon, the Star Ferry Bus Terminal is the most crucial, with buses to the KCR station and points in eastern and western Kowloon.

The terminals have signs listing the route number, destinations, stops served en route and fare. But if you're at a regular bus stop it can be tricky to figure out where buses go,

as signs there list only route numbers, not destinations. Unfortunately there is not much in the way of good bus maps, and Citybus is often out of stock of route maps at their information point just outside the Central Star Ferry terminal (see under Maps in the Facts for the Visitor chapter for some other possibilities).

All is not lost however. Most visitors are likely to only make use of several major bus terminals. A quick browse through the signs will show you where the buses end up and what stops they make along the way. And of course all buses have destinations listed in English, as well as Chinese, on the front. What's useful to note is that any bus number ending with the letter K (78K, 69K etc) means that the route connects to the KCR. Similarly, bus numbers ending with M (51M, 68M etc) go to the MTR stations. Those ending with R are recreational buses and normally run on Sunday, public holidays or for special events like horse-racing at Happy Valley. Buses with an X are express.

If you can't find the bus you need, the HKTA has leaflets and an information hotline (☎ 2807-6177) that should get you on your way. You can also contact China Motor Bus (☎ 2565-8556), Citybus (☎ 2873-0818) or Kowloon Motor Bus (☎ 2745-4466). For buses to specific sights around Hong Kong, see the relevant section in the Things to See & Do chapter.

**Cross-Harbour Bus**

These buses deserve special mention, as they are pretty much the only cheap way to get from Hong Kong Island to Kowloon after the MTR shuts down at 1 am. Bus routes numbered in the 100s, 300s or 600s denote services between Hong Kong Island and Kowloon or the New Territories, via the cross-harbour tunnel. During the day the only reasons for visitors to take a cross-harbour bus are to get a glimpse of Hong Kong and save a few Hong Kong dollars. Traffic around the tunnel is nearly always backed up. If you want to get across the harbour quickly take the MTR, which serves most of the same destinations as the cross-harbour buses.

However, if it's after 1 am and you find yourself caught on the wrong side of the harbour, you might consider the No 121 and 122 buses, which operate through the cross-harbour tunnel every 15 minutes from 12.45 am to 5 am. No 121 runs from the Macau ferry terminal in Sheung Wan on Hong Kong Island, along Des Voeux, Hennessy and Morrison Hill Rds, through the tunnel to Chatham Rd in Tsim Sha Tsui East and then on to Choi Hung on the east side of the airport. No 122 runs from North Point on Hong Kong Island, along King's, Causeway and Hennessy Rds, through the cross-harbour tunnel to Chatham Rd in Tsim Sha Tsui East, and then continues up the northern part of Nathan Rd on to Lai Chi Kok and Mei Foo in north-western Kowloon.

## Minibus

Minibuses are cream coloured with a red roof or stripe down the side, and seat 16 people. Unless the roads are congested, minibuses are very swift; but can be difficult for visitors to use. For one, the destination is displayed in the front in largish Chinese characters: there is sometimes a smaller English translation below, but it can be hard to read. The price to the final destination is also displayed on a card propped up in the window, but this is often in Chinese as well.

It can also be awkward to board one. Like taxis, minibuses stop almost anywhere to pick up or let off passengers. But Hong Kong's complex traffic rules and myriad no-stopping zones make things complicated. If minibuses keep passing you by, look down to see if there's a single or double yellow line on the street next to the kerb. If there is, you are in a restricted stopping zone, and neither minibuses nor cabs will stop for you. CMB, Citybus and KMB bus stops are also off limits. Minibuses are most plentiful at rush hours and all stop in packs.

The real trick is getting off. There are no buttons or bells: you must call out the stop you wish to alight at. This is not easy if you're not really sure where you want to get

### The Terror of Minibuses

A ride on a Hong Kong bus can lift the pulse, but it's the minibuses that really gets the heart in the throat. I used to take the minibus from Wan Chai to Kennedy Town every night after work – it was like being strapped to a rail-gun and being shot blindly into the night. The ride usually started off quite slowly, the minibus purring along while the driver looked for fares to fill up the last few seats. But as soon as the last seat was filled (always the worst seat at the back over the wheel arch), it's as though the driver became possessed with the urge to speed like a Grand Prix driver – the streets of Wan Chai and Central would blur into a stream of lights. Packs of minibuses raced each other, the driver slapping his thigh as he cut up the opposition.

I read an interview once with a Hong Kong minibus driver who said that he loved his job because of 'the thrill and the sheer skill needed – you never know what the traffic's going to throw at you next'. Say no more.

**Damian Harper**

off. Moreover, minibus drivers rarely speak English, so they may not understand you. If you call out 'stop here please' chances are they will, but if not you can try the Cantonese version, which sounds like '*yow lok*'. Despite all these drawbacks minibuses can be handy to go short distances such as from Central to Wan Chai or Causeway Bay. Another good thing is that you always get a seat, as standing passengers are not allowed by law.

Fares range from HK$2 to HK$10, but tend to increase on rainy days and at night. You pay the driver when you get off, and they can change bills for you if you don't have the exact change (which often makes them preferable to buses).

If you're in Central, the best place to catch minibuses to Wan Chai and points east is at the bottom of Exchange Square. If heading west towards Kennedy Town, walk up to Stanley St, near Lan Kwai Fong. There are a few buses that cross the harbour late at night, running between Wan Chai and Mong Kok. On Hong Kong Island, they can be found on Hennessy and Fleming Rds. In Kowloon you may have to trudge up Nathan Rd as far as Mong Kok before you'll find one.

One last point. If you're in a hurry, do not jump on an empty or near-empty minibus. Drivers will sit for as long as 20 minutes waiting for passengers, and if they still don't fill up they will cruise the streets, stopping constantly to try and pull in riders. When this happens, you're better off taking the bus, the MTR, or walking.

### Green Minibus

Also known as maxicabs, these have a green stripe and operate on fixed routes and stop at designated places. Fares vary according to the distance – anywhere from HK$1.50 to HK$18. You pay when you get on and no change is given. In Tsim Sha Tsui the No 1 green minibus runs from the Star Ferry Terminal to Tsim Sha Tsui East every five minutes or so between 7.20 am and 10.20 pm. The fare is HK$2.50. On Hong Kong Island, another useful route is from Edinburgh Place (near City Hall and the Star Ferry Terminal) to the Peak. Hours of operation are 7 am to midnight.

### TRAM

One of the world's great travel bargains, Hong Kong's trams are tall, narrow, double-decker streetcars that trundle along the northern side of Hong Kong Island.

The tram line was built in 1904 on what was then the shoreline of Hong Kong Island, which helps one appreciate just how much land Hong Kong has reclaimed from the sea. Although the tram has been in operation since then, the vehicles now in service were built later.

The trams are not fast but they are cheap and fun. For a flat fare of HK$1.60 (dropped in a box beside the driver when you leave – no change is given so have the right change) you can go as far as you like, whether it's one block or the end of the line. The fare is due to rise to HK$2 in the summer of 1998. Trams operate between 6 am and 1 am. They can be slow, especially at rush hour, but go pretty swiftly at night. On each route they run with a frequency from two to seven minutes,

but often arrive bunched together. If the wait is much longer then there's probably been a backup somewhere down the line, so be prepared to elbow your way through the crowd to squeeze aboard when it arrives. Try to get a seat at the front window upstairs to enjoy a first-class view of life in Hong Kong while rattling through the crowded streets. If it's packed, start squeezing ahead to the front well ahead of your stop as it's often difficult to alight. Passengers over six feet tall will find it uncomfortable standing up as the ceiling is low, but you can stand at the very back where you get on, which has more space. Watch out for trams when crossing the road; although most make a grinding sound which alerts you to their lumbering approach, some are stealth versions and the driver may not be looking ahead carefully (they often eat their lunch and dinner while driving).

The routes often overlap. Some start from Kennedy Town and run to Shau Kei Wan, but others run only part of the way and one turns south to Happy Valley. The longest run, from Shau Kei Wan to Kennedy Town, takes about 1½ hours. The eight routes are as follows:

| From (west) | To (east) |
| --- | --- |
| Kennedy Town | Causeway Bay |
| Kennedy Town | Happy Valley |
| Kennedy Town | North Point |
| Kennedy Town | Shau Kei Wan |
| Shau Kei Wan | Happy Valley |
| Western Market | Causeway Bay |
| Western Market | Shau Kei Wan |
| Whitty St | North Point |

### BOAT

Hong Kong has an extensive network of ferries. As long as you aren't prone to seasickness, the boats are fun and the harbour views magnificent when the weather is co-operative. Fares are very reasonable, and there are discounts for children under 12. Though you'll find that many people break the rules, smoking is prohibited on all ferries and the fine for violating this is HK$5000.

### Star Ferry

A ride on the Star Ferry, with its spectacular views of Hong Kong Island and Kowloon, is a must for visitors. It is also an essential mode of transport for commuters. All the ferries have names like Morning Star, Evening Star, Celestial Star, Twinkling Star, etc.

There are three Star Ferry routes, but by far the most popular is the one running between Tsim Sha Tsui and Central. The trip takes seven minutes, enough time to knock off some great photos. There are frequent departures, leaving every five to 10 minutes at peak time. Fares for the lower and upper deck are HK$1.70 and HK$2.20 respectively. Those 65 years of age and older ride for free. The coin-operated turnstiles do not give change but you can get change from the ticket window. A special tourist ticket is available for HK$20, which allows unlimited rides on the Star Ferry and Hong Kong's trams. Seeing how cheap the normal fare is, you'd have to do at least 14 trips in four days to make this worthwhile. The Star Ferry also links Tsim Sha Tsui with Wan Chai, and Central with Hung Hom. Operating hours are as follows:

Central (Edinburgh Place) – Hung Hom: every 12 to 20 minutes (every 20 minutes on Sundays and holidays) from 7 am to 7.20 pm
Central (Edinburgh Place) – Tsim Sha Tsui: every five to 10 minutes from 6.30 am to 11.30 pm
Wan Chai – Tsim Sha Tsui: every 10 to 20 minutes from 7.30 am to 11 pm

## Hong Kong Island-Kowloon-New Territories Ferries

The Hong Kong & Yaumatei Ferry Company (HKF) operates many large and medium-size conventional and hovercraft ferries which serve Hong Kong Island, Kowloon, the New Territories and many of the Outlying Islands. The routes between Hong Kong Island and Kowloon/New Territories are as follows:

*Ferry*
Central – Yau Ma Tei (Jordan Rd): every 15 to 20 minutes from 6.10 am to midnight
North Point – Hung Hom: every 20 minutes from 6.55 am to 9 pm

North Point – Kowloon City: every 20 minutes from 6.50 am to 8.50 pm
North Point – Kwun Tong: every 20 minutes from 7 am to 8 pm
Wan Chai – Hung Hom: Monday to Friday every 15 to 20 minutes from 7 am to 8 pm; Saturday every 20 to 30 minutes from 7.10 am to 8.15 pm

There are also sporadic early morning ordinary ferry departures from Wan Chai, via Central to Tuen Mun and vice-versa; another service operates from Tsuen Wan to Central and Wan Chai via Tsing Yi.

*Hovercraft (Hoverferry)*
Central (Queen's Pier) – Tsim Sha Tsui East: every 20 minutes from 8 am to 8 pm
Central (Outlying Islands ferry piers) – Tsuen Wan: every 20 minutes from 7 am to 6.40 pm
Central (Outlying Islands ferry piers) – Tuen Mun: every 15 to 20 minutes from 6.45 am to 8.30 pm
Central – Tuen Mun by jet catamaran – four services every morning between 7.20 and 8.35 am

## Outlying Islands Ferries

These are large vessels run by HKF that serve Hong Kong's more populous islands, including Lantau, Cheung Chau, Peng Chau and Lamma islands. Departures are from the Outlying Islands ferry piers, which sit on a plot of newly reclaimed land in front of Exchange Square in Central. They are all clearly signposted. On weekends there are a few ferries to Lantau and Cheung Chau from the Star Ferry Terminal in Tsim Sha Tsui.

The larger boats are separated into ordinary and deluxe classes. The latter comprises an air-conditioned top deck that can induce frostbite, and a small open-air deck on the fantail. This last spot is one of the nicest places to be in Hong Kong on a warm sunny day, and is the main reason why you'd want to shell out extra for the deluxe ticket.

Fares are generally reasonable, except on weekends, when prices nearly double. From Monday to Saturday morning, adult fares to Mui Wo (Lantau) are HK$9.70 (HK$17 deluxe); on Saturday afternoons and Sundays they rise to HK$17 and HK$32 respectively. Ferries to Lamma cost HK$9.20 (H$17 deluxe) from Monday to Saturday morning and HK$12.50 (HK$32 deluxe) on Saturday afternoons and Sunday. Prices for children and senior citizens are about half.

Beverages and snacks are available on board. If you decide to venture out to one of the islands, try and do so during the week, as it's cheaper and boats are packed to the gunwales on weekends. For more information on the Outlying Islands, see the Excursions chapter.

Lantau is also served by ferries linking Central with Discovery Bay, a bedroom community on the eastern side of the island. Ferries run every 20 minutes during the day and every hour or so throughout the night. The one-way fare is HK$20, and boats depart from the eastern side of the Star Ferry Terminal in Central.

Amusingly (or not), ferries from Central occasionally have a problem navigating the short distances involved. A ferry en route to Lamma Island recently got lost in fog and strayed into Chinese waters, where its engine caught fire and had to be escorted back to Hong Kong by a Chinese vessel. Another ferry from Lamma Island to Aberdeen decided to go the long way round, via Stanley on the south of Hong Kong Island. Apparently this is not uncommon behaviour.

Basic schedules for some of the major Outlying Islands ferries are listed below. Times are subject to change. For the latest information, pick up a seasonal schedule at the HKF information office next to the Outlying Islands ferry piers in Central or phone the HKF inquiries hotline (☎ 2542-3081). HKTA information centres also have up-to-date ferry schedules.

Central – Cheung Chau: approximately hourly from 5.35 am to 12.30 pm, with more frequent sailings during rush hours

Central – Cheung Chau: five hovercraft services in either direction between 8.50 am and 4.50 pm Monday to Friday

Tsim Sha Tsui – Cheung Chau: one sailing to Cheung Chau at 4 pm Saturday; sailings to Cheung Chau at 8 and 10 am Sunday; one sailing to Tsim Sha Tsui at 12.45 pm Sunday

Central – Lantau (Mui Wo): approximately hourly from 6.10 am to 12.20 am

Central – Lantau (Mui Wo) via Peng Chau: four hovercraft services a day each way from 9.40 am and 5.10 pm

Tsim Sha Tsui – Lantau (Mui Wo): every one to two hours from 1 to 7 pm Saturday and from 9 am to 7 pm Sunday

Central – Lantau (Tai O): two services a day at 9.15 am and 2.15 pm on Saturday; one service a day at 8.15 am Sunday and public holidays

Central – Peng Chau: approximately hourly from 6.30 am to 12.20 am

Central – Peng Chau: four hoverferry services each way between 9.40 am and 5.20 pm Monday to Friday

Central – Lamma Island (Yung Shue Wan): approximately every 1½ hours from 6.20 am to 12.30 am

Central – Lamma Island (Sok Kwu Wan): every two to three hours from 6.50 am to 11 pm

Yung Shue Wan on Lamma Island is also connected to Central by Pollyferries during the morning and evening rush hours; there is also a boat from Yung Shue Wan to Pak Kok Tsuen and Kennedy Town which leaves approximately every two hours. There are also occasional boats from Pak Kok Tsuen to Central.

### Kaidos & Sampans

A *kaido* is a small to medium-sized ferry which can make short runs on the open sea, for example from Cheung Chau to Lantau (about HK$100 for three people). Few kaido routes operate on regular schedules, preferring to adjust supply according to demand. Kaidos run mostly on weekends and holidays when everyone tries to 'get away from it all', though some make weekday runs on more popular routes, such as Aberdeen to Lamma Island. If you are island hopping it's also worth checking public noticeboards for off-the-cuff ferry services, so you don't have to go via Central.

A *sampan* is a motorised launch which can only accommodate a few people. A sampan is too small to be considered truly seaworthy, but can safely zip you around typhoon shelters like Aberdeen Harbour.

Bigger than a sampan, but smaller than a kaido, is a *walla walla*. These operate as water taxis on Victoria Harbour. Most of the customers are sailors working on vessels anchored in the harbour.

### TAXI

Though prices continue to rise, Hong Kong taxis are still not too expensive compared with other major developed cities. And with more than 18,000 cruising the roads, they're usually easy to flag down.

When a taxi is available, there should be a red 'For Hire' sign displayed in the windscreen and the 'Taxi' sign on the roof will be lit up at night. It's important to realise that taxis cannot stop at bus stops or where a yellow line is painted next to the kerb, which denotes a restricted stopping zone.

In Kowloon and Hong Kong Island, taxis are red with silver tops. In the New Territories they are green with white tops. New Territories taxis are not permitted to pick up or put down passengers in Kowloon or Hong Kong Island. On Lantau Island, taxis are blue. Hong Kong Island taxis and Kowloon taxis tend to avoid each other's territory as they are really not that sure of street geography on the other side of the water.

In Hong Kong and Kowloon, the flagfall is HK$14.50 for the first 2km and HK$1.30 for every additional 200m. In the New Territories, flagfall is HK$12 for the first 2km, and HK$1.20 for every 0.2km thereafter. Prices are due to rise some time in 1998. There is a luggage fee of HK$5 per bag but not all drivers insist on this. Most drivers carry very little change so keep a supply of coins and HK$10 bills.

If you go through either the cross-harbour or eastern harbour tunnels, you'll be charged an extra HK$20. The toll is only HK$10, but the driver is allowed to assume that he won't get a fare back so you have to pay for his return toll as well. You will be charged a mammoth HK$45 for using the new Western Harbour Tunnel. There is no double charge for other tunnels, tolls for which are as follows: Aberdeen HK$5; Lion Rock HK$6; Shing Mun HK$5; Tate's Cairn HK$4; Tseung Kwan O HK$3.

It's often hard to get taxis during rush hour, when it rains or during driver shift changes (around 4 pm). Taxis are also in higher demand after midnight. Officially, there are no extra late-night charges and no extra passenger charges. Unofficially, during heavy rains and after midnight some drivers try to charge double, which is illegal – just pretend you don't understand and pay the meter fare.

Many taxis have a card on which the top 50 destinations are listed in Cantonese, English and Japanese – very useful as many taxi drivers don't speak English. Even if the card doesn't list your specific destination, it will certainly have some place nearby. However, it's never a bad idea to have your destination written down in Chinese if possible.

If you feel a taxi driver has ripped you off, get the taxi number and call the police hotline ☎ 2527-7177 to lodge a complaint with the relevant details about when, where and how much.

## CAR & MOTORCYCLE

Driving is on the left side of the road, the same as in Australia and the UK, but the opposite to China. Seat belts must be worn by the driver and all front seat passengers. Police are strict and give out traffic tickets at the drop of a hat.

Driving in crowded Hong Kong brings little joy. Traffic often slows to a crawl and finding parking is a nightmare. On top of that, the government has deliberately made driving expensive in order to discourage it. For a local resident to get a driving licence, he or she must take an expensive driving course and wait about 18 months. The motor vehicle import tax is 100% and the petrol tax is more than 100%. Vehicle registration (based on engine size) averages about HK$8000 annually and liability insurance is compulsory. Top it all off with the fact that public transport is generally excellent in Hong Kong and driving becomes even less attractive.

As for foreigners, anyone over the age of 18 with a valid driving licence from their home country, or an international driving licence, can drive in Hong Kong for up to 12 months. If you're staying longer, or if you are a Hong Kong resident, you'll need a Hong Kong licence.

### Car Rental

There's not much need to rent a car in Hong Kong, unless you are planning an excursion to the New Territories. Even then, unless the place is quite out of the way, you may do better with public transport. It still can be fun though.

Car rental firms require either an international driver's licence or one from your home country, as well as a credit card deposit of HK$5000 and up (the slip is torn up upon return of the undamaged vehicle). Drivers must be at least 25 years old. Daily rates run from HK$650 for a small car like a Honda Civic to HK$2500 for a flashy Mercedes or BMW. Two of the more reputable car rental outfits in Hong Kong include: Ace (☎ 2560-8689) in Happy Valley and Avis (☎ 2890-6988) in Causeway Bay.

### Motorcycle

It's impossible to rent motorcycles in Hong Kong, but if you're staying for a while you can buy one. In truth, Hong Kong is not a great place to ride; traffic is fierce, exhaust fumes heavy and other drivers don't give a damn about motorcyclists. Registration is expensive and a bit of a hassle. But when the weekend comes, all that slips away as you speed down to the beaches or up to the New Territories.

The best place to look for a motorcycle, new or used, is on Caroline Hill Rd in Causeway Bay. There is a string of shops, most of which have at least one English speaker. Unless you have a high income, you may only be able to window-shop; Hong Kong's soaring import duties make motorcycles ridiculously expensive.

### BICYCLE

Bicycling in Kowloon or Central is suicidal, but in quiet areas of the islands or the New Territories a bike can be quite a nice way of getting around.

Some places where you can rent bikes and ride in safety include: Shek O on Hong Kong Island; Sha Tin and Tai Mei Tuk (near Tai Po) in the New Territories; on the island of Cheung Chau; and Mui Wo (Silvermine Bay) on Lantau Island. The bike rental places tend to run out of bikes early on weekends however.

### HELICOPTER

If you want a spectacular flight over the city, Heliservices (☎ 2802-0200) is on hand to whirl you up to get a different perspective on the Bank of China Tower, though you have to charter the chopper for at least 30 minutes. A 45 minute flight to Lantau Island and back is a mere HK$11,205.

### WALKING

Much of Hong Kong is best seen on foot. However, walking around isn't necessarily easy or relaxing, especially in the business districts. Poorly designed pedestrian crossings, crushing masses of people and hurtling buses can make your stroll anything but casual. The pedestrian flyovers around Central, Admiralty and Wan Chai can drive visitors insane with their complexity – but there's often no other way to cross the road. If it seems you can't cross the road, look up and you will probably see a flyover nearby.

---

#### The World's Longest Escalator

Along with its other diverse forms of transport, Hong Kong is also home to the world's longest escalator. Officially dubbed the 'Hillside Escalator Link', this novel idea looks like something borrowed from Paris' Pompidou Centre. Consisting of covered escalators and moving walkways elevated above street level, the entire system is 800m long. It also has a rather strange design: it only goes one way. When the city was presented an estimate of what it would cost to build a two-way system, it balked and opted for a single lane that moved down in the morning during rush hour, and up from 10 am onward.

The escalator was built to alleviate traffic in the Mid-Levels, home to many of Hong Kong's well-to-do commuters. Although it's not that far a walk to Central's business district, it's a steep one, which means a strenuous climb at the end of the day that few are willing to make.

The escalator is worth a try just for the novelty, though the Mid-Levels themselves make for fairly dull exploring. It can, however, take you to the heart of Soho, if you are in need of a decent meal. There is no fee to use it. Although the system moves at a snail's pace, many people stand, so if you want to get there quickly, you'll end up walking anyway. ■

But finding the stairs can be bewilderingly difficult; they are often inside neighbouring buildings. Sometimes it seems that the other side of the road is completely inaccessible. You also have to constantly be on your guard against the dangers of traffic – the heat, humidity and general chaos of the streets of Hong Kong can create a stubborn lethargy in the shopper that can be as lethal as some of the driving. But if you persevere you will be rewarded with the sights, sounds and smells that define Hong Kong.

Rural Hong Kong offers some outstanding walks and hikes. Try the 100km MacLehose Trail for starters. Even Hong Kong Island has a 50km Hong Kong Trail that spans the length of the island and takes you up and out of the city and into the trees and hills. If that daunts you, just stick to the 3.5km circuit around the Peak or head out to the islands. For more information on city and rural walks, see the Things To See & Do and Excursions chapters.

### ORGANISED TOURS

Tourism is one of Hong Kong's main money earners, so it's no surprise that there is a mind-boggling number of tours available. Along with specialised tour operators, hotels, bus and ferry companies, and even the MTR all offer tours to just about anywhere in Hong Kong. Listing them all would require a separate book.

Of all the options out there, some of the best are offered by the HKTA. While it tends to sugar-coat Hong Kong somewhat, it has done its homework. Tours take in some genuinely worthwhile sights, and are well run. If you only have a short time in Hong Kong, or are not in the mood to deal with public transport, these may be just what you're looking for. Some tours are standard excursions covering major sights on Hong Kong Island such as Victoria Peak, while other tours take you on harbour cruises, out to the islands, or through the New Territories.

The HKTA also has a series of thematic tours covering subjects such as horse-racing, Chinese folk customs and lifestyles, sports and recreation, and life in Hong Kong's public housing estates, where you visit a Chinese family. Prices range from about HK$275 to HK$500 per person, and there are discounts for children and seniors. The HKTA also arranges tours of Macau and Guangdong Province. For further details pick up a copy of the *HKTA Tours* pamphlet at a HKTA information centre or call the tour operations department (☎ 2807-6390; Web site www.hkta.org) Monday to Saturday from 9 am to 5 pm, (☎ 2807-6177, 9 am to 5 pm Sundays and public holidays). Another operator with trips around Hong Kong and to Macau, Shenzhen and Guangzhou is Gray Line (☎ 2368-7111).

Watertours is owned by the venerable Hong Kong trading conglomerate Jardine Matheson. The company offers nearly 20 different harbour tours, island excursions and dinner and cocktail cruises. Prices range from HK$200 for the Afternoon Eastern Harbour Cruise to HK$630 for the Highlight of the Night Cruise. You can book straight through Watertours (☎ 2118-6235), a travel agent or, in many cases, your hotel.

The Star Ferry Company (☎ 2118-6241, 2118-6242) runs seven ferry tours a day, costing HK$180 for adults, HK$140 for children 12 and under. You can even hire a Star Ferry by the hour for HK$1300.

Hong Kong Tramways offers open-top tram tours, which use special luxury trams. Tours leave five times daily (there is one evening departure) and cost HK$180 for adults, and HK$140 for kids. For information and bookings, call ☎ 2118-6235. You can also hire a tram for a party, costing HK$530 per hour, unless you go for the antique version which is HK$830 per hour. You often see them trundling down the streets at night, with balloons, music and laughter spilling from the upper deck.

# Things to See & Do

Since the handover, the changes to Hong Kong have been largely symbolic, such as the occasional red and gold flag of the People's Republic of China fluttering in the breeze. Snatches of Mandarin can be heard, before being swallowed up by the chorus of Cantonese. But for the traveller, Hong Kong is the same – a city where preserved historical relics are hemmed in by an upwardly mobile skyline of dazzling modernity and prosperity.

The presence of mainland China is so clandestine that Hong Kong continues with a life all its own, still full of self-assurance and almost oblivious to the significance of the transferral of sovereignty.

Hong Kong is not so much worth visiting for sights as for spectacle. With a few exceptions – the stunning night-time view from the Peak or the frenzy of Victoria Harbour seen from the Star Ferry – your sharpest memories are likely to be not of individual sights but the frantic fusion of colours, sounds and scents that make up this vibrant city.

Of course many of Hong Kong's attractions are still fun to visit. They are quite spread out, but excellent public transport makes them easy to reach. Try and take your time. Often getting to and from a sight, or nosing around the surrounding neighbourhood, offers as much if not more than the sight itself.

## HIGHLIGHTS

It has become clichéd to describe Hong Kong as a blend of old and new, tradition and modernity. But this is a genuine part of the territory's appeal, and unless you stay rooted in Central for your entire stay, you're bound to notice it.

It's not a bad idea to kick off your visit with a trip up to Victoria Peak, more often referred to as simply 'the Peak'. Not only do you get a spectacular view, weather permitting, but you can also acquire a good feel for the geography and layout of Hong Kong.

The Peak area also has some fine walking trails that take you to shady groves of trees, and stunning views of the western and southern parts of Hong Kong Island. The Peak at night also offers a stunning spectacle of glittering Central below, one of the most moving vistas in the whole of Hong Kong.

From there it depends on what you're looking for. If you're in the mood to experience Hong Kong's modernity and dynamism, take a walk through Central, passing the magnificent Hongkong and Shanghai Bank Building and the totemic Bank of China Tower. This area is a forest of architectural treasures. Or hop on the MTR to Causeway Bay, home to some of Asia's most sophisticated department stores outside of Tokyo.

To really see what urban Hong Kong looked like a century ago, you'll have to visit the Hong Kong Museum of History. But you can get a feel for the old days by wandering the streets and alleys of Sheung Wan on Hong Kong Island, or Yau Ma Tei and Mong Kok in Kowloon. A visit to one or two of Hong Kong's scattered Chinese temples offers the chance to soak up some traditional atmosphere and incense.

Tsim Sha Tsui, Hong Kong's main tourist district, is where you throw yourself into the thick of it. Jam-packed with people at any time of day, the streets are lined with shady electronics shops, high-fashion clothing stores, hole-in-the-wall restaurants and bars and a hotel on nearly every block.

When you've had your fill of urban excitement, head out to the beaches and country parks on the south side of Hong Kong Island. Sun yourself on the beaches at Shek O or Repulse Bay, shop for cheap clothing and tacky trinkets at the Stanley market or go hiking in Aberdeen Country Park. If the bus ride over didn't give you enough ups and downs, try Ocean Park, Hong Kong's very own amusement park, complete with roller coaster, log flume, marine mammal shows

## Hong Kong's Top Ten

1. **The Peak** (pages 109-11) – spectacular views of Victoria Harbour from the top of Hong Kong Island
2. **Hong Kong Island tram ride** (pages 87) – a slow but picturesque trundle through the heart of Hong Kong
3. **Cheung Chau** (page 211) **and Lamma Island** (page 213) – two splendid islands sheltering some fine, sandy beaches and captivating walks
4. **Stanley** (pages 114-5) – a lively market and relaxing seaside getaway
5. **Shek O** (page 115) – one of the best beaches on Hong Kong Island, almost deserted during the week
6. **Tsim Sha Tsui Promenade** (page 118) – more spectacular views, this time of Hong Kong Island's high-rises; go at night
7. **Hong Kong Museum of History** (page 118) – a great way to revisit old Hong Kong
8. **Wong Tai Sin Temple** (page 120-1) – a lively and colourful Taoist temple in Kowloon
9. **Yuen Po St Bird Garden** (page 120) – Hong Kong's singing garden of feathered friends
10. **Afternoon Tea at The Peninsula** (page 148) – bask once more in post-colonial luxury

## Hong Kong's Ten Worst

1. **The lifts at Chungking Mansions** – if you ever get stuck in one of these, say your prayers and chew on that cyanide capsule
2. **The stairwells at Chungking Mansions** – on view among the centuries of litter are a species of roach specific to the mansions (*roachus guesthousus*), noted for their humungous size and voracious appetite
3. **Nathan Rd camera shops**
4. **Low-hanging street signs** especially the sharp ones
5. **The 'no change given' policy on Hong Kong buses**
6. **Hong Kong air conditioners** that constantly drip on to your head as you walk down the street
7. **The coffee on Hong Kong ferries**
8. **The words 'copy Rolex' shouted into your ear on Nathan Rd**
9. **Hong Kong's roads being endlessly dug up**
10. **Cockroaches that fly in summer** (don't worry, only the big ones get off the ground)

and more, all set on a promontory overlooking the South China Sea.

Then take time, I almost insist, to go to one or two of the Outlying Islands. Lamma Island is a verdant alternative to cosmopolitan Hong Kong; you'll find a sense of quiet and beauty you never associated with Hong Kong.

## HONG KONG ISLAND

Though the island makes up only 7% of Hong Kong's land area, it is the territory's centre of gravity. This, after all, is the site of the original colonial settlement, Victoria. Most of the major businesses, government offices, top-end hotels and restaurants and upper crust residential neighbourhoods are here. The island is home to the governor's mansion, the stock exchange, the legislature,

the territory's premier shopping district, the original horse-racing track and a host of other places that define Hong Kong's character. Not surprisingly, a good deal of Hong Kong's sights are also on the island.

Looking across from Tsim Sha Tsui shows how unbelievably crowded the northern side of the island is. About the only natural places left to build on are the steep hills rising up behind the skyscrapers. As well as moving up, Hong Kong keeps on moving out. Reclamation along the harbour edge continues to add the odd 250m every so often, and buildings once on the waterfront are now several hundred metres back. The latest round is altering the shorelines of the Sheung Wan, Central, Admiralty and Wan Chai districts, leaving some wags to predict that the harbour will soon be completely filled.

THINGS TO SEE & DO

One of the best ways to see the north side is to jump on one of the wobbly double-decker trams that trundle between Kennedy Town and Shau Kei Wan. Try and go during mid-morning or mid-afternoon, when there's a better chance of grabbing a front seat on the upper deck. The trams take their time, moving slower than almost every other form of traffic. While this may not be great for rushed commuters, if you want to sit back and get a feel for Hong Kong city life, this is just the ticket. And for HK$1.60 (rising to HK$2 in the summer of 1998), it's also one of the best bargains out there.

The south side of Hong Kong Island has a completely different character to the north. For one thing, there are some fine beaches here, and the water is just about clean enough for swimming. The best beaches are at Big Wave Bay, Deep Water Bay, Shek O and Repulse Bay. Incredibly expensive villas are perched on the hillsides, though these are being joined more and more by soaring, and usually ugly, multistorey apartment blocks.

It's easy to circumnavigate the island by public transport, starting from Central and taking a bus over the hills to Stanley, then heading clockwise along the coast via Aberdeen back to the Star Ferry Terminal.

### Central (Map 6)

Nearly every visitor to Hong Kong passes through Central whether for sightseeing, taking care of errands such as changing money, or en route to the bars and restaurants of Lan Kwai Fong. Many business travellers spend all their time in this district, where most of Hong Kong's larger international companies have their offices. Being the business centre, Central has some impressive architecture which can appear quite magnificent, especially in the right light conditions. Historical remnants, churches, parks and gardens contribute to surprising harmonies of ancient and modern themes.

A good place to start exploring Central is the Star Ferry Terminal. As you exit the terminal, you will see the last surviving **rickshaws** in Hong Kong. There are fewer and fewer of the rickshaws left, and their ancient owners only pose for photos (for a fee). They certainly won't take you to the Peak! Rickshaws were introduced from Japan in the 19th century and are called *yanlikche* in Cantonese (miniature models of rickshaws for HK$270 can be found at Chinese Arts & Crafts stores – see Arts, Crafts & Antiques in the Shopping chapter for information).

Exiting the terminal on the right-hand side, you'll find **Jardine House**, a 40 storey silver monolith covered with circular port-hole-style windows. This is the headquarters of Hong Kong's venerable trading house-turned-conglomerate, Jardine Matheson. In honour of the building's appearance (and, some say, of the more snobbish employees working within) this structure has been nick-named the 'House of a Thousand Orifices' though it also goes by a more off-colour epithet.

Aside from this distinction, the building's basement is also where you will find the Hong Kong Island HKTA information centre. Here you can pick up scores of leaflets on sights, accommodation, public transport and just about anything else relating to visiting Hong Kong. To the east of the building is the sculpture *Double Oval*, by Henry Moore. The former Jardine House was on the south-west corner of Pedder St, and was demolished in 1982.

West of Jardine House is **Exchange Square**, home to the Stock Exchange of Hong Kong and one of Central's more elegantly designed structures. The entire complex of three office towers is elevated. Access is via a pedestrian walkway network that stretches west to Sheung Wan and which also links Exchange Square to many of the buildings on the other side of Connaught Rd. The ground level is given over to the Exchange Square Bus Terminus and minibus stop. The stock exchange is at the main entrance to towers One and Two.

Tours of the stock exchange (☎ 2840-3859) are possible, but they generally take business groups and are not really geared up for a flood of tourists, so don't be surprised if they turn you down.

*continued on page 97*

# Where have all the Rickshaws gone?

Rickshaws must have appeared in Hong Kong soon after their invention as the Japanese *jinriksha*. There were already 700 registered and licensed in the colony by 1895 and there were probably more than 5000 by WWI. In the mid-1920s here, despite competition from buses, trams and other mechanised transport, they still numbered more than 3000 and were a vital part of the colony's transport network. Over the next 15 years they dwindled away until there were only a few hundred left at the start of WWII, but their numbers must have swollen dramatically during the war and in the tough years that followed because there were about 8000 registered in the late 1940s. It was the peak before a rapid decline as taxis and increased traffic congestion swept them off the roads in the 1950s and 1960s. By the early 1970s rickshaws had ceased to be a means of transport and become a pure and simple tourist attraction.

It's said the last rickshaw licence was issued in 1975, when there were still nearly 100 left in the colony, but the rickshaw pullers still seem to have current licences that cost them HK$50 a year. Although there is no campaign to get rid of them the remaining rickshaw 'boys' are now old men, and ready to entertain offers from any rickshaw collector who might care to buy their steeds. At their peak rickshaws were not simply public transport, businesses and well-off families often kept a rickshaw much as they would a car today. Towards the end of WWI there were even 60 rickshaws registered in the name of brothels. These were used to deliver courtesans to their customers.

Rickshaws could still be found on both the Hong Kong Island and Kowloon side of the Star Ferry run and there was a busy trade to the bars and brothels of Wan Chai for a time during the Vietnam R&R years of the 1960s and into the 1970s. By the early 1980s the numbers had dropped to less than 50 and they eventually contracted to the small group which hangs out at the Star Ferry pier on the Hong Kong Island side, waiting to take visitors on a short jog around the car park or to pose for photographs. By the early 1990s their numbers had fallen to less than 20 and by late 1997 they were truly an endangered species, just eight rickshaws remained and a 'For Sale' sign hung over the whole collection, indicating their days were truly numbered.

**Tony Wheeler**

*The number of rickshaws in Hong Kong has faded from a postwar peak of around 8000 to only a handful today.*

BOTH PHOTOGRAPHS BY RICHARD I'ANSON

*continued from page 95*

Outside Exchange Square I and II is a seating area surrounding a fountain which can be an excellent place to relax, especially in the early evening. The huge statue facing you in front of the Forum shopping mall is of a taijiquan posture known as 'Snake creeps down', although the sculpture is simply called *Taiji*. The work is by the Taiwanese sculptor, Zhu Ming.

Take the pedestrian walkway over Connaught Rd and you will find yourself in the heart of Central. Most of the buildings are office towers, but those with an eye towards shopping can check out Prince's Building and the Landmark shopping centre, both of which cater to more well-heeled consumers.

Going past the Landmark, tucked uphill is **Lan Kwai Fong,** a densely packed cluster of bars and restaurants in Central's south. Formerly an expatriate drinking ghetto, the area has now become popular with locals as well. The bars are nothing to get too excited about, but it's a fun place to do a little pub-crawling. There are a number of good places to eat too, and at lunchtime during the week Lan Kwai Fong becomes a swirling, dizzy mass of office workers trying to squeeze a decent meal into a pitifully short lunchbreak. For more details, see the Places to Eat and Entertainment chapters.

Right next to Prince's Building lies **Statue Square**, which used to display effigies of England's royalty, including Queen Victoria, Queen Alexandra, King Edward VII, King George V and the Duke of Connaught. The statues were taken down and spirited away by the Japanese when they occupied Hong Kong during WWII. Though they were found intact in Japan after the war, colonialism was on the defensive and only Queen Victoria was restored, not in Central but in Causeway Bay's Victoria Park.

Fittingly the sole survivor in the square is a bronze likeness of Sir Thomas Jackson, a particularly successful Victorian-era head of the Hongkong and Shanghai Bank (he was recently the victim of a red paint attack by a demonstrator who then crossed the road and did the same to one of the Chinese lions

outside the old Bank of China Tower, for good measure).

On the north side of Chater Rd, in a smaller section of Statue Square is the cenotaph dedicated to Hong Kong residents who died in both world wars. The pre-handover raising and lowering of the flags of the forces is no longer performed, except on Remembrance Day.

Statue Square is now best known in Hong Kong as the spot where thousands of Filipino migrant workers congregate on the weekends to picnic, sing, dance and generally celebrate a respite from their often dreary jobs as domestic helpers or factory workers.

The ornate colonial building on the east side of the square is the former Supreme Court, which now serves as the **Legislative Council Chamber**. In the front is a blindfolded statue of the Greek goddess Themis, representing justice. This is a good place to watch Hong Kong's grassroots political movements in action: they routinely stage protests outside the east entrance; watch out for the April 5th Action Group and its long-haired leader (Leung Kwok-hung) who often try to storm the place.

East of the Legislative Council is **Chater Garden**, which is a good place to watch Chinese practising taijiquan exercises in the early morning.

### Hongkong and Shanghai Bank Building

Emblazoned on most Hong Kong dollar notes, this headquarters of the territory's most famous and powerful bank has come to symbolise modern Hong Kong: daring, innovative and frightfully expensive.

Sitting south of Statue Square, this bizarre yet graceful jumble of steel, glass and aluminium occupies the same spot as every preceding headquarters since the bank's founding in 1865. Indeed the need to fit a huge office tower on the original site is what pushed renowned British architect Norman Foster to adopt such a unique design. Most of the building's major components were assembled overseas and brought together on site, requiring an unprecedented degree of engineering and assembly precision.

By using bridge engineering techniques and locating all services in prefabricated modules hung on the east and west sides of the building, Foster eliminated the need for a central core. The result is a striking atrium that soars upward 11 stories from the ground level. A computer-controlled bank of 480 mirrors hung on the south side of the building reflect natural light into the atrium, adding to the sweeping, open feeling.

Perhaps most incredibly, on orders from the bank, Foster designed the building to be expandable; the front and side sections can support a 30% weight increase in the form of additional floors and service modules. There aren't too many other buildings that can actually grow. Not surprisingly, this was not a cheap project. It cost nearly US$1 billion, making it the world's most expensive building at the time of its completion in 1985.

It's definitely worth riding up the escalator to the 1st floor to gaze at the cathedral-like atrium and the natural light filtering through. The bank does not conduct tours of its masterpiece, but staff are accustomed to tourists wandering in; there is a reception desk on the 1st floor where you can pick up a booklet on the building. The bank is open from 9.00 am to 4.30 pm Monday to Friday, and from 9.00 am to 12.30 pm Saturday.

**Bank of China Tower** Vying with the Hongkong and Shanghai Bank Building for the mastery of Hong Kong's financial district is the soaring Bank of China Tower. When built, it was the tallest building in Hong Kong at 74 storeys, though it has since been eclipsed by the hulking 78 storey Central Plaza in Wan Chai. See the Bank of China Tower section on page 100 for more details.

Take the express lift to the 43rd floor (it doesn't stop at any other floor) for an eagle eye's view from a panoramic window. From here you are at about the same height as the roof of the Hongkong and Shanghai Bank Building. You can't go any higher than the 43rd floor, which is a shame, as it's very exciting when the wind blows (the building is designed to sway several feet at the very top).

**Tsui Museum of Art** The pet project of a Hong Kong tycoon, this museum (☎ 2868-2688) can be found on the 4th floor of the Henley Building, 5 Queen's Rd, Central. The collection is interesting though modest in size, with a good display of *sancai* (or three colour) pottery from the Tang Dynasty (618-907 AD), bronzes from as far back as the late Shang Dynasty (1700-1100 BC) and a few paintings and calligraphy scrolls. Admission is HK$30 for adults, HK$15 for children; operating hours are from 10 am to 6 pm weekdays and from 10 am to 2 pm Saturday.

**St John's Cathedral** Built in 1847, this is one of the few truly colonial structures left in Hong Kong. Criticised for marring the landscape of the colony when it was built, this Anglican church is now lost in the forest of skyscrapers that make up Central.

Services have been held continuously since the church opened, save from 1942 to 1944 when the Japanese Imperial Army used it as a social club. The building was ravaged during the occupation, and the wooden front doors were rebuilt after the war, using timber salvaged from HMS *Tamar*, a British warship that formerly guarded the entrance to Victoria Harbour.

The church is still quite active, and in addition to weekly services runs a number of community and social services, as well as a small bookstore. Behind the cathedral is the **French Mission Building,** a charming structure dating from 1917 and now home to Hong Kong's new Court of Final Appeal. Both the cathedral and the French Mission Building are on Battery Path, a tree-lined walk that takes you back into the heart of Central. A flight of steps opposite the southern face of Hongkong and Shanghai Bank Building takes you up to the cathedral and the French Mission.

**Government House** This is the former residence of the governor of Hong Kong, on Upper Albert Rd, opposite the Zoological & Botanical Gardens. The original sections of the building date back to 1858. Other features were added by the Japanese during their WWII occupation, including the rectangular tower.

Government House is closed to the public except for one day in March (always a Sunday) when the azaleas are in bloom. It really should be opened up as a museum, but the idea has been cold-shouldered by the powers that be; hopefully this will change. From the outside it's interesting to look in at what was the last seat of colonial administrative power in Hong Kong, but to be allowed inside would be much better.

**Zoological & Botanical Gardens** First established in 1864, these excellent gardens are a pleasant collection of fountains, sculptures, greenhouses, aviaries, a zoo and a playground. There are hundreds of species of birds, exotic trees, plants and shrubs on display. The zoo is surprisingly comprehensive and is also one of the world's leading centres for breeding endangered species.

The gardens are divided by Albany Rd, with the plants and aviaries in the first section, off Garden Rd, and most of the animals in the other. The black jaguar is a beautiful specimen, while the Emperor tamarins are gorgeous primates that communicate in high squeaks. Also check out the lion-tailed macaque and the orangutans – there's a grumpy male who sits with his face pressed against the wire, surrounded by his wives and offspring. If you go to the gardens before 8 am the place will be packed with people toning up with a bit of taijiquan before heading off to work. Opening hours are from 6 am to 10 pm daily (6 am to 7 pm for the zoo). Admission is free.

The gardens are at the top end of Garden Rd – an easy walk, but you can also take bus No 3 or 12 from the stop in front of Jardine House on Connaught Rd. The bus takes you along Upper Albert and Caine Rds on the northern boundary of the gardens. Get off in front of the Caritas Centre (at the junction of Upper Albert and Caine Rds) and follow the path uphill to the gardens.

**Hong Kong Park** This unusual park seems designed to look anything but natural.

Rather, the park stresses synthetic creations such as its fountain plaza, conservatory, aviary, artificial waterfall, rubber-floored playground, viewing tower, amphitheatre, museum and the Taichi Garden. For all that, the park is a beautiful oasis in the heart of a rather intense urban setting, and makes for dramatic photography with skyscrapers on one side and mountains on the other.

There is a marriage registry located on the grounds, conveniently allowing newlyweds to sign the papers and get on with the all-important business of wedding photos near the waterfall.

Within the park is the **Flagstaff House Museum** (☎ 2869-0690), the oldest building from the colonial era still standing, dating from 1846. The museum houses a Chinese tea-ware collection, including pieces dating from the Warring States period (473-221 BC) to the present. There is also a gallery exhibiting some rare Chinese ceramics and seals. It is open daily except Monday (and some public holidays), from 10 am to 5 pm. Admission is free.

Perhaps the best feature of the park is the **aviary**. Home to more than 600 birds (and 30 different species), the aviary is huge, and the feeling is like wandering into a world of birds. Visitors walk along a wooden bridge suspended about 10m above ground, putting one eye level with the tree branches, where most of the birds are to be found.

Hong Kong Park is an easy walk from either Central or Admiralty. Bus No 3, 12, 23, 23B, 40 and 103 will also get you there. Alight at the first stop on Cotton Tree Dr.

**Li Yuen St** Actually this is two streets: Li Yuen St East and Li Yuen St West, which run parallel to each other between Des Voeux and Queen's Rds, opposite the Lane Crawford Department Store. Closed to motorised traffic, these two lanes are crammed with shops selling clothing, handbags, fabrics and assorted knick-knacks. Nearby Pottinger St, with old cobbled steps and equally ancient-looking street hawkers, is also worth looking into.

*continued on page 102*

**THINGS TO SEE & DO**

# IM Pei's Bank of China Tower

NICKO GONCHAROFF

The design of the Bank of China Tower is imbued with symbols, metaphors and purpose. In purely physical terms, the building dominates not just its immediate environment, but also lords it over the whole Hong Kong skyline. Its geometric, crystalline purity is intended to personify prosperity, dynamism and optimism; but according to the principles of fung shui it does the opposite.

Opened in 1988, the tower had to be bigger than the nearby Hong Kong and Shanghai Bank Building, in order to represent the new power about town (the PRC) and dwarf the symbol of the exiting power (Great Britain). The previous stone Bank of China building had been looked down upon by Norman Foster's Hongkong and Shanghai Bank Building since 1986. Despite being smaller, Foster's building has a few advantages due to its position. The Bank of China Tower is impeded by its location, caught in a web of flyovers and

*IM Pei's starkly geometric Bank of China Tower has been criticised for ignoring the rules of geomancy or fung shui.*

GLENN BEANLAND

*The Bank of China Tower lords it over not only the rival Hongkong and Shanghai Bank Building but the entire skyline of Central as well.*

TED CARROLL

not easily accessible to the pedestrian, while the Hongkong and Shanghai Bank sits on enviable ground near an MTR station and facing Statue Square.

The Chinese-American architect, IM Pei, largely eliminated Chinese elements from the design; muted homage is paid to China in the lobby, with its tomb-like suggestions, and the gardens on either side of the building take inspiration from Chinese landscape painting. A notable absence for a building of this size is the lack of Chinese lions by the main door (the old Bank of China building has *two* sets, one traditional, the other, Art Deco). Even the Hongkong and Shanghai Bank Building has a pair of huge bronze lions, reclining on the north side of the building. Other Chinese inclusions are less clear and rely on explanation for effect; the square sections of the building ascend in a way analogous to bamboo sections, which signify growth and prosperity.

Westerners have no problem accepting the structure in the way the architect desired. However, many Hong Kongers (especially fung shui experts) see the building as a violation of fung shui, the laws that govern the physical world and influence the lives of people.

For starters, the bank's four triangular prisms are negative symbols in the fung shui lexicon; being the opposite to circles, they contradict what circles suggest – money, perfection and prosperity. Furthermore, the huge crosses on the sides of the building suggest negativity. Although the building is impressive, it imposes on its surrounding environment, and the shape has been likened to that of a praying mantis (with the radio masts representing the insect's antennae), a threatening symbol.

Even more sinister are the triangular angles on the surface of the building that are associated with daggers or blades that cut into neighbouring buildings. For example, one angle cuts across the former governor's residence, which was taken to explain the run of bad luck that afflicted the last governors.

Rather than being a deliberate fung shui attack on nearby buildings (Norman Foster's Hongkong and Shanghai Bank Building would also have been adversely affected), it was probably more a case of the architect being unfamiliar or unconcerned with fung shui, despite the respect paid to it in Hong Kong.

*continued from page 99*

**Central Market** You shouldn't have any trouble finding the Central Market – just sniff the air. The market is a large four storey affair between Des Voeux and Queen's Rds. It's more a zoo than a market, with everything from chickens and quail to eels and crabs, alive or freshly slaughtered. It may not merit a separate visit, but it's worth a look if you're not too squeamish and don't have time to make it to any of Hong Kong's older districts like Sheung Wan or Yau Ma Tei. The upper floor of the market has been converted into the lower terminus of the Hillside Escalator Link, which stretches up 800m into the heart of the Mid-Levels.

### Sheung Wan (Map 6)

This district lying just west of Central, once had the feel of old Shanghai. A steady onslaught of jackhammers and cement mixers has stripped a lot of this away, and old stairway streets once cluttered with stalls and street sellers have been cleared to make

---

### Master of Taijiquan

'Relaxation is most important' breathes Zhang Yunfa, leading me through the movements of pushing hands, an exercise in the martial art of taijiquan. We are in Hong Kong Park and have been here since well before the first flourish of the dawn which is now bringing a blush of colour to the steel and glass skyline. His movements are lithe, boneless and sure; he steps like a ghost, yet there is a power and solidity deep down. I can feel it.

Pushing hands is a two-person training routine that educates the timeless principles of taijiquan into the student. You face your partner, link your hands at the wrist and while your partner pushes towards your centre you yield, absorbing his pressure and then you push back, trying to unbalance him. If you don't yield adroitly enough, the ground evaporates under your feet and you are launched into space.

I land about five foot away, step forward and link wrists again. 'Just relax.' He has said this I don't know how many times this morning already. He has this secret, a fluid and deep awareness of himself that is like an unfathomable lake; all you can see is a placid surface, a skin of water that reflects what is without, and hides what is within. That is the heart of the art of taijiquan – to suddenly reveal its depth, and catch the opponent offguard.

Zhang Yunfa escaped from China during the murderous excesses of the Cultural Revolution. He smuggled himself over the border to join the community that was born from escaping China. He doesn't talk much of his experiences in China during the mid-1960s and his silence reflects a deep and punishing grief. But on the subject of taijiquan, he is loquacious.

'In English you say you roll with the punch – well that is so true of taijiquan. The height of the art is to allow no resistance to your attacker – if there is resistance the punch lands, without resistance it cannot land. The fist needs something to hit. If your attacker punches air all the time, he will quickly tire and then you attack. You wait till he is off balance and then it is a simple task to floor him'. With that I go flying again.

This says a lot about passivity in people, I muse. Passivity gives you time to analyse the situation, calmly. Passivity has a scheming side to it, a thoughtfulness that reaches deep conclusions like the profound progress of a championship chess match. Long, measured thoughts reach to their conclusion without commotion; then a winning move appears, as if from nowhere. Such a deep and boundless passivity has become essential in today's Hong Kong, I muse further. Life in Hong Kong appears to continue as before, but the real differences lie in the collected depth of feelings in 6.4 million people; the situation is being carefully studied by a people who are well aware of the stakes and the nature of the opponent. The game needs the reserves that passivity can give for the stakes are as high as they come. So far it is all going well, but in Hong Kong they don't forget how quickly an opponent's smile can turn into something far more malignant.

The passivity of taijiquan masks a searching by your opponent for your weak spot; what appears calm is calm, but also harboured is a rapidly deepening knowledge of the situation. At the first touch of the wrists, he knows of any weakness in your foundation, and it is that which he is going to work mercilessly on. I look Mr Zhang in the eye and see a flicker of something like mischieviousness appear from some subterranean quarter. There I go again, falling backwards as if I've got a real penchant for it.

**Damian Harper**

room for new buildings. It's hard to tell, for instance, that the neighbourhood of Shek Tong Tsui (near Kennedy Town) was once the brothel centre of Victorian Hong Kong.

Nevertheless the area is still worth exploring. There aren't many sights per se: it's best to just start walking (see the boxed text Sheung Wan Walking Tour on the next page). Take a tram down Des Voeux Rd West, past all the shops selling dried seafood, Chinese medicine and flattened, preserved ducks. Get off at the terminus in Kennedy Town for a look at the barges and river boats unloading fresh vegetables, pigs and other cargo from China. Or take a stroll through the narrow alleys and backstreets of Sheung Wan, where there are still a few shops that carry on business the same way they've done for decades.

**Western Market** Almost directly opposite Shun Tak Centre and the Macau ferry terminal is the Western Market. This four storey Edwardian building, first built in 1906, was fully renovated and reopened in 1991 as (surprise, surprise) a shopping centre. It's filled with modern shops selling all kinds of small antiques, collectables and embroideries – there's even an aromatherapist. An unusual theme here is that the ground floor shops must present one-of-a-kind merchandise – the idea is to prevent the usual boring overlap of near-indentical products sold in most Hong Kong shopping malls. There's also an excellent café, the *Six Bugs Antiques and Café* (☎ 2581-4754). Spot the old London telephone boxes. The 1st floor is a 'cloth alley', similar to the fast-disappearing outdoor markets. Some good silks can be bought here. Shops are open from 10 am to 7 pm.

**Man Mo Temple** This temple, on the corner of Hollywood Rd and Ladder St, is one of the oldest and most famous in Hong Kong. The Man Mo – literally meaning 'civil' and 'military' – is dedicated to two deities. The civil deity is a Chinese statesman of the 3rd century AD and the military deity is Kuan Ti, a soldier born in the 2nd century AD and now worshipped as the God of War.

The civil deity (Man) is dressed in a red robe, holding a writing brush. Kuan Ti is dressed in green, a sword in hand. To the left of the main altar is Pau Kung, the black-faced god of justice. To the right is Shing Wong, the god of cities, a kind of protector of urban dwellers.

Outside the entrance are four gilt plaques on poles which are carried at procession times. Two plaques describe the gods being worshipped and the others request quietness and respect, and warn menstruating women to keep away. Inside the temple are two antique chairs shaped like houses, used to carry the two gods at festival time. The coils suspended from the roof are incense cones burnt by worshippers. A large bell on the right is dated 1846 and the smaller ones on the left, 1897. The exact date of the temple's construction has never been agreed on, but it's certain it was already standing when the British arrived to claim the island. The present temple was renovated in the middle of the last century.

The area around Man Mo Temple was used extensively for location shots in the film *The World of Suzie Wong*. The building to the right of the temple was used as Suzie's hotel. Actually, the real hotel in the novel (the Luk Kwok, alias the Nam Kok) was in Wan Chai, a few kilometres to the east. The temple is open from 8 am to 6 pm. Take bus No 26 from in front of the Hongkong and Shanghai Bank building, and get off at the second stop on Hollywood Rd, facing the temple.

**Fung Ping Shan Museum** This museum (☎ 2859-2114) is located on the campus of Hong Kong University, which sits on the hills above the neighbourhood of Shek Tong Tsui, west of Central. The campus is nothing special to look at, but the museum is one of the best of its kind in Hong Kong. The collection consists mainly of ceramics and bronzes, plus a lesser number of paintings and carvings.

The bronzes are in three groups: Shang and Zhou Dynasty ritual vessels; decorative mirrors from the Warring States period to the

THINGS TO SEE & DO

## Sheung Wan Walking Tour

Walking through the streets of Sheung Wan (Map 6) hardly takes you back in time: scores of new high-rise apartment blocks and the steady traffic keep you firmly rooted in the present. But there are traces here and there of late 19th and early 20th century Hong Kong, and if you use a bit of imagination you may get a feel for the way things used to be. If you do the whole route, this walking tour should take you a leisurely two to three hours.

Start off by taking a tram westwards along **Des Voeux Rd**. (Trams headed to either Whitty St or Kennedy Town will do, but Western Market trams stop too early.) Get off at Sutherland St, the third stop after Western Market. Take a little look around Des Voeux Rd West, sticking your head (and nose) into the occasional **dried seafood shop**. Here you can find preserved oysters, shrimp, mussels, squid and all sorts of fish. Some shops also sell preserved ducks, which have been flattened so that they look as if a truck ran over them.

Head off Des Voeux Rd West up Sutherland St to **Ko Shing St**, where there are a few traditional Chinese **herbal wholesalers** still in action. Life moves pretty slowly behind these walls: conversation seems to be the chief activity (though they're probably at least talking about business).

Continue down to the end of Ko Shing St, briefly back onto Des Voeux Rd and turn right onto **Bonham Strand West**, which is lined with wholesale *ginseng sellers* and more Chinese medicinal herb shops. Though some of the shops have modernised, others appear to have retained equipment for decades, giving an idea of what the Chinese trading houses of 1930s Shanghai might have looked like.

Hook a left onto **Bonham Strand** and walk up to the intersection with Queen's Rd West. To the left you'll find shops selling **bird's nests** (for the soup!) as well as paper offerings. The latter are replicas of homes, cars, furniture and bank notes which are burnt at funerals to ensure the deceased doesn't head into the afterlife without the necessary creature comforts. Also at this intersection is Kaffa Kaldi Coffee, where you can recharge if your energy is flagging.

Diagonally across Queen's Rd is **Possession St**, the spot where Captain Charles Elliot first planted the Union Jack in 1841, formally annexing Hong Kong. Aside from the street name, there's nothing else to indicate the event

Kuan Yin, goddess of mercy and compassion

---

Tang, Song, Ming and Qing dynasties; and Nestorian crosses from the Yuan Dynasty. Its collection of Yuan Dynasty bronzes is the largest in the world. A collection of ceramics includes Han Dynasty tomb pottery and recent works from the Chinese pottery centres of Jingdezhen and Shiwan in the PRC.

Take bus No 3 from Edinburgh Place (adjacent to City Hall) in Central, or No 23 or 103 coming from Causeway Bay, and get off at the university campus on Bonham Rd, opposite St Paul's College.

The museum is open Monday to Saturday, from 9.30 am to 6 pm, and on some public holidays. Admission is free.

### Admiralty (Map 6)

Heading just east of Central brings you to Admiralty, a clump of office towers, hotels and shopping centres. There are no sights took place here. In fact, reclamation has pushed the shoreline so far out, it's hard to believe this used to be the coast.

Climbing Pound Lane to where it meets **Tai Ping Shan St**, look to the right to find the **Pak Sing Temple** (Citizens Temple). This shrine was built in the 1850s to hold ancestral tablets brought over from China by some of Hong Kong's first Chinese inhabitants. There are still some 3000 ancestor tablets in this diminutive structure.

Up the steps on Tai Ping Shan St is the small neighbourhood **Kuan Yin Temple**, which is worth a quick look. Descend Upper Station St back to **Hollywood Rd**, where you will run into a string of Chinese **antique shops**. Here at the western end of Hollywood Rd the shops tend a bit more suspect: prices are easily knocked down, and a lot of shopowners somehow seem to have gotten hold of the same priceless artefacts.

Continuing east on Hollywood Rd will bring you to **Man Mo Temple** (see the relevant section on page 103 for more details). The extremely steep flight of steps next to the temple is **Ladder St**. Well over 100 years old, this unique cobbled thoroughfare used to be one of the best remaining examples of old Hong Kong, crammed with stalls and shops. Now it's been paved over with concrete.

A short hop down Ladder St is **Upper Lascar Row**, home of the overrated **Cat St market** and **antique galleries**. There are a few nice pieces to be found here, but most of the stuff displayed on the pavement is trash. Most of the antique merchants have moved into the Cat Street Galleries, a four storey building on Lok Ku Rd.

Taking Ladder St all the way down will bring you to Queen's Rd again, which you can cross over to get to **Hillier St**. This narrow street has all sorts of **street stalls** selling noodles, dim sum and other snacks. Stay away from anything with too much meat in it: people have been known to get sick from eating here. Even if you don't eat, it's still fun to watch the action.

Down onto Bonham Strand, heading east you'll come across **Man Wa Lane**. This is the place to go if you want to have a traditional chop made. Chops, or seals, have long been used in Chinese to endorse documents, and the more elaborate designs are quite beautiful.

Heading further east will bring you back again to Queen's Rd. Cross over and hike up **Wellington St**, which is home to a number of **mahjong parlours** and shops selling mahjong pieces and tables. While the action in a mahjong parlour is great to watch, it's not a good idea to stop and stare too long, as players may take serious offence.

Up on **Graham St** you'll find a fresh food market set up on the steps, where it looks as if very little has changed in decades (except for the food of course). One block further, on **Cochrane St**, there are a series of street-side tailors as well as a shop selling snake blood, which is supposed to bolster strength and male virility. If you're hungry, the **food market** on Stanley St is a good place to get a steaming plate of fried noodles or veggies.

Back down to Queen's Rd, head west briefly to check out **Eu-Yan Sang Pharmacy**, a Chinese medicine shop where the prescriptions are written out in a little booth in one corner of the store and then sent buzzing across a little wire-pulley system to the clerks behind the counter. It's definitely more interesting than Watson's.

To wind up the tour, cut through the narrow confines of **Wing Kut St**, where you can buy (or chuckle at) a bizarre array of **costume jewellery**, which is pretty much all they sell here. On the other side of Wing Kut St lies **Des Voeux Rd**, where you can catch a tram at the stop ahead and to the right, or head left to the MTR station. If you need to sit down and rest those weary feet, there is an Oliver's Super Sandwiches right near the MTR station. ■

here, but the **Pacific Place Shopping Mall** is one of the nicest in Hong Kong, with both mid-priced and expensive shops, restaurants and one of Hong Kong's biggest cinemas, the UA Queensway. You can also get to Hong Kong Park by taking the escalators up at the west side of the mall, near the pedestrian bridge spanning Queensway.

Across Queensway, the **Lippo Centre** (the work of architect Paul Rudolph) makes an interesting addition to Hong Kong's skyline, although it's not that fascinating inside.

Sitting on the hill above Pacific Place are the JW Marriot, Conrad and Island Shangri-La hotels, probably the main reason why visitors make it to Admiralty.

### Wan Chai (Map 7)

To those familiar with Hong Kong, Wan Chai (the name means 'little bay' in Cantonese)

THINGS TO SEE & DO

still brings to mind visions of topless bars, hookers working the pavements and drunken sailors on the prowl. In its sleazy heyday, as an R&R destination for the US and UK navies it was all that, and more. And in many people's minds Wan Chai is still *The World of Suzie Wong*, even though Richard Mason's tale of the kind-hearted Hong Kong prostitute dates back to 1957.

Though Wan Chai today is mostly office towers and shopping centres, it is still a pretty interesting place to poke around. The rows of narrow streets sandwiched between Johnston Rd and Queen's Rd East harbour all sorts of interesting shops and mini factories where you can see the real Hong Kong at work; watchmakers, blacksmiths, shoemakers, printers, sign-makers and so on.

Nestled in an alley on the south side of Queen's Rd East, is the **Tai Wong Temple**, also known as Hung Sing Temple, where fortune-tellers used to do a brisk trade. It is still active, if somewhat subdued.

Just east of the temple, also on Queen's Rd East, the **Hopewell Centre** is one of Hong Kong's more unusual office towers. Basically a 40 storey cylinder, it is the flagship building of Hong Kong property and construction magnate Gordon Wu. There is a tacky revolving restaurant at the top, which is reached by two bubble-shaped external elevators. Though it's a short trip, riding up these elevators is a great way to get an overhead view of Wan Chai.

The area between Hennessy and Gloucester Rds, north of the Hopewell Centre, has become one of Hong Kong's main entertainment districts. There is a slew of rather good restaurants and an impressive number of bars, many of which stay open until just before sunrise. See the Places to Eat and Entertainment chapters to find out more.

Wan Chai North, which lies on the other side of Gloucester Rd, is a fairly sterile group of high-rise office blocks and hotels, including the Grand Hyatt. In this strange setting you'll find the **Hong Kong Academy for Performing Arts** (☎ 2584-8514) at 1 Gloucester Rd, which stages local and overseas performances of dance, drama and music.

The building was designed by local architect Simon Kwan. Right next door at 2 Harbour Rd is the **Hong Kong Arts Centre** (☎ 2582-0200). The Pao Galleries on the 4th and 5th floors feature international and local exhibitions year round with an emphasis on contemporary art. Opening hours are from 10 am to 8 pm daily. Admission is free.

East of the Arts Centre, looming over Wan Chai like a malevolent giant postmodern hypodermic is the 78 storey **Central Plaza**. Take a ride in the escalator to the Sky Lobby (a vast, marble-clad lobby on the 46th floor) for sweeping views of Hong Kong Island and lower Kowloon, from 8 am to 6 pm.

Across from Central Plaza, facing the harbour, is the **Hong Kong Convention & Exhibition Centre**, an enormous building that boasts the world's largest 'glass curtain', a window seven storeys high. Expanded onto a massive chunk of reclaimed land for the handover ceremony in June 1997, the building now reaches out into Victoria Harbour. The design of the extension is spectacular, symbolizing a bird in flight, although this impression is only really available if you view the building from above (pop into Central Plaza and dart up to the 46th floor). The curves, rolls and overall aerodynamism of the building's roof makes one wonder if it will really take wing in a major typhoon. Come here on a fine day and you can walk along the clean and modern promenade and look out over to both Kowloon and Central. The centre is almost constantly hosting trade shows or other major events, and it's worth popping in to see what's on.

Housed in the Causeway Centre within the China Resources Building complex, the **Museum of Chinese Historical Relics** (☎ 2827-4692) houses cultural treasures from China unearthed in archaeological digs. Two special exhibitions each year focus on artefacts from specific provinces. It's touch and go: sometimes the exhibits are interesting; other times you'd do better wandering through the adjacent gift shop. Operating hours are from 10 am to 6 pm on weekdays and Saturday, 1 to 6 pm on Sunday and holidays. Admission is free.

To get to any of the above spots in Wan Chai North, you can take the MTR to Wan Chai station, which connects with a pedestrian walkway that crosses Gloucester Rd to Central Plaza. Alternatively, from Central take bus No 10A, 20 or 21.

### Causeway Bay (Map 7)
Along with Tsim Sha Tsui, Causeway Bay is where Hong Kong goes to shop. A cluster of Japanese department stores – Sogo, Daimaru, Matsuzakaya and Mitsukoshi – draw in the masses. If crowds bother you, steer clear of Causeway Bay on weekends.

Causeway Bay is called *Tung Lo Wan* in Cantonese, meaning 'Copper Gong Bay'. In either language, the namesake has almost disappeared due to repeated reclamation. This area was the site of a British settlement in the 1840s and was once a *godown* (warehouse) area for merchants. Jardine Matheson set up shop here, which explains some of the street names: Jardine's Bazaar, Jardine's Crescent and Yee Wo St (Yee Wo is Jardine Matheson's Chinese name).

Shopping is not confined to the department stores. Jardine's Crescent, Jardine's Bazaar and the area south of there are filled with shops peddling cheap clothing, luggage and electronics. For more information see the Shopping chapter.

In addition to buying things, people come to Causeway Bay to dine out and, to a lesser extent, go drinking. The rush of consumers, diners and drinkers gives this district a vibrant feel at almost any time of the day or night. Several shopping centres can be found south of Hennessy Rd, chief among these is **Times Square**, an enormous retail/office/restaurant complex that jars sharply with the decrepit 1950s low-rise tenements around it. Defying critics who said the location would doom the project, Times Square and its shops, restaurants, cinema and office towers have created a second centre of gravity in Causeway Bay.

One of the few vestiges of the district's colonial past is the **noon day gun**, a recoil-mounted three-pounder built by Hotchkiss in Portsmouth in 1901. It stands in a small garden in front of the Excelsior Hotel on Gloucester Rd, accessible via a tunnel under the road from the World Trade Centre, and is fired daily at noon. Exactly how this tradition started is unknown. Noel Coward made the gun famous with his satirical 1924 song *Mad Dogs and Englishmen* about colonists who braved the heat of the noon day sun while the natives stayed indoors:

*In Hong Kong they strike a gong, and fire a noon day gun, to reprimand each inmate, who's in late.*

The noon day gun overlooks the Causeway Bay **typhoon shelter**, a busy mass of junks, fishing boats, yachts and sampans huddling behind a large breakwater. Occasionally you can get a glimpse of the boat people, a few of whom moor their homes in the shelter. The little arm of land jutting out to the side is **Kellett Island**, which was actually an island until a causeway was built in 1956. Further land reclamation turned it into a peninsula. Now it's the headquarters of the Royal Hong Kong Yacht Club.

**Victoria Park** One of the biggest patches of green grass on the northern side of Hong Kong Island, Victoria Park is one of the territory's most popular parks. Football matches are played on weekends and the Urban Services League puts on music and acrobatic shows. Also in the park is a statue of Queen Victoria that used to sit in Statue Square.

Victoria Park is the sight of the annual Tiananmen Square massacre remembrance held on the evening of 4 June, which saw a record turnout for the last event before the handover. The occasion is very moving, and is usually accompanied by songs and speeches, while everyone sits on the ground with candles. Whether 1998 and beyond will see as many people coming, or if it will continue at all, is speculative at best.

The best time to stroll around the park is daytime during the week. Early in the morning it's an excellent place to watch the slow-motion choreography of practitioners of taijiquan. The evening is given over to

Hong Kong's young lovers. Between April and October you can take a dip in the Victoria Park swimming pool for HK$17. Do the backstroke and you'll get a good view of the Causeway Bay skyline.

Victoria Park becomes a flower market a few days before the Chinese New Year. The park is also worth a visit during the evening of the Mid-Autumn (Moon) Festival when people turn out en masse carrying lanterns. Other events in the park include the Hong Kong Tennis Classic and the Hong Kong International Kart Grand Prix.

**Tin Hau Temple** Just east of the park, dwarfed by surrounding high-rises, is the tiny Tin Hau temple on Tin Hau Temple Rd at the junction with Dragon Rd (near Tin Hau MTR station). Before reclamation, the temple to the seafarers' goddess stood on the waterfront. Staff say it has been a site of worship for 300 years, though the current structure is only about 200 years old. A painting on the outside of the temple, left of the main entrance, shows the original building as it looked 300 years ago. There is also an old bell inside dating back to the 15th century. Adjacent to the temple is a little park with a fountain and benches.

**Tiger Balm Gardens** Not actually in Causeway Bay but in the adjacent Tai Hang district are the famous (infamous?) Tiger Balm Gardens, officially known as the Aw Boon Haw Gardens. A pale relative of the better known park of the same name in Singapore, Hong Kong's Tiger Balm Gardens are three hectares of grotesque statuary in appalling taste. These concrete gardens were built at a cost of HK$16 million (and that was in 1935!) by Aw Boon Haw, who made his fortune from the Tiger Balm cure-everything medication. Boon Haw is widely described as having been a philanthropist, though perhaps his millions could have been put to a more philanthropic use. Still, his creation has at least provided some amusement for untold numbers of visitors.

The gardens are just off Tai Hang Rd, within walking distance of Causeway Bay. Alternatively take bus No 11 from Admiralty MTR station or Exchange Square in Central. The gardens are open daily from 9.30 am to 4 pm and admission is free.

### Happy Valley (Map 3)
This quiet residential suburb has one claim to fame: the **Happy Valley horse-racing track**. On race days (either Wednesday, Saturday or Sunday) it seems as though half of Hong Kong swoops down to this little hamlet to indulge in the territory's favourite sport: betting. Going to the races can be a lot of fun, especially if you win. The racing season is from late September to May. For details, see the Entertainment chapter.

Across the street from the spectator stands are **cemeteries** that make for an interesting history lesson. They are divided into Catholic, Protestant and Muslim sections and date back to the founding of the colony. Their placement is somewhat ironic, as is Happy Valley's name, for the area was a malaria-infested bog that led to a fair number of fatalities before the swamps were drained. Many of the victims of the huge fire at Happy Valley racecourse 80 years ago are buried here. There is also a beautifully kept Parsee (Zoroastrian) cemetery adjacent.

Racing buffs can wallow in history at the **Hong Kong Racing Museum** (☎ 2966-8065) on the 2nd floor of the Happy Valley Stand at the racecourse. It's open Tuesday to Saturday from 10 am to 5 pm, on Sunday from 1 to 5 pm and closed Monday. Entry is free.

The easiest way to Happy Valley is by tram. Trams marked Happy Valley run in both directions. Bus No 1 and 5 will get you here from Central.

### Eastern Hong Kong Island (Map 3)
Sights really start to thin out east of Causeway Bay, with the landscape dominated by apartment towers and industrial blocks. **Quarry Bay**, however, is the home of the Cityplaza Shopping Centre, one of Hong

Kong's biggest malls and the only one with an ice-skating rink. If you're out to shop this is a much more relaxed environment than Tsim Sha Tsui. To get here take the MTR to Tai Koo station from where there is an exit leading directly into the shopping mall.

Some travellers make it out to **Shau Kei Wan**, either to catch the No 9 bus to Shek O or because it's the eastern terminus of the tram line. If you do, you might consider a stroll through the **Ah Kung Ngam wharf area**, which is about 10 minutes walk from Shau Kei Wan MTR station.

This spot has long been the site of a small fishing community, though high-rise apartments and a sewage treatment plant have now invaded. But a stroll down Ah Kung Ngam Village Rd and Shau Kei Wan Main St still reveals some traces of traditional lifestyle, and the area has a decided port feel to it. On Shau Kei Wan Main St there's even a Tin Hau temple that in the past has welcomed both the last Hong Kong Governor Chris Patten and former UK prime minister Margaret Thatcher. Opposite Ah Kung Ngam Village Rd is access to the Shau Kei Wan Typhoon Shelter. Pop down to the jetty for a glimpse of the working fishers and boat people. Sampans are constantly shuttling inhabitants or sailors out to their boats, and you may be able to hire one to take you around. At the very least it's less touristy than Aberdeen. Near the jetty is the Tan Kung Temple, built in 1905.

To get to Ah Kung Ngam, walk from Shau Kei Wan MTR station toward Tung Hei Rd, which runs under the elevated freeway. Follow it north-east for about 10 minutes until you reach Ah Kung Ngam Village Rd on the right hand side. The jetty and temple are to the left, across Tung Hei Rd.

**Chai Wan**, the easternmost district on the north side of Hong Kong Island, is another forest of stark apartment towers and multistorey factories. But if you make it out here, stop by the **Law Uk Folk Museum** (☎ 2896-7006), a 200-year-old Hakka home that has been restored to a sparkling version of its original state, complete with furniture and farm tools. The museum is located at 14 Kut

Shing St and is open from 10 am to 1 pm and 2 to 6 pm Tuesday to Saturday and from 1 to 6 pm Sunday and some public holidays. Entry is free.

### The Peak (Map 8)

The Peak is one sight that should not be missed. You may feel like every tourist in town is going up there with you, but there's a good reason. The view is spectacular. It's also a good way to get Hong Kong into perspective. It's worth repeating the Peak trip at night – the illuminated view is something else. Bring a tripod for your camera if you wish to get some sensational night photos.

Unfortunately, developers couldn't resist throwing up an overblown, overpriced, four-level shopping plaza at the top, the **Peak Galleria**. This robbed the area of some of its charm. Not only that, but the structure doesn't really afford 360° views. Looking like a huge titanium anvil is the seven storey **Peak Tower**, a further questionable addition to the Peak skyline. Restaurants, cafés, shops and entertainment centres draw in the hordes from outside. For most, however, a walk around the surrounding area still rewards with great views and pretty tree-lined paths.

The Peak has been *the* place to live ever since the British moved in. The taipans built their summer houses here to escape the heat and humidity (it's usually about 5°C cooler than down below), although they spent three months swathed in mist for their efforts. It's still the most fashionable place to live in Hong Kong, as reflected by the astronomical real estate prices: homes up here routinely sell for millions of US dollars.

The top of the tram line is at 400m elevation. Getting off the tram will see you inside the Peak Tower. This could be a place to bring the kids – there are a couple of adventure simulators, the 'Peak Explorer' (a futuristic ride in space and time) and the 'Rise of the Dragon' (a car ride through Hong Kong's history) plus 'Ripley's Believe it or Not!' (an odditorium) that could keep them amused.

Apart from that, there are loads of shops and restaurants, a viewing terrace and even a post office. The Peak Galleria is right next to the terminus. The place is designed to withstand winds of over 270km/h, hopefully more than the theoretical maximum that can be generated by typhoons. The viewing deck is reached by taking escalators up to the 3rd level.

Inside the mall you'll find a number of expensive restaurants and all number of retail shops, from art galleries to duty-free. If you're looking for a bite to eat, see if there's a free table at the Peak Café, which is a much better dining experience. See the Places to Eat chapter.

Just north of the mall, down Findlay Rd, is **Lions Pavilion**, a lookout point that gives a 180° perspective on Hong Kong Island, the harbour and Kowloon. It's often packed, but the view is hard to beat.

When people refer to the Peak, this generally means the Peak Galleria and surrounding residential area. The actual summit is **Victoria Peak**, about half a kilometre to the west and 140m higher. You can hike up here by following the narrow road rising up next to the Peak Tram terminus. At the top are gardens, playing fields, benches and a little stand selling cold drinks.

Just below the summit are the remains of the **old governor's mountain lodge**. This building was burnt to the ground by the Japanese during WWII, but the gardens remain and are open to the public. The views are particularly good.

If you're going to the Peak, you should go by the **Peak Tram** – at least one way. It's an incredibly steep ride, and the floor is angled to help passengers getting off at the midway stations. In the summer, packed with people, the inside of these trams can get pretty hot though.

The tram terminal is in Garden Rd, Central, behind Citibank Plaza, 650m from the Star Ferry Terminal. Once every 20 minutes there is a free shuttle bus between the Star Ferry and the Peak Tram terminal from 9 am to 7 pm (8 pm on Sunday and holidays); it is often late however. Between 8.05 and 11.35 pm, the No 15C shuttle bus can race you to the terminal. The tram trip

takes about eight minutes and costs HK$18 one way, or HK$28 for a round trip (HK$5/8 for children under 12; HK$6/12 for people over 65). The tram operates daily from 7 am to midnight, and runs about every 10 minutes with three stops along the way. Avoid going on a Sunday when there are usually long queues. Alternatively, bus No 15 from the Exchange Square Bus Terminus in Central will take you on a 40 minute trip around the seemingly perilous road to the top. The trip down is even more hair-raising. Bus No 15B runs from Causeway Bay (Yee Wo St) to the Peak.

**Peak Walks** The best way to appreciate the Peak is to walk around it. One particularly pleasant (and popular) route is a 3.5km loop on Harlech and Lugard Rds. Harlech Rd, on the south side, takes you past a small waterfall and offers great views of southern Hong Kong Island and Lamma Island beyond. When you reach a playground/barbecue area turn right onto Lugard Rd, which weaves through lush forest and takes you onto a pedestrian causeway jutting out from the side of the hill that gives amazing views northward. It's often misty up on the Peak, which ruins the view, but makes any walks cool and fresh.

Another pleasant hike that is only a bit more strenuous is the Governor's Walk, which can be accessed from either the Victoria Peak summit area or near the intersection of Harlech and Lugard Rds.

For a downhill hike you can walk about 2km from the Peak to Pok Fu Lam Reservoir. This route starts at Peak Rd across from the car park exit, and winds down Pok Fu Lam Reservoir Rd past the reservoir to the artery of Pok Fu Lam Rd where you can get the No 7 bus to Aberdeen or back to Central.

If you're feeling energetic, you can drop off Pok Fu Lam Reservoir Rd onto the Family Walk, which takes you through actual forests, past a small stream, several picnic tables and some very pleasant scenery. The main trail winds up at a lookout point at the end of Harlech Rd. The entire loop, back to the Peak Tram terminus, is around 6km.

Another good walk is from the Peak to Hong Kong University. First walk to the west side of Victoria Peak by taking either Lugard or Harlech Rds. After reaching Hatton Rd on the west side of Victoria Peak, follow it down. The descent is steep but the pathway clearly marked. It eventually leads to the university and Kotewall Rd, where you can catch a minibus to Central. Alternatively walk down through the university to Pok Fu Lam or Bonham Rds, both of which have bus stops with frequent buses to Central.

Also check at the Peak Galleria for charity walks that may be happening around the Peak area while you are in Hong Kong.

### Aberdeen (Map 9)

Aberdeen is rated as one of Hong Kong's top tourist attractions, but when you get here you may wonder why. The urban area is not much more than a cluster of dingy apartments, shopping centres and industrial buildings. The main lure is **Aberdeen Harbour**, where several thousand people still live or work on junks anchored there. The other main draw

is a string of three palace-like **floating restaurants**, the most famous of which is the Jumbo. Cheaper meals can be had at one of the myriad houseboat seafood restaurants moored next to the promenade.

This being the case, the best way to see Aberdeen Harbour is by sampan, which can weave in and out of the rows of boats and bring you close to the action: Tanka women preparing food, racks of fish drying in the sun, kids playing in the water and so on.

Sampan tours can be arranged at the Aberdeen Promenade. You have your choice of private operators, which generally mill around the eastern end of the promenade, or licensed operators, sponsored by the HKTA, like the Aberdeen Sampan Co (☎ 2873-0310). The private sampans usually charge HK$50 to HK$60 per person for a 30 minute ride, though you should easily be able to bargain this down if there are several of you. If you are by yourself, just hang out by the harbour as the old women who operate the boats will leap on you and try to get you to join a tour. On one of the tours you can get a

---

### The Hong Kong Trail

Victoria Peak is the starting point for the 50km Hong Kong Trail (see Map 3), which spans the entire length of Hong Kong Island. Obviously doing the whole thing at once is only for the fittest of hikers. But the route is divided into eight sections, which offer walks of varying length and difficulty.

The trail winds through five country parks, zigzagging along the ridgetops until it finally descends to end at Shek O, at the south-eastern tip of the island. The eight sections are divided as follows, with details of the buses to go to or from the trail sections:

| Section | Km | Hrs | Difficulty | Bus No |
|---|---|---|---|---|
| 1. The Peak | 7.0 | 2 | Medium | 15 |
| 2. Pok Fu Lam | 4.5 | 1+ | Medium | 4,7,37,40 |
| 3. Aberdeen | 6.5 | 1 | Medium | 7, 38, 70, 78, 95 |
| 4. Wong Chuk Hang | 7.5 | 2 | Easy | 15 |
| 5. Jardine's Lookout | 4.0 | 1+ | Hard | 6, 41, 61, 262 |
| 6. Tai Tam | 4.5 | 1+ | Easy | 2, 20, 21, 22, 80, 102 |
| 7. Tai Tam Bay | 7.5 | 2 | Easy | 14 |
| 8. Tai Long Wan | 8.5 | 2+ | Hard | 9 |

If you're attempting this or any other long hike in summer, be sure to bring lots of water. Though humid, Hong Kong's heat can still dehydrate. And while it's not a major concern, do be aware that you're sharing these trails with native inhabitants of the country parks, including snakes.

For detailed information on this hike, pick up the *Hong Kong Trail* map published by the Country Parks Authority. Another good map is *Countryside Series Sheet No 1: Hong Kong Island*, which shows many details of the streets and topography not on the hiking map. Both maps are available from the Government Publications Office (see the Maps section in the Facts for the Visitor chapter). ■

close up of the *xhuga teng* or houseboats. Watertours (☎ 2118-6235) does a 25 minute trip around the harbour for about HK$50 per person, but it's more fun to charter a sampan. If you don't mind missing out on close-up shots of boat life, you can get a free 10 minute tour by hopping on one of the boats out to the floating restaurants and then riding back. They leave every four or five minutes.

On the south side of the harbour is the island of **Ap Lei Chau** (Duck's Tongue Island). There's not much to see there, but a walk across the bridge to Ap Lei Chau affords good views of the harbour and some nocturnal shots of the fiery lights of the Jumbo restaurant. Alternatively, you can get a boat across for HK$1.50.

If you've got the time, a walk through Aberdeen will bring you to the **Tin Hau temple**, at the junction of Aberdeen Main and Aberdeen Reservoir Rds. Built in 1851, it's a sleepy spot, but still an active place of worship. It's also one of Hong Kong's more important altars to the patron deity of Hong Kong's boat people, given Aberdeen's harbour community. Down near Aberdeen Main Rd is the Hung Hsing Shrine, a collection of ramshackle altars and incense pots.

If you're feeling vigorous, the entrance to Aberdeen Country Park and Pok Fu Lam Country Park is about a 15 minute walk up Aberdeen Reservoir Rd. From here you can hike up to the Peak and catch the Peak Tram or the bus down to Central.

Chinese junks, one of the classic symbols of Hong Kong, can still be seen occasionally in the waters around the territory and can even be hired to tour the Outlying Islands.

RICHARD I'ANSON

TED CARROLL

RICHARD I'ANSON

RICHARD I'ANSON

Top Left: Looking across Victoria Harbour to Hong Kong Island's skyline.
Top Right: Fireworks mark a new era as Hong Kong returns to China on 30 June 1997.
Bottom Left: The Temple St night market in Yau Ma Tei, a great place to hunt for bargains.
Bottom Right: The Legislative Council building in the midst of the bustle, Central.

# Hong Kong's Vanishing Pink Dolphins

Although called Chinese White Dolphins (*Sousa chinensis*), these dolphins are actually pink in colour. About 100 to 150 of these lovely mammals inhabit the coastal waters around Hong Kong, finding the brackish waters in the vicinity a perfect habitat. The dolphin population however faces a great threat from environmental pollution, and numbers are dwindling.

This threat comes in many forms, but the most prevalent and direct dangers are: sewage – about 150,000 cubic metres of raw sewage is dumped into the western harbour every day (predicted to increase to 700,000 cubic metres per day by 2010); chemical pollutants – DDT and PCBs – have been found in very high concentrations in tissue samples from dolphins; overfishing – several dead dolphins have shown signs of having been entangled in fishing nets; boat traffic – despite the dolphins' skill at sensing and avoiding surface vessels, some show signs of collision.

The habitat of the dolphins is also being diminished by the erosion of the natural coastline of Lantau Island to make way for the new Chek Lap Kok airport. The construction of the airport has led to the reclamation of approximately 9 sq km of seabed and the destruction of many kilometres of natural coastline. The north Lantau expressway has also consumed about 10km of natural coastline. Further environmental threats are waiting to threaten the dolphins' habitat.

Hong Kong Dolphinwatch was founded in 1995 to raise awareness of these dolphins and the dangers they face. Promoting a policy of responsible ecotourism, Dolphinwatch offers cruises to tourists to see the pink dolphins in their natural habitat. Cruises leave on Sunday (adults: HK$350, children under 12: HK$175) and weekdays (adults: HK$400, children under 12: HK$200). About 95% of Dolphinwatch cruises result in the sighting of a pink dolphin. If no dolphin is seen, passengers are offered a free trip next time. Contact Hong Kong Dolphinwatch (☎ 2984-1414; fax 2984-7799; email dolphins@hk.super.net; Internet www.zianet.com/dolphins). ■

*The habitat of the pink dolphin in Hong Kong's waters is under threat from pollution, boat traffic and the reclamation of the natural coastline.*

BOTH PHOTOGRAPHS BY HONG KONG DOLPHINWATCH

Getting to Aberdeen is fairly easy. From the Exchange Square Bus Terminus in Central, take bus No 7 or 70. No 7 goes via Hong Kong University and western Hong Kong Island, and No 70 goes via the Aberdeen tunnel, which runs from Wan Chai to Wong Chuk Hang, just east of Aberdeen. The No 70 terminates at the Aberdeen bus station, the No 7 passes by there.

**Ocean Park & Water World** A stimulating cultural experience this is not. But these two fun parks are set in a pleasant location just to the east of Aberdeen and are quite entertaining. They are also good places to see modern Hong Kong at play.

Hong Kongers are quite proud of Ocean Park (information and inquiries ☎ 2552-0291), a fully-fledged amusement park, complete with roller coaster, space wheel, octopus, swinging ship and other stomach-turning rides. It is also something of a marine park, with a wave cove housing seals, sea lions and penguins, daily dolphin and killer whale shows and an aquarium that features a walk-through shark tank and atoll reef. The atoll reef is particularly impressive, with around 4000 fish on display including the mammoth Napoleon fish, tawny nurse shark, white tip reef shark and cowtail stingray – you can get right up close. The shark tank has hundreds of sharks on view and scores of stingrays. The park also caters for bird-watchers, with aviaries and a flamingo pond.

The complex is built on two sides of a steep hill, and is linked by a very scenic seven minute-long cable car ride. The park entrance is on the 'lowland' side, which also has children's attractions like a dinosaur discovery trail, kid's world and mini-rides. The park's main section sits on the 'headlands' and affords a beautiful view of the South China Sea and southern Hong Kong Island. This is where you'll find the rides and marine attractions. McDonald's is on hand for swift refreshment.

At the rear entrance is the Middle Kingdom, a sort of Chinese cultural village with temples, pagodas, traditional street scenes and staff dressed in period garments. There are also arts and crafts demonstrations, live theatre and Cantonese opera. This is a highly whitewashed version of ancient China, but it's harmless enough.

Entrance fees are HK$140 for adults, or HK$70 for kids aged three to 11. Opening hours are from 10 am to 6 pm daily. It's best to go on weekdays; weekends are amazingly crowded. A map comes with the ticket, so it's not difficult to find your way around.

Water World is right next to the front entrance of Ocean Park. A collection of swimming pools, water slides and diving platforms, it's a great place to go and splash around in the searing heat of summer. Water World is open from June to October. During July and August, operating hours are from 9 am to 9 pm. During June, September and October it is open from 10 am to 6 pm. Admission for adults/children costs HK$65/33 during the daytime, but in evenings falls to HK$44/22.

Probably the most convenient way to get to Ocean Park and Water World is via a special Citybus service that leaves from the bus station next to Admiralty MTR station. Buses leave every 15 to 20 minutes from 9.10 am and cost HK$11, children's tickets are HK$5.50. Citybus sells a package ticket that includes transportation and admission to Ocean Park for HK$150 for adults, HK$75 for children (which doesn't actually save you a whole load). A special Ocean Park Citybus also leaves from the Star Ferry Terminal which costs the same as the above and leaves every 15 to 20 minutes from 10 am to 3.30 pm; the last bus back to the Star Ferry Terminal is at 4.30 pm except on Sunday, when it's 6.30 pm.

A cheaper way to get there is to catch bus No 70 from the Exchange Square Bus Terminus in Central and get off at the first stop after the tunnel. From there it's a 10 minute walk. The No 6 green minibus (HK$7.5) from Central's Star Ferry Terminal takes you directly to Ocean Park and Water World, but does not run on Sunday and holidays. Bus No 73 connects Ocean Park with Aberdeen to the west and Repulse Bay and Stanley to the east.

THINGS TO SEE & DO

### Deep Water Bay

This is a quiet little beach with a generous dose of shade trees located a few kilometres east of Aberdeen. There are a few nice places to eat and have a drink and there is a barbecue pit at the eastern end of the beach. If you want a dip in the water, this spot is usually less crowded than Repulse Bay (see below).

To get here from Central, take bus No 6A, 260 or 262 from the Exchange Square Bus Terminus. Bus No 73 connects Deep Water Bay with Aberdeen to the west and Repulse Bay and Stanley to the east.

### Repulse Bay (Map 3)

Repulse Bay's long, somewhat white beach is the most popular on Hong Kong Island. Packed on weekends, it's good for people-watching, but bad if you're hoping for solitude. In the summer even the weekdays see a big turnout. Middle Bay and South Bay, about a 10 minute and 30 minute walk respectively along the shore to the east, also have beaches and are usually less crowded. The water is pretty murky and the slimy feel underfoot is enough to make you a landlubber for life.

Toward the eastern end of Repulse Bay beach is an unusual **Tin Hau temple** popularly known as the Life Saver's Club. The temple area is full of statues and mosaics of Kuan Yin (also called Guan Yam), the goddess of mercy and inside is a café and the headquarters of the Royal Life-Saving Society. The sprawling temple is an amazing assembly of deities and figures, including a four-faced Buddha and statues draped in pearl necklaces and ornaments. It's garish, but fascinating. In front of the temple is Longevity Bridge – crossing it is supposed to add three days to your life.

Repulse Bay is also home to some of Hong Kong's rich and famous, and the hills behind the beach are saturated with luxury apartment towers. One worth noting is the pink, purple and yellow monstrosity with a giant square cut out of the middle. Apparently this unique design feature was added at the behest of a fung shui expert, though in Hong Kong such a stunt might also work to push up the value of the property. The **Repulse Bay Shopping Arcade** at 109 Repulse Bay Rd is a busy place, many with shops and restaurants.

Bus No 6, 6A, 61, 260 and 262 from Central's Exchange Square Bus Terminus all pass by Repulse Bay. Shuttle buses to Repulse Bay leave every 15 minutes (peak time) from a stop just to the left as you exit Central's Star Ferry Terminal. To get to Repulse Bay from Aberdeen take bus No 73.

### Stanley (Map 10)

Here lies another one of Hong Kong's top tourist destinations. Most people come to Stanley to swarm through **Stanley Market**, several covered blocks of cheap (and not-so-cheap) clothing, sporting goods, low grade jewellery and art, and the usual smattering of trinkets and souvenirs.

The market is fairly entertaining, at least for a while. But it's worth visiting Stanley for the relaxed atmosphere. Wander down Stanley Main St to the waterfront restaurants for a drink or a bite to eat. Or head over to the other side of the isthmus to Stanley Main Beach and kick back on the sand. A lot of Hong Kong's wealthier commuters live here to enjoy the laid-back atmosphere.

About 2000 people lived here when the British took over in 1841, making it one of the largest settlements on the island at the time. The army set up a garrison here, a presence that continued until 1997. The colonial government also built a prison near the village in 1937 – just in time to be used by the Japanese (called 'turnip heads' by the Cantonese) to intern expatriates.

From the Stanley Bus Terminal it's a two minute walk down to Stanley Market. On weekends it's bursting with both tourists and locals, so it's better to come on a weekday. The market is open daily from 10 am to 7 pm. A short walk out of town along Stanley Main St is yet another Tin Hau Temple, which dates back to 1767. However, the building has undergone complete renovation, and is now a bit of a concrete hulk, although the interior is traditional. Behind the temple a huge residential estate is being built, but if you follow the path that passes the Tin Hau Temple and continue up the hill, you reach the Kuan Yin temple. This temple, with its complement of nuns (who are often in prayer, so be respectful) displays a 48-armed figure of Kuan Yin (the goddess of mercy and compassion, usually worshipped by women). Above the temple is a pavilion which houses a massive statue of Kuan Yin looking out to sea.

From town you can walk south along Wong Ma Kok Rd to **St Stephen's Beach**, which has a café, first aid unit, shower and toilet facilities, umbrella rental and boat and windsurfer hire (in summer months); lording over it all is a lifeguard. The lovely walk takes about 25 minutes. Turn right when you come to a small road leading down to a jetty. At the end of the small road turn left, and walk past the boathouse to reach the beach. You can also hop on bus No 73A, which takes you close to the intersection with the small road. Opposite the bus stop is a **military cemetery**; the oldest graves date from 1843, and the cemetery was reopened in 1942 for the burial of those who died in WWII and during internment at the hands of the Japanese.

To get to Stanley from Central take bus No 6, 6A, 6X or 260X from the Exchange Square Bus Terminus. The No 6 bus climbs over the hills separating the north and south sides of the island, which makes for a scenic, winding ride. Bus No 260, which goes via the Aberdeen tunnel is quicker, and perhaps better for those prone to motion sickness. From Hoi Ping Rd in Causeway Bay you can take the No 40 green minibus. If you're coming from Shau Kei Wan (the eastern terminus of the tram), an exciting ride comes in the form of bus No 14 which takes you to Stanley, via the Tai Tam Tuk reservoir. Bus No 73 connects Stanley with Repulse Bay and Aberdeen.

One note of warning. If you visit Stanley during the weekend, you may have a tough time catching a bus back to Central between 5 and 8 pm, when everybody else is trying to get home. If queues for the No 6 and 260 buses are too long to endure, consider the No 73 to

Aberdeen. Or check the queue for the No 40 green minibus to Causeway Bay.

### Shek O (Map 3)

Shek O, on the south-eastern coast, has one of the best beaches on Hong Kong Island. And because it takes around two hours to get here, it's usually less crowded than the other south island spots. On weekdays the town is sometimes almost deserted, and it's easy to spend the afternoon lazing on the beach, snacking at the open-air restaurants or gawking at the mansions dotting the Shek O headlands.

Shek O is a small village so it's easy to get your bearings. From the bus stop walk five minutes and you're on the beach. En route you'll pass a few good restaurants (see the Places to Eat chapter). If you take the road leading off to the left you'll enter a maze of small homes, which gradually grow in size and luxury as you head up the peninsula that juts out east of the beach. This is the **Shek O headlands**, home to some of Hong Kong's wealthiest families. If you traipse down to the tip of the peninsula you'll come to a viewpoint where you can look out over the South China Sea; next stop, the Philippines.

There are some hikes around Shek O beach, though the terrain is steep and the underbrush quite thick in spots. Better yet, take advantage of the bicycle rental shops and peddle down to **Big Wave Bay**, another fine beach located 2km to the north of Shek O. To get there just follow the road out of town, past Shek O Country Club and Golf Course, bear right at the traffic circle and keep going until the road ends.

To get to Shek O, take the MTR or tram to Shau Kei Wan, and from Shau Kei Wan take bus No 9 to the last stop. It's a long ride but scenic and, depending on your driver, quite exciting.

### KOWLOON

Kowloon presents another face of Hong Kong, quite different from that of the former colonial outpost across Victoria Harbour. Leave the glittering hotels and shopping malls of Tsim Sha Tsui and you begin to see where Hong Kong and China come together, culturally at least. East doesn't really meet west in Kowloon: it swallows it up. While Hong Kong Island has its share of gritty neighbourhoods, there's something in them that feels familiar to western eyes. Not so here. While English signs abound, they look decidedly secondary. Hong Kong Island is home to big business and government. Kowloon is home to shopkeepers and Triads.

Kowloon's districts are best seen on foot. There aren't too many fantastic sights here; it's the overall experience that's worth taking in. However, there are a few good destinations, and travelling to them should give you plenty of chance to soak up the atmosphere.

Strictly speaking, Kowloon (as annexed in 1860) is the 12 sq km extending from Tsim Sha Tsui north to Boundary St. The remainder of the peninsula, up to the hills that form the effective border with the New Territories, is officially called New Kowloon, which the British gained in 1898. However nowadays few people note the distinction, and the entire peninsula is referred to as Kowloon.

### Tsim Sha Tsui (Map 5)

Perched at the very edge of the peninsula, Tsim Sha Tsui is Hong Kong's tourist ghetto. Countless clothing and shoe stores, restaurants, pubs, sleazy bars, fast-food outlets, camera and electronics stores and hotels are somehow crammed into a few square kilometres. This is one of Hong Kong's key shopping districts and is also a good place to avoid on weekends if you don't enjoy dense crowds.

Next to the Star Ferry Terminal and the Hong Kong Cultural Centre stands one of Kowloon's few remaining examples of colonial architecture, a 45m-high **clock tower**. This is all that has been preserved from the original southern terminus of the Kowloon-Canton Railway (KCR), which was built in 1916 and torn down in 1978. The old station was a colonial-style building adorned with columns, but it became too small to handle passenger traffic, which soared with the development of the New Territories. The new station at Hung Hom, where travellers now begin their journey to China, is much larger but far less appealing.

On the other side of the Star Ferry Terminal is **Ocean Terminal/Harbour City**, a labyrinth of swanky retail shops, hotels and office towers. Ocean Terminal is the long building jutting out into the harbour, which is also Hong Kong's sole pier for cruise liners. The sheer size and number of stores make this mega-mall interesting, but if you're one of those people that doesn't like shopping, you'll hate this place.

A few blocks east along Salisbury Rd stands one of Hong Kong's landmarks, the famous hotel **The Peninsula**. Although it now has plenty of worthy competitors, for many this is still the place to stay when in Hong Kong. Land reclamation has robbed the hotel of its prestigious waterfront location, but the breathtaking interior is worth a visit. Take in the exclusive shops and the main lobby, which are usually packed with tourists rather than guests. Afternoon tea here is still one the best experiences in town. If you can ever afford to stay here, do it; there is a commitment to excellence that makes it special. For more details on The Peninsula, see the Places to Stay chapter.

The area behind The Peninsula, including Ashley, Hankow and Lock Rds, is a warren of cheap (and often shady) shops, restaurants and bars. It's a fun area to wander around, particularly in the evening. And of course no visit to Kowloon is complete without at least a brief stroll down **Nathan Rd**. This artery was named after a governor, Sir Matthew Nathan, who held office at the start of this century. It was promptly titled Nathan's Folly, since in those times Kowloon was sparsely populated and such a wide road seemed unnecessary. The southern section is known as the 'Golden Mile', which refers to both the price of real estate and also its ability to suck money out of the pockets of tourists.

Dominating the intersection of Nathan and Cameron Rds is the **Kowloon Mosque and Islamic Centre**, the largest mosque in Hong Kong. The present building was completed in 1984 and occupies the site of a previous mosque built in 1896 for Muslim

Indian troops who were garrisoned in barracks at what is now Kowloon Park. The mosque is interesting to admire from the outside, but you can't simply wander in and take photos. If you are a Muslim, you can participate in their religious activities; otherwise you must obtain permission.

**Hong Kong Cultural Centre Complex** The government chose a worthy, if perhaps not very attractive, successor for the prime plot of waterfront land formerly occupied by the KCR station. The **Hong Kong Cultural Centre** (☎ 2734-2009) was built as 'a high-technology nail in the coffin of the long-dead cliche that Hong Kong is a cultural desert'. Or so the government says. It's a world-class venue, including a 2100-seat concert hall, a theatre that seats 1800, a smaller 300-seat theatre, rehearsal studios, an arts library and a pretty impressive main lobby. The concert hall even has an organ with 8000 pipes, the largest in South-East Asia. The advent of the cultural centre has enabled Hong Kong to regularly book high-profile international artists. The cultural centre is open from 9 am to 11 pm on weekdays and Saturday, and from 1 pm to 11 pm on Sunday and public holidays. There are daily tours except Sunday and public holidays, of the cultural centre from 12.30 pm to 1 pm; tickets for adults are HK$10, for children, disabled and senior citizens, HK$5. Call ☎ 2734-2009 for more information.

Adjacent to the cultural centre and grabbing probably one of the nicest views in town is the **Hong Kong Museum of Art** (☎ 2734-2167). It's easy to spend an afternoon wandering around here. There are six galleries exhibiting Chinese antiquities; Chinese fine arts; paintings and lithographs of old Hong Kong; and the Xubaizhi collection of painting and calligraphy. The sixth gallery has rotating international exhibits. The exhibits are quite tastefully displayed, giving one the feeling that funding isn't a major problem for this particular museum. When your feet are sore, take a seat in the hallway and enjoy the harbour vista. There is a shop on the ground floor that has a commendable collection of art books and prints, including an extensive section on Chinese art. The museum is closed Monday, otherwise operating hours are weekdays and Saturday from 10 am to 6 pm, and Sunday and holidays from 1 pm to 6 pm. Admission is HK$10 for adults, HK$5 for kids and seniors, but free Wednesday.

Behind the art museum, looking like a giant golf ball, is the **Hong Kong Space Museum** (☎ 2734-2722). It's divided into three parts; the Space Theatre (planetarium), the Hall of Space Science and the Hall of Astronomy. Exhibits include ancient astronomy, early rockets, plans for future space programmes, manned space flight and solar and stellar science. The displays are in general quite interesting and in many cases interactive. Though most of the spacecraft shown are models, the museum did manage to snare the Mercury space capsule piloted by the American astronaut Scott Carpenter in 1962. Opening times for the exhibition halls are weekdays (closed Monday) from 1 pm to 9 pm, and from 10 am to 9 pm weekends and holidays. Admission is HK$10 for adults and kids, HK$5 for students and seniors.

The Space Theatre has several 'skyshows' daily (except Monday), some in English and some in Cantonese. Headphone translations are available for all shows. The museum also shows Omnimax, or giant-screen, films. However the films, which are intended for a semi-circular screen, are projected onto the rounded dome of the theatre, and the effect is more laughable than dramatic. Space Theatre shows generally start at 11.30 am, with the last show usually at 8.30 pm. Both skyshows and Omnimax films cost HK$30 for adults and HK$15 for children. To find out what's playing and when, stop by the ticket window or call the museum. Advance bookings can be made up to one hour before showtime by calling ☎ 2734-9009.

**Kowloon Park** Once the site of the Whitfield Barracks for British and Indian troops, this area has been reborn as an oasis of green and a refreshing escape from the clutter and bustle of Nathan Rd. Pathways and walls crisscross the grass, birds hop around in cages, and towers and viewpoints dot the landscape. The **Sculpture Walk** is an interesting addition, featuring works by local sculptors. The Hong Kong Museum of History is here (see below), as well as an excellent indoor/outdoor pool complex complete with waterfalls. If you want to swim (between April and October when the pools are open), go in the morning or afternoon on a weekday; on weekends there are so many bathers it's tough to make out the water. The park is open from 6 am to midnight.

**Hong Kong Museum of History** A visit here is essential for anyone who hopes to gain a deeper understanding of Hong Kong. This excellent museum (☎ 2367-1124) is located in the grounds of Kowloon Park, not far from the Haiphong Rd entrance. The museum takes the visitor on a fascinating walk through Hong Kong from about 6000 years ago to today. As well as a big collection of 19th and early 20th century photographs, there are replicas of village dwellings, traditional Chinese costumes and a re-creation of an entire street block from 1881, including an old Chinese medicine store.

The museum is open Tuesday to Saturday from 10 am to 6 pm, and Sunday and public holidays from 1 pm to 6 pm. It is closed on Monday. Admission costs HK$10, HK$5 for students and seniors, but it's free Wednesday.

**Tsim Sha Tsui East (Map 5)**
This triangular block of land east of Chatham Rd didn't even exist until 1980. Built entirely on reclaimed land, Tsim Sha Tsui East is a cluster of shopping malls, hotels, theatres, restaurants and nightclubs. Everything is new – there are none of the old, crumbling buildings of Tsim Sha Tsui. The area has a few office towers, but mainly caters to more affluent shoppers, diners and night owls.

**Tsim Sha Tsui Promenade** Along with the Peak, this waterfront walkway offers some of the best views in Hong Kong. A lovely place to stroll during the day, at night the view of Central lit up in neon is mesmerizing. You'll find yourself accompanied by

lovers, joggers, musicians, photographers with tripods, fellow visitors and, believe or not, people fishing right off the promenade (didn't think anything could survive in that water, did you?). The promenade becomes a sea of people during the Chinese New Year fireworks display and again during the Dragon Boat Festival.

The promenade officially starts at the New World Centre, though you can walk along the shore from the Star Ferry Terminal. It goes all the way to the Hong Kong Coliseum and Kowloon KCR station. Midway along is a ferry pier, where you can catch a hovercraft across the harbour to Hong Kong Island.

**Hong Kong Science Museum** This is a good place to take the kids. The museum (☎ 2732-3232) is near the corner of Chatham and Granville Rds, about 10 minutes walk north from the Promenade. It's a multi-level complex with more than 500 exhibits on computers, energy, physics, robotics, communications, transportation and more. About 60% of the exhibits are 'hands-on', which helps to keep the younger visitors interested.

Admission costs HK$25 for adults, and HK$12.50 for kids, students and seniors. Operating hours are 1 pm to 9 pm Tuesday to Friday, and 10 am to 9 pm weekends and holidays. The museum is closed on Monday.

**Yau Ma Tei (Map 4)**
In Cantonese Yau Ma Tei means 'place of sesame plants'. The name obviously dates from years gone by. Now the only plants you'll find in this heavily urban district are in the window boxes of grimy, crumbling tenements. The narrow streets and alleys of Yau Ma Tei are a good place to check out Hong Kong's more traditional urban society. Within the square bordered by Kansu, Woosung, Nanking and Ferry Sts you'll stumble across old pawn shops, outdoor fresh food markets, Chinese pharmacies, mahjong parlours and other retailers practising their time-honoured trades. To see some weird items, poke your nose into one of the dried food stores – fancy dried lizard on a stick? How about bat?

The best way to see this area is to just set off by foot and take whichever turn beckons. Everything is just a short walk from Yau Ma Tei MTR station. If you want a detailed guided tour, pick up a copy of the HKTA's *Yau Ma Tei Walking Tour*, available at HKTA information centres for HK$35.

**Jade Market** Hong Kong tourist literature really hypes up this place, but it's actually fairly dull.

There are several hundred stalls selling all varieties and grades of jade from inside a large tent. Jade is a traditional symbol of longevity for the Chinese, and this market definitely works better for locals than tourists. Some sellers are reasonable, other dishonest. Unless you really know your jade, it's probably not wise to buy any really pricey pieces here. For more information see Jade in the Shopping chapter.

The market is located near the junction of Battery and Kansu Sts under a flyover. It's open daily between 10 am and 3.30 pm, but go early as you may find the sellers packing up and leaving at about 1 pm. To get there take bus No 9 from the Kowloon Star Ferry Bus Terminal in Tsim Sha Tsui, get off at Kowloon Central Post Office and walk down to Kansu St. You can also take the MTR and get off at either Jordan or Yau Ma Tei MTR stations.

**Tin Hau Temple** East of Public Square St, a block or two to the north of the Jade Market, is a large Tin Hau temple, dedicated to the patron goddess of seafarers. Off to the right as you face the main temple you can find a row of fortune-tellers, some of whom speak English, so you can get that *Yikging* (*I Ching*) reading you've always wanted. The temple complex also houses an altar dedicated to Shing Wong (the city god) and To Tei Kung (the earth god). The temple is open daily from 8 am to 6 pm.

**Temple St** The liveliest night market in Hong Kong, Temple St (named after the Tin Hau Temple, above) is the place to go for cheap clothes, cheap food, watches, pirate CDs, fake labels, footwear, cookware and everyday items; everything seems to end up here. It used to be known as 'Men's St' because the market only sold men's clothing. Though there are still a lot of men's items on sale, vendors don't discriminate – anyone's money will do.

For street food, head to the section of Temple St north of the Tin Hau Temple. At night you can get anything from a simple bowl of noodles to a full meal, served at your very own table on the street. There are also a few seafood and hotpot restaurants around here. The Temple St hawkers set up at 6 pm and leave by midnight. The market is at its best in the evening from about 8 to 11 pm when it's clogged with stalls and people.

**Mong Kok (Map 4)**
This district has one of the highest population densities of any place in the world, a point that hits home as soon as you arrive. Aside from housing a ridiculous number of people in shabby apartment blocks, Mong Kok is also one of Hong Kong's busiest shopping districts: the name in Cantonese aptly means 'prosperous corner'. But this is not a place for designer fashion, ritzy jewellery and hovering salespeople. This is where

---

**Illegal Structures**

Because Hong Kong is so starved of space, flats seem to grow extra rooms and balconies. These are illegally added to the sides of buildings, supported on rickety frames and waiting for the opportunity to plummet to earth. In fact, large chunks of masonry and concrete regularly descend to flatten some poor hawker, prompting TV advertisements to remind the hoi-polloi not to build such structures.

A casual glance up above street level in any part of Hong Kong other than the really ritzy areas will reveal many buildings in a pitiful state. Crumbling through neglect and the unrelenting humidity, it's amazing they stay up at all. Every now and then bamboo scaffolding goes up to give the terminal cases an overdue face-lift; unfortunately, the bamboo poles have a nasty habit of coming loose and spearing passing pedestrians. ■

THINGS TO SEE & DO

locals come to buy everyday items like jeans, tennis shoes, kitchen supplies, computer accessories and so on. Take a look at Fife St, which has an amazing collection of stalls selling old records, music scores, machinery, ceramics and books. This is also a good place to buy backpacks, hiking boots and other travel gear (see the Shopping chapter). Even if none of these items are on your shopping list, it's worth taking a look.

Most of the action is east of Nathan Rd. Two blocks walk from Mong Kok MTR station, Tung Choi St throws up a nightly street market you can wade through. Similar to Temple St market in Yau Ma Tei, but not as much fun, Tung Choi St used to also be known as 'Women's St' selling only goods for females. Like Temple St, it now happily caters to both sexes.

The streets west of Nathan Rd reveal Hong Kong's seamier side, for here is where you'll find some of the city's seediest brothels. Mostly run by Triads, these places are often veritable prisons for young women and teenage girls, usually brought to Hong Kong on false pretences and then forced into prostitution. The police routinely raid these places, but a look at the rows of brightly coloured signs shows that business goes on as usual. This is not a great part of town to hang around after midnight, though there's little risk of violent crime.

**Yuen Po St Bird Garden** The bird market has flown its original location from Hong Lok St and has alighted in the Yuen Po St Bird Garden, not too far away. Chinese have long favoured birds as pets; you can often see local men walking around airing their feathered pets. They especially like birds that can sing and the singing prowess of a bird often determines its price. Some birds are also considered harbingers of good fortune, which is why you'll see some men carrying birds to the horse races.

Aside from the hundreds of birds on display, elaborate cages carved from teak and bamboo, and ceramic water and food dishes are also on sale. The birds seem to live pretty well; the Chinese use chopsticks to

RICHARD I'ANSON

The Yuen Po St bird garden is Hong Kong's biggest market for feathered pets.

feed live grasshoppers to their feathered friends, and give them honey nectar to gild their vocal cords.

To get to the Bird Garden, take the MTR to Prince Edward station, come out of the Prince Edward Rd West exit and walk east for about 10 minutes.

**Other Kowloon Sights**
Most of Kowloon's other districts, such as Sham Shui Po, Kowloon City or Kwun Tong are vast tracts of featureless public housing estates, residential towers and industrial buildings. However there are a few sights worthy of mention scattered about. And though some are not that fascinating, getting there and back will definitely add to your perspective on Hong Kong.

**Wong Tai Sin Temple** This Taoist temple is one of the largest and liveliest in Hong Kong, and is worth visiting mainly to see the crowds. The buildings and gardens, dating from 1973, are attractive enough, but not really inspirational.

According to legend, Wong Tai Sin (also known as Huang Chu Ping) was a shepherd who lived in a remote section of Zhejiang Province in the 4th century AD. At the age of 15 he was apprenticed to an immortal and through his studies concocted a medicine that cured all illnesses. Not surprisingly he is worshipped by those concerned about their health. The statue of Wong Tai Sin in the main temple was brought to Hong Kong from China and installed in its present site in 1921.

Like most Chinese temples, this one is an explosion of colour, with red pillars, bright yellow roofs and blue latticework all around. Bright flowers and shrubs add to the effect. If you come in the late afternoon or early evening, you can watch hordes of business people and secretaries praying and divining the future with *chim*, sticks that must be shaken out of a box onto the ground and then read. Friday evening is the busiest time for such worshippers. Behind the main temple are the Good Wish Gardens, replete with some colourful (though concrete) pavilions, curved pathways and an artificial waterway. Adjacent to the temple is an arcade filled with dozens of booths operated by fortune-tellers. Some of them speak good English, so if you really want to know what fate has in store for you, this is your chance to find out. Just off to one side of the arcade is a small open area where you can look up and get a magnificent view of Lion Rock, one of Hong Kong's prominent natural landmarks.

The temple is open daily from 7 am to 5.30 pm. The busiest times are around the Chinese New Year, Wong Tai Sin's birthday and weekends. There is no admission fee for visiting this or any other temple in Hong Kong, but they've become used to tourists dropping a few coins (HK$1 will do) into the donation box by the entrance. Getting there is easy. Take the MTR to Wong Tai Sin station, take exit B and follow the signs.

**Lei Cheng Uk Museum & Han Tomb** This burial vault dating from the Eastern Han Dynasty (25-220 AD) is Hong Kong's earliest historical monument. It was discovered in 1955 when workers were levelling the hillside for a housing estate. The tomb consists of four barrel-vaulted brick chambers in the form of a cross, around a domed central chamber. While somewhat interesting, it's kind of a long way to come for an anticlimactic peek through plexiglass.

The museum (☎ 2386-2863), a branch of the Hong Kong Museum of History, is at 41 Tonkin St, Lei Cheng Uk Estate, Sham Shui Po. It is open daily (except Monday) from 10 am to 1 pm and from 2 to 6 pm. On Sunday and most public holidays it's open from 1 to 6 pm. Admission is free.

To get there, take bus No 2 from the Kowloon Star Ferry Bus Terminal in Tsim Sha Tsui and get off at Tonkin St. The nearest MTR station is Cheung Sha Wan, a five minute walk from the tomb. Just follow the signs.

**Lei Yue Mun** East of Kai Tak airport, the little village of Lei Yue Mun ('carp gate') is a popular spot for Hong Kong seafood lovers. The neighbourhood is quaint and very lively at night when the diners arrive en masse. Although the seafood isn't necessarily better here than anywhere else, it makes for a nice eating excursion. You can get there on bus No 14C from Kwun Tong MTR station – take it to the end of the line (Sam Ka Tsuen Terminal).

## NEW TERRITORIES (Map 2)

This city guide focuses on Hong Kong Island and Kowloon, and does not pretend to do justice to the New Territories. However, the following museums, temples and monasteries can be reached fairly quickly from the urban area, and thus are included here. Several day trips into the New Territories are also covered in the Excursions chapter.

For a look at life among the landowning clans of 200 years ago, you should check out the **Sam Tung Uk Museum** (☎ 2411-2001). This rather simple museum houses a restoration of a village founded by the Chan clan in 1786. Within the museum grounds are eight furnished houses plus an ancestral hall. The museum is a five minute walk to the east of

Tsuen Wan MTR station (just follow the signs) and is open from 9 am to 4 pm daily except Tuesday. Admission is free.

The **Chinese University Art Museum** (☎ 2609-7416) is a four-level museum housing local collections as well as exhibits from museums in mainland China. There's an enormous exhibit of paintings and calligraphy by Guangdong artists from the Ming Dynasty (1368-1644 AD) to modern times, as well as a collection of 2000-year-old bronze seals and a large collection of jade flower carvings. The gallery is open weekdays and Saturday from 10 am to 4.30 pm, and Sunday and public holidays from 12.30 pm to 4.30 pm (closed on some public holidays). Admission is free. To get there, take the KCR to University station. A free bus outside the station runs through the campus to the top of the hill. It's easiest to take the bus uphill and then walk back to the station.

Also on the KCR line is the **Hong Kong Railway Museum** (☎ 2653-3339), which is housed in a restored 1913 railway station. Inside there are photos and illustrated explanations dating back to the start of rail travel in the colony and China. Lined up outdoors are a series of old trains dating back as far as 1911. The museum is open daily (except Tuesday) from 9 am to 5 pm. Admission is free. The museum is a 10 minute walk northwest along the KCR tracks from Tai Po Market station. The museum is on On Fu Rd and there are signs pointing the way.

If you're up in Tai Po to visit the railway museum, there is a **Man Mo temple** about 200m away on Fu Shin St. Like the Man Mo temple in Sheung Wan, Hong Kong Island, this place is dedicated to two Taoist deities representing the pen and the sword, although it is much smaller. Although small, it adjoins a bustling street market of interest.

Further up the KCR line, at Fanling, you'll find the **Fung Ying Sin Kwun Temple**, a Taoist temple for the dead. The ashes of the departed are deposited here in what might be described as miniature tombs. It's an interesting place to look around, but be respectful of worshippers. The temple is located across from Fanling KCR station.

The New Territories offer the chance to see a few working Buddhist monasteries as well as some nicely appointed temples. One of the most impressive is the **Chuk Lam Sim Yuen**, or 'Bamboo Forest Monastery'. Founded in 1927, it boasts three of the largest Buddha statues in Hong Kong. There are also a couple of smaller monasteries nearby. Two are on the hillside just above Chuk Lam Sim Yuen, and a third, Tung Lam Nien Temple, is across the road. To reach the monastery and temple complex, take green minibus No 85 from Shiu Wo St, two blocks south of Tsuen Wan MTR station.

Just 1.5km north-east of the Tsuen Wan MTR station is the **Yuen Yuen Institute**, a large complex with Taoist, Buddhist and Confucian temples. The main building is a replica of the Temple of Heaven in Beijing. There is also a vegetarian restaurant on site. The **Western Monastery** is also nearby. To get there, take green minibus No 81 from Shiu Wo St, two blocks south of Tsuen Wan MTR station. Alternatively, take a taxi from the Tsuen Wan MTR station, which is not expensive. If you want to walk, you can take

The rural backwaters of the New Territories offer a glimpse of traditional country life.

the pedestrian bridge (400m west of the MTR station) which will get you across Cheung Pei Shan Rd and in the right direction.

If you want to look out over the world's longest combined rail and road suspension bridge and work your way through elaborate set models of the airport and peripheral projects connected with it, the **Airport Core Programme Exhibition Centre** will be up your street. The show is actually reasonably interesting, but it's aimed more at locals and visiting mainland Chinese, who find massive civil engineering projects spellbinding. It's not that easy to reach, but you first go to Tsuen Wan and take either bus 234B or 53 from the Ferry Pier. The No 96 green minibus also goes by the exhibition centre; you can also get aboard at the Ferry Pier. The address of the centre is 410 Castle Peak Rd and opening times are 10 am to 5 pm Tuesday to Friday, and 10 am to 6.30 pm Saturday, Sunday and holidays. Entry is free.

If you're big on Buddhas, head for the **Temple of Ten Thousand Buddhas**, which sits on a hillside about 500m west of Sha Tin. Built in the 1950s, it actually has 12,800 miniature Buddha statues, all of similar height but striking slightly different poses along the walls of the main temple. There is a nine-level pagoda and statues of Buddha's followers in front of the temple. From the main monastery area, walk up more steps to find a smaller temple housing the embalmed body of the founding monk, who died in 1965. His body was encased in gold leaf and is now displayed in a glass case. It is considered polite to put a donation in the box next to the case. The temple is open from 8 am to 6.30 pm.

It's easy to reach; just take the KCR to Sha Tin station and go through the left-hand exit, following the signs. However from here on you'll need some strong legs to climb the 40-odd steps up to the complex. Take note that the monastery may be shut, as it was undergoing repairs due to mud slides in the vicinity when we were last there. Check with the HKTA (☎ 2807-6177) for more information.

On the western side of the New Territories in Lam Tei you'll find the **Miu Fat Buddhist Monastery**, which houses three large golden Buddhas on the 3rd floor. This is an active monastery which preserves more of a traditional character than many smaller temples. On the 2nd floor is an excellent vegetarian restaurant. It is easily reached by taking the LRT to Lam Tei from Tuen Mun, and then it's a five minute walk along Castle Peak Rd from the Lam Tei LRT station (Tuen Mun can be reached by taking the hovercraft ferry from Central).

## ACTIVITIES
### Participation Sports
Hong Kong may be a jumble of concrete and asphalt, but there are a surprising number of ways to keep fit and have fun.

One excellent year-round option is the South China Athletic Association (Map 7; ☎ 2577-6932), 88 Caroline Hill Rd, Causeway Bay. The SCAA has numerous indoor facilities for billiards, bowling, tennis, squash, ping pong, gymnastics, fencing, yoga, judo, karate and dancing. Outdoor activities include golf, and there is also a women's activities section. Membership is very cheap and there is a discounted short-term membership available for visitors (HK$50 per month).

Another terrific place you can contact is the Hong Kong Amateur Athletic Association (☎ 2504-8215; fax 2577-5322), Room 1017, Sports House, 1 Stadium Path, So Kon Po, Causeway Bay. All sorts of sports clubs have activities or hold meetings here.

In general, gyms and fitness centres are prohibitively expensive, and there's often a very long queue to join (one exception is the SCAA). So if your exercise routine involves fitness training, you may want to find an alternative, unless your hotel has a gym.

For information on martial arts, see the Courses section at the end of this chapter.

**Cricket** This most British of sports is also increasingly popular with locals, but club waiting lists are very long, joining is very expensive and you may have to be recommended; this is only worth considering if your stay is long-term.

On Hong Kong Island, north of Deep Water Bay, is the Hong Kong Cricket Club (☎ 2574-6266). On the other side of Victoria Harbour lies the Kowloon Cricket Club (☎ 2367-4141), a wonderful patch of greenery in Yau Ma Tei. There's not just cricket on the menu here, there are also facilities for squash, tennis, hockey, soccer, swimming, tenpin bowling, snooker, darts and lawn bowls. Additional information may be obtained by contacting the Hong Kong Cricket Association (☎ 2859-2414). Lamma Island has its own cricket club (☎ 2723-8721) who may be able to help.

**Cycling** There are bicycle paths in the New Territories, mostly around Tolo Harbour. The paths run from Sha Tin to Tai Po and continue up to Tai Mei Tuk. You can rent bicycles in these three places, but they get very crowded on weekends. On a weekday you may have the paths to yourself. Bicycle rentals are also available at Shek O on Hong Kong Island, and Mui Wo on Lantau Island. Try contacting the Hong Kong Cycling Association (☎ 2573-3861) for information, although they mainly organise races. To find out about good mountain biking areas or for equipment, try asking the staff at Flying Ball Bicycle Co (☎ 2381-3661) at 201 Tung Choi St in Mong Kok. Another decent area for purchasing cycling gear and accessories is Garden St in Mong Kok and Wan Chai Rd in Wan Chai.

**Fishing** Sport fishing from boats is popular with expats and locals alike. To organise an excursion, contact the Hong Kong Amateur Fishing Society (☎ 2730-0442), Yau Ma Tei. While there are virtually no restrictions on sea fishing, it's a different story with fishing at reservoirs. There are limits on the quantity and size of fish taken from reservoirs, and the fishing season runs from September through March. A licence (HK$24) is required, valid for six months from September 1 to March 31, which can be obtained from the Water Supplies Department (☎ 2824-5000), Wan Chai.

**Fitness Centres** Getting fit is big business in Hong Kong, with the larger slices of the pie shared out between a few big names. The TLC Fitness chain of gyms have branches in Admiralty (☎ 2866-9968), Causeway Bay (☎ 2576-7668) and Jordan (☎ 2730-5038) and their monthly subscription starts at HK$415. Ray Wilson California Fitness Centre has two branches, one at 1 Wellington St in Central (☎ 2522-5229) and one at 88 Gloucester Rd in Wan Chai (☎ 2877-7070). New York Fitness (☎ 2543-2280) in Hollywood Rd offers aerobics, personal training, physiotherapy, massage and beauty therapy.

**Soccer** The 'Great Game' has caught the imagination of the Chinese, so competition for playing fields is keen. If you want to get serious about competing in matches, contact the Football Association (☎ 2712-9122), Kowloon. The association also maintains a women's division.

**Golf** There are five golf courses in Hong Kong. Green fees vary for visitors, but range anywhere from HK$450 (Deep Water Bay Golf Club) to HK$1400 (Fanling) for an 18 hole course. If you are signed in by a member, it can be considerably cheaper. On weekends, the courses are crowded and you pay more.

The Hong Kong Golf Club has two golf courses. The less expensive one is the nine hole course at Deep Water Bay (☎ 2812-7070), on the south side of Hong Kong Island. Considerably nicer is the course at Fanling (☎ 2670-1211) in the New Territories. The Discovery Bay Golf Club (☎ 2987-7271) on Lantau Island is perched high on a hill, offering some impressive views. So does the Shek O Country Club (☎ 2809-4458), which sits at the south-eastern tip of Hong Kong Island. The Clearwater Bay Golf & Country Club (☎ 2719-1595) is on the Sai Kung Peninsula in the New Territories.

If you want to purchase golf equipment, then try Nevada Bob's Golf stores which can be found in Central and Kowloon (☎ 2868-4234, 2368-6805).

**Hiking** Hiking is one of Hong Kong's best outdoor activities. The scenery is beautiful and the trails, most of which are in Country Parks, are well maintained. Lantau Island and the MacLehose Trail in the New Territories offer some outstanding hikes. Hiking is very popular, and many trails are very crowded on weekends. But on weekdays many trails are deserted.

The Government Publications Office (see Maps in the Facts for the Visitor chapter) has a series of excellent topographical maps. The Universal Publications maps of the New Territories and Outlying Islands are really worth pursuing as they are detailed, easy to read and waterproof. The Country Parks Authority (☎ 2733-2132) in Kowloon and the HKTA also have useful leaflets detailing good hikes. If you really want to scour the trails, consider picking up a copy of Kaarlo Schepel's *Magic Walks in Hong Kong*, which has three different volumes; another helpful volume is *Hong Kong Pathfinder* by Martin Williams, available in most Hong Kong bookshops.

If you're planning to hike a good distance, take into account the merciless sun, high heat and humidity during spring and summer. Even if there is cloud cover and no visible sun, you can still get bad sunburn at this latitude. November to March are the best months for strenuous treks. Hong Kong's countryside is also home to a variety of snakes, some poisonous. There's not a big chance that you'll run into one, especially if you stick to trails and avoid walking to dense underbrush. If you see a snake, the best thing to do is to walk away from it.

To contact hiking clubs, call the Federation of Hong Kong Hiking & Outdoor Activities Groups (☎ 2720-4042) in Sham Shui Po. More serious climbers should try the Hong Kong Mountaineering Union (☎ 2747-7003; fax 2770-7115) which runs training courses in climbing for sport, leisure, rock climbing and mountain craft. Also contact the YMCA (☎ 2369-2211) and the YWCA (☎ 2522-3101), who regularly arrange a series of adventurous walks around such areas as Silvermine Bay to Pui O, Shek

O to Chai Wan and other popular routes. The Green Lantau Association (☎ 2985-5099) organises walks on Lantau Island.

Serious walkers can join in the annual Trailwalker event, which is a race across the MacLehose Trail in the New Territories. This 100km walk is a real challenge, but it cuts through some of the most exciting countryside in Hong Kong. For more information, call the Trailwalker Charitable Trust c/o Oxfam (☎ 2520-2525).

**Horse-riding** Hong Kong's small size limits the opportunities for horse-riding. The Hong Kong Riding Union (☎ 2488-6886), Kowloon Tong, organises rides through the New Territories. On Hong Kong Island, riding lessons are available at the Pok Fu Lam Riding School (☎ 2550-1359). Classes are HK$340 per hour but they have a long waiting list. Other possibilities include the Lo Wu Saddle Club (☎ 2673-0066) and the Hong Kong Rider Club (☎ 2522-2142); the latter organises outings for two days and one night for HK$880.

**Ice-Skating** The rink on the 1st floor of the Cityplaza Shopping Centre (☎ 2885-4697) in Quarry Bay is a fine place to skate. Other rinks include the Whampoa Super Ice (☎ 2774-4899) at Whampoa Gardens in Hung Hom and Riviera Ice Chalet (☎ 2407-1100) at Riviera Plaza in Tsuen Wan.

**Parachuting** It's not the cheapest of sports, but you can't beat it for thrills. If you get your jollies by diving out of aircraft, contact the Hong Kong Parachute Association (☎ 2791-4550). Jumps take place almost any day when the weather is good.

**Running** If you'd like a morning jog with spectacular views, nothing beats the path around Victoria Peak on Harlech and Lugard Rds. Part of this is a 'fitness trail' with various exercise machines (parallel bars and the like). Almost as spectacular is the jog along Bowen Rd, which is closed to traffic and runs in an east-west direction in the hills above Wan Chai. As long as there are no races at the time, the horse-racing track at Happy Valley is an excellent place to run. There is also a running track in Victoria Park in Causeway Bay. On the Kowloon side, a popular place to run is the waterfront Promenade in Tsim Sha Tsui East. The problem here is that it's not a very long run, but the views are good and it's close to many of the hotels.

If you take running seriously, contact the Triathlon Association (☎ 2504-8282), who can fill you in on competitions. The Hong Kong International Marathon is held on the second day of the Chinese New Year. This has become a cross-border event, with part of the running course passing through China. The Coast of China Marathon is held in March. Contact the HKTA for more information on upcoming marathons.

**Sauna & Massage** OK, so it's not much of a sport. But it's a great way to relax following any activity, whether it's been a strenuous hike through the hills or a frantic day of dodging fellow shoppers in Causeway Bay. Sauna baths are popular in Hong Kong and many offer a legitimate massage service. Most are only for men, but the hotels and a few of the saunas have facilities for women as well.

On Hong Kong Island one of the biggest places is the New Paradise Health Club (☎ 2574-8807), 414 Lockhart Rd, Wan Chai. Services include sauna, steam room, jacuzzi and massage for both men and women; sauna and massage, plus one drink costs HK$238. Nearby the elaborate Sunny Paradise Sauna (☎ 2831-0123), 339-347 Lockhart Rd, only takes men, but it's legitimate. Saunas start at HK$340. One of the oldest places in town is the funky Hong Kong Sauna (☎ 2572-8325) at 388 Jaffe Rd, Wan Chai. This place is tiny and looks really seedy, but it's on the up and up. Again, it only takes men and a one hour sauna and massage will cost you HK$218.

Over in Kowloon, another reputable establishment is Crystal Spa (☎ 2722-6600), Basement 2, Harbour Crystal Centre, 100 Granville Rd, Tsim Sha Tsui. Go with a friend for HK$480. In pricey Tsim Sha Tsui

East is VIP Sauna (☎ 2311-2288), 13th floor, Autoplaza, 65 Mody Rd.

**Scuba Diving** Diving in Hong Kong is not very rewarding as pollution has killed off most of the interesting sea life and muddied the water. But there are organisations which put together dives near reefs and islands further out from Hong Kong. Bunn's Diving Equipment (☎ 2893-7899) in Wan Chai organises dives every Sunday from 9 am to 4.30 pm at a cost of HK$280; most of the dives are off the Sai Kung Peninsula. Bunn's also have branches in Mong Kok (☎ 2380-5344) and Kowloon (☎ 2382-0828). Other contacts to try are Scubamania (☎ 2792-0805) at 269 Hennessy Rd. Mandarin Divers (☎ 2554-7110) offers advanced, rescue, Divemaster and instructor courses as well as a whole range of other diving activities. Another company that can provide an array of courses from beginner to advanced is Pro Dive Education Centre (☎ 2890-4889; Web site www.divehk.com), 2nd floor, 27 Paterson St, Causeway Bay. Equipment can be bought at Ming's Sports Co (☎ 2376-0031) in Kowloon.

**Snooker and Pool** The Kowloon Cricket Club (☎ 2367-4141) has snooker tables, although the cost of joining the club may be prohibitive, unless you take the game seriously and plan to stay in Hong Kong for a while. Two bars in the same building in Wan Chai, the Flying Pig (☎ 2865-3730) and Ridgways (☎ 2865-6608), have pool tables (see the Entertainment chapter for details).

**Squash** There are about 600 public squash courts in Hong Kong. These become totally full in the evening or on holidays. The most modern facilities are to be found at the Hong Kong Squash Centre (☎ 2521-5072), next to Hong Kong Park in Central. They charge HK$27 per half hour, but you should book in advance. This is also the home of the Hong Kong Squash Rackets Association, which has done much to promote the sport. There are also squash courts in the Queen Elizabeth Stadium (☎ 2591-1331) in Wan Chai. In Sha

Tin in the New Territories, you can play squash at the Jubilee Sports Centre (☎ 2605-1212). Other venues include Kowloon Tsai Park (☎ 2336-7878) and the Lai Chi Kok Indoor Sports Games Hall (☎ 2745-2796) in Kowloon. Also in Kowloon, the Kowloon Cricket Club (☎ 2367-4141) has squash facilities. The event of the year is the Hong Kong Squash Open, held in September.

**Surfing** Not strictly allowed in Hong Kong, you do however find surfers at Big Wave Bay, Shek O. If you want to find out the state of play (before you fork out for that board), phone the Hong Kong Surfing Association (☎ 2858-5288).

**Swimming** Except for Kowloon and the north side of Hong Kong Island, there are good beaches spread throughout the territory. The most accessible beaches are on the south side of Hong Kong Island but some of these are becoming increasingly polluted. The best beaches can be found on the Outlying Islands and in the New Territories. The longest beach in Hong Kong is Cheung Sha on Lantau Island. Some beaches verge on the idyllic – Hung Shing Ye beach on Lamma Island in the early morning is wonderfully serene, despite the hulking power station opposite (see the Excursions chapter for more details). The other thing to be wary of are shark attacks. The major beaches all have shark nets (some in a state of disrepair), but you should think twice about swimming wherever you feel like it (eg off the side of a pleasure boat).

There is an official swimming season from 1 April to 31 October. At this time, the 42 gazetted public beaches in Hong Kong are staffed with lifeguards. When the swimming season is officially declared finished, the beaches become deserted no matter how hot the weather. Conversely, from the first day of the official swimming season until the last, expect the beaches to be chock-a-block on weekends and holidays. On weekdays, it's not bad at all. At most of the beaches you will find toilets, showers, changing rooms, snack stalls and sometimes restaurants.

Hong Kong's Urban Council also operates 13 public swimming pools. There are excellent pools in Kowloon Park (Tsim Sha Tsui) and Victoria Park (Causeway Bay). Many pools shut for the winter, but heated pools do exist, for example at the South China Athletic Association (☎ 2890-7736), 88 Caroline Hill Rd, Causeway Bay, and Morrison Hill Swimming Pool (☎ 2575-3028), 7 Oi Kwan Rd, Wan Chai. Try contacting the Amateur Swimming Association (☎ 2572-8594) in Wan Chai for more information.

**Tennis** The Hong Kong Tennis Centre (☎ 2574-9122) is at Wong Nai Chung Gap, a spectacular pass in the hills between Happy Valley and Deep Water Bay on Hong Kong Island. It's open from 7 am until 11 pm, but it's only easy to get a court during working hours; charges are HK$42 per hour (day) and HK$57 (night).

There are 14 courts in Victoria Park (☎ 2570-6186) in Causeway Bay which can be booked and are open from 7 am until 10 pm (again, very busy at night). There are four courts open from 7 am until 5 pm at Bowen Road Sports Ground (☎ 2528-2983) in the Mid-Levels; the charge is HK$42 per hour. The South China Athletic Association (☎ 2577-6932) also operates the tennis courts at King's Park, Yau Ma Tei.

Other facilities in Kowloon are at Tin Kwong Rd Playground in Kowloon City and at Kowloon Tsai Park in Shek Kip Mei. In the New Territories, you can play tennis at the Jubilee Sports Centre (☎ 2605-1212) in Sha Tin.

The Hong Kong Tennis Association (☎ 2504-8266) is in Victoria Park. This is the place to ask questions about available facilities and upcoming events. Spectators may be interested in the Hong Kong Open Tennis Championship, held every September. In October, there's the Hong Kong Tennis Classic in Victoria Park.

**Water-Skiing** The main venues for water-skiing are on the south side of Hong Kong Island at Deep Water Bay, Repulse Bay, Stanley and Tai Tam. The south side of

Lamma Island also attracts water-skiers. The Deep Water Bay Speedboat Company (☎ 2812-0391) charges HK$580 per hour for boat and ski hire. Contact the Hong Kong Waterski Association (☎ 2504-8168) for more help.

**Windsurfing** Windsurfing is extremely popular in Hong Kong, giving the territory its first Olympic gold medal at Atlanta in 1996. The best months for windsurfing are September to December when a steady north-east monsoon gets blowing. Windsurfing during a typhoon is *not* recommended! Rental fees are typically from HK$60 to HK$80 per hour. Around December, Stanley becomes the venue of the Hong Kong Open Windsurfing Championship.

At Stanley Main Beach on Hong Kong Island you can try the Pro Shop (☎ 2723-6816), who have a windsurfing course for HK$800 (four to five hours), or you can just rent a board hourly for much less. The Stanley Windsurfing Centre (☎ 2813-2882) is an alternative. Shek O is another good place on Hong Kong Island for windsurfing.

Equipment rentals are available in the New Territories at the Windsurfing Centre (☎ 2792-5605), Sha Ha (just past Sai Kung). They also sell second-hand equipment. On Cheung Chau you could try the Cheung Chau Windsurfing Centre (☎ 2981-8316), Tung Wan Beach; they are cheap but communication can be a problem. Try also phoning the Windsurfing Association of Hong Kong (☎ 2504-8255) who have courses from HK$800 (for youngsters), and should be able to fill you in on the action.

**Yachting & Sailing** With water on all sides, it makes sense that this is an extremely popular activity in Hong Kong. Bearing witness to this are seven major yacht clubs. The most prominent is the Royal Hong Kong Yacht Club, which has facilities throughout the territory. Even if you're not a member, check with any of the following clubs to see if races are being held and whether a ride on an entrant vessels is possible: Aberdeen Boat Club (☎ 2552-8182), Aberdeen Marina Club

(☎ 2555 8321), Hebe Haven Yacht Club (☎ 2719-9682), Royal Hong Kong Yacht Club (☎ 2832-2817) and the Hong Kong Yachting Association (☎ 2504- 8158). Some clubs hire vessels, others just let you use club facilities where you can moor your boat.

If smaller sailboats or hobie cats are more your style, you may be able to rent one down at St Stephen's Beach, near Stanley. Hobies rent for around HK$150 to HK$200 per hour, depending on the size.

If there is a group of you, you may also want to consider hiring a traditional Chinese junk for a day or evening. This is a great way to see the New Territories, or you could sail out to Lamma or Lantau islands for seafood lunches or dinners. Usually included in the price is eight hours of vessel hire, plus a captain and deckhand.

Charterboats (☎ 2555-8377) in Aberdeen hire out junks for HK$2500 (weekdays) and HK$3500 (weekends), which gives you a vessel that can seat 35 people. They also hire out cruisers that can take up to 60 people.

More expensive is the Aberdeen Marina Club (☎ 2555-8321), who hire out junks for HK$5200 (weekdays) and HK$6200 (weekends). Nowadays, junks are just rather mundane-looking diesel-powered boats, and many are made of fibreglass. Other outfits that rent out junks include; The Boatique (☎ 2555-9355), Aberdeen and Rent-A-Junk (☎ 2780-0387), Mong Kok.

One of the major events on the sailing calendar is the Hong Kong-Manila yacht race, which takes place every two years. Phone the Royal Hong Kong Yacht Club for more details (☎ 2832-2817).

## COURSES

Hong Kong is a good place to brush up on Chinese culture, be it learning how to make a decent pot of hot-and-sour soup, paint a classic landscape or jabber away in Cantonese. The following list includes some options for study. If you can't find what you're after, the Community Advice Bureau (☎ 2524-5444) is a volunteer-staffed operation that puts people together with the organisations they seek. Both the YMCA (☎ 2369-2211)

Mahjong is a Chinese game for four people, using tiles of various designs.

and YWCA (☎ 2522-3101) offer a broad range of cultural classes and three month courses. The courses include just about anything you can think of: basic Cantonese, continuing Cantonese, cooking, mahjong, watercolour painting, card games, computer courses, taijiquan, wine tasting, tennis and loads more. For the visual arts, check with the Hong Kong Museum of Art (☎ 2734-2167, 2734-2141) or the Hong Kong Arts Centre (☎ 2582-0219).

**Calligraphy** Most calligraphy courses in Hong Kong are given in Cantonese, but the Hong Kong Arts Centre has some in English as well. You can also check with the School of Professional and Continuing Education at Hong Kong University (☎ 2547-2225) and get them to send you a prospectus.

**Chinese Painting** Classes come and go with demand, but you can check with the Hong Kong Arts Centre (☎ 2582-0219) and the School of Professional and Continuing Education at Hong Kong University (☎ 2547-2225).

**Cuisine** Oddly enough, among the most regular providers of Chinese cooking lessons are two of Hong Kong's utility companies. Continuous classes spanning a vast range of Chinese, Thai and western cuisines are offered by the Towngas Cooking Centre (☎ 2576-1535), in Causeway Bay. The Home Management Centre (☎ 2510-2828) in North Point has classes on Wednesday morning, where you can learn three Chinese dishes in two hours for HK$85. For strictly Chinese/Asian fare, try the Oriental Culinary Institute (☎ 2882-3000) in Pok Fu Lam which offers basic and advanced courses, including dim sum, abalone and bird's nest soup plus the ever useful stir-fry. Classes cost HK$200 and are taught in Cantonese and English. In Mong Kok, Chinese cooking lessons are given at the Chopsticks Cooking Centre (☎ 2336-8433). If you want to learn how to cook the perfect cake, try Baker's Dozen (☎ 2826-9283) at Room 403, Yu Yuet Lai Building, 43-55 Wyndham St, Central.

**Dance** The Jean M Wong School of Ballet (☎ 2886-3992) has seven schools across the territory where you can study Chinese ethnic minority dances as well as Balinese dance, ballet, jazz dance and other western styles. Prices are reasonable at HK$150 per hour. Salsa, Latin, ballroom, rock 'n' roll and disco classes are all on offer at Teresa Woods Dance Studios (☎ 2987-0592; Web site www.teresawood.com), 18-20 Lyndhurst Terrace, Central. Check the classified pages of *HK Magazine* for other schools and individuals that teach even more exotic dance routines like belly dancing.

**Language** Not many people take the time and considerable effort needed to learn Cantonese, but there are a number of schools where you can learn. With China's economy booming, demand for Mandarin classes has soared. However, outside of the classroom, Hong Kong is a not a good place to learn Mandarin as you may pick up an atrocious accent. However, Hong Kongers prefer to use Mandarin rather than Cantonese with visitors, so they can practise at the same time.

The Chinese University in Hong Kong has courses in Cantonese and Mandarin. Classes can be arranged through the New Asia Yale centre in the China Language Institute, which

---

### Kung Fu

Many people have been bewitched by the spell of kung fu, plunging into its world of legends and mystery. For the novice, however, it promises a way that becomes more labyrinthine with every step, and the skills it promises seem ever more distant. But for those who take to it, kung fu becomes a rewarding journey with a unique destination. Often misinterpreted as simply a way to fight, kung fu teaches an approach to life that stresses patience, endurance, magnanimity and humility. When two people discover they share an interest in martial arts, it's the cue for an endless exchange of techniques and anecdotes. It's a club mentality for members only.

The first well-known modern missionary of this ancient art was Bruce Lee, who displayed skills up there with the likes of the Silver Surfer. Despite having a genuine skill, his films projected little more than a violent cinematic form of kung fu, a distortion of the original. Kung fu literally means skill, and can be applied to any artistic achievement that has been reached through hard work. It's the difficult journey towards mastery that gives kung fu its mystery, grace and skill. The films of Bruce Lee are intriguing, but kung fu is more than flares and sideburns. It's not a simple, just-add-water formula but a heady brew made from discipline, patience and hard work.

One thing that keeps adherents on the gruelling path to achievement are the stories and legends that circulate around the martial arts community. Have you heard about the Malaysian Five Ancestors master who broke the leg of a Thai boxer – with his finger? No way! Or what about Sun Lutang, the famous taijiquan, xingyi and bagua master who could stand with one side of his body flush against the wall, from the side of his foot to his shoulder, and lift the other leg without losing his balance! Are you kidding!?

**Wing Chun Kung Fu** Wing chun is a ferocious and dynamic system that promises reasonably quick results for those who study it. It was invented by a nun named Ng Wai from the famous Shaolin Monastery in Henan Province, who taught her skills to a young girl named Wing Chun. This was the style that Bruce Lee studied, and although he developed his own style, wing chun had an enormous influence on him.

---

is associated with the university. There are three terms a year – one 10-week summer term and two regular 15-week terms. Classes are also held by the School of Professional and Continuing Education at Hong Kong University (☎ 2547- 2225). The British Council (☎ 2913-5500) is also a good place to study Cantonese and Mandarin. Classes are also held in both languages by the YMCA (☎ 2369-2211) and the YWCA (☎ 2522-3101). Venture (☎ 2507-4985), 163 Hennessy Rd, is a British-run school which offers lessons for learning Cantonese; the school is small, but attractive and welcoming.

There are a number of private language schools which cater to individuals or companies. These informal schools offer more flexibility and will even dispatch a teacher to a company to teach the whole staff if need be. Considering all the native Chinese speakers in town, tuition is not cheap at these places, often running at around H\$300 plus per lesson for one-on-one instruction. Some to consider include the Chinese Language Institute of Hong Kong (☎ 2524-8678) in Central, and the Chinese Language Society of Hong Kong (☎ 2529-1638) in Wan Chai.

Another way is to look through the classifieds sections of the *South China Morning Post*, *Hong Kong Standard* and English-language magazines for schools and individual teachers. Alternatively, you could advertise yourself, looking for a teacher. This could be a good idea, as you could get either a language partner or very cheap tuition.

**Martial Arts** Chinese *gongfu*, or kung fu as it's often called, has formed the basis for many Asian martial arts. There are several organisations offering training in various schools of Chinese martial arts *(wushu)*, as well as other Asian disciplines. Popular Chinese arts include taijiquan and Wing Chun kung fu, while karate, judo and aikido are Japanese, and taekwando is Korean. A good idea is to check the classifieds pages of the English newspapers and magazines for contact numbers of teachers, or go to the

Wing chun suits people with a slim build, as it emphasises speed rather than strength. Evasion, subterfuge and rapid strikes are the hallmarks of the wing chun system; the forms are simple and direct, doing away with the pretty flourishes that characterise other styles. While some say that this makes the art unattractive, it is typical of wing chun that it stresses effectiveness rather than glamour.

The theory of wing chun is enshrined in its 'centre-line theory', which concentrates attacks and blocks on an imaginary line down the centre of the body. The line runs through the sensitive regions: eyes, nose, lips, mouth, throat, heart, solar plexus and groin. Any blow that lands on any of these points is debilitating and dangerous; the three 'empty hand' forms train arm and leg movements that both attack and defend this line. None of the blocks stray beyond the width of the shoulders, as this limits the range of possible attacks, and punches follow the same theory. This gives the forms of wing chun its distinctive simplicity. The sweeps of western boxers are removed and instead the punch takes its strength mainly from the shoulders, elbows and wrist. Punches are delivered in a straight line, along the shortest distances between puncher and punched, with great rapidity. A training routine for two called *chi sau* or 'sticking hands' teaches the student how to be soft in response to attacks; softness promotes relaxation in the practitioner and fosters speedy counterattacks.

Weapons in the wing chun arsenal include the twin wing chun butterfly knives, which are sharp and heavy, and the extremely long pole, which requires considerable strength to handle with skill. The philosophy of simplicity also belongs to weapon skills, so once the empty hand forms are learned, ability with weapons falls into place.

Despite being an excellent system for self-defence, wing chun practitioners often tend to be over-confident and cocky, which is contrary to the spirit of the system. Wing chun forms are not especially strenuous and often do not build up the stamina necessary for students who want to compete professionally. For your average punter, however, the study of wing chun can provide a whole range of useful skills. See the listings at the end of the Martial Arts sections for some associations that teach wing chun and kung fu. ∎

parks in the early morning in search of someone who will teach you. Among those listed below, the Hong Kong Taichi Union charges HK$500 a month for weekly classes (but their English is not good) and the Hong Kong Wushu Union only has classes for children. Relevant addresses include:

*Chinese Martial Arts Association* – (☎ 2504-8164)

*Hong Kong Amateur Karatedo Association* – (☎ 2891-9705) Room 1006, Queen Elizabeth Stadium, 18 Oi Kwan Rd, Wan Chai

*Hong Kong Chinese Martial Arts Association* – (☎ 2394-4803) 9th floor, 687A Nathan Rd, Kowloon

*Hong Kong Taekwondo Association* – (☎ 2504-8116) Room 1014, Sports House, No 1, Stadium Path, Causeway Bay

*Hong Kong Taichi Association* – (☎ 2395-4884) 11th floor, 60 Argyle St, Kowloon

*Hong Kong Wushu Union* – (☎ 2504-8226) 3rd floor, 62 Castle Peak Rd, Kowloon

*South China Athletic Association* – (☎ 2577-6932) 88 Caroline Hill Rd, Causeway Bay

*Wing Chun Kung Fu Club* (☎ 2385-5908) – 1st floor, No 12, Man Yuen House, Jordan Ferry Point, Kowloon

*Wing Tsun Martial Arts Association* – (☎ 2385-7115) Block A, 8th floor, 440-442 Nathan Rd, Kowloon

*YMCA* – (☎ 2369-2211) 41 Salisbury Rd, Tsim Sha Tsui

**Pottery** The Pottery Workshop (☎ 2525-7949) at the Fringe Club, 2 Lower Albert Rd in Central has classes as well as exhibitions. The art auction house Christie's (☎ 2521-5396) occasionally organises classes on Chinese ceramics that take you into the refined world of porcelain.

THINGS TO SEE & DO

# Places to Stay

Though Hong Kong caters to hordes of visitors, the territory does not have very diverse accommodation options. There are three basic categories: cramped guesthouses; adequate but uninspiring mid-range hotels; and luxury hotels, some of which are considered the world's finest. Recently there also has been a decline in the number of hotel rooms.

Prices, even for budget accommodation, are higher than most other Asian cities and you don't get a whole lot for your money, except in some of the top-end places. At the same time, within each category there is a good deal of choice, and you should be able to find a comfortable place to stay. The sharp turnaround in prices during late 1997 and early 1998 is worth bearing in mind. Due to the sharp fall-off in tourists visiting the ex-colony after the handover (especially from Japan and South Korea), many mid-range and luxury hotels were offering 'winter packages' in a bid to attract customers. Many hotels were slashing up to 50% off their prices or offering other benefits to their guests – it's worth phoning around first or booking through a travel agent who can advise on cheap options. The general consensus is that if the tourist slump continues, prices will drop permanently. The prices below are therefore really just a general guide, since the market has been so unpredictable since the handover.

Dominating the lower end of the market are the so-called guesthouses, usually a block of tiny rooms squeezed into a converted apartment or two. Often there are several guesthouses operating out of the same building. Even the cheapest option, a dormitory bed at one of the youth hostels, is no bargain at HK$50. The picture brightens up a bit if there are two of you. Find a double room in a clean guesthouse for around HK$200 and your accommodation cost falls to a more bearable level. Although the room may be a glorified closet, at least it's yours. Prices are much cheaper in Macau at the budget end – it could well be more fun to pop over to Macau on the ferry, spend a few days there and head back (just don't gamble away your savings in the process!). Try and haggle and find out what the best offer is; a lot of places may be very eager to fill up rooms.

Hong Kong's mid-range hotels are as expensive as top-end places in many other cities. Prices range anywhere from HK$600 (relatively scarce) to over HK$2000 for a double room. Singles are sometimes priced a bit lower. The average price you're likely to encounter is HK$1000. This will usually buy you a somewhat small room with bath and shower, TV, air-con and the other amenities. The best thing about these hotels is that there is a lot of them – several dozen in fact – so you can find one in almost any part of urban Hong Kong.

For those who can afford HK$2000 or more for a room, a stay in one of Hong Kong's luxury hotels is an experience worth savouring. Of course one must be selective: there are plenty of average hotels that charge top-end rates, but a few – such as The Peninsula, Island Shangri-La and Regent – offer comfort, amenities and service that can compete with the world's finest five-star hotels.

In the past, during the peak tourist seasons of September to January and March to June mid-range and top-end hotel rates would rise by between 10% and 30%. As mentioned previously, the tourist downfall has had a dramatic impact on room prices. Of course predicting the future popularity of Hong Kong as a tourist destination is impossible, but if the downward trend continues, bargains may regularly become available. Prices given in this chapter represent low season, or standard, rates – you could well find the price much lower when you visit Hong Kong.

If you arrive needing somewehere to stay, the Hong Kong Hotels Association (☎ 2383-8380; email hkha@att.net.hk; Web site www.hkta.org.hkha) has reservation centres at Kai Tak and Chek Lap Kok airports. They can find you a mid-range or luxury room at a rate up to 50% lower than if you were to just walk up to the front desk. They deal with 75 hotels and have a selection of brochures for each, so you can compare facilities. They also do reasonable last-minute booking deals. The centre does not handle any budget accommodation.

Booking hotels through a travel agent can also garner substantial discounts – sometimes as much as 40% off the walk-in price. If you want to book either a mid-range or luxury hotel, you can call Phoenix Services (☎ 2722-7378; fax 2369-8884), Room A, 7th floor, Milton Mansion, 96 Nathan Rd, Tsim Sha Tsui, who can often get you 20% to 30% off what you would expect at the hotel. Another place that handles hotel bookings is Traveller Services (☎ 2375-2222; fax 2375-2233; Web site www.traveler.com.hk), Room 1012, Silvercord Tower 1, 30 Canton Rd, Tsim Sha Tsui. At the time of writing, many airlines and hotels were in cahoots to attract business. Airlines such as British Airways and Cathay Pacific were offering super-cheap return flights (for one or two) to Hong Kong with a set number of nights in a hotel.

The Hong Kong Tourist Association (HKTA) publishes a *Hotel Guide* that lists more than 80 hotels, complete with prices and photos. To get hold of this before you leave, contact the nearest HKTA overseas office (see the Tourist Offices section of the Facts for the Visitor chapter). You can also get a list of hotels by fax from the HKTA by contacting their fax information service.

### WHERE TO STAY
For the most part, Central and Tsim Sha Tsui are the most convenient for public transport. However, between the MTR and the bus network, almost anywhere is pretty easy to get to, so this need not be a major consideration. At any rate Central and Admiralty have only luxury hotels (with one exception), so you can pretty much rule these districts out if that's beyond your budget.

Staying in Tsim Sha Tsui, Causeway Bay or Wan Chai puts you close to a wide choice of restaurants, bars and shopping, and all have good transport connections. Price or room availability may push you out a bit further to areas like Mong Kok, or North Point on Hong Kong Island; while these areas aren't as cosmopolitan, they have their own gritty charm, and will give you a chance to see where average Hong Kongers live.

Most of the budget accommodation is clustered in Tsim Sha Tsui, and to a lesser degree in Causeway Bay. Mid-range hotels are all over the place, but the majority are in Kowloon, from Tsim Sha Tsui to Mong Kok. There are also quite a few in Wan Chai. It's easy to pick out the luxury accommodation: just look for the hotels with the fantastic harbour views.

If you need easy access to Kai Tak airport, you can't get much closer than at the *Regal Airport Hotel* (☎ 2718-0333; fax 2718-4111; email regalrah@navigator.com), Sa Po Rd, Kowloon. The hotel is linked to the airport by a pedestrian overpass, so you can walk from your room right to the boarding gate. The hotel will close shortly after the opening of Chek Lap Kok, and a new one set up at the new airport. It will be renamed the *Regal Bauhinia Airport Hotel*. Doubles and twins range from HK$1300 to HK$2050.

### PLACES TO STAY – BUDGET
Dormitory beds in the Chungking Mansions and Mirador Arcade will cost you HK$60 and up, and there is a shrinking number of guesthouses that have such accommodation. A few, like the Garden Hostel in Mirador Arcade (see under Dormitories following) have women-only dormitories. The average double room in a guesthouse is slightly larger than a shoe box, with the bed taking up most of the floor space. Almost all rooms come with TV and air-conditioning. The price difference between singles and doubles ranges from HK$50 to HK$100. The cheapest rooms have no attached bath, and cost anywhere from HK$120 to HK$300. Rooms with a private washroom range from HK$160 to HK$550. Often the 'washroom'

is little more than a shower cubicle with a sink and toilet crammed in it. Triple rooms are available in some places, and there are a few places that still have dormitory accommodation. If you're looking to pay HK$450 or more for a double room, consider some of the cheapest mid-range hotels: for an extra HK$100 you'll likely get a much better environment. Remember that when business is slow these places are fishing for customers, so you can haggle the price down if they seem desperate. There are loads of guesthouses about, so move on to the next one if you think you might find something offering better value for money.

Before handing over any money, first check the room – especially the plumbing and air-con. Standards of cleanliness vary wildly from place to place, and also check out the facilities – some guesthouses have email and charge fair rates for usage (although the majority are not wired up) while others offer a laundry service and have a small kitchen.

In general it's safe to leave your luggage in your room provided there's a lock on the door. In some places you can keep your bags in a storage closet, but never leave valuables unattended, even for a few minutes. Another warning: be wary of touts who hang around the airport to lure backpackers with offers of cheap rooms. If they insist on escorting you to their guesthouse, it's probably best to decline. Some touts will even flash name cards of hostels and guesthouses which have been highly recommended in Lonely Planet or other guidebooks, and then they take you to some other dump. If they persist, grab their business card and tell them you will go yourself and check the place out. These characters also work the airport bus stops, particularly in Tsim Sha Tsui.

## Youth Hostels

The cheapest accommodation is through a member hotel of the Hong Kong Youth Hostels Association (HKYHA), which have cheap dorm beds for both members and non-members. It is cheaper to be a member (annual membership HK$180), although if you pay the non-member rate (HK$30 more) for six nights, then you will automatically get membership.

There is only one youth hostel close to the city, the *Ma Wui Hall* (☎/fax 2817-5715), perched atop Mt Davis, near Kennedy Town on Hong Kong Island. From Central it's about a 20 to 30 minute bus ride, and then a 30 minute hike from the bus stop to the hostel. On the other hand, this place is clean, quiet, has great views of the harbour and costs only HK$65 (members) or HK$95 (non-members) per night. There are cooking facilities, secure lockers and a TV and recreation room. The hostel has 112 beds and is open from 7 am to 11 pm. Call ahead to make sure there's a bed before you make the trek out here.

The hostel now offers a shuttle bus from the Macau ferry terminal in Sheung Wan, but there are only four departures a day from the hostel, so phone first and get the time of the next service. To get to the Macau ferry terminal from the airport, take the A2 airport bus. Otherwise take bus No 5B, 47 or 77 and get off at Felix Villas (the 5B terminus) on Victoria Rd. (Note: the 5B only runs from 5.55 am to 10.15 am and from 4.40 pm to 8.20 pm.) From the bus stop, walk back 100m. Look for the YHA sign and follow Mt Davis Path (not to be confused with Mt Davis Rd) – there is a shortcut which is signposted halfway up the hill. The walk takes 20 to 30 minutes. If you come from the airport, take the A2 bus to Central, then change to the 5B or 47 bus. Bus No 5B runs from Paterson St in Causeway Bay to Felix Villas. Bus No 47 starts at the Exchange Square Bus Terminus. You're least likely to use bus No 77, which runs westwards through to Aberdeen.

## Dormitories

These are dwindling in number, but there are still a few left in Kowloon. At 33 Hankow Rd is the *Victoria Hostel* (Map 5; ☎ 2376-0621; fax 2376-2609; email vhostel@ hkstar.com; Web site www.hkstar.com/ vhostel) which has dorm beds starting at HK$90. Reasonable singles start at HK$350 and doubles at HK$450. The hostel offers free email access and you get a 15% discount if you book your room through their Web site.

The *STB Hostel* (Map 4; ☎ 2710-9199; fax 2385-0153; email stbhoste@netvigator.com), operated by the Hong Kong Student Travel Bureau, has 12 dorm beds for HK$160 each per night (eight male, four female). It also has doubles/triples with bathroom for HK$460/540. Suites cost HK$600. It's clean and relatively quiet and decent English is spoken, although some travellers have encountered less than friendly management in the past. If you have an ISIC card you can get a 10% discount. Lockers are available (for a fee), and they have a photocopier, fax and email facilities for guest use, as well as a small library. The hostel is on floors 1-3, Great Eastern Mansion, 255-261 Reclamation St, Mong Kok, just to the west of Yau Ma Tei MTR station.

On the 16th floor of A Block in Chungking Mansions (refer to the following Guesthouses section) is the popular *Travellers' Hostel* (Map 5; ☎ 2368-7710), which has mixed dormitory accommodation for HK$70. Cooking facilities are available. There are also double rooms with/without attached bath for HK$150/170. This place attracts a steady stream of travellers, and has a useful bulletin board.

*Garden Hostel* (Map 5; ☎ 2721-8567), 3rd floor, Flat F4, Mirador Arcade, 58 Nathan Rd, Tsim Sha Tsui, has dorm beds for HK$60. There's also separate dorms for men and women, and a large balcony where you can crack open a beer. If you want to go upmarket, there's doubles with showers for HK$170. Excellent English is spoken here, the atmosphere is good and they have phonecards for sale.

If you want something different, *Tung O Bay Homestay* on Lamma Island has dorm beds for HK$100 and up (see the Other Guesthouses entry under the next section).

## Guesthouses

Tsim Sha Tsui is the place to go for the cheapest guesthouses. Although the area can be noisy, at least you are close to inexpensive noodle shops and fast food places, as well as several useful bus routes, airport bus stops, the MTR and the Star Ferry Terminal. It's only a short stroll down to splendid nocturnal views across Victoria Harbour to Central. Some of the guesthouses offer a discount if you stay for more than one week, so ask.

**Chungking Mansions (Map 5)** The very mention of this name can strike horror into some backpackers, while others look back with a twisted sort of fondness. Creaking with the weight of dozens of guesthouses, this enormous high-rise dump sits at 30 Nathan Rd, in the heart of Tsim Sha Tsui. It may not be pretty, but it's about the cheapest place to stay in Hong Kong. To really get in the mood, watch the film *Chungking Express* before heading to Hong Kong. It was partly shot in the mansions and captures its disorientating scale and weirdness.

Some of the guesthouses are actually quite nice inside. It's getting to them that makes for the Chungking Mansions experience. Greeting visitors at the Nathan Rd entrance is the ever-present pack of shiftless indolents who apparently have nothing better to do than eye you and your possessions while scheming ways to score quick cash. Make your way past rows of tiny shops – selling everything from tailored suits to trashy novels – to find the lifts labelled for the block you're headed to. This is the really fun part. There are only two tiny overworked lifts for each 17 storey block, often giving you a choice between a long line or a sweaty walk up the fire stairs. If the lift ever breaks down when full, God help you. Lines for the A and B blocks are the worst. The lifts for the C, D and E blocks have much less traffic. Sooner or later the antiquated lifts will force you to use the fire stairs. This could be your clearest memory of Chungking Mansions: the grime, grease and trash that line some of these staircases seem to predate the building itself.

Adding to the fun are the occasional midnight raids by the police. Mostly they are looking for illegal immigrants – if your passport is at a consulate getting visa stamps, this could create a problem. At least try to have a photocopy of your passport and some other picture ID card.

There have been calls to raze Chungking Mansions because it's an eyesore and a fire-trap. The place is actually improving somewhat, though it's not in danger of losing its notoriety. After a 1993 fire, there was a crackdown on safety violations, and many guesthouses were shut down. Others survived by raising their standards. Even so, the stairwells remain hellish and the filth is almost surreal.

It's usually possible to bargain for a bed, especially when business is slack. You can often negotiate a cheaper price if you stay a long time, but never do that on the first night. Stay one night and find out how you like it before handing over two weeks' rent. Once you pay, there are no refunds, and be certain to get a receipt. Below is just a sampling of the dozens of Chungking Mansions guest-houses. The prices listed are only a guide and vary with the season, peaking in summer and during certain holidays such as Easter.

### A Block:
*Chungking House* – (☎ 2366-5362) 4th & 5th floors; not very friendly; quiet singles with attached bath for HK$230, and doubles for HK$345

*Park Guesthouse* – (☎ 2368-1689) 15th floor; clean and friendly; singles from HK$100 (no shower) to HK$150 (with shower/air-con) and doubles from HK$200

*Peking Guesthouse* – (☎ 2723-8320) 12th floor; friendly management, clean and cheery; singles/doubles (with bath) for HK$180/200

*Tom's Guesthouse* – (☎ 2722-4956) 8th floor; has bright, airy singles/doubles with attached bath from HK$160/180

### B Block:
*Amar Guesthouse* – (☎ 2368-4869) 17th floor; poorly spoken English; singles/doubles for HK$180

*Hong Kong Guesthouse* – (☎ 2723-7842) 12th floor; quite friendly; singles/doubles from HK$150/220

*New Washington Guesthouse* – (☎ 2366-5798) 13th floor; friendly, clean and popular; singles for HK$130 (without shower), HK$150 (with) and doubles for HK$200 (with shower)

*Tom's Guesthouse* (2nd branch) – (☎ 2367-9258) 16th floor; not a lot of English spoken; clean rooms; singles/doubles for HK$150/200

### C Block:
*Garden Guesthouse* – (☎ 2368-0981) 16th floor; excellent but more pricey; singles/doubles with private bath for HK$200/300 (there's also a branch on the 7th floor)

*New Chungking Guesthouse* – (☎ 2368-0981) 7th floor; pleasant and friendly place; singles/doubles for HK$200/300

*New Grand Guesthouse* and *Osaka Guesthouse* – (☎ 2311-1702) both on 13th floor, run by the same owner; singles/doubles for HK$180/250; also has a fax machine

*Tom's Guesthouse* (3rd branch) – (☎ 2367-9258) 16th floor; clean, quiet and friendly; singles/doubles HK$200/250

### D Block:
*Fortuna Guesthouse* – (☎ 2366-4524) 8th floor; not a lot of English spoken; singles/doubles HK$160/200

*Royal Plaza Inn* – (☎ 2367-1424) 5th floor; rooms with shared bath for HK$180 to HK$250

### E Block:
*Mandarin Guesthouse* – (☎ 2366-0073) 13th floor; clean and nice rooms; singles with/without bath for HK$180/150, and doubles from HK$180

*Regent Inn Guesthouse* – (☎ 2722-08330) 6th floor; quite nice, each room has its own phone; singles with/without bath from HK$220/200

**Other Guesthouses** If you just can't stomach staying at Chungking Mansions, don't despair. There are other options, both

---

**Unmansionables**

For a real-life vision of hell, take a look down the light wells of Chungking Mansions' D block. It's dark, dirty, festooned with pipes and wires and covered in what looks like the debris of half a century. Why put rubbish in the bin when it's so much easier to throw it out the window? Discarded plastic bags fall only halfway before lodging on a ledge or drainpipe. Soon they're joined by old newspapers, used toilet paper, underwear, half-eaten food, an expired rat (was it too dirty for him too?).

As for the lifts, they're a little slice of hell all their own. A buzzer sounds when too many people have clambered aboard them and a sign inside one helpfully announces: 'The Irresponsible for Accident due to Overloading'.

**Robert Storey**

in Tsim Sha Tsui and Causeway Bay. If you want a quieter and more mundane visit (at a higher price) the guesthouses listed below can help. Also bear in mind that prices fluctuate when business is bad for guesthouses, so ask for their cheapest offer; the prices could well be lower than those quoted below.

In Tsim Sha Tsui, *Mirador Arcade* (Map 5) at 58 Nathan Rd is like a scaled-down version of Chungking Mansions, but considerably cleaner and roomier. It's on Nathan Rd between Mody and Carnarvon Rds, one block north of Chungking. A reasonably clean and cheap option here is *Man Hing Lung Guesthouse* (☎ 2722-0678) on the 14th floor in Flat F2. All rooms come with air-con and TV and most have private baths. Singles usually cost HK$280 to HK$300, but at time of writing were going for HK$150.

On the 13th floor is the *Kowloon Hotel* (☎ 2311-2523) and *New Garden Hotel* (same phone and owner). Singles or doubles with shared bath are HK$150 to HK$300. Doubles with private bath and refrigerator cost HK$300 to HK$450. Ask about discounts if you want to rent long-term. Also up on the 13th floor is the *Ajit Guesthouse* (☎ 2369-1201) which has clean single rooms with shared bath for HK$150. On the 6th floor, Flat A3, is the *Oriental Pearl Hostel* (☎ 2723-3439) which has singles with shower for HK$200 and doubles with bath for HK$200/300.

There are more guesthouses to be found in Tsim Sha Tsui along Cameron Rd, near the intersection with Chatham Rd. The Lyton Building, 32-40 Mody Rd, also has several average guesthouses, all with private bath, air-con and TV. Examples include the *Frank Mody House* (☎ 2724-4113) on the 7th floor (take lift No 4 at the back) which has doubles/triples with shower for HK$400/500 and the *Lyton House Inn* (☎ 2367-3791) on the 6th floor, with doubles from HK$300.

In Hankow Rd you can find the *Lucky Hotel* (Map 5; ☎ 2926-3220) whose friendly owner offers doubles with shared showers for HK$300.

Further north in Yau Ma Tei, the *New Lucky Mansions* at 300 Nathan Rd (entrance on Jordan Rd) is in a fairly decent neighbourhood and has a number of places to choose from in different price ranges.

Causeway Bay has a number of decent guesthouses, though they are generally more expensive than those in Tsim Sha Tsui. One which gets great reviews from travellers is the *Noble Hostel* (Map 7; ☎ 2808-0117), Flat A3, 17th floor, Great George Building, 27 Paterson St. Singles with private bath are HK$380, doubles with shared bath are HK$320 to HK$340, and doubles with private bath are HK$420. The rooms are small but very clean, and the lobby has a small lending library.

About one block north is the friendly and sparkling clean *Payless Inn* (Map 7; ☎ 2808-1030), Flat A, 5th floor, Fairview Mansion, 51 Paterson St. Singles/doubles without bath are HK$280/350, and doubles with bath HK$500. One floor below is the *Jetvan Traveller's House* (Map 7; ☎ 2890-8133). This place isn't bad, but not as comfortable as the Payless Inn, and the beds are tiny. Singles/doubles without bath are HK$300/400.

On the southern side of Causeway Bay and next door to a church is the *Causeway Bay Guest House* (Map 7; ☎ 2895-2013), Flat B, 1st floor, Lai Yee Building, 44A-D, Leighton Lane. With only seven rooms, it's easily filled up, but if you can get one you'll probably be happy with it. All are quite clean and have attached bathrooms. Singles are HK$400 (with shower), doubles HK$500 and triples HK$600. The owner speaks good English; the guesthouse is quite near the No 10 stop of the A3 airport bus.

Nearby, the Phoenix Apartments building (Map 7), 70 Lee Garden Rd, has a plethora of somewhat sleazier guesthouses. Most are 'love hotels' where rooms are rented by the hour; ambiguous messages like 'special for after midnight' decorate their business cards. Nevertheless, they are also available for more legitimate overnight stays, if you can put up with the pink wallpaper, mirrored ceilings, circular beds and chrome furniture that some entice you with. Prices here depend on whether you stay during the week or at weekends – it's far more expensive on weekends, as this is the time that the 'love-weekenders' come out to play and the rooms are full; the staff are usually not that friendly and the spoken English is pretty diabolical. The hostels also charge by the day which is far more expensive – get it across that you want it just for the night, if that's what you want; be sure to confirm the checkout time before paying, as it can be early. One of the cheapest places is the *Wah Lai Villa,* on the 4th floor, where HK$220 will get you a round bed with mirror headboard for the night. The *Garden Guest House* (☎ 2577-7391) is a quiet, clean establishment with doubles at HK$450. *Dragon Inn* (☎ 2576-3849) in Flat G on the 2nd floor has Monday to Friday doubles at HK$380. There are also more guesthouses/love motels in the Leishun Court building at 116 Leighton Rd, and at 14-20 Pak Sha Rd. Be warned, these places have little character and few facilities to support those staying more than a few nights.

Adventurous travellers can make it out to the *Tung O Bay Homestay* (Map 11; ☎ 2982-8461; fax 2982-8424) on Lamma Island. It features spacious dorms (HK$100 per bed), double rooms (HK$350), meals, hot tubs and a sandy beach to boot. A full breakfast is included in the price. The energetic owner throws together dinner as well if you want (and the dinners are cheap). The hot tub can seat a party and is situated on the beach, fired up by driftwood. To get there, take the ferry from Aberdeen to Mo Tat Wan, turn left at the Coral Restaurant and follow the path for 25 minutes to the beach. It's also possible to get there from Sok Kwu Wan over the hills, but the walk is more strenuous and it's easy to get lost.

## PLACES TO STAY – MIDDLE

Mid-priced accommodation consists mainly of business/tourist hotels. There is little to distinguish one from another. At the very least, rooms will have a bathroom with shower, bath and toilet; air-con; telephone; and TV. Some hotels also have in-house cable TV, refrigerators, toiletries and other small amenities. Many have business centres and email facilities.

Be warned that some hotels charge for local calls. If you are going to make local calls, you may get charged HK$5 a call, which is ridiculous considering the hotel does not get charged. Often this is not clearly stated, so ask beforehand. Before you decide to stay in a better class mid-range hotel, it's worth bearing in mind that heavily discounted packages were being offered by many top-end hotels in early 1998.

Surprisingly few hotels have swimming pools. If this is something you want, on Hong Kong Island check out the *City Garden*, *Empire*, *Newton Hong Kong* and *Wharney* hotels. In Kowloon, the *Metropole*, *Miramar* and *Prudential* are the only mid-range hotels with pools (needless to say, we're not talking Olympic-size here).

In comparison with most other major cities, almost none of the mid-range hotels in Hong Kong offer good value for money. High demand and soaring property values keep accommodation costs high, and there's really no way of getting around it. There are a few places that might be considered better deals though. On Hong Kong Island, the *Newton Hotel Hong Kong* in North Point is quite nicely furnished and, once you're inside, feels a bit like a luxury hotel. It also has a rooftop pool with a great view. Over in Kowloon, the *Eaton Hotel* has quite comfortable rooms and good service despite its relatively low rates. Staying at the *Kowloon Hotel* (which is run by the Peninsula group) allows you to use the fantastic pool, health club and other gorgeous facilities at the nearby Peninsula. If you can manage to book a room at the *Salisbury YMCA* you'll be rewarded with their courteous, professional service, a comfortable room and excellent exercise facilities.

Within the mid-priced category are a few places that deserve special mention for their low prices, all located in Kowloon. The *New Kings Hotel* has recently had a facelift and has singles for HK$550 and doubles for HK$650 to HK$750. The *International Hotel* has similarly priced rooms.

Also reasonably cheap is the hostel accommodation offered several non-profit organisations, such as the Salvation Army's *Booth Lodge* in Yau Ma Tei. There is also the *Caritas Bianchi Lodge* in Yau Ma Tei and Mong Kok. The *YMCA International House* in Yau Ma Tei and the *Anne Black Guest House (YWCA)* in Mong Kok are two other options.

The hotels listed below are divided by area and in as many cases as possible are indicated on the appropriate area maps. Prices for double rooms refer to twin rooms as well. Some hotels that have only double rooms give a lower rate for single occupancy. The rates do not include the 10% service charge or 5% government tax.

### Central (Map 6)

There is only one place near this district that falls outside the luxury hotel category. The YWCA's *Garden View International House* (☎ 2877-3737; fax 2845-6263) at 1 MacDonnell Rd hovers on the border between Central and the Mid-Levels and overlooks the Zoological & Botanical Gardens. Twin rooms range from HK$880 to HK$990 and suites range from HK$1512 to HK$1815. There is a fast-food restaurant on the ground floor.

### Wan Chai & Causeway Bay (Map 7)

Hotels in these districts tend to be a bit more expensive than similar places in Kowloon or eastern Hong Kong Island. This is due to their proximity to Central. If you stay here, you're paying for the location. A few of these hotels offer nice harbour views, but you have to pay for them.

*Charterhouse Hotel* – (☎ 2833-5566; fax 2833-5888; email info@charterhouse.com; Web site www.charterhouse.com); 209-219 Wan Chai Rd, Wan Chai; singles/doubles from HK$1400/1750 to HK$1750/1850 and suites from HK$2500

*Empire Hotel* – (☎ 2866-9111; fax 2861-3121; email booking@empire-hotel.com; Internet www.empire-hotel.com); 33 Hennessy Rd, Wan Chai; doubles from HK$1400 to HK$2200 and suites from HK$2800

*Harbour View International House* – (☎ 2802-1111; fax 2802-9063); 4 Harbour Rd, Wan Chai; doubles from HK$1050 to HK$1550

*Hotel New Harbour* – (☎ 2861-1166; fax 2865-6111); 41-49 Hennessy Rd, Wan Chai; doubles from HK$1080 to HK$1680 and suites from HK$1980

*Luk Kwok Hotel* – (☎ 2866-2166; fax 2866-2622; email lukkwok@lukkwokhotel.com); 72 Gloucester Rd, Wan Chai; singles/doubles from HK$1700/1880 to HK$1980/2180 and suites from HK$4000

*New Cathay Hotel* – (☎ 2577-8211; fax 2576-9365); 17 Tung Lo Wan Rd, Causeway Bay; singles HK$700, doubles from HK$980 to HK$1130, and suites from HK$1870

*South Pacific Hotel* – (☎ 2572-3838; fax 2893-7773; email hinfo@southpacifichotel.com.hk; Web site www.southpacifichotel.com.hk); 23 Morrison Hill Rd, Wan Chai; singles/doubles from HK$1550/1700 to HK$2200/2200 and suites from HK$3900

*Wharney Hotel* – (☎ 2861-1000; fax 2529-5133); 57-33 Lockhart Rd, Wan Chai; singles/doubles from HK$1400/1500 to HK$4500

### Eastern Hong Kong Island

There are more mid-range hotels spread between North Point and Quarry Bay. For the most part, their prices aren't much cheaper than similar places in Wan Chai or Causeway Bay, possibly because all are close to MTR stations.

*City Garden Hotel* – (☎ 2887-2888; fax 2887-1111); 9 City Garden Rd, North Point (Fortress Hill MTR); doubles from HK$1700 to HK$3500

*Grand Plaza Hotel* – (☎ 2886-0011; fax 2886-1738); 2 Kornhill Rd, Quarry Bay (Tai Koo MTR); twins from HK$1500

*Newton Hotel Hong Kong* – (☎ 2807-2333; fax 2807-1221); 218 Electric Rd, North Point (Fortress Hill MTR); doubles from HK$1400 to HK$1950

*South China Hotel* – (☎ 2503-1168; fax 2512-8698); 67-75 Java Rd, North Point (North Point MTR); doubles from HK$1610 to HK$1800

### Tsim Sha Tsui (Map 5)

This district almost sinks under the weight of all the hotels clustered around here. Prices are generally lower than those on Hong Kong Island, though some of the hotels are also a bit more seedy. At some of the cheaper places you may find that only the front-desk staff speak English. (Note: a few hotels list their address as Yau Ma Tei, but are located on the border of Tsim Sha Tsui and so are included here.)

*Bangkok Royal Hotel* – (☎ 2535-9181; fax 2730-2209); 2-12 Pilkem St, Yau Ma Tei; singles from HK$500 to HK$660, doubles from HK$580 to HK$740

*BP International House* – (☎ 2376-1111; fax 2376-1333); 8 Austin Rd, Tsim Sha Tsui; doubles from HK$1300 to HK$1900 and family rooms from HK$1050 to HK$1230

*Eaton Hotel* – (☎ 2782-1818; fax 2782-5563); 380 Nathan Rd, Yau Ma Tei; doubles from HK$1350 to HK$2700

*Imperial Hotel* – (☎ 2366-2201; fax 2311-2360; email imperial@imperialhotel.com.hk; Web site www.imperialhotel.com.hk); 30-34 Nathan Rd, Tsim Sha Tsui; singles/doubles from HK$950/1100 to HK$1700/2000

*International Hotel* – (☎ 2366-3381; fax 2369-5381); 33 Cameron Rd, Tsim Sha Tsui; singles/doubles from HK$580/780 to HK$880/1080

*Kimberley Hotel* – (☎ 2723-3888; fax 2723-1318); 28 Kimberley Rd, Tsim Sha Tsui; singles/doubles from HK$1550/1650 to HK$2050/2150 and suites from HK$2450

*Kowloon Hotel* – (☎ 2369-8698; fax 2739-9811; email khh@peninsula.com.hk); 19-21 Nathan Rd, Tsim Sha Tsui; singles/doubles from HK$1500/1600 to HK$2550/2650, suites from HK$3600

*Majestic Hotel* – (☎ 2781-1333; fax 2781-1773); 348 Nathan Rd, Yau Ma Tei; doubles from HK$1450 to HK$1900

*Metropole Hotel* – (☎ 2761-1711; fax 2761-0769); 75 Waterloo Rd, Yau Ma Tei; doubles from HK$1330 to HK$1650

*Miramar Hotel* – (☎ 2368-1111; fax 2369-1788); 118-130 Nathan Rd, Tsim Sha Tsui; doubles from HK$1800 to HK$2200

*Nathan Hotel* – (☎ 2388-5141; fax 2770-4262); 378 Nathan Rd, Yau Ma Tei; singles/doubles/triples from HK$780/880/1200

*New Astor Hotel* – (☎ 2366-7261; fax 2722-7122); 11 Carnarvon Rd, Tsim Sha Tsui; doubles from HK$880 to HK$1800 and suites from HK$3600

*Park Hotel* – (☎ 2366-1371; fax 2739-7259); 61-65 Chatham Rd South, Tsim Sha Tsui; singles/doubles from HK$1200/1300 to HK$2100/2200

*Prudential Hotel* – (☎ 2311-8222; fax 2311-4760); 222 Nathan Rd, Yau Ma Tei; doubles from HK$1480 to HK$2980

*Ramada Hotel Kowloon* – (☎ 2311-1100; fax 2311-6000; email hotel@ramada-kowloon.com.hk); 73-75 Chatham Rd South, Tsim Sha Tsui; doubles from HK$1300 to HK$2050 and suites from HK$2800

*Royal Pacific Hotel & Towers* – (☎ 2736-1188; fax 2736-1212; email htl@royalpacific.com.hk; Web site www.royalpacific.com.hk); 33 Canton Rd, Tsim Sha Tsui; singles/doubles from HK$1300/1500 to HK$2450/2650 and suites from HK$2500

*Salisbury YMCA* – (☎ 2369-2211; fax 2739-9315); 41 Salisbury Rd, Tsim Sha Tsui; singles HK$880, doubles from HK$1030 to HK$1270 and suites from HK$1720

*Shamrock Hotel* – (☎ 2735-2271; fax 2736-7354); 223 Nathan Rd, Yau Ma Tei; doubles from HK$630 to HK$1070

*Stanford Hillview Hotel* – (☎ 2722-7822; fax 2723-3718; email sfhvhkg@netvigator.com.hk); 13-17 Observatory Rd, Tsim Sha Tsui; doubles from HK$910 to HK$1310

*Windsor Hotel* – (☎ 2739-5665; fax 2311-5101; email windsor@windsorhotel.com.hk; Web site www.windsorhotel.com.hk); 39-43A Kimberley Rd, Tsim Sha Tsui; doubles from HK$1400 to HK$1800 and suites from HK$2900

### Yau Ma Tei & Mong Kok (Map 4)

Although further from the action, hotels in these two districts are not much cheaper than those in Tsim Sha Tsui. All of them are close to an MTR station, however, and put you in a fairly interesting, if gritty, part of town.

*Anne Black Guest House (YWCA)* – (☎ 2713-9211; fax 2761-1269); 5 Man Fuk Rd, Mong Kok; singles from HK$363 to HK$600, doubles start at HK$550

*Booth Lodge* – (☎ 2771-9266; 2385-1140); 11 Wing Shing Lane, Yau Ma Tei; doubles and twins from HK$620 to HK$1200

*Caritas Bianchi Lodge* – (☎ 2388-1111; fax 2770-6669); 4 Cliff Rd, Yau Ma Tei; singles/doubles/triples for HK$720/820/1020

*Concourse Hotel* – (☎ 2397-6683; fax 2381-3768); 22 Lai Chi Kok Rd, Mong Kok; doubles from HK$1280 to HK$1580

*Grand Tower Hotel* – (☎ 2789-0011; fax 2789-0945); 627-641 Nathan Rd, Mong Kok; doubles from HK$1500 to HK$2300

*New Kings Hotel* – (☎ 2780-1281; fax 2782-1833); 473 Nathan Rd; singles/doubles from HK$550/650 to HK$600/750

*Newton Hotel Kowloon* – (☎ 2787-2338; fax 2789-0688); 58-66 Boundary St, Mong Kok; doubles from HK$1060 to HK$1640

*Pearl Seaview Hotel* – (☎ 2782-0882; fax 2388-1803); 268 Shanghai St, Yau Ma Tei; singles/doubles from HK$880/1280 to HK$1280/1580 and suites from HK$2400

*Stanford Hotel* – (☎ 2781-1881; fax 2388-3733; email sfhkg@netvigator.com.hk); 118 Soy St, Mong Kok; singles from HK$1200, doubles from HK$1800

*YMCA International House* (☎ 2771-9111; fax 2388-5926; email ymcares1@netvigator.com.hk); 23 Waterloo Rd, Yau Ma Tei; singles from HK$680; doubles from HK$1100 and suites from HK$1300

## PLACES TO STAY – TOP END

Prices for Hong Kong's luxury hotels are as high as anywhere on earth. In some cases, the money you spend brings a level of comfort and service not often matched elsewhere. Hong Kong's top hoteliers are constantly trying to better their peers in Bangkok, London, New York, Paris and Tokyo; so far they're doing a fine job.

This assessment does not extend to all the hotels in the top-end category. Some merely have top-end prices: their amenities, location and service are good, but not outstanding. If you're going to spend this amount of money anyway, try and book one of the six or seven hotels that take service to that next rarefied level.

Mention Hong Kong and many people think of *The Peninsula,* which opened in 1928 and has become the patriarch of the territory's luxury hotels. Lording over the tip of the Kowloon Peninsula, the place still evokes a feeling of colonial elegance, and from the outside resembles a huge throne. The lifts quickly whisk you away from the lobby and take you to classic European-style rooms which boast features such as faxes, video, CD players and marble bathrooms. The suites are out of this world, and the last word in elegance, equipping you with everything you need to enjoy the experience. The health facilities, which include pool, sauna, jacuzzi and weights, are probably what Nero would have ordered were he ruling Rome today. Due to a new 20 storey addition, many more of the hotel's rooms offer spectacular views of Hong Kong Island, Kowloon or the New Territories.

Near the Peninsula is *The Regent,* flagship hotel of the Regal International Hotels chain. It is much more modern in feel, though like the Peninsula, it bows to a few colonial traditions, such as a fleet of Rolls-Royces and Daimlers. This hotel is a favourite with business travellers, and its outdoor swimming pool has outstanding views.

Other Kowloon notables include the *New World Hotel,* which has an outdoor pool set in a huge garden with a spectacular view, and the *Hotel Nikko Hong Kong,* where you'll find all the amenities and attention typical of fine Japanese hotels.

The Peninsula's counterpart on Hong Kong Island is the *Mandarin Oriental,* owned by none other than Jardine Matheson, Hong Kong's most famous trading house. The Mandarin has a healthy dose of old-world charm. The styling is subdued (and in some rooms a bit outdated) and one gets the feeling that the hotel is riding a bit on its reputation. However, the service, food and facilities are still excellent, and you get all the atmosphere that comes with staying at one of Hong Kong's landmarks.

A glittering and crisp exterior conceals an elegant sophistication at the *Island Shangri-La.* Placing a strong emphasis on personal service, this is the kind of hotel that will find you a guitar, your favourite book, even a pet if you really want it: staff seem genuinely interested in making your stay pleasant. This tasteful hotel has some nice touches, like a library where you can take afternoon tea, an outdoor jacuzzi and a 24 hour business centre. Shopping is a breeze with the adjacent Pacific Place shopping mall which embraces a huge collection of fashionable stores.

Its glistening twin next door is the *Conrad International Hong Kong,* a member of the Hilton Hotels group. While not quite as elegant as the Island Shangri-La, the hotel has gotten enthusiastic reviews for its attention to business travellers' needs.

Winning the prize for the most overblown lobby is the *Grand Hyatt.* A swirl of black marble, oriental rugs and palm trees, this vast foyer inspires either admiration or amusement, but the hotel itself can be taken seriously. The rooms are tastefully and comprehensively furnished, the service attentive and the recreation facilities among the most complete of any hotel.

Hong Kong used to have a Hilton Hotel that boasted one of the best locations in the city, but unfortunately it was bought by Hong Kong tycoon Li Ka-shing, who tore it down to make way for another office tower. Li also built his own luxury hotel, the *Harbour Plaza,* curiously located in Hung Hom in Kowloon (though it *is* on the waterfront). Most of the former Hilton staff moved to the Harbour Plaza, but the Hilton's elegance failed to follow.

Prices for double rooms in the hotels listed below refer to twin rooms as well. Some hotels that only have double rooms give a lower rate for single occupancy. Rates do not include the 10% service charge or 5% government tax.

## Hong Kong Island

*Century Hong Kong Hotel* – (Map 7; ☎ 2598-8888; fax 2598-8866); 238 Jaffe Rd, Wan Chai; singles/doubles from HK$1850/2050 to HK$2050/2150

*Conrad International Hong Kong* – (Map 6; ☎ 2521-3838; fax 2521-3888; email info@conrad. com; Web site www.conrad.com.hk); Pacific Place, 88 Queensway, Admiralty; singles/doubles from HK$2850/3050 to HK$3900/4150 and suites from HK$5200 to HK$25,000

*Excelsior* – (Map 7; ☎ 2894-8888; fax 2895-6459); 281 Gloucester Rd, Causeway Bay; doubles from HK$2400 to HK$3400 and suites from HK$4200 to HK$8500

*Furama Kempinski Hong Kong* – (Map 6; ☎ 2525-5111; fax 2845-9339; email furamahk.china. com); 1 Connaught Rd, Central; doubles from HK$2500 to HK$3500 and suites from HK$3700 to HK$10,000

*Grand Hyatt* – (Map 7; ☎ 2588-1234; fax 2802-0677; Web site www.hyatt.com.hk); 1 Harbour Rd, Wan Chai; singles/doubles from HK$2900/3150 to HK$25,000

*Island Shangri-La Hong Kong* – (Map 6; ☎ 2877-3838; fax 2521-8742; Web site www.shangri-la.com); Pacific Place, Supreme Court Rd, Admiralty; doubles from HK$2700 to HK$3850 and suites from HK$5300 to HK$26,000

*JW Marriot Hotel Hong Kong* – (Map 6; ☎ 2841-3000; fax 2845-0737); Pacific Place, 88 Queensway, Admiralty; doubles from HK$2800 to HK$3950 and suites from HK$6000

*Mandarin Oriental* – (Map 6; ☎ 2522-0111; fax 2810-6190); 5 Connaught Rd, Central; doubles from HK$3300 to HK$5300 and suites from HK$7000 to HK$25,000

*New World Harbour View* – (Map 7; ☎ 2802-8888; fax 2802-8833); 1 Harbour Rd, Wan Chai; singles from HK$2700 to HK$18800 (add on HK$300 for price of double)

*Park Lane* – (Map 7; ☎ 2890-3355; fax 2576-7853; email info@parklane.com.hk); 310 Gloucester Rd, Causeway Bay; singles/doubles from HK$2480/2780 to HK$3680/3980 and suites from HK$4880

*Regal Hongkong Hotel* – (Map 7; ☎ 2890-6633; fax 2881-0777; email rhk@regal-hotel.com; Web site www.regal-hotels.com); 88 Yee Wo St, Causeway Bay; doubles from HK$2800 to HK$3800, suites from HK$6000 to HK$22,000

*Ritz-Carlton Hong Kong* – (Map 6; ☎ 2877-6666; fax 2877-6778; email ritzrchk@hk.super.net; Web site www.ritz-carlton-hongkong.com); 3 Connaught Rd Central, Central; singles/doubles from HK$2850 to HK$4200 and suites from HK$4500

## Kowloon

*Grand Stanford Harbour View* – (Map 5; ☎ 2721-5161; fax 2732-2233); 70 Mody Rd, Tsim Sha Tsui East; singles/doubles from HK$2350/2500 to HK$3250/3400 and suites from HK$4800

*Harbour Plaza* – (Map 5; ☎ 2621-3188; fax 2621-3311); 20 Tak Fung St, Hung Hom; doubles from HK$2200 to HK$2850

*Holiday Inn Golden Mile* – (Map 5; ☎ 2369-3111; fax 2369-8016; email goldenmile@asianvoyage. com; Web site www.goldenmile.com); 50 Nathan Rd, Tsim Sha Tsui; singles/doubles from HK$1900/2300 to HK$2450/2550 and suites from HK$5500

*Hong Kong Hotel* – (Map 5; ☎ 2113-0088; fax 2113-0011; email mphkh97@asiaonline.net; Internet www.marcopolohotels.com); Harbour City, Canton Rd, Tsim Sha Tsui; singles/doubles from HK$2300/2400 to HK$3530/3630 and suites from HK$3960 to HK$15,000

*Hong Kong Renaissance Hotel* – (Map 5; ☎ 2375-1133; fax 2375-6611); 8 Peking Rd, Tsim Sha Tsui; doubles from HK$2600 to HK$3600

*Hotel Nikko Hong Kong* – (Map 5; ☎ 2739-1111; fax 2311-3122; email nikko@hotelnikko.com.hk); 72 Mody Rd, Tsim Sha Tsui East; doubles from HK$2200 to HK$3100

*Hyatt Regency* – (Map 5; ☎ 2311-1234; fax 2739-8701; email general@hyattregency.com.hk); 67 Nathan Rd, Tsim Sha Tsui; doubles from HK$2800 to HK$3600 and suites from HK$4400

*Kowloon Shangri-La* – (Map 5; ☎ 2721-2111; fax 2723-8686; Web site www.shangri-la.com); 64 Mody Rd, Tsim Sha Tsui East; singles/doubles from HK$2300/2550 to HK$3600/3850 and suites from HK$4400 to HK$17,000

*Marco Polo Hotel* – (Map 5; ☎ 2113-0088; fax 2113-0022; email mphkgbc@wlink.net); Harbour City, Canton Rd, Tsim Sha Tsui; singles/doubles from HK$1950/2050 to HK$2200/2300 and suites from HK$3450

*New World Hotel* – (Map 5; ☎ 2369-4111; fax 2369-9387); 22 Salisbury Rd, Tsim Sha Tsui; singles/doubles from HK$2200/2350 to HK$2850/2850 and suites from HK$3300 to HK$7500

*Omni Prince Hotel* – (Map 5; ☎ 2113-1888; fax 2113-0066); Harbour City, Canton Rd, Tsim Sha Tsui; doubles from HK$2050 to HK$2400

*The Peninsula* – (Map 5; ☎ 2366-6251; fax 2722-4170; email pen@peninsula.com); Salisbury Rd, Tsim Sha Tsui; doubles from HK$2900 to HK$4600, suites from HK$5200 to HK$39,000

*Regal Kowloon Hotel* – (Map 5; ☎ 2722-1818; fax 2369-6950; email rkh@regalhotels.com; Web site www.regalhotels.com); 71 Mody Rd, Tsim Sha Tsui East; singles/doubles from HK$2100/2200 to HK$2900/3050 and suites from HK$5000 to HK$12,000

*The Regent* – (Map 5; ☎ 2721-1211; fax 2739-4546); Salisbury Rd, Tsim Sha Tsui; doubles from HK$2600 to HK$4150 and suites from HK$4650

*The Royal Garden Hotel* – (Map 5; ☎ 2721-5215; fax 2369-9976; email htlinfo@theroyalgardenhotel.com.hk; Web site www.theroyalgardenhotel.com.hk); 69 Mody Rd, Tsim Sha Tsui East; singles/doubles from HK$2300/2450 to HK$2900/3050 and suites from HK$4000 to HK$15,600

*Sheraton Hong Kong Hotel* – (Map 5; ☎ 2369-1111; fax 2739-8707); 20 Nathan Rd, Tsim Sha Tsui; doubles from HK$2800 to HK$3400

## LONG TERM
### Rental Accommodation

Finding an apartment in Hong Kong is usually not a lot of fun, especially if it's hot and humid and you are dragging your belongings around with you. Finding what you want for a reasonable price can take weeks of scurrying up and down lifts and stairwells, all the while staving off your estate agent, who is used to clinching several deals daily. At the same time, it's a lot easier for foreigners here than in other Asian cities. English is widely spoken, and there are literally thousands of real estate agencies – in many areas, it seems every other shop is an estate agency (eg Kennedy Town). Taking along a Cantonese-speaking friend in your hunt will definitely help you negotiate a good price. One thing that is very important is spending a decent amount of time finding a place to live – a large number of expats make the mistake of choosing inadequate and characterless housing because they are too impetuous. Take your time and mull over a selection before committing yourself.

You can look for a place by yourself by checking the property sections of the English-language newspapers, the classifieds section of *HK Magazine* or bulletin boards at expatriate associations like the Royal Hong Kong Yacht Club.

Many people end up going through an estate agent, who can scour through the reams of Chinese-language rental ads and notices. It's best to go with one of the bigger outfits, such as L&D or Centaline Property, though there are plenty of smaller agencies that are reliable as well. Check the *Yellow Pages for Businesses* for a complete listing. The vast number of estate agents in Hong Kong reflects the mobility of the populace and the spell that the property market exercises over locals.

The agent's fee is generally equivalent to one month's rent. Other initial expenses will include a deposit, usually equal to two months' rent, and the first month's rental payment. This can add up to a lot of money, as rents in Hong Kong are very steep, on a par with those in New York, London and, in some cases, Tokyo. Also remember that the majority of flats in Hong Kong are unfurnished, so furnishing costs also must be considered. Luckily there are many cheap furniture outlets around, but it will still all add up.

A one bedroom apartment in the Mid-Levels will cost anywhere from HK$15,000 to HK$50,000 per month. That same flat will go for somewhat less in Tsim Sha Tsui or Wan Chai. More affordable are districts on eastern Hong Kong Island, western Hong Kong Island (eg. Kennedy Town, which is quite a popular expat refuge) and north-eastern or north-western Kowloon, where you may be able to find a 600 sq foot one-bedroom flat for HK$8000 per month. The most expensive place is the Peak, where rents can easily top HK$100,000 per month (nearly US$13,000).

It's worth remembering that the Hong Kong Chinese prefer to live in the tall, modern lift-equipped high-rises (which all have monthly management fees) and shun the old, smaller *tonglau*, or 'Tang buildings' which are usually five to seven stories tall and often do not have lifts. Tonglau are, however, much cheaper than the high-rises and often have more character (as they are older) even though they are generally not as clean. They have no management fee, usually just a monthly cleaning fee which is only about HK$100. Tonglau buildings also give you the opportunity to find a flat at the top which will give you a terrace on the roof the same area as the flat. The Hong Kong Chinese are not wild about having a rooftop terrace, so they are not difficult to find and are only marginally more expensive than a flat without a terrace. This gives you double the space (essential in Hong Kong) plus the chance to hold barbecues.

Hong Kong people are used to living in small apartments and, unless you can spend several thousand US dollars a month on rent, you'll have to learn to adapt as well. Most places have (in western terms) closet-sized bathrooms, bathroom-sized kitchens and bedroom-sized living rooms. Of course there

are exceptions, which you may be lucky enough to stumble upon; the further out you go from the city centre, the better your chances are. If you're willing to go as far as the Outlying Islands, such as Lamma or Lantau, or the New Territories, you'll get a lot more for your money.

The Outlying Islands options, while not at the hub of the action, give you splendid surroundings – jump aboard a ferry and head over to Lamma Island and search out a room for much less money than you would pay in Kowloon or Hong Kong Island. You can get a three bedroom flat on Lamma, plus roof terrace, for less than HK$8000 per month. Rooms and flats easily can be found by scanning the property pages of the English-language papers or, even better, by glancing at the advertisement wall just beyond the ferry terminal at Yung Shue Wan, which is usually plastered with offers. Here you can get a flat-share or a room in a house for as little as HK$1600 a month – the cheapest Chungking Mansions dive would be twice that. Factors to weigh up are the 45 minute ferry trip to Lamma (HK$9.20 weekdays;

## Living Conditions

How can anyone stand living in Hong Kong? How can anyone in their right mind live in a roach infested, coffin-sized flat, cheek-by-jowl with an air-conditioning machine that sounds like a jet taking off? How can you live somewhere where your best clothes sprout mould practically overnight, unless you've invested in a vast, humming dehumidifier? How can anyone live in a place where a 55 sq metre Mid-Levels flat (and that is *small*) will cost you HK$4 million to buy (US$500,000) or up to HK$18,000 a month to rent? Surely, for that price you would expect some solace in the view, like a priceless spectacle of Victoria Harbour? Wrong. The usual view is a row of identikit concrete housing block monstrosities. These housing blocks that Hong Kong residents queue up for are for the underprivileged in any other country. Yet in Hong Kong they are a status symbol, something to reach for and aspire to. At least when a new block goes up, the roaches take a couple of years to make it up to the top floors.

The fact is that you have no choice. Building in Hong Kong is vertical; the only answer to the shortage of land. The best flats are on the upper floors – if you manage to get a thin sliver of a sea view through the concrete curtain, your flat is worth more.

The property market in Hong Kong inspires incredulity. The 36 floor Entertainment Building in Central was sold in November 1996 for HK$3.6 billion (US$470 million). This works out at HK$170,000 per sq metre. Anyone who questions this insatiable desire for property in Hong Kong only has to listen to the orchestra of jackhammers, or notice that in certain parts of Hong Kong every other shop is a real estate agency. The 50,000 Chinese immigrants a year that come to Hong Kong always need somewhere to live. Needless to say, many wealthy Hong Kongers have built their fortunes on the property market. But not everyone: in 1997, a couple bought a garden flat for HK$3.25 million, only to discover that the tenant who sold them the property had impersonated the university professor who really owned it. They had to leave immediately, and face the real professor who was suing them for damages and wrongful occupation. ■

HK$12.50 weekends) and that the last ferry leaves at 12.30pm. This is offset by the joy of living in an almost unspoilt Eden of banana trees and dense grasses, rolling hills, beautiful, neat fields, and total silence apart from croaking frogs. If you're going to live in Hong Kong for a month or so, this is an excellent place to do it; the island has quite a large community of expats and offers a jaunty nightlife scene with relatively cheap beer and good food. You can often hear expats in Lamma bars complaining that 'if only I'd known Lamma was so cheap and tranquil, I would never had lived in Sha Tin for two years'.

Also worth looking out for are the 'flats' advertised almost daily in the property pages of the English press, starting at around HK$4000 per month (usually in the Kowloon area). These are actually rooms with bathroom (no kitchen), TV, air-con and telephone in apartment blocks that have been converted by landlords into makeshift temporary accommodation. They are not very attractive, not very clean and not worth the money, but they are central – if that's what you want.

### Serviced Apartments

If you're only going to be based in Hong Kong for a month or more (and the company is footing the bill) serviced apartments are worth considering. A complete list can be found in the *Yellow Pages for Consumers*. Occasionally the property sections of the English-language newspapers also carry advertisements.

Most serviced apartments are part of hotels, such as *Grand Plaza Apartments* in the Grand Plaza Hotel at Quarry Bay on the eastern side of Hong Kong Island. Monthly rents in places like this run anywhere from HK$32,000 for a 400 sq foot studio through HK$45,000 for a 700 sq foot one bedroom apartment to HK$65,000 for a two bedroom suite. The price generally includes the management fees, electricity, linen service and other charges.

Serviced apartments are also available at the *Hong Kong Convention & Exhibition Centre* in Central and at *Parkview*, a luxury residential complex located near Wong Ngai Chung Gap on Hong Kong Island. These apartments are more luxurious, and monthly rents are well over HK$60,000. Check the property pages of the *South China Morning Post*, which usually carries advertisements for serviced apartments.

Most of the serviced apartment providers require a minimum lease of one month, a deposit equivalent to one month's rent, and the first month's rent paid in advance.

# Places to Eat

Hong Kong's reputation as a shopper's paradise may be in question, but there's no doubt that this place is a food lover's heaven. The territory is said to have the world's highest per capita ratio of restaurants. Small wonder, for the Chinese truly live to eat: any night of the week you will find restaurants, banquet halls or tiny noodle shops crammed with customers. The frenetic pace and long hours of work in Hong Kong also make eating out a necessity for many.

For the visitor this translates into an exciting range of choices. Almost all the different styles of Chinese cooking are represented in Hong Kong, as well as a dazzling number of foreign cuisines. The more you can spend, the greater the variety you will enjoy.

It's easy to eat on a budget in Hong Kong. Almost every neighbourhood has cheap noodle shops. During lunchtime keep an eye peeled for signs advertising set lunches. These usually belong to restaurants serving western fare: you can get soup, an entrée, dessert and a cup of tea or coffee for as little as HK$30, although HK$35 is usually closer to the average.

There are also some interesting options on the fast-food front. In addition to international chains like McDonald's and KFC, there are several local chains that dish up passable Chinese and western food. Oliver's Super Sandwiches offers tasty sandwiches, bagels, soups, salads and baked potatoes with prices from HK$12 to HK$40. A more recent arrival is Genroku Sushi, which has sushi for as little as HK$9. Jack In The Box is another local fast-food franchise, tempting customers with the blurb 'Jacks are better than Mac's'. Another cheap option is Indian restaurants, although these aren't the bargain they once were. Still, in some Indian places you can get dinner for around HK$50 to HK$60.

The best hunting grounds for budget diners are the little backstreets uphill from Central (such as Stanley and Wellington Sts),

Sheung Wan, Wan Chai, Causeway Bay and Tsim Sha Tsui. Most of these areas have the steady flow of commuters or residents needed to support a large number of noodle shops, fast-food joints and so on.

All these areas also have plenty of mid-range restaurants, and this is where Hong Kong truly comes into its own. You can find almost any Asian or western cuisine, from Portuguese to Vietnamese. Unfortunately, like its hotels, Hong Kong's mid-priced restaurants charge more than one might expect. Lunch at a nice Chinese or western restaurant can easily cost HK$600 for three people.

Hong Kong's bent for conspicuous consumption extends to dining, and there are plenty of spots where you can spend astronomical sums indulging your palate. But as with the top-end hotels, only some of these high-priced restaurants can turn out a meal that is truly worth the money.

Dedicated diners may want to pick up the annual *HK Magazine Restaurant Guide*. Covering more than 500 restaurants, this is one of the best, and liveliest guides to dining out in Hong Kong and Macau. Some of the guide's favourite places are included in this chapter. At HK$50 a copy, it's well worth the money if you plan to really go restaurant hunting. To get a copy, call *HK Magazine's* editorial office (☎ 2850-5065; fax 2543-4964; email asiacity@hk.super.net). The Hong Kong Tourist Association (HKTA) also puts out an *Official Dining and Entertainment Guide* which includes many of its member restaurants, but as all the reviews are uniformly upbeat, it's hard to get a feel for which places are worth going to.

## DRINKS
### Alcoholic Drinks
Beer is by far the most popular alcoholic beverage, and there's a wide range of choice in bars, convenience stores and supermarkets. Hong Kong has two major breweries, one each owned by Carlsberg (Denmark)

146

and San Miguel (Philippines). In addition to producing their own brands, they brew other beers under licence, including Löwenbrau and Kirin. Carlsberg and San Miguel are the two most widely available brands, which is unfortunate, since they are among the worst to drink.

All is not lost however, as microbrewery or boutique beers are served at a number of bars. Hong Kong's original micro-brewery, the South China Brewing Company, brews a selection of concoctions that you may see about town. These include Red Dawn, Tai Koo Brew, Aldrich Bay Pale Ale, Stonecutter's Lager and Dragon's Back India Pale Ale.

Imported beers are very popular, and most bars have many kinds, mostly in bottles but in some cases on tap as well. There are some good English bitters and ales on draught, though their taste sometimes suffers a bit from having spent several weeks in a cargo ship. Irish and German beers are also available. Tsingtao, China's main export beer, is sold everywhere. Beer drinking in bars is ridiculously expensive, unless you target happy hour. Buying beers at the supermarket, however, is cheap and cans of beer can cost as little as HK$2!

Among the more well-heeled drinkers, Cognac brandy is the liquor of choice. It's hard to believe, but Hong Kong accounts for nearly 11% of the world's Cognac market, and has the world's highest per capita consumption. Locals generally drink it neat, but rarely sip it: sometimes you'll even see a group of enthusiastic diners downing it shot-style! No wonder they go through so much of it.

Supermarkets, department stores, restaurants and bars usually have a decent selection of other spirits and wines. Certain spirits can also be cheap if bought at supermarkets, which stock very cheap no-name brands. Some blended whiskies are not bad and can sell for as little as HK$50 for 750mL. Well-known brands of spirits are generally expensive, however.

Wine is becoming increasingly popular. A list of vintners appears in the Wine section of the Shopping chapter.

If you want to try Chinese alcohol, it's most commonly available in restaurants (few bars deal with it). Easiest on the palate is probably *siu hing jau,* more commonly known by its name in Mandarin, *shao xing jiu.* Other options may not go down so smoothly. Though Chinese tend to translate all their alcohols as 'wine' in English, the majority are hard spirits distilled from rice, sorghum or millet. Most are quite potent, colourless and extremely volatile. The best known, and most expensive, is *mao tai,* distilled from millet. Another searing delicacy is *goh leung* (*gao liang* in Mandarin), which is made from sorghum. Have fun with these, but if your dining companions start repeating the phrase *gon bui* (drain your glass), you may want to start scouting out escape routes.

## Non-Alcoholic Drinks

A consumer's paradise, Hong Kong has a large selection of non-alcoholic beverages. In any convenience store or supermarket you'll find a whole range of juice, soft drink and milk products. Most restaurants have cola and juice at the very least.

Of course tea is everywhere. In Chinese restaurants tea is often served free of charge, or at most you'll pay HK$2 for a large pot with endless refills of water. There are three basic types of tea: green or unfermented (*luk cha*); fermented (*bolei*), also known as black tea; and semi-fermented (*oolong*). Within these categories fall dozens of varieties. One of the most well known is jasmine (*heung pin*), a blend of tea and flowers. Chinese teas are drunk straight, without milk or sugar. If you want a pot refill in a restaurant, put the lid half-on, half-off and the waiter will get the message.

There are also some pretty good English teas to be drunk, though you usually must go to a nice hotel if you wish it to be served properly. Some Chinese places also serve western-style tea, but with a Hong Kong twist. Milk tea (*nai cha*) uses an extremely strong brew so the flavour can punch through the heavy dose of condensed milk. Lemon tea (*ningmeng cha*) is also strong, and is often served with several slices of lemon.

PLACES TO EAT

## Morning Coffee & High Tea

The tradition of afternoon tea is dying out in frantic, business-crazed Hong Kong, but a few of the upmarket hotels still make a good show of it. Undoubtedly the best known of these is *The Peninsula* (Map 5) in Tsim Sha Tsui, where silent, immaculately clad waiters painstakingly prepare your pot of tea and serve up an impressive array of finger sandwiches and pastries. The best place to enjoy this experience is on the mezzanine level, which spares you the noise and distraction of the constant crowds in the lobby.

The *Regent Hotel* (Map 5), also in Tsim Sha Tsui, lacks the colonial air of The Peninsula, but offers nice harbour views along with your tea. In Central, the *Mandarin Oriental* (Map 6) serves afternoon tea in its mezzanine level café, which is also a good spot to watch the mix of tourists and business types parading through the lobby below.

Coffee has undergone a renaissance in Hong Kong in the past several years, to the relief of the western and Japanese expat community, many of whom have long suffered under the tyranny of instant coffee. Most restaurants now do a much better job of brewing up fresh pots for their customers, and cappuccino/espresso machines can be found all over the place.

Best of all, coffee stands and shops offering a variety of tasty straight brews and speciality coffees have started appearing in more and more areas. They're thickest on the ground in Central, though Wan Chai and Tsim Sha Tsui are beginning to sprout their own branches. Prices vary. Many places sell their regular brews for between HK$8 and HK$20. Cappuccino, café latte and espresso drinks average between HK$15 and HK$30 for the larger servings. Here's a list of some places where you can get your daily dose of caffeine. Some of these places also sell coffee beans.

*Espresso Americano* – ground floor, Star House (Map 5), Salisbury Rd, Tsim Sha Tsui
    shop 131, 1st floor, Hutchison House (Map 6), Central; coffee from HK$12 to HK$33
*Fauchon* – (Map 6) shops 4 and 5, The Forum, Exchange Square Tower III, 8 Connaught Place,
    Central; small coffee HK$15
*Kona Coffee Specialists* – shop 5, ground floor, Cameron Lane, Tsim Sha Tsui; 14 coffee types, blue
    mountain HK$32, espresso HK$15

---

Coffee is also widely available, and more and more cafés are opening up. Cafés are expensive in Hong Kong, but offer a blessed escape from the streets. The last few years have seen tremendous growth in the number of cafés, and the range of coffee now available is quite rich. Locals also enjoy chilled coffee (*dong gafei*), which can also be bought everywhere in cans, usually made by Nescafé. The cans come in gradations of strength and consistency.

In the summer Hong Kongers like to have a sweet cold drink called a 'fleecy'. This is quite tasty, and is most often made with milk and red or green beans (it tastes better than it sounds). Sometimes fruit is used instead.

Road-side stalls sell a whole range of made-on-the-spot fruit juices that sell for about HK$7. You can custom make your own brew according to the fruits they stock. Sugar-cane juice is delicious but a real tooth-rotter; the cane is stripped with a knife and pulverised in a grinder for its juice.

## PLACES TO EAT – BUDGET

It's easy to go budget dining in Hong Kong. Every neighbourhood has cheap spots of one sort or another to cater for workers and local residents. The most common option is the noodle shop; for the more adventurous there are the street markets.

Restaurants in this section are arranged according to type, and within that type, eateries on Hong Kong Island are first and then those in Kowloon. If the restaurant is marked on a map, the map number appears before the phone number, but if the restaurant is in a hotel or shopping mall, the map number appears after the name of the building.

Most of the interesting and decent restaurants are on the Hong Kong Island side, and that is where you should go if you want to be rewarded with variety and originality.

### Breakfast

You can go western or Chinese on this one. Don't forget that dim sum is what the Can-

*Martino Coffee Shop* – (Map 7) 66 Paterson St, Causeway Bay; coffee HK$35
*Pacific Coffee Co* – ground floor, Bank of America Tower (Map 6), Central
    Shop 404, Pacific Place (Map 6), Admiralty
    Star Ferry Pier (Map 6), Central
    Star Ferry Terminal (Map 5), Tsim Sha Tsui
    1st floor, Devon House, Quarry Bay; takeaway coffee from HK$12 to HK$29
*Pasticceria* – ground floor, Landmark shopping centre (Map 6), 15 Queen's Rd, Central; cappuccino $35
*Peak Café* – (Map 8)121 Peak Rd, The Peak; cappuccino HK$33, café latte HK$35
*Six Bugs Antiques and Café* – shop 2, ground floor, Western Market (Map 6), 323 Des Voeux Rd, Sheung Wan; cappuccino HK$35
*TW Café* – (Map 6) ground floor, Capitol Plaza, 2-10 Lyndhurst Terrace, Central
    mezzanine, 2 Queen Victoria St, Central

In addition to these places, Oliver's Super Sandwiches (see the Fast Food section under Places to Eat – Budget) makes an acceptable cup of brewed coffee, and has cappuccino as well. La Rose Noire Patisserie (see French restaurants under Places to Eat – Middle) has excellent coffee, including the best café au lait in Hong Kong. La Trattoria, the Italian restaurant in the Landmark shopping centre (see Italian restaurants under Places to Eat – Middle), has an adjacent coffee shop. For those who take coffee drinking as seriously as drinking wine, *Coffee Lover's Guide to Hong Kong* by Geri Clisby & Sheryl Coughlin is a commendable book that weighs up all the best cafés in the territory. It is available from most bookshops in Hong Kong for HK$70.

All of these places serve pastries. Some, like La Rose Noire Patisserie and La Trattoria, have treats that can be addictive; others like Pacific Coffee Co, do a good job of satisfying the sweet tooth, but that's about all.

For ice cream, Haagen-Dazs is, as always, ridiculously expensive, but it's damn good. There are a few branches around town: Pedder St, Central; Kingston St, Causeway Bay; and the Peak Galleria, the Peak. ■

tonese breakfast is all about, and if you want to go native and really relish this morning treat, check the list of dim sum eateries recommended in the earlier Chinese Cuisine section. Dim sum is extremely addictive and very rich, so you probably don't want to overdo it, but you should try it at least once.

Western breakfasts can be found at *Delifrance*, a chain that serves croissants, sandwiches and coffee, all at reasonable prices. They also provide free newspapers for the use of their customers. *Oliver's Super Sandwiches* serves western-style breakfast until 11 am, and dishes up excellent snacks throughout the day. *Hardee's* serves a fastfood breakfast that is really not so bad. See under Fast Food in this section for more details of these three eateries.

### Noodle Shops

These are absolutely everywhere, and while some are larger shops, most occupy a little hole in the wall and hold only eight to 10 tables. If you go to these places for every meal you will soon get bored: though the menus look long, the selections are basically variations on a few basic themes. Here you can usually get a bowl of soup noodles for between HK$15 and HK$25, and often a plate of steamed vegetables with oyster sauce from HK$11 to HK$14. It's pretty easy to spot these places, as the noodle vats ·are usually right by the front window.

Recommending particular shops is no easy task. There are literally hundreds, if not thousands, of noodle shops. The selection below represents shops that have become well known in their neighbourhoods.

*Cosmic Noodle Bar & Café* – noodles plus salads, pancakes, muffins, burgers and other goodies (from HK$25 to HK$40); 8-12 Hennessy Rd, Wan Chai (Map 7)
*Happy Garden Noodle & Congee Kitchen* – good soup noodles and congee (from HK$28 to HK$30); 76 Canton Rd, Tsim Sha Tsui (Map 5)

*Jim Chai Kee Noodle Shop* – famous for king prawn dumpling noodles (from HK$15); 98 Wellington St, Central (near Sheung Wan; Map 6) and 36 Stanley St, Central (Map 6)

*Law Fu Kee Noodle Shop* – famous for dumpling noodles (HK$14); 144 Des Voeux Rd, Central (near Sheung Wan; Map 6)

*Taiwan Beef Noodle* – chain with good Taiwan-style beef noodles (HK$26); 78-80 Canton Rd, Tsim Sha Tsui (Map 5), and 13 King Kwong St, Happy Valley

### Japanese Ramen Shops

This is a very tasty and relatively inexpensive option. Several shops serving Japanese ramen noodles have sprung up around town, but two in particular are highly recommended by local Japanese. In Central there is *Miyoshiya,* 39 Lyndhurst Terrace (near Sheung Wan, Map 6). The owner prepares all the ramen himself, and you can choose from either pork or soy sauce-based broth. A bowl will cost you around HK$35.

The other expert's choice is *Ichibantei* which has specialities like the fiery 'bomb hot noodles' loaded with chilli and garlic, as well as a wide assortment of rice dishes and appetisers. This place specialises in miso-based broth. Ramen ranges from HK$35 to HK$52 per bowl. Ichibantei is in a tiny shop at 17 Morrison Hill Rd, Wan Chai (Map 7).

### Vegetarian

In certain pockets of Hong Kong you can find the occasional cramped and cheap vegetarian restaurant.

In the Central/Sheung Wan area, try *Fat Heung Lam,* (Map 6; ☎ 2543-0404) on Wellington St.

*Vegi-Table* (☎ 2877-0901), at 1 Tun Wo Lane, Central has cheap, no-nonsense food, and no MSG. To get there walk under the Mid-Levels escalator as it cuts between Lyndhurst Terrace and Hollywood Rd. Tun Wo Lane to the left as you walk uphill.

The *Fringe Club* (Map 6; ☎ 2521-7251), at 2 Lower Albert Rd, does a vegetarian lunch buffet where you can crunch your way through salads.

Also in the Central/Sheung Wan district is *The Original Health Café* (☎ 2815-0398) at

2702-3, 27th floor, Wing Shan Tower, 173 Des Voeux Rd. This is where you want to be if high-fibre new age meals on the cheap give you a buzz. The meals here are cooked up in an organic frenzy of wholesome puritanism.

In Causeway Bay is the excellent and usually packed out *Kung Tak Lam* (Map 7; ☎ 2890-3127), which seems to hold hostage most of the vegetarian population at 31 Yee Wo St. Inexpensive, well-prepared Shanghai vegetarian food from a huge menu is on offer. The dishes are prepared to resemble meat in appearance and texture, but without a shred of the real thing. The mock goose, mock duck, and sweet and sour fish are recommended. All the vegetables are grown organically, and the food is free of MSG. The only drawback is the noise. There is another branch (Map 5; ☎ 2367-7881) in Tsim Sha Tsui at 45-47 Carnarvon Rd.

The *Vegi Food Kitchen* (Map 7), off Gloucester Rd, is less of a budget option. It has a brass sign forbidding anyone from carrying meat into the restaurant! Check your Big Mac at the front desk.

There are a string of budget vegetarian places on Jardine's Bazaar in Causeway Bay (Map 7). The *Fat Mun Lam* is said to have good dishes, but all the places look the same.

Johnston Rd in Wan Chai (Map 7) has a few vegetarian eateries. At 128 Johnston Rd, the *Vegetarian Garden* (☎ 2833-9128) is one of the plentiful Buddhist restaurants in town. It has takeaway dishes on the ground floor, and downstairs the restaurant serves a great range (English menu) of vegetarian meals. Two dishes will cost about HK$100. Also found in Wan Chai is the *Healthy Vegetarian Restaurant* (Map 7; ☎ 2363-5723), a good Buddhist establishment.

On the Kowloon side, earn karma credit points with a trip to *The Higher Taste Vegetarian Dining Club* (Map 5; ☎ 2723-0260), on the 6th floor, 27 Chatham Rd. Here you are invited to take off your shoes (and sandals) before munching through cheap vegetable offerings. You can pass on the street dance if you want, but the food is excellent, great value and the restaurant attracts a colourful assortment of types.

Cheap Indian meat-free meals are cooked up at *Woodlands* (☎ 2369-3718), 5-6 Mirror Tower, 61 Mody Rd. The setting is unpretentious, simple and fun, and the food is good. See also Club Sri Lanka in the Indian section, following.

Don't forget that many temples have vegetarian restaurants, where you can get decent Buddhist food; one example is the *Miu Fat Buddhist Temple* in Lam Tei (in the New Territories) which has a popular Buddhist restaurant on the 2nd floor, with set meals for HK$75 (see the Things to See & Do chapter for more details on how to get there).

### Indian

Indian food used to be one of the great budget options in town, but ridiculously high rents and stiff competition from fast-food joints have taken their toll. A good lunch or dinner will cost between HK$60 and HK$90 at the cheaper places. There are also some fancier Indian places: for details see the Places to Eat – Middle section later in this chapter.

The very mention of Chungking Mansions (Map 5) may fill you with horror, yet it is home to some authentic and cheap Indian food. Chungking Mansions has an avid fan base, so why not give it a bash. *The Taj Mahal Club* (☎ 2722-5454), 3rd floor, B block, is a popular destination for those who like to leave with red eyes, a swollen tongue and money still in their wallet. The chicken masala costs HK$38 and is excellent value. On the 3rd floor of C block is *The Delhi Club* (☎ 2368-1682), which serves Indian and Nepali food. This really is good value dining – try the chicken tandoori for HK$20. Also in C block, on the 4th floor, is the *Islamabad Club* (☎ 2721-5362), a spartan place that fills you up without emptying your pockets.

The *Koh-I-Noor* (Map 5; ☎ 2368-3065), part of a chain of restaurants, has a presence in Tsim Sha Tsui, at 3-4 Peninsula Mansion, 1st floor, 16C Mody Rd. This place is cheaper and less stylish than its counterpart in Central, but the food is still great and the staff are friendly. Their emphasis is on North Indian food, although they often stage buffets from different regions which are

value for money. See the Vegetarian section earlier in this chapter for information on *Woodlands*, where you can eat vegetarian Indian cuisine.

On the Hong Kong Island side, there is a cluster of Indian places along Wellington St, in the Central and Sheung Wan districts. The *Spice Island Club,* at 63-69 Wellington St, serves good Indian and Nepali food. Their prices are quite reasonable for lunch, but not so great for dinner.

Nestled on the 3rd floor of the Winner Building at 10 Wing Wah Lane, next door to Club 64 in Lan Kwai Fong is *The Curry Club* (Map 6; ☎ 2523-2203). It is another cheap, long-standing expat hangout, and with good reason. The food is good value for money and the staff are always obliging. Also in Lan Kwai Fong is *Koh-I-Noor* (☎ 2568-8757), on the 1st floor of the California Entertainment Building (Map 6).

Costing a bit more but worth it is *Club Sri Lanka* (Map 6; ☎ 2526-6559), basement, 17 Hollywood Rd, Sheung Wan. This place features an excellent Sri Lankan buffet for around HK$85. There's also a vegetarian buffet that costs a bit less. Note that alcohol is not served on the premises, but you can take your own.

Over in Wan Chai (Map 7) there is a good Indian place, though you need to order carefully if you want to stay in true budget range. *Jo Jo Mess Club,* 1st floor, 86-90 Johnston Rd, suffers from somewhat dreary decor, but you can sit by the window and watch the Wan Chai action while you enjoy your meal.

If you want to combine Indian with a Lamma Island venture, *Toochkas* (Map 11; ☎ 2982-0159) could be the place, at 44 Main St, Yung Shu Wan. Get off the ferry, follow the hordes down Main St for about five minutes and it's on your left on a corner. Indian food is just one of a global concoction of cuisines they serve here.

### Street Markets

Though not the epitome of hygiene, these street-side markets (known as *dai pai dong*) can whip up some pretty tasty dishes in no time, and the prices are quite reasonable.

Ordering is also no problem: just point at what you want. Meals are eaten at folding tables set up on the sidewalk or street. These are not for everyone, but for what it's worth, the wok is subjected to such searing heat that it should kill any nasty bacteria.

Most dai pai dong don't start hopping until night-time, but there are a few where you can grab lunch or an afternoon snack. Hong Kong's best known dai pai dong is at the northern section of the Temple St market in Yau Ma Tei (Map 4).

### Set Lunches

One good way to fill up for a relatively little price is the set lunch. In Sheung Wan, Wan Chai and parts of Tsim Sha Tsui you will stumble across signs advertising soup or salad, entrée, dessert and tea or coffee for HK$30 and up. Even if the sign is in Chinese you should be able to get the idea, and most of these places have English-language menus. Set lunches are a staple of Hong Kong-style western restaurants. Most also have Chinese dishes on the menu, but these are not usually part of the set lunches.

There are no places worth recommending in particular, as they all have pretty much the same menus. The food isn't all that bad, and it gives you a chance to sit down and relax. One of the most popular chains in this category is the *Farm House* group of restaurants. There's one in nearly every district and they are easy to recognise by their yellow and green motif. You can get a set meal here (such as borsch for starters, roast chicken, chips, vegetables and a coffee) for HK$43.

### Fast Food

The scene is not as bleak as the label might suggest. In Hong Kong people do everything quickly, so there's a good market for places that can turn out quality food in a hurry.

Of course the usual international offenders are here: McDonald's, KFC, Hardee's etc. In fact Hong Kong has earned a special place on the McDonald's corporate map: at last count seven of the world's 10 busiest McDonald's restaurants were here. 'Golden Arches' is unusually cheap in Hong Kong,

with set meals (Big Mac, fries and soft drink) for HK$17.

Hong Kong has several home-grown fast-food chains, serving both western and Chinese food. Breakfast usually features congee (gruel made from boiled rice), fried noodles, and ham and eggs. For lunch and dinner there is a slew of different dishes, ranging from pepper steak to home-style bean curd. Most chains also have afternoon tea menus: a chicken leg, hot dog or fried radish cake with tea or coffee. Breakfasts average around HK$20, lunch and dinner cost from HK$35 to HK$50.

The four major chains are *Café de Coral, Fairwood, Dai Ga Lok* and *Maxim's*, all similar in price and quality. Westerners are notably absent from these places, but that's not to say they are not worth trying. Some, like Maxim's, have special value meals after 5.30 pm (they mainly cater for the lunch crowd), where you can get a deep bowl of vermicelli noodles with pork strips in a tasty soup for only HK$15.

One of the brightest spots on the fast-food scene is the *Oliver's Super Sandwiches* chain. Originally a gourmet food store in Central, Oliver's has evolved into a growing network of clean, reasonably priced sandwich shops. The ingredients are fresh and the sandwiches tasty, put together in front of you by staff wearing surgical gloves. Breakfast (till 11 am) is excellent; they also serve waffles, soup, baked potatoes, salads, and toasted sandwiches. In Central (Map 6), Oliver's has branches in Exchange Square, Prince's Building and Citibank Plaza. In Causeway Bay (Map 7) there's an Oliver's in Windsor House. For other locations, check the Tsim Sha Tsui map (Map 5).

*Delifrance* is a chain of outlets selling decent coffee and tea, sandwiches, croissants, cheese puffs, soup and other tit-bits. The restaurants are spacious and clean, and newspapers on wooden rods are available for customers to thumb through. There are branches in Central, Sheung Wan and Wan Chai (see Maps 6 & 7).

An excellent place to tuck into filling sandwiches, daily set meals (such as cottage pie, quiche lorraine and pasta) and great coffee is *Pier One* (Map 6; ☎ 2526-3061), in the arcade under Jardine House, Central.

Wan Chai is also home to many thriving, hole-in-the-wall sandwich shops where westerners swarm during their lunch break. They are all pretty good and serve great nosh and decent coffee. *Little Italy* has made a name for itself at 88 Lockhart Rd and is open till 6 am on Saturday and Sunday mornings. There is another branch at 13 Lan Kwai Fong (Map 6); perfect for post-club munchies. *Fidi* does the same sort of fare at 87-91 Lockhart Rd, Wan Chai.

The *Chop Chop Café* (Map 6; ☎ 2537-7288), 17 Wing Wah Lane, Lan Kwai Fong, is a midget cheap eatery where you can fill up on baked potatoes and other quick meals. Nearby, *Midnight Express* (Map 6; ☎ 2525-5010), 3 Lan Kwai Fong Lane, cooks Greek, Indian and Italian favourites late into the night. *HK Baguette* (Map 6) a few doors away specialises in sandwiches.

Winning the prize for the most exotic fast-food is *Genroku Sushi*. Though not in the same league as a good Japanese restaurant, the sushi is still OK. The only drawback is that there can be long queues for seats, especially during the 1 to 2 pm lunch hour. For locations of some Genroku Sushi branches, check the Central, Causeway Bay and Tsim Sha Tsui maps.

More speedy Japanese food can be found at *Yoshinoya Beef Bowl* (Map 6) which specialises in big bowls of steamed rice with sliced beef or chicken for HK$27 to HK$35. There's a branch opposite Arsenal St on Hennessy Rd, Wan Chai.

### Self-Catering
*Wellcome* and *Park n' Shop*, the two major supermarket chains, have branches all over Hong Kong. They stock all the major staples, like bread, milk, eggs, tinned and frozen foods, as well as wine and spirits. The selection is generally large. *7-Eleven* convenience stores are ubiquitous and open 24 hours, but prices are high.

Upmarket self-caterers may want to check out the basement floors of the Japanese department stores in Causeway Bay. The supermarkets here have all manner of exotic items and high-quality foods, as reflected by the prices. The basement level of the Seibu department store, in the Pacific Place shopping mall (Map 6) in Admiralty has one of the best markets in town, with dozens of imported cheeses, meats, and luxury foods.

Delicatessens are blossoming in Hong Kong. Gastronomes can head to a number of quality outlets, rich with the aroma of herbs, spices, cheeses, dried sausages, patés and fine wines. *Oliver's Food Stores,* associated with the sandwich fast-food chain, is stuffed with European delicacies, though prices are steep. There are Oliver's Food Stores in the Prince's Building (Map 6) in Central, Harbour City (Map 5) in Tsim Sha Tsui and the Repulse Bay shopping arcade.

Other delis to look out for are *Vino and Olio* (Map 6; ☎ 2523-4483) at 54 D'Aguilar St, Lan Kwai Fong, and the *Wyndham Street Deli* (Map 6; ☎ 2522-3499), a smart deli/restaurant at 36 Wyndham St, Central.

Wan Chai features on the cholesterol map of Hong Kong with *Castello del Vino Italian Wine Shop and Delicatessen* (☎ 2866-0587) at 12 Anton St.

Up in Mid-Levels, you can find *L'Epicerie* (☎ 2522-1577) at 31-37 Mosque St.

Other good delis include *Monsieur Chatté* (☎ 2889-5628), shop 132, West Wing, Heng Fa Chuen and *Superitalia* (☎ 2554-6203), Unit 1013-14, 10th floor, Horizon Plaza, 2 Lei Wing St, Ap Lei Chau.

If you want fresh bread and wholemeal ingredients, *The Source of Health* (☎ 2869-7383) obliges with a pastoral selection of breads and cakes including blueberry muffins, banana and raisin muffins, organic whole wheat loaves and French baguettes. Follow the crispy aroma to the Yip Fung Building, 18 D'Aguilar St, Central.

### PLACES TO EAT – MIDDLE
This is where you can really start to enjoy what Hong Kong has to offer. In addition to the numerous types of Chinese restaurants, consider trying out some other Asian cuisines on offer.

PLACES TO EAT

PLACES TO EAT

## HONG KONG RESTAURANT INDEX

### Chinese Cuisine

**CENTRAL & ADMIRALTY (Map 6)**

| | |
|---|---|
| Cantonese | Jade Garden, Luk Yu, Noble House, Tai Woo, Yung Kee |
| Chiu Chow | Chiu Chow Garden |
| Hunan | Hunan Garden |
| Peking | Peking Garden |
| Shanghai | Ning Po Residents Association, Shanghai Garden, Shanghai Shanghai |
| Sichuan | Sichuan Garden |

**SHEUNG WAN (Map 6)**

| | |
|---|---|
| Cantonese | Ho Choi Seafood Restaurant, Hsin Kuang, Golden Snow Garden |
| Chiu Chow | Leung Hing Chiu Chau Seafood Restaurant |
| Shanghai | South and North |
| Vegetarian | Fat Heung Lam, Vegi-Table |

**WAN CHAI & CAUSEWAY BAY (Map 7)**

| | |
|---|---|
| Cantonese | Dynasty, Fook Golden East Lake, Golden East Lake Chinese Cuisine Restaurant, Lam Moon, Lung Moon, One Harbour Road, Steam & Stew Inn |
| Chiu Chow | Carriana Chiu Chow |
| Peking | American |
| Shanghai | Lao Ching Hing, Shanghai Village, Wu Kong |
| Sichuan | Red Pepper, Sze Chuen Lau, Yin King Lau |
| Taiwan | Forever Green |
| Vegetarian | Fat Mun Lam, Kung Tak Lam, Vegetarian Garden, Vegi Food Kitchen |
| Yunnan | Yunnan Kitchen |

**ABERDEEN (Map 9)**

| | |
|---|---|
| Cantonese | Jumbo, Jumbo Palace, Tai Pak |

**HONG KONG ISLAND SOUTH (Map 3)**

| | |
|---|---|
| Cantonese | Hei Fung Terrace (Repulse Bay), Shek O Chinese-Thai (Shek O) |
| Sichuan | Welcome Garden (Shek O) |

**TSIM SHA TSUI (Map 5)**

| | |
|---|---|
| Cantonese | Dynasty, Fook Lam Moon, Jade Garden, Lai Ching Heen, North Sea Fishing Village, Oriental Harbour, Shark's Fin, Siu Lam Kung, Sun Tung Luk, The Chinese Restaurant |
| Chiu Chow | Chiu Chow Garden, Delicious Food Co Chiu Chow |
| Peking | Peking Restaurant, Spring Deer, Tai Fung Lau |
| Shanghai | Great Shanghai, Shanghai Restaurant, Snow Garden |
| Vegetarian | Kung Tak Lam |

**YAU MA TEI & MONG KOK (Map 4)**

| | |
|---|---|
| Cantonese | House of Tang, Yat Tung |

### International Cuisine

**CENTRAL & ADMIRALTY (Map 6)**

| | |
|---|---|
| American | American Pie, Dan Ryan's, Hard Rock Café, Tony Roma's, Trio's |
| British | Bentley's Seafood, Bull and Bear Pub |
| Continental | Jimmy's Kitchen, M at the Fringe, Post 97 |
| French | Aujourd'hui, La Rose Noire Patisserie, Le Fauchon, Papillon, Petrus |
| German | Bit Point, Mozart Stub'n, Schnurrbart |
| Indian | Ashoka, India Curry Club, Koh-I-Noor, Mughal Room, Spice Island Club, Tandoor, The Village |
| Italian | Grappa's, La Trattoria, Tutto Meglio, Va Bene |
| Japanese | Agehan, Fukuki, Genroku Sushi, Hanagushi, Sakaegawa, Tokio Joe, Yorohachi |
| Mexican | Zona Rosa |
| Pan-Asian | Vong |
| South-East Asian | Tiger's |

---

International restaurants can be found in abundance in this price range; in fact a revolution of sorts has occurred over the past year or so, with a clutch of snazzy new restaurants opening in the area christened as Soho (south of Hollywood Rd), centred on Staunton and Elgin Sts. Jostling for attention are a whole host of international eateries – this whole area is seriously challenging Lan Kwai Fong's hold on fashionable food and nightlife. It hasn't all gone smoothly, however; local residents, panicking at the

## HONG KONG RESTAURANT INDEX

*Note: Not all entries are shown on maps. Check text under district and cuisine headings for addresses and directions.*

**PLACES TO EAT**

sudden appearance of a noisy Lan Kwai Fong clone in their neighbourhood, have managed to make it an uphill struggle for many of the new places to get liquor licences. Still, you can take your own booze – get your wine from *Hop Hing Vintners* (Map 6)

nearby at 29 Staunton St – to those restaurants still waiting for a liquor licence, and delight in some novel flavours, from New Orleans to Nepal, from Spain to India. Soho's growth is set to continue, with more restaurant openings on the cards.

## Chinese

**Central & Admiralty (Map 6)** This district is better for non-Chinese food, but there are a few places worth recommending. Most are packed to the walls during the working week from 1 to 2 pm, but if you go around noon to 12.30 pm, you should be able to get a table.

Sitting between the towers of Exchange Square on the 3rd floor of the Forum shopping mall and feeding the suits from above at lunchtime, is *Hunan Garden* (☎ 2868-2880). This elegant, somewhat expensive place specialises in spicy Hunanese cuisine. The fried chicken with chilli is excellent, their seafood dishes (unusual in Hunanese cuisine) are recommended, and the setting, looking out over the harbour or the heart of Central, adds to the atmosphere.

Hunan Garden is part of a chain run by Maxim's, a local restaurant and food service company. The names usually reflect the style of Chinese cuisine. There's a *Chiu Chow Garden* (☎ 2525-8246) in the basement of Jardine House (and another one on the ground floor of the Lippo Centre), a *Shanghai Garden* (☎ 2524-8181) on the 1st floor of Hutchison House and a *Peking Garden* (☎ 2526-6456) in the basement of Alexandra House. *Sichuan Garden* (☎ 2521-4433) is on the 3rd floor of Gloucester Tower, The Landmark, Central. There are exceptions to the regional names: *Jade Garden* serves decent quality Cantonese food in Swire House (☎ 2526-3031) and Jardine House, Central (☎ 2524-5098), among other places. The food at all of these restaurants is usually tasty, and the presentation is good as well. Hunan Garden is the most expensive; prices at the others tend to be quite reasonable.

Classy (but pricey) Cantonese flavours can be indulged in at the *Island* restaurant (☎ 2848-7305) on the 4th floor of the Furama Kempinski Hotel on Connaught Rd. If you want to let your hair down and spend with abandon, try the deep fried squid stuffed with mashed shrimp or the sliced pigeon with bamboo shoots – delicious. A very popular and cheap dim sum venue is the long-standing *Luk Yu* (☎ 2523-5464) at 24-26 Stanley St.

Near Lan Kwai Fong at 32-40 Wellington St is the reigning patriarch of Cantonese restaurants, the *Yung Kee* (☎ 2522-1624). The roast goose here has been the talk of the town for 50 years, and their dim sum is also excellent.

Shanghainese food cooked as if flown straight in from the Bund gives *Shanghai Shanghai* (☎ 2869-0328) a commendable authenticity that makes the rather huge bill all worth while. You can find it in the basement of the Ritz-Carlton Hotel.

**Sheung Wan (Map 6)** The province of cheap eats and noodle shops, this area also has a few good mid-priced restaurants. A popular destination for dim sum and Cantonese seafood is the *Ho Choi Seafood Restaurant* (☎ 2850-6722) at 287-291 Des Voeux Rd, Central. The menu here is just a maze of Chinese characters so get pointing and join in the fray. For the full aircraft-hanger Cantonese restaurant experience, try the *Hsin Kuang Restaurant* (☎ 2541-3233), a multi-storey affair next to the Western Market. The food isn't all that memorable, but the atmosphere is pure Hong Kong. Next door is the *Golden Snow Garden Restaurant* (☎ 2815-8128), steeped in the flavours of Shanghai, with traditional aromas from Sichuan and Beijing adding to the complete Chinese experience. Dim sum is served from 11 am to 3 pm.

Shanghai cuisine is also the speciality at the *South and North Restaurant* (☎ 2816-6421) at 480 Queen's Rd West, west of Sheung Wan. Little more than a hole-in-the-wall restaurant, there are lots of tasty little treats on offer here: the Shanghai dumplings are especially good, as are the filling pork chop soup noodles. Although the sign out front is in English, the menu is not, so be prepared to point. The food is very cheap and the place is usually packed.

For Chiu Chow food, head to *Leung Hing Chiu Chau Seafood Restaurant* (☎ 2850-6666) at 27 Queen's Rd West. This restaurant uses the main cooking ingredients of the region – seafood, goose and duck – and prepares them delectably. Try the classic (cold) sliced goose and soya in vinegar, and revel in the lip-smacking desserts.

The *Red Star Bar & Café* (☎ 2804-6939), on the Central/Sheung Wan borders, is difficult to categorise. A product of the strange culture of handover 1997, this place serves postmodern Chinese food against a trendy backdrop of TV sets, geometric tables and poseurs. This is Chinese food with a western kick. It's in trendy Soho, of course, at 26-30 Elgin St.

**Wan Chai & Causeway Bay (Map 7)** Both these districts are brimming with all types of restaurants. Johnston Rd in Wan Chai has a couple of really traditional spots that are popular. Eating at the *Lung Moon Restaurant* (☎ 2572-9888) is probably similar to what it was like in the 1950s, and the prices, while not at 1950s levels, are still pretty reasonable. Not a lot of English is spoken here.

Nearby, the *Steam and Stew Inn* (☎ 2529-3913), at 21-23 Tai Wong St East, serves 'homestyle' Cantonese food, most of which is steamed, stewed or boiled. Pinned to the windows are some yellowing photos of the last governor, Chris Patten, chomping away on location. The food is good and free of MSG; try the steamed mushroom stuffed with minced pork and crab meat sauce. The place is popular, so it may be a good idea to reserve a table in advance.

Excellent Beijing food can be found at *American* (☎ 2527-1000), 20 Lockhart Rd. Don't be put off by the name, or by its grimy appearance; the restaurant has been around for over 50 years and most of its customers are regulars. Peking specialities can also be found at the *King Heung Peking Restaurant* (☎ 2577-1035) in the Riviera Mansions, Gloucester Rd, Causeway Bay.

If you don't mind a steeper bill, *One Harbour Road* (☎ 2588-1234) is a beautifully designed Cantonese restaurant in the Grand Hyatt Hotel. In addition to a harbour view, you can choose from a six page menu of gourmet dishes and dine in spacious surroundings. Not a bad combination. You'll need little tempting to sample the pan-fried beancurd stuffed with shrimp mousse, but go easy on the abalone unless you've endless credit. Another gem is *Dynasty* (☎ 2802-8888), in the New World Harbour View Hotel, where you can eat great dim sum.

For Chiu Chow food, the *Carriana Chiu Chow Restaurant* (☎ 2511-1282) on Tonnochy Rd, Wan Chai, rates right up there. Try the cold dishes (goose slices and cold crab), pork with tofu, or chiujiew chicken. The restaurant is usually crowded, but there are a lot of tables, so you shouldn't have to wait.

*Lao Ching Hing* (☎ 2598-6080), in the basement of the Century Hong Kong Hotel, has been consistently serving outstanding Shanghainese cooking since 1955. Sauteed fresh water shrimps are among the delicacies that will have you shaking the chef's hand.

Spicy Sichuan aromas are not hard to detect in Wan Chai and Causeway Bay. Popular with expats and Chinese alike, a number of restaurants specialise in this fiery food. However, despite their popularity, the *Yin King Lau Restaurant* (☎ 2520-0106), 113 Lockhart Rd, and way down at the other end of the same road in Causeway Bay, the *Sze Chuan Lau Restaurant* (☎ 2891-9027), will leave the real Sichuan food fan asking for a more authentic restaurant. The best Sichuan food I found was in Macau, which is a fair way to go for the experience – see the Excursions chapter for more on Macau.

Much better, but more expensive, is the long-established *Red Pepper* (☎ 2577-3811) restaurant at 7 Lan Fong Rd. If you want to set your palate aflame and sear your tonsils, try their sliced pork in chilli sauce, accompanied by Sichuan *dan dan min* noodles.

Spicy food lovers may also want to try the *Yunnan Kitchen* (☎ 2506-3309), in a vertical food court (you'll understand when you see it) on the 12th floor of the Times Square shopping complex. This place does a pretty good job of capturing the taste of Yunnanese cuisine: specialities include Yunnan ham, fried vermicelli Dali-style and fresh prawns stuffed in bamboo. Like all the restaurants in Times Square, this one's a bit pricey, but the midday buffet is good value at HK$78.

The *3.6.9. Restaurants* are worth a visit for reasonably priced, traditional Shanghai food

PLACES TO EAT

and polite and resourceful (although a bit doddery) service. The tangy hot and sour soup is thick with chunks of chicken, mushroom, tofu strips and peas – almost a meal itself. The aubergine fried with garlic is excellent. There are two branches in Wan Chai: one on O'Brien Rd and the other on Queen's Rd East, across from the Hopewell Centre.

Up on the 12th floor of Times Square, the *Wu Kong Shanghai Restaurant* (☎ 2366-7244), has a deserved reputation for serving excellent Shanghainese specialities, including pigeon with wine sauce and delicious crab dishes.

Finally, the best place in town to go for Taiwanese food is *Forever Green* (☎ 2890-3448) on Leighton Rd in Causeway Bay. This place does a good job with traditional Taiwanese specialities like oyster omelette, fried bean curd and three-cup chicken (*sanbeiji*). The prices are fairly high.

**Aberdeen (Map 9)** Restaurants have pretty much made Aberdeen world famous. This little harbour city is home to three of the largest, gaudiest and most unique eateries anywhere: the floating restaurants. Chief of these is *Jumbo* (☎ 2553-9111), a massive four-storey blaze of neon, gold lettering and ersatz pagoda roofing. The interior looks like Beijing's Imperial Palace crossbred with a Las Vegas casino. The Jumbo has played host to dignitaries from around the world, featured in several movies (including one James Bond film) and fed tourists for three decades. It's not so much a restaurant as an institution. That's how you should view it if you go to eat there, because the food has received bad press. The neighbouring *Jumbo Palace* is considerably more expensive. On the other side is *Tai Pak,* which has prices and standards similar to Jumbo.

Transport to and from the restaurants is via boats, which regularly run between piers at the Aberdeen Promenade and next to the Aberdeen Marina Club.

If dining on water-borne warehouses is not for you, there are also a few good Chinese and Thai restaurants on Old Main St. For details on getting to Aberdeen, see the Things to See & Do chapter.

**Southern Hong Kong Island (Map 3)** There is not much in the way of notable Chinese restaurants on the south side of the island. If you're in Repulse Bay and in the mood for dim sum or a fancy Cantonese meal you can try *Hei Fung Terrace Chinese Restaurant* (☎ 2812-2622), on the 1st floor of the Repulse Bay shopping arcade.

In Stanley, *Stanley's Oriental* (Map 10; ☎ 2813-9988), 90B Stanley Main St, serves Chinese and Thai food as well as a whole host of other Asian dishes. A whole concoction of flavours makes the waterfront location of this restaurant even more unique and memorable.

If you've made it all the way out to Shek O, you can try the *Welcome Garden* (☎ 2809-2836), a little Sichuan place that, while roofed, has a pleasant open-air feel to it. The food is generally well prepared and the prices are reasonable. The restaurant is on the left side of the main road as you enter town.

Across the street, the *Shek O Chinese-Thai Seafood Restaurant* (☎ 2809-4426) does a booming trade, but is known more for its Thai dishes than Chinese cuisine.

**Tsim Sha Tsui (Map 5)** This area is inundated with Cantonese restaurants, and once you get away from Nathan Rd, a lot of them are quite good. Prices are generally a bit lower than on Hong Kong Island.

The *Siu Lam Kung Seafood Restaurant* (☎ 2721-6168), at 17-21 Minden Ave, has long been a local favourite and is known for its shellfish specialities. This place is a bit more expensive than most, but that doesn't deter the crowds, so you may want to book in advance.

Also frequented by local seafood lovers is the *North Sea Fishing Village Restaurant* (☎ 2723-6843), in the 1st basement of the Auto Plaza, 65 Mody Rd, Tsim Sha Tsui East. Don't worry about the cheesy nautical decor: this place really is all right. It also serves good dim sum.

*continued on page 167*

# Hong Kong's Chinese Cuisine

*Title page: The fine art of shopping for groceries, at the Reclamation St market, Yau Ma Tei. (Photograph by Richard l'Anson)*

*Box: Hong Kong offers an abundance of both Chinese and western ingredients, making it one of the food capitals of Asia. (Photograph by Tony Wheeler)*

**Using Chopsticks**

*Place first chopstick between base of thumb and top of ring finger. (Bend fingers slightly.)*

*Hold second chopstick between the top of the thumb and tops of middle and index fingers.*

*Keeping the first chopstick and thumb still, move the other one up and down using middle and index fingers.*

# CHINESE FOOD

Chinese food is without doubt one of the finest aspects of this venerable culture. The diversity of flavours, cooking styles and ingredients, and the thousands of different dishes show that chefs have kept busy throughout China's 5000 year history.

The various types of Chinese cuisine are classified by region, and the ingredients tend to reflect what is available in each area. For example, northern China is suitable for raising wheat, so noodles, dumplings and other wheat-based dishes are most common. In the south, where the climate is warm and wet, rice is the basic staple. The Sichuan area, where spices grow well, is famous for fiery hot dishes.

The dominant style of cooking is Cantonese and, to a lesser extent, Chiu Chow, named after a coastal area in eastern Guangdong Province. But there are also plenty of restaurants serving other types of Chinese food. Of course, Sichuan, Beijing and Shanghai cuisine is generally better at the true place of origin, despite the claims of the Hong Kong Chinese, but there's plenty of outstanding food to be had here, and making it to a Chinese restaurant is one essential experience.

Following is a brief introduction to Chinese food etiquette and some of the styles of Chinese food available in Hong Kong, along with the names of a few notable dishes. The names of all regional dishes are romanised into Cantonese.

# Food Etiquette

The Chinese are by and large casual about etiquette at the table, and they don't expect foreigners to understand all of their dining customs. But there are a few rules that are good to know.

Chinese meals are social events. Typically, a group of people sit at a round table and order dishes (at least one per person) from which everyone partakes. Ordering a dish just for yourself appears selfish, unless you're with close friends. Most Chinese pick food from these communal dishes with their own chopsticks. But if you notice someone carefully placing a pair next to each plate of food, then use these 'public chopsticks' to serve yourself. Some dishes will come with a serving spoon, in which case use this.

Toasts in Hong Kong are not usually the variety with tedious speeches that occasionally befalls western diners, but are considerably more succinct. Sometimes a toast is limited to the words *yam seng*, which roughly translates to 'down the hatch!'. Raising your tea or water glass is not very respectful, so unless you have deep-rooted convictions against alcohol, it's best to drink your booze with the rest of the crowd. If you are the guest of honour at dinner, don't be surprised if you're called on to down a few glasses.

When the food is served, it's best to wait for some signal from the host before digging in. You will likely be invited to take the first piece if you are the invited guest. Often your host will serve it to you, placing a piece of meat, fish or chicken in your bowl. When eating fish, don't be surprised if the head gets placed on your plate: the head is considered to have the tastiest meat. It's all right if you decline, as someone else will gladly devour it.

Apart from the communal dishes, everyone gets an individual bowl of rice or a small soup bowl. It's considered polite to hold the bowl near your lips and shovel the contents into your mouth with chopsticks (or a spoon for soup). Soup is usually eaten at the end of a meal, rather than as an appetiser.

Eating is generally a hearty affair and often there is a big mess after the end of a meal. Restaurants are prepared for this – they change the tablecloth after each customer leaves. In Hong Kong it is also acceptable for Chinese diners – depending on the situation of course – to spit the bones from their food out on to the tablecloth.

Another good rule to remember is not to stick your chopsticks upright into your rice – this is how rice is offered to the dead, and the connotations at

Dried, fried, or baked – Chinese cooking makes use of raw ingredients such as squid, in this case dried, in many different ways.

Crispy, oily and juicy, plum-flavoured Peking duck is one of Chinese cuisine's most famous achievements.

Hotpot dishes originate from the colder northern regions of China, such as Inner Mongolia and Manchuria.

*Sichuan cuisine is renowned for being the most fiery type of Chinese food, allowing dishes to soak up chilli powder, as well as using other spices such as pepper.*

GLENN BEANLAND

*Noodle dishes originated from the wheat-growing belt of northern China, but can be found nowadays in many regional cuisines.*

JULIET COOMBE/LA BELLE AURORE

meal time are not pleasant for Chinese people. Chinese habitually make use of toothpicks after dinner, and even between courses. The polite way is to cover one's mouth with one hand while using the toothpick with the other.

Finally, if you absolutely can't manage chopsticks, don't be afraid to ask for a fork. Nearly all Chinese restaurants have them. Better a little humility and a full belly than intact pride and an empty stomach.

# Cantonese

Originating in neighbouring Guangdong Province, Cantonese food is the most popular in the city. Flavours are more subtle than other Chinese cooking styles, sauces are rarely strong, and some dishes almost have a sweet taste to them. There is almost no spicy Cantonese fare. All Chinese stress the importance of fresh ingredients, but the Cantonese are almost religious about it. Thus it is common to see fish tanks in most seafood restaurants. Those familiar with the sights of Chinatowns around the world will recognise the practice of stir-frying using a wok over a searing hot flame. This is known in Cantonese as 'wok hei'.

| | |
|---|---|
| *chā sīuh* | 叉燒 |
| barbecued pork | |
| *cháuh dahùhmihùh* | 炒豆苗 |
| stir-fried pea sprouts | |
| *chīngcháuh gaihlán* | 清炒芥蘭 |
| stir-fried kale (cabbage) | |
| *chīngjīng sehkbānyùhèh* | 清蒸石斑魚 |
| steamed garoupa (fish) with soy sauce dressing | |
| *jīuhyihm ngaùhpaih* | 椒鹽牛排 |
| deep-fried salt-and-pepper spareribs | |
| *sihjīuh ngaùhhó* | 豉椒牛河 |
| fried rice noodles with beef and green peppers | |
| *sāihlanfā daihjí* | 西蘭花帶子 |
| stir-fried broccoli with scallops | |
| *sāng sīuh gap* | 生燒鴿 |
| roast pigeon | |
| *sīnnìhng jīnyùèhngāih* | 鮮檸煎軟雞 |
| pan-fried lemon chicken | |
| *taìhbahk juihyūng hā* | 大白醉翁蝦 |
| 'drunken' prawns (steamed in rice wine) | |

**Dim Sum** These famous Cantonese delicacies are normally served steamed in a small bamboo basket, or on a little plate, during breakfast and lunch hours. Typically, each basket or plate contains three to four identical pieces and does the rounds of restaurant tables via a pushcart. Various stir-fried and steamed vegetable dishes, as well as some tasty sweets, are also available and nicely complement the dim sum. Though you can usually point to what you want, the following list gives you an idea of what's on offer.

| | |
|---|---|
| *chā sīuh bāùh* | 叉燒包 |
| barbecued pork buns | |
| *chéùhng fén* | 腸粉 |
| steamed rice flour rolls with shrimp, beef or pork | |
| *chīng cháuh sihchohih* | 清炒時菜 |
| fried green vegetable of the day | |
| *chūn gúèhn* | 春卷 |
| fried spring rolls | |
| *fuhng jáùh* | 鳳爪 |
| fried chicken's feet | |
| *fún gwó* | 粉果 |
| steamed dumplings with pork, shrimp and bamboo shoots | |

## The Ritual of Dim Sum

The best known of Hong Kong's culinary traditions, dim sum blends China's ancient traditions of tea drinking with the Cantonese penchant for snacking. The term *dim sum* refers to 'little snacks', although more literally translated it means 'to touch the heart'.

When Cantonese go for dim sum, they often describe it as going to drink tea *(yam cha)*. Although tea does play a major role, it's the array of different, delicious little snacks which make dim sum so much fun. That, and the places where you eat it. Hong Kong dim sum restaurants are mostly huge, boisterous affairs – the scene of constant action. Diners usually go in large groups, which makes for a wider variety of snacks, and more lively conversation.

In a cavernous room where they must compete with several hundred other diners, as well as the constant crash of clearing plates and teacups from tables, the noise level has to be heard to be believed. Even the decor seems loud. But if you're in the mood for it, this is all part of the experience, for it's the sound of people relaxing and enjoying themselves. Obviously the best way to participate is to come in a group yourself. Dim sum alone is not much fun, especially because on your own you can't sample a whole range of snacks: they fill you up very quickly.

It takes time to get used to the whole ritual. Don't be afraid to wave or call over the people with the pushcarts. Each pushcart has a different selection, so take your time and order a few things from the different carts. It's estimated that there's about 2000 dim sum dishes, though a restaurant will only prepare 100 on any given day. You pay by the

number of plates and baskets you order. When the cart comes by, feel free to lift up the lids to see what is underneath. It's not considered rude. If you want more tea, remove the lid and let it hang from the cord attaching it to the pot. Someone will see it, and refill

| | | |
|---|---|---|
| *gāihsī cháùhmihn* | 雞絲炒麵 | |
| fried crispy noodles with shredded chicken | | |
| *gōn sīùh yīmihn* | 干燒伊麵 | |
| dry-fried noodles | | |
| *hā gáùh* | 蝦餃 | |
| shrimp dumplings | | |
| *ham sùih gohk* | 鹹水角 | |
| fried rice flour triangles (usually with pork inside) | | |
| *hòh yihp fahn* | 荷葉飯 | |
| rice wrapped in lotus leaf | | |
| *paih gwāt* | 排骨 | |
| steamed spare ribs | | |
| *sān jūk ngaùh yohk* | 山竹牛肉 | |
| steamed minced beef balls | | |

the pot with hot water for you.

Usually dim sum is not expensive – HK$30 per person is about average for breakfast, or perhaps HK$50 for a decent lunch. However if you venture into one of the restaurants in the hotels, or a very traditional looking place loaded with rosewood chairs and ceiling fans, expect prices to be much higher.

Restaurants normally open about 6 am and close about 2.30 pm, with many also shutting down between 10 and 11.30 am. Arriving after lunch is probably not a good idea as the best food will be gone. This is also true of mid-morning. Operating hours are often extended on weekends and holidays, though it can also get very crowded at these times. Listing all the dim sum places in town would fill several volumes, but the places below should get you started.

*Canton Court* – (☎ 2739-3311) Guangdong Hotel, 18 Prat Ave, Tsim Sha Tsui; under HK$100 per person, dim sum served from 7 am to 2 pm

*Harbour View Seafood Restaurant* – (☎ 2722-5888) 3rd floor, Tsim Sha Tsui Centre, West Wing, 66 Mody Rd, Tsim Sha Tsui East; under HK$100 per person, dim sum served from 11 am to 5 pm

*Lai Ching Heen* – (☎ 2721- 1211) Regent Hotel, 18 Salisbury Rd, Tsim Sha Tsui; HK$200 to HK$300 per person, dim sum served from noon to 2.30 pm

*Luk Yu Teahouse* – (☎ 2523-5464) 26 Stanley St, Central; one of Hong Kong's oldest dim sum venues, prices range from HK$200 to HK$300 per person, dim sum served from 7 am to 6 pm

*Serenade Chinese Restaurant* – (☎ 2722-0932) 1st and 2nd floors, Restaurant Block, Hong Kong Cultural Centre, 10 Salisbury Rd, Tsim Sha Tsui; HK$100 to HK$200 per person, dim sum served from 11 am to 3 pm

*Steam and Stew Inn* – (☎ 2529-3913) ground floor, Hing Wong Court, 21-23 Tai Wong St East, Wan Chai; under HK$100 per person, dim sum served from 11.30 am to 2.30 pm

*Summer Palace* – (☎ 2820-8552) 5th floor, Island Shangri-La Hotel, Pacific Place, Supreme Court Rd, Admiralty; HK$200 to HK$300 per person, dim sum served from noon to 3 pm

*Tai Woo Restaurant* – (☎ 2524-5618) 17-19 Wellington St, Central; under HK$100 per person, dim sum served from 10 am to 1 pm

*Yat Tung Chinese Restaurant* – (☎ 2710-1093) Eaton Hotel, 380 Nathan Rd, Yau Ma Tei; HK$100 to HK$200 per person, dim sum served from 11 am to 3 pm

*Yung Kee Restaurant* – (☎ 2522-1624) 32-40 Wellington St, Central; HK$50 to HK$100 per person, dim sum served from 2 to 5 pm

*sìuh maih*　　　　　　　烧賣
　　pork and shrimp dumplings
*wohòh gohk*　　　　　　芋角
　　deep-fried taro puffs

# Chiu Chow

Chiu Chow dishes are in some cases lighter than Cantonese, and make heavy use of seafood. Sauces sometimes border on sweet, using orange, tangerine or sweet beans for flavour. Among the most famous specialities are shark's fin and bird's nest, but duck and goose, cooked in an aromatic sauce that is used again and again (known as 'lo sui', or old water) are also popular. Chiu Chow chefs are known for their skills in carving raw vegetables into fancy floral designs.

*Hong Kong's top restaurants have many different types of shark fin soup, priced accordingly. (Photograph by Glenn Beanland)*

*bākgū sāihlanfā* 北菇西蘭花
stewed broccoli with black mushrooms
*bīngfā gōngyin* 冰花宮燕
cold sweet bird's nest soup (dessert)
*chùhèhnjiùh gohklùhnghā* 川椒焗龍蝦
baked lobster in light pepper sauce
*chīngjiùh ngaùhyohksī* 清椒牛肉絲
fried shredded beef with green pepper
*dahih yùhèhchi tōng* 大魚翅湯
shark's fin soup
*fōngyùhèh gailán* 方魚芥蘭
fried kale with dried fish
*gāihyùhng sihùhchohih* 雞茸紹菜
stewed Tianjin cabbage with minced chicken
*jīng háih* 蒸蟹
steamed crab
*ja nghēùhng ngap* 炸五香鴨
deep-fried spiced duck
*seihsēk pingpún* 四色拼盤
cold appetiser platter of four meats/seafood

## Peking (Beijing) & Northern Cuisine

Peking cuisine, also referred to as northern-style food, originated in China's wheat belt, so steamed bread, dumplings and noodles figure more prominently than rice. Dishes feature stronger spices such as peppers, garlic and coriander.

The most famous speciality is Peking duck, often carved in front of you, which you place on a wafer thin pancake with strips of spring onion, cover it all in plum sauce and roll it up. The duck is crispy, oily and juicy and quite wonderful. Often a broth made from the bones of the duck are served alongside. Lamb and mutton hotpots are also popular. Another popular dish is beggar's chicken (see the boxed text on this dish later in this chapter).

*bākgīng tihnngap* 北京填鴨
Peking duck
*bākgīng fūngcháùh lāihmihn* 北京風炒拉麵
noodles fried with shredded pork and bean sprouts
*bākgūpa jūnbahkchohih* 北菇扒津白菜
Tianjin cabbage and black mushrooms
*chōngyaùh béng* 蔥油餅
pan-fried spring onion cakes
*fohòhgwaih gāih* 富貴雞
beggar's chicken
*gōncháùh ngaùhyohksī* 干炒牛肉絲
fried shredded beef with chilli sauce
*gōngbaùh dahihhā* 宮爆大蝦
sauteed prawns in chilli sauce
*sāmsīn tōng* 三鮮湯
clear soup with chicken, prawn and abalone
*sīnyohk siùhlòhng bāùh* 鮮肉小龍包
steamed minced pork dumplings

## Shanghai

*Pan-fried fish or spring onion cakes are a common form of snack food on Hong Kong streets. (Photograph by Marie Cambon)*

Shanghainese cooking (including Hangzhou and Suzhou) is generally richer, sweeter and oilier than other Chinese cuisines and strong flavours are paramount. Seafood is widely used, as are preserved vegetables, pickles and salted meats. Like Peking food, there are a lot of dumplings on the menu.

*chīngcháuh dahùhmihùh*　清炒豆苗
  sauteed pea sprouts
*fehihchuih yùhèhdaih*　翡翠玉帶
  sauteed scallops with vegetables
*fótuìh siùhchohih*　火腿小菜
  Shanghai cabbage with ham
*hóhngsiùh sijiitaùh*　紅燒獅子頭
  braised minced pork balls with vegetables
*ja jigāih*　炸子雞
  deep-fried chicken
*juih gāih*　醉雞
  'drunken' chicken in cold rice wine marinade
*nghēùhng ngaùhyohk*　五香牛肉
  cold spiced beef
*sehùhnghóih chōcháùh*　上海粗炒
  fried Shanghai noodles with pork
*sūèhnlaht tōng*　酸辣湯
  hot-and-sour soup
*sùhngsùèh wòhngyùhèh*　松鼠黃魚
  sweet-and-sour yellow croaker fish

# Sichuan (Szechuan) & Hunan

This area is known for having the most fiery food in China. Simmering and soaking are used more than in other Chinese cuisines, which really gives the chilli peppers time to work their way into the food. In addition to chilli, common spices include aniseed, coriander, fennel seed, garlic and peppercorns. Not all dishes from Sichuan are hot however (such as Camphor smoked duck) and there is a fair amount of mild flavouring at work as well. Hunanese cooking, on the other hand, is generally excruciatingly hot, and ideal for those who love hot food. These provinces are miles from the sea, so pork, chicken and beef act as staple meats. Hubei is also noted for its spicy food.

*chīngjiùh ngaùhyohksī*　清椒牛肉絲
  sauteed shredded beef and green pepper
*dan dan mihn*　擔擔麵
  noodles in spicy peanut soup
*chuihpèhih wòhngyùhèhpin*　脆皮黃魚片
  fried fish in sweet-and-sour sauce
*gönbīn seihgwaih dahùh*　干煸四季豆
  pan-fried spicy string beans
*gōngbaùh gāihdīng*　宮爆雞丁
  sauteed diced chicken and peanuts in chilli sauce
*gōngbaùh mihnghā*　宮爆明蝦
  sauteed shrimp in chilli sauce
*jēùhngcha háùh ngap*　樟茶烤鴨
  duck smoked in camphor wood
*mapòh dahùhfohòh*　麻婆豆腐
  'grandma's beancurd' in spicy sauce
*sūèhnlaht tōng*　酸辣湯
  peppery hot-and-sour soup with shredded meat
*yùhèhhēùhng kéihjí*　魚香茄子
  sauteed eggplant in spicy fish sauce

# Other

**Vegetarian** The Chinese are masters at the art of adding variety to vegetarian cooking. Even if you are not a vegetarian it is worth giving one of the excellent vegetarian restaurants a try. Vegetarian food is largely based on soybean curd – but the Chinese do some miraculous things with it. 'Pork' or 'chicken' can be made by layering pieces of dried bean curd or can be fashioned from mashed taro root. It may not always taste like meat, but is sure looks real. Mushrooms are also widely used.

| | |
|---|---|
| *bōlòh cháùhfahn* | 菠蘿炒飯 |
|   fried rice with diced pineapple | |
| *chīngdūn bākgū tōng* | 清燉北菰湯 |
|   black mushroom soup | |
| *chūn gúèhn* | 春卷 |
|   spring rolls | |
| *fohòhpèhih gúèhn* | 腐皮卷 |
|   spicy bean-curd rolls | |
| *gūmgū súnjīm* | 金菇筍尖 |
|   braised bamboo shoots and black mushrooms | |
| *jāihlóùhmehih* | 齊鹵味 |
|   mock chicken, barbecued pork or roast duck | |
| *lòhhohn chohih* | 羅漢菜 |
|   stewed mixed vegetables | |
| *lòhhohnjāih yīmihn* | 羅漢齊伊麵 |
|   fried noodles with vegetables | |
| *yèhhchohih gúèhn* | 椰菜卷 |
|   cabbage rolls | |

**Noodles** Most noodle shops have several types of soup noodles, fried noodles and a few small dishes, such as steamed vegetables with oyster sauce or shrimp dumplings. Some shops also serve congee, a savoury rice porridge usually flavoured with pork, fish and pickled egg. The more deluxe places also serve full-blown Chinese dishes like fried beef and green pepper, curry chicken rice or sauted prawns. Regular thin noodles *(min)* can be substituted with thick rice noodles *(ho fun)*. A few variations are listed here (the more common dishes are first).

| | |
|---|---|
| *yùhèhdán mihn* | 魚蛋麵 |
|   fishball noodles | |
| *ngaùhyúèhn hó* | 牛河丸 |
|   beef balls with rice noodles | |
| *sīnhā wùhntūn mihn* | 鮮蝦雲吞麵 |
|   shrimp dumpling noodles | |
| *chohihyúèhn mihn* | 菜遠麵 |
|   vegetable noodles | |
| *sēùhngyúèhn hó* | 雙丸河 |
|   fish and beef balls with rice noodles | |
| *hòhyaùh yechohih* | 蠔油野菜 |
|   steamed vegetables with oyster sauce | |
| *yùhpin jūk* | 魚片粥 |
|   congee with fish slices | |
| *sīngjäùh cháùhmáih* | 星洲炒米 |
|   Singapore fried noodles (spicy) | |
| *yèhùhngjäùh cháùhfahn* | 楊州炒飯 |
|   fried rice with egg, shrimp and spring onion | |
| *gāléih ngaùhyohk fahn* | 咖喱牛肉飯 |
|   curried beef on white rice | |

*continued from page 158*

Not a bad deal for the money is the *Jade Garden Restaurant* (☎ 2730-6888), up on the 4th floor of Star House (across from the Tsim Sha Tsui Star Ferry Terminal). The restaurant has a consistently fine choice of Cantonese dishes including pan-fried stuffed bean curd.

The traditional rosewood furniture and ambience of *Dynasty* (☎ 2369-4111) at the New World Hotel is part of the authentic Cantonese dining experience you can enjoy at this restaurant. Though not cheap, specialities include steamed sliced pork with preserved shrimp paste and fresh salmon with rice noodle strips.

On the 2nd floor of the Tsim Sha Tsui Centre is the Kowloon branch of Maxim's *Chiu Chow Garden* (☎ 2368-7266), where you can taste this lighter, more subtle variation of Cantonese cooking for a modest sum.

The *Delicious Food Co Chiu Chow Restaurant* on Prat Ave, Tsim Sha Tsui, is also worth trying, though the decor is a bit more basic.

Next door is the *Shanghai Restaurant* (☎ 2739-7083), which presents its food the authentic Shanghai way: heavy with lots of oil. If you don't mind that, and a somewhat high bill, it's probably worth trying.

One door over, the *Great Shanghai Restaurant* (☎ 2366-8158), while a bit more touristy and less authentic, is somewhat cheaper and easier to negotiate for non-Chinese speakers. The stir-fried freshwater shrimps are a speciality.

The *Snow Garden* (☎ 2736-4341), 10th floor, 219 Nathan Rd is another popular venue for Shanghai food – come here for drunken pigeon, braised sea cucumber and sauteed fresh water shrimps, or *siu long bao*, traditional Shanghai meat-filled buns that are cooked in a steamer.

The *Shanghai No 1 Restaurant* (☎ 2316-2517), 5-9 Hart Avenue, is clean, cheap and fun, and serves extremely good siu long bao – once eaten, forever smitten.

Tsim Sha Tsui is home to what is probably Hong Kong's most famous Peking restaurant, *Spring Deer* (☎ 2366-4012). Tucked away in a nondescript building at 42 Mody

---

**Beggar's Chicken**

Towards the end of the Qing Dynasty (1644-1911), a chef, by the name of Wang Si, in Jiangsu Province was preparing a chicken, but accidentally broke the only pot in his kitchen. Out wandering alone, deep in contrition, he smelled the aroma of chicken, and spied a beggar cooking what appeared to be a lump of clay over a fire.

Wang was spellbound as the man broke open the clay to reveal a whole chicken sizzling inside. The beggar then spilt the beans. He had stolen a chicken, but had no pot in which to cook it, so he cooked it smothered in clay. Wang immediately saw the answer to his problem, and upgraded the beggar's recipe by first marinating the chicken in wine, ginger and spring onion, wrapping the chicken in a few lotus leaves to keep it clean, and then adding all sorts of special ingredients and stuffings. Since then, the dish has become a classic of Peking (Beijing) cuisine. ∎

---

Rd, this place serves some of the crispiest Peking duck in town. At HK$280 for a whole bird, it's not exactly budget dining, but won't break the bank either. This place is extremely popular, so you may have to book several days in advance.

If you can't get in at Spring Deer, try the *Tai Fung Lau Peking Restaurant* (☎ 2366-2494), 29-31 Chatham Rd, Tsim Sha Tsui, which also does a fine job on the northern specialities; HK$240 for a whole Peking duck. If it's full, try the lamb hot-pot restaurant next door for more north Chinese cooking.

At 227 Nathan Rd the inexpensive *Peking Restaurant* (☎ 2730-1315) keeps the fans of Peking duck merrily chomping away.

**Yau Ma Tei & Mong Kok (Map 4)** Most of the mid-range places in these areas are seafood restaurants that cater for locals and don't have English menus. If you're feeling adventurous, stroll the streets west of Nathan Rd and take a chance. If you don't feel like battling the language barrier, some of the hotel restaurants are worth a shot. The *Yat Tung Chinese Restaurant* (☎ 2710-1093) in the basement of the Eaton Hotel (Map 5) has an interesting menu, and the service is usually friendly and attentive.

For a slightly more refined atmosphere, you can try the wood-panelled *House of Tang* (☎ 2761-1711) in the Metropole Hotel (Map 4), which serves a mix of traditional and nouveau Cantonese cuisine.

### International

**American** The 1990s saw an eruption of American restaurants in Hong Kong. There are now so many it's almost ludicrous, but they all have one thing in common: high prices. The first, and still one of the best places, is *Dan Ryan's Chicago Grill*. There are two branches: the original (☎ 2845-4600) in the Pacific Place shopping mall (Map 6) in Admiralty; and a newer Tsim Sha Tsui counterpart (☎ 2735-6111) at Ocean Terminal (Map 5). The food is consistently good, the portions huge and the service excellent. The burgers here are universally acknowledged as excellent, as are the potato skins and chicken strips.

One of the other top picks is *American Pie* (☎ 2877-9779), hidden away on the 4th floor of the California Entertainment Building (Map 6) in Lan Kwai Fong. Featuring more homestyle dishes like turkey with gravy, fresh salads and even meatloaf, this place has become so popular you almost always need to book a table in advance. Try their Sunday brunch, a real bargain.

If you're craving a fat slab of ribs, hit *Tony Roma's* (☎ 2521-0292), next door on the 1st floor of the California Tower (Map 6).

Also in Lan Kwai Fong is *Al's Diner* (Map 6; ☎ 2521-8714), 27-39 D'Aguilar St, a retro throwback of chrome and 1950s curves; the burger prices are more up-to-date though.

*Paper Moon* (Map 7; ☎ 2881-5070), at 8 Kingston St, Causeway Bay, has jarring decor but scores on the food front, and has a decent kiddies menu. This restaurant has a live band in the evening.

On the Hong Kong Island side, *Trio's* (Map 6; ☎ 2877-9773), on Wo On Lane near Lan Kwai Fong, is for lovers of Maine lobster, clam chowder and oysters (flown in from Canada). The place is cosy, but tiny, so reservations are recommended.

US pop culture has elbowed its way into the restaurant scene with the arrival of *Planet Hollywood* and the *Hard Rock Café*. Planet Hollywood (☎ 2377-7888), near the bottom of Canton Rd in Tsim Sha Tsui, sees long queues trying to sample its standard American fare – but it's really the stunning ambience they're all in line for. The Hard Rock Café is a stamping ground for homesick Americans, burger and beer in hand and baseball cap screwed on tight. There is one branch (Map 6; ☎ 2377-8168) at Swire House, Chater Rd, Central and another branch (Map 5; ☎ 2377-8118) at 100 Canton Rd, Tsim Sha Tsui. Of the two, the Central restaurant is better: the Kowloon branch doubles as a dance club and the service suffers for it.

The *San Francisco Steak House* (☎ 2735-7576), 7 Ashley Rd, Tsim Sha Tsui, specialises in surf-and-turf, setting you up for the night with steaks, barbecue ribs, lobsters, kebabs, burgers, clams et al. This restaurant is only for the serious carnivore.

**Australian** A far-flung outpost of the Australian food empire takes on all comers at *The Continental* (☎ 2563-2209) in Quarry Bay. *HK Magazine* has heaped praise upon praise for its carrot soup and rigatoni pasta. An imaginative menu keeps all and sundry drifting back. The restaurant is on the ground floor, 2 Hoi Wan St. To get there, take the MTR to Quarry Bay, take the exit to Tong Chong St and Devon House. Hoi Wan St is near the end of Tong Chong St on the left.

Over in Wan Chai, *Brett's Seafood Restaurant* (Map 7; ☎ 2866-6608), at 72-86B Lockhart Rd, is nothing fancy: formica and fish and chips are the order of the day. The point is that the fish aren't dragged from the sludge of Victoria Harbour, but flown in from Oz.

**British** Pubs are everywhere, though many have 'gone native'. One place that stays true to its roots is the *Bull & Bear Pub* (Map 6; ☎ 2525-7436) on the ground floor of Hutchison House in Central. All the standards are on the menu, at prices even the English should be able to stomach.

Rather more expensive is *Bentley's Seafood Restaurant and Oyster Bar* (☎ 2868-0881), in the basement of the Prince's Building (Map 6) in Central. Among the medley of seafood served is lobster bisque, oyster and mushroom pie and fresh Scottish salmon.

For Hong Kong's best fish and chips, there's no contender to *Harry Ramsden's* (Map 7; ☎ 2832-9626), at 213 Queen's Rd East, Wan Chai. The service is a bit slow and sloppy, but the fish is excellent and a bargain. For HK$98 you get a fine haddock and chips, and a soft drink. Brits trip over each other to get in. This place is highly recommended.

**Burmese** The only show in town is the *Rangoon Restaurant* (☎ 2893-2281), at 265 Gloucester Rd, near the corner of Cannon St, in Causeway Bay. Don't expect the place to echo old Burma, the decor plays second fiddle to the wide selection of Burmese food. Vegetarians will find more than enough to make the trip worthwhile.

**Cajun/New Orleans** A popular new name in the Soho neighbourhood is *The Bayou* (Map 6; ☎ 2526-2118) at 9-13 Shelley St. This new establishment has gone down well with expats, picking up good reviews although it's not cheap. Try the Cajun barbecue ribs or the voodoo pasta.

**Continental** Many an eatery goes for the 'European' moniker, without confessing to one national cuisine. What's more, among the Euro-fare restaurants lurk a few oriental and nondescript intruders, so 'continental' is a woolly description at best.

Big on nostalgia and one of the oldest names in the game is *Jimmy's Kitchen* (Map 6; ☎ 2526-5293), at 1 Wyndham St, Central, which at 60 years of age has become an institution. Although the emphasis is on British food, even the fussiest eclectic diner will pause for breath confronted by the varied menu. Specialities include char-grilled king prawns, baked onion soup, black

pepper steak and a whole medley of desserts. There's also a branch in Tsim Sha Tsui (☎ 2376-0327) on the 1st floor, Kowloon Centre (Map 5), 29 Ashley Rd.

For stunning views over Victoria Harbour and Central and groovy decor, try the new *Port Café* (Map 7; ☎ 2582-7731), set in the Hong Kong Convention and Exhibition Centre. This is a stylish, sophisticated addition to the dining scene; relaxed and quiet with fine Euro/Italian dishes. On a similar note is the *Trader's Grill* (☎ 2582-8888), also in the exhibition centre. Trader's is a sleek, stylish and good value restaurant with efficient service. The emphasis is on seafood and quiet dining, the only noise being the odd rattle of pans from the open kitchen.

*Camargue* (☎ 2525-7997), near bb's in Wan Chai at 128 Lockhart Rd, offers outstanding meals. *HK Magazine* routinely gives this place its highest 'not to be missed' rating, so perhaps you should take their advice. Prices are on the high side.

Also in this category falls one of Hong Kong's most relaxing, laid-back café/restaurants, *Post 97* (Map 6; ☎ 2810-9333), 1st floor, 9 Lan Kwai Fong. Truth be told, the food and service can disappoint sometimes. But good music, plush comfy couches and chairs, and muted decor make it easy to sip your wine, read a book and contemplate a nice relaxing nap, although during lunch, dinner and weekend nights it gets pretty lively.

Off the beaten track and in the (relative) wilds of Hung Hom is the goal of many a Europhile diner, *The Grill* (☎ 2996-8433). Don't be put off by the uninspired name, the food and service make up for it. It's at the Harbour Plaza Hotel, 20 Tak Fung St.

A smattering of European delights (with a lightweight menu but low prices) awaits at *Lucy's* (Map 10; ☎ 2813-9055), 64 Stanley Main St, Stanley, in the south of Hong Kong Island. Winning consistent praise from diners, few are let down. French, Italian and Mediterranean flavours are combined here to create new twists and surprises.

Down in Repulse Bay you can find *The Verandah* (☎ 2812-2722) at 109 Repulse

Bay Rd, although you may have to book well in advance, as it's popular (and rightly so).

*Q* (☎ 2960-0994), at 33 Tong Chong St, Quarry Bay, is a reasonably recent arrival that has attracted attention due to its good value and ever-changing continental menu (with strong Italian tendencies).

**Filipino** Wan Chai is the part of town where you can find *Cinta* (Map 7; ☎ 2529-9752) at 41 Hennessy Rd, which serves Indonesian favourites like satay as well as Filipino delights. *Cinta-J* (Map 7; ☎ 2529-4183), at Malaysia Building, 50 Gloucester Rd, offers the same.

**French** There are a fair number of French restaurants in town, but most fall into the 'Things to Eat – Astronomical End' category. *Le Fauchon* (Map 6; ☎ 2526-2136), at 6 Staunton St near Central, won't require a bank loan, but the bill may inspire beads of sweat on the forehead and palpitations. Even so the food and mood are almost certain to satisfy.

Friendlier to the wallet and just as nice to the palate is *Papillon* (Map 6; ☎ 2526-5965), hidden near the end of Wo On Lane, next to Lan Kwai Fong. The place has a relaxed feel and the food is excellent. The lunchtime set menu is good value, but you may need to book a table in advance.

Another attractive French landmark at 30-32 D'Aguilar St in Lan Kwai Fong is *Café des Artistes* (Map 6; ☎ 2526-3880), which has won considerable praise for what it cooks up.

Unpretentious yet refined French dining can be had in Central at *Aujourd'hui* (Map 6; ☎ 2869-1132), 4-6 On Lan St, an attractive side street off Wyndham St. This relative newcomer is a touch on the expensive side, but has proved popular.

Authentic French food is also on offer in the smart *2 Sardines* (Map 6; ☎ 2973-6618) at 43 Elgin St in Soho.

For breakfast, it's hard to beat a bowl (that's right, bowl) of café au lait and pastries at *La Rose Noire Patisserie* (☎ 2877-0118) on the 3rd floor of the Pacific Place shopping mall (Map 6) in Admiralty. Lunch and dinner menus feature a delicious range of cheap salads (Hungarian, Hawaiian, Greek and more), quiches, puffs and pizzas, plus an extravaganza of cakes, muffins, doughnuts and pastries. Busy people can order food online (www.la-rose-noire.com.hk) and pick up later. There is another branch in Tsim Sha Tsui (☎ 2956-1222), on the ground floor of the Gateway at 254 Canton Rd.

If you're in Pacific Place, you can also check out *La Cité* (☎ 2522-8830), a bistro of sorts on the basement level. The fixed lunch menu is a good deal, and the cappuccino provides a fine reason to sit back and rest your feet.

Returning to the more pricey, high-class establishments, a trip to Stanley on southern Hong Kong Island will bring you to *Stanley's French* (Map 10; ☎ 2813-8873), 86 Stanley Main St. The seaside setting, the attentive staff and above all the fine food can more than justify the trip out here. Dishes include spinach and lobster bisque, braised veal shank in creamy potato purée and a vegetarian set lunch.

**German/Austrian** If you're yearning for a tasty bockwurst and maybe even some German conversation, there are places on both sides of the harbour that can oblige. In Lan Kwai Fong (Map 6) both *Schnurrbart* (☎ 2523-4700) and *Bit Point* (☎ 2523-7436) serve hearty fare, but they are bars however, where German beer drinking is taken seriously and the cigarette smoke can get pretty thick at times.

If so, hike up 8 Glenealy St to *Mozart Stub'n* (Map 6; ☎ 2522-1763) in Central, a cosy little Austrian spot with good food and wines and a delightful atmosphere.

In Tsim Sha Tsui more German pub grub is available at the *Biergarten* (Map 5; ☎ 2721-2302), 8 Hanoi Rd, and the Kowloon branch of *Schnurrbart* (Map 5; ☎ 2366-2986), at 9 Prat Ave.

**Indian** While most Indian restaurants fall into the budget price range (see earlier in this chapter) there are some places that offer a more refined setting. Perched above Lan Kwai Fong at 47-59 Wyndham St is *Ashoka* (Map 6; ☎ 2524-9623). This long-serving survivor still garners tributes for its use of fresh ingredients.

*The Mughal Room* (☎ 2524-0107), 75-77 Wyndham St, serves idyllic samosas and the rest of the menu is an exercise in harmonic flavouring. Recommended dishes include the dahi papri chat and the paneer dilbahar.

*Greenlands India Club* (Map 6; ☎ 2522-6098), 1st floor, Yu Wing Building, 64-66 Wellington St, Central, is an old standby, but it pushes it a bit by proclaiming itself 'Best Indian Cuisine in Town'.

*Tandoor* (Map 6; ☎ 2845-2299), 3rd floor, On Hing Building, 1-9 On Hing Terrace in Central, is another local favourite, and has an open kitchen so you can see how it's all done. Prices are a bit high, but not unreasonable.

*India Today* (☎ 2801-5959), at 26-30 Elgin St, is a new arrival in the self-fuelling 'How many restaurants can you get on one street?' competition that has galvanised the area south of eastern Hollywood Rd.

The venerable *Gaylord* (Map 5; ☎ 2376-1001) in Ashley Rd, Tsim Sha Tsui, has been going strong since 1972. Dim lighting, booth seating and live Indian music ushers you into a cosy world of spicy dining. You will hardly be able to tear yourself away from the remains of chicken tikka and pappadum crumbs on your plate and return to the real world.

**Indonesian** If you don't mind a bit of formica and fake wood panelling, go for an authentic meal at the *Indonesian Restaurant* (Map 7; ☎ 2577-9981), at 28 Leighton Rd in Causeway Bay. The service won't have you jumping for joy, but the fried chicken and super-spicy roasted fish with chilli might. There are also a couple of Indonesian hole-in-the-wall places on Lockhart Rd, just west of the Sogo department store, that may be worth a try.

Over in Wan Chai, the *Shinta* (☎ 2527-8780) is a dimly lit, laid-back spot that serves a pretty good nasi goreng. It's on the 1st floor of the Kar Yau Building, 36-44 Queen's Rd

East, near the intersection with Hennessy Rd.

If you're in Tsim Sha Tsui, the *Java Rijsttafel* (☎ 2367-1230), at 38 Hankow Rd, packs a lot of restaurant into a tiny room. The menu is extensive, but if you get overwhelmed just order the rijsttafel, which gives you 16 tasty dishes for under HK$150.

**Irish** *Delaney's* is about as close to real Irish pub grub and silky smooth draught Guinness as you're going to get outside of Dublin. There are two branches of this popular bar/restaurant: in Wan Chai (Map 7; ☎ 2804-2880), 2nd floor, One Capital Place, 18 Luard Rd; and in Tsim Sha Tsui (Map 5; ☎ 2301-3980), 3-7 Prat Ave. The Tsim Sha Tsui branch, which has an impressive long bar that stretches the length of the restaurant, has the better atmosphere. But the food in both places is always reliable. Delaney's Irish Ale is on tap, which is specially brewed for the bar by the South China Brewing Co.

**Italian** Along with American restaurants, a bevy of new Italian places have flooded onto the scene in recent years. Most aren't bad, but there are only a few that justify the money you must shell out.

In Lan Kwai Fong, *Tutto Meglio* (Map 6; ☎ 2869-7833) is beautifully decorated, and the food excellent, hailing principally from Florence. Tutto Meglio has a sister restaurant in the northern section of Tsim Sha Tsui: *Tutto Bene* (Map 5; ☎ 2316-2116) at 7 Knutsford Terrace. This spot has the added benefit of outdoor seating under giant umbrellas: throw in a nice spring day and you could well be in Florence.

*Tutta Luna* (Map 6; ☎ 2537-7288), 12 Lan Kwai Fong Lane, will surprise with a rich range of dishes, at prices that won't have the waiter prising your credit card from your vice-like grip.

Also in Lan Kwai Fong is *Va Bene* (Map 6; ☎ 2845-5577), at the top end of Lan Kwai Fong. Elegantly appointed, with pastel walls and wooden venetian blinds, the (decent) food is compromised by a hefty price tag.

*Il Mercato* (Map 6; ☎ 2868-3068), 34-36

D'Aguilar St, Lan Kwai Fong, is a bit of a squeeze inside but the food prices are nice and the food doesn't disappoint.

In the Landmark shopping centre (Map 6) in Central is the attractive but rather expensive *La Trattoria* (☎ 2524-0111). Spaghetti with clams in white wine sauce, duck lasagne and other exotic Italian dishes make this a rare treat.

*Club Casa Nova* (Map 6; ☎ 2869-1218), 46B Elgin St, is a popular place, but the servings are minuscule for what you pay (and we were overcharged).

Hounded by rave reviews for their pizzas, *Pepperoni's* (☎ 2792-2083) is a pilgrimage spot for devotees of their fresher-than-fresh ingredients. Amazing considering they are based in Sai Kung town, at 1592 Po Tung Rd.

*Beaches* (Map 10; ☎ 2813-7213), at 92B Main St, Stanley, is a more than serviceable Italian option at the very end of Main St. Also in Stanley is a branch of *Domino's Pizza* (☎ 2813-9239) at 30A Main St.

In Wan Chai, *La Bella Donna* (☎ 2802-9907) is a low cost option. The food is not spectacular, but you should walk away full and happy. It's on the 1st floor of the Shui On Centre (Map 7), 8 Harbour Rd.

Italy is not forgotten in Tsim Sha Tsui – the green, red and white flag flies outside *Valentino* (Map 5; ☎ 2721-6449) at 16 Hanoi Rd. The food and service are both very good.

**Japanese** There are countless numbers of Japanese places to choose from, the best of which are, not surprisingly, run by native Japanese. These restaurants support a large Japanese expatriate community, so you stand a good chance of getting a high-quality meal, though you will pay for it. Some Japanese venture that Hong Kong's Japanese fare is sometimes more expensive than Tokyo's in terms of what you get for your money. One way around this is to go for the set luncheons. They are priced from around HK$100 to HK$150, and include soup, pickles and other appetisers, all served together. Go at night, start enjoying the sake, and your bill can easily soar past HK$1000.

Two great places for lunch in Central are

*Hanagushi* and *Fukuki,* both in the Lan Kwai Fong area. Hanagushi (Map 6; ☎ 2521-0868) is a bit cramped and really fills up from 1 to 2 pm weekdays, but the yakitori, soba noodles and sushi are all crowd-pleasers. Fukuki (Map 6; ☎ 2877-6668) is rather more refined, with tatami mats and private dining enclaves; it also costs more.

A chopstick throw away *Tokio Joe's* (Map 6; ☎ 2525-1889), 16 Lan Kwai Fong Lane, makes Japanese food accessible to initiates and is not fiercely expensive. Also in the area at 5-6 Lan Kwai Fong (spoilt for choice?) is *Yorohachi* (Map 6; ☎ 2524-1251), which offers an excellent teppanyaki grill and great value lunch boxes. *Kiyotaki* (Map 6; ☎ 2877-1772), 19 D'Aguilar St, is another popular spot in the vicinity.

Two other decent lunch spots in Central are *Sakaegawa* (☎ 2522-0230) in the basement of the Ritz-Carlton Hotel (Map 6) and *Agehan* (☎ 2523-4332), in the basement of the Furama Kempinski Hotel (Map 6).

Not cheap, but up there with the best is *Isshin* (☎ 2506-2220) in Times Square (Map 7), Causeway Bay. The teppanyaki and sashimi bars are impressive and a complete spread of Japanese dishes will satisfy the most searching palate.

For a more down-to-earth atmosphere, try *Ichiban* (Map 7; ☎ 2890-7720), 21 Lan Fong Rd, Causeway Bay. The mood is more like an *izakaya,* Japan's ubiquitous pubs. Over in Tsim Sha Tsui is *Osaka* (Map 5; ☎ 2363-8323), 3rd, Ashley Building, 14 Ashley Rd, a comfortable place with great sushi.

It's also worth checking out the basement levels of the Japanese department stores Daimaru, Matsuzakaya, Mitsukoshi, Seibu and Sogo. With the exception of Seibu, in the Pacific Place shopping mall in Admiralty, all these stores are clustered together in Causeway Bay. The restaurants are usually pretty authentic and have good set lunches.

**Korean** If you don't mind hiking over to Sheung Wan, you can eat where the local Korean expats do. In the Korean Centre Building, 119-21 Connaught Rd, you'll find *Korea House Restaurant* (Map 6; ☎ 2544-

0007), acknowledged as having some of the most authentic Korean barbecue, kimchi and appetiser plates in Hong Kong. Prices are very reasonable too. Enter from Man Wa Lane. In the same building, the *Korea Garden* also seems to draw a steady crowd of Korean diners.

*Secret Garden* (Map 6; ☎ 2801-7990), shop 5, ground floor, Bank of America Tower, Harcourt Rd, Central, is often packed out, and you may find yourself at the end of a salivating queue.

In Times Square, Causeway Bay (Map 7) is *Arirang* (☎ 2506-3298), a large, brightly lit restaurant that may not be the place for a romantic dinner for two, but great for a group. It's a specialist barbecue outfit, and why not, they're a lot of fun. Get a plateload of *segyubsahl gooi* (pork belly slices) or the *boolgogi* (marinated beef slices) and sizzle up. Arirang has another branch at 210 the Gateway, 25 Canton Rd, Tsim Sha Tsui (☎ 2956-3288). Also on the Tsim Sha Tsui side is the small, but sizzlingly popular *Three-Five Korean Restaurant* (☎ 2376-1545), 6 Ashley Rd.

**Mediterranean** *Bacchus* (Map 6; ☎ 2529-9032), basement, 8 Hennessy Rd, Wan Chai, is a place to go and have a good time: the food is deliciously different and the service friendly and upbeat. Some nights there is live entertainment and on Tuesday you can smash a plate in honour of Greek party night. The experience will cost you, but it's almost always worth it.

**Mexican** Several places in town claim to serve Mexican food. With the following exceptions, they should all be given a wide berth, unless you enjoy throwing away money. In Lan Kwai Fong *Zona Rosa* (Map 6; ☎ 2801-5885) has impressed serious Mexican food fans. The food is fresh, and the sauces and chillies quite hot, but the high prices may cool you down a bit. A cosy and intimate Mexican evening can be had at the new *Caramba!* (Map 6; ☎ 2530-9963) in the heart of Soho at 26-30 Elgin St. Flush those scrummy tortilla chips and nachos down with a choice from a blinding selection of tequilas.

**Middle Eastern** *Desert Sky* (Map 6; ☎ 2810-7318), 36 Elgin St, is an oasis of Arabic spices and shades, hidden away among the Staunton/Elgin Sts Soho axis. Stars glint from the ceiling onto diners tucking into Middle Eastern grills. It offers a buffet lunch for HK$78 and a belly dancer goes into action on Tuesday nights.

At 27-39 D'Aguilar St in Lan Kwai Fong, *Beirut* (Map 6; ☎ 2804-6611) continues to serve excellent, and extremely filling, Lebanese food. There is another branch (Map 7; ☎ 2865-7271) over at 48-50 Lockhart Rd, Wan Chai.

**Mongolian** *Kublai's* is a fast growing chain of places that does a refined version of Mongolian barbecue. Head to the food counter, pick out whatever meat, vegetables, spices and sauces you want (there's a lot to choose from), hand it through a hole in the wall to the cook, and return to your table to await your creation. It's all you can eat for HK$98 (lunch) and HK$138 (dinner), and for the taste and the experience, this is a fine price. It's best if you can go with a group, as it's a very social atmosphere. Diners are allotted time blocks (two hours after 9.30 pm) due to the high demand, so call ahead to book your spot. An Internet access area exists for those eager to fraternise with distant nomads online. There are three branches: (☎ 2529-9117), 3rd floor, One Capital Place, 18 Luard Rd, Wan Chai; (Map 7; ☎ 2882-3282), 1 Keswick St, Causeway Bay; and (☎ 2722-0733), 55 Kimberley Rd, Tsim Sha Tsui.

**Nepalese/Himalayan** At the hub of the new Soho restaurant zone in Hong Kong is *Nepal* (Map 6; ☎ 2869-6212). Open the dagger-handled door of 14 Staunton St to a feast of Nepalese wonders, including such novelties as chicken lali gurash, mutton gorkhali, steamed vegetable dumplings and yak cheese; the set dinner comes in at a healthy HK$178. Waiters rush across the road with loaded plates to sister restaurant *Sherpa*

(Map 6; ☎ 2973-6886) opposite, which shares the same menu. The restaurants also sell Nepalese souvenirs.

**Pan-Asian/East Meets West** King of the pan-Asian genre is the *Peak Café* (Map 8; ☎ 2849-7868), which sits across the top end of the Peak Tram. The food is always delicious, and includes Chinese, Indian, Thai and some western dishes (the Indian food is usually the best pick). But what really makes this place is its amazing setting, vaulted ceiling, elegant decor and one of Hong Kong's best looking bars. It's also perfect for outdoor dining and voted by readers of *HK Magazine* in 1997 as the most romantic dining experience.

Across the road, housed in the hulking Peak Galleria (Map 8), is the *Café Deco Bar and Grill* (☎ 2849-5111). This place also does the pan-Asian thing, though with neither the class nor the warmth of the Peak Café. Still the food is good, if overpriced, and you can't argue with the jaw-dropping view of Hong Kong and Kowloon, especially the glittering version at night.

*Vong* (☎ 2825-4028), on the 25th floor of the Mandarin Oriental Hotel (Map 6) in Central, is a newcomer with Vietnamese, French and Thai food on the menu. Go easy, otherwise the bill can quickly get carried away with itself, although you may think it's worth it, what with the view.

A funky option is the glorious *Viceroy* (☎ 2827-7777) which goes overboard on its mixed-Asian lunch buffet: a swish blend of Indian, Vietnamese, Thai and Indonesian dishes await the imaginative diner. You can find it on the 2nd floor of the Sun Hung Kai Centre (Map 7), 30 Harbour Rd, Wan Chai.

*The Open Kitchen* (Map 7; ☎ 2827-2923) is a new addition to this eclectic option, serving Indian, Malaysian, Japanese and Italian food from a well-lit, smart restaurant on the 6th floor of the Arts Centre, 2 Harbour Rd, Wan Chai. If you're taking in a show or a play at the Arts Centre, this is an excellent spot to meet friends and have dinner.

One of the great bargains in town is the lunch/dinner buffet at *Salisbury's Dining Room* (☎ 2369-2211) on the 4th floor of the Salisbury YMCA (Map 5) in Tsim Sha Tsui. The food is not exquisite, but it's value for money. The cheery atmosphere and the prime location over Salisbury Rd make it stand out.

**Portuguese** If you don't have the time to make it to Macau, you might consider the *Casa Lisboa* (Map 6; ☎ 2869-9631), at 21 Elgin St near the Central/Sheung Wan border. Where better to chomp your way through roast suckling pig, African chicken, ribs and baked seafood rice? It costs a lot more than a Portuguese meal in Macau, but then you don't have to buy a ferry ticket.

*Portucale* (Map 7; ☎ 2527-9266), at 33 Lockhart Rd, Wan Chai, is nothing to shout about, but the relaxing interior and honest food still makes it worth putting on your map.

All is not lost on the Tsim Sha Tsui side. *Hideaway* (☎ 2926-3098), 86-98 Canton Rd stumbles a bit with the decor, but gets smoothly in step with genuine Portuguese food.

**Scandinavian** Yes, there is a Scandinavian restaurant, and, of course, it's part of the invasion of restaurants that has taken Soho by storm. It's called *Club Scandinavia* (Map 6; ☎ 2525-2621) and as you can imagine, strongly features seafood. You can find it at 15 Staunton St.

**South-East Asian** Amid all the glitter and lights of the Pacific Place shopping mall (Map 6) is *Tiger's* (☎ 2537-4682). The decor is a bit off-beat, but the food is right on target. Satay, Thai, Indian and other South-East Asian cuisine all get the workover here; the buffet is reasonable value at HK$138 (lunch) and HK$198 (dinner).

Eastern Hong Kong Island features an enclave of South-East Asian spice at *Wild Orchids* (☎ 2856-9848), ground floor, 39 Tong Chong St. Work your way through a veritable map of South-East Asian cuisine, from Hainan Island through Vietnam, Thailand, Indonesia to Malaysia and beyond.

A trip to Lantau Island can also net yourself some fine South-East Asian cooking at *Chili n' Spice* (☎ 2987-9191), shop 102, Discovery Bay Plaza. A popular spot for Thai, Indonesian and Singaporean dishes, this place is packed at weekends, so book ahead or go during the week.

**Spanish** A long-time favourite with expats, *El Cid* (Map 5; ☎ 2312-1989), 14 Knutsford Terrace, Tsim Sha Tsui, does justice to classics such as paella and fritas, and has an excellent assortment of tapas (appetisers that go great with drinking). On hand is a healthy selection of Spanish wine. Actually there are two restaurants, one just dishing up tapas and the other with both tapas and entrées.

A Lan Kwai Fong landmark for many years, *La Bodega* (Map 6; ☎ 2877-5472) serves quirky Spanish food in large helpings. The menu is a blackboard brought to your table. You can work your way through pasta with vegetables and garlic prawns, seafood paella and barramundi with green tomatoes.

*La Comida* (Map 6; ☎ 2530-3118) is a cosy little affair waving the Spanish flag at 22 Staunton St. *Rico's* (☎ 2840-0937), 44 Robinson Rd, takes tapas to the Mid-Levels. Always a refreshing dining experience, the gazpacho is zingy, the paella just right and the Mediterranean atmosphere spot on.

**Steak House** Get those steak knives ready, because *W's Entrecote* (☎ 2506-0133) does steak and only steak. Included in the price is bread, a salad and vinaigrette, and as many fries as you can squeeze on your plate. You can find the restaurant at shop 1303 in the Food Forum, Times Square (Map 7), Causeway Bay.

**Thai** A glut of Thai eateries spoils the diner for choice.

In Central at 13 Wing Wah Lane is the *Good Luck Thai* (Map 6; ☎ 2877-2971) restaurant. You can sink a few beers at Club 64, fight your way out (at weekends) and plonk yourself down on a wobbly stool at the Thai restaurant opposite, which spills over into the street. It's cheap, chaotic and fun and

only a glance away from further beers at Club 64, or the rest of Lan Kwai Fong.

Also in Lan Kwai Fong but at the other end of the spectrum is *Supatra's* (Map 6; ☎ 2522-5073), 50 D'Aguilar St. This place is trendy, but the food is good. It gets a bit loud when the after-work crowd starts flowing in, but the mood is cheerful enough.

*Lemongrass* (Map 6; ☎ 2905-1688), in the basement of the California Tower at 30-32 D'Aguilar St, is a smart and polite place that serves such treats as pomelo salad, spicy green Papaya salad and mussels in red curry.

Surrounding yourself with Thai artefacts and elegance is the way to enjoy fantastic Thai food at the *Golden Elephant* (☎ 2522-8696) at Pacific Place (Map 7), Queensway. Go as a group so you can order a table-load of dishes from the extensive menu. There are two other branches: one (☎ 2506-1333) in Times Square (Map 7), Causeway Bay; and the other (☎ 2735-0733) in Harbour City (Map 5), Kowloon.

The *Chili Club* (☎ 2527-2872), on the 1st floor, 88 Lockhart Rd, Wan Chai, is another old haunt of Thai aficionados. Some say it's slipped a few notches, but it's still a popular destination on the Hong Kong spice route.

Nearby at 44 Hennessy Rd, *Thai Delicacy* (Map 7; ☎ 2527-2598) certainly has some of Hong Kong's most authentic Thai food, and at prices that few other places can match. The decor is strictly utilitarian, but you'll probably be too busy feasting to notice.

In the Mid-Levels all is not lost with *Phukets* (☎ 2868-9672), at 30-32 Robinson Rd. This cosy spot has a mural of a Thai beach to lure you into its way of thinking. The food is good (mainly seafood) and the menu regularly expands.

On the Kowloon side you can find authentic, flavoursome Thai food at the *Red Chilli Thai Food Restaurant* (☎ 2363-5723) at 27 Man Tai St, Hung Hom. Another popular place is *Sawadee Thai Restaurant* (Map 5; ☎ 2363-3299), 6 Ichang St.

**Vietnamese** There's good Vietnamese food in Hong Kong, thanks to a large community of Chinese migrants from Vietnam.

At the budget end, *Bon Appetit* (Map 6; ☎ 2525-3553), 14B Wing Wah Lane, Lan Kwai Fong, serves good, cheap meals. In the same area is the inexpensive *Pearl Vietnamese Restaurant* (Map 6; ☎ 2523-5233), 7 Wo On Lane, off D'Aguilar St.

One of the best and most well-known places is *Saigon Beach* (Map 7; ☎ 2529-7823) at 66 Lockhart Rd, Wan Chai. If it's crowded and there are only one or two of you, chances are you'll be sharing your table with strangers. Don't worry; it's all worth it. Prices are higher than you might expect for a place of this size and appearance, but if you don't want to pay, there are plenty of others who will grab your seat.

Colonial Vietnamese elegance ushers you into another world at *Indochine 1929* (Map 6; ☎ 2869-7399), on the 2nd floor of the California Tower in Lan Kwai Fong. The old photographs, lighting and memorabilia are appetisers for the remarkable food that follows. Try the spring rolls, and the beef and papaya salad.

The Soho clique of eateries wouldn't be complete without the Vietnamese elegance that *Café Au Lac* (Map 6; ☎ 2526-8889) brings to this international fraternity of kitchens. Authentic Vietnamese food for the well-heeled – the traditional garb on the waitresses adds to a rarefied atmosphere. You can find it at 20 Staunton St.

Causeway Bay hosts the often packed *Yuet Hing Yuen* (Map 7; ☎ 2832-2863), at 17 Cannon St, an establishment that makes few concessions to decor, but the food is a triumph. It's a bit noisy and chaotic, but the price is right and you could well find yourself going back for seconds. The deep-fried butter garlic chicken wings is a good choice.

If Yuet Hing Yuen is packed out, just across the street is the *Yinping Vietnamese Restaurant* (Map 7; ☎ 2832-9038) at 24 Cannon St.

## PLACES TO EAT – TOP END

Often in Hong Kong the price difference between a top-end and a mid-range meal is a matter of what you order on the menu. There are numerous restaurants in the preceding section where dinner for two can cost HK$1000 or more. Likewise, in the places listed in this section, you may be able to get out for less than HK$1000 for two. But not if you really want to go for it, which after all is what top-end dining should be all about.

Many of Hong Kong's finest restaurants are in the luxury hotels. Those staying in one of the five-star hotels will find top-end restaurants without even having to venture outside. The following is a fairly selective list that includes a few of the top picks.

### Chinese

There aren't too many really high-priced Chinese places, perhaps because there's so much good food already available for less money. At the few really expensive restaurants you're usually paying more for the setting, decor or reputation, rather than the food.

At the *Golden East Lake Chinese Cuisine Restaurant* (☎ 2576-2008) you will find yourself surrounded by carved wooden screens, frosted glass, small trees and fountains. The idea is to put your mind and body at ease, and focus all your attention on the elaborate Cantonese seafood dishes that the chefs have laboured over. The restaurant is on the ground and 1st floors of Eton Tower, 8 Hysan Ave, Causeway Bay.

Long known as one of Hong Kong's top Cantonese restaurants, the *Fook Lam Moon* makes sure you're taken care of from the minute you walk in the door – *cheong-sam* clad hostesses escort you in and out of the elevator that brings you to the dining room. Once you've been comfortably seated you will be faced with an intimidating menu that's designed for shock value, by listing prices for shark's fin on the first page. Sample the pan-fried lobster balls, the house speciality. Portions are not very large, but they are filled with flavour. There are two branches: (☎ 2866-0663), 35 Johnston Rd, Wan Chai; and (☎ 2366-0286), 1st floor, 55 Kimberley Rd, Tsim Sha Tsui.

For conspicuous consumption, it's hard to beat the *Sun Tung Luk Shark's Fin Restaurant*. This is where business executives go to

Whether you're on board the Jumbo floating restaurant on Aberdeen Harbour (top), at the food stalls in Temple St, Yau Ma Tei (middle left), surveying the night from a busy fast-food eatery (bottom left) or walking around the fruit and vegetable stalls at the Gresson St market, Wan Chai (bottom right), eating out in Hong Kong is a culinary education.

GLENN BEANLAND

RICHARD I'ANSON

RICHARD I'ANSON

GLENN BEANLAND

RICHARD I'ANSON

Shopping in Hong Kong is a buyer's paradise: hunt for clothes on Li Yuen St, Central (top left); trade at the bird market – birds are a particular favourite choice of pet (top right); wander under the neon signs of Nathan Road, Kowloon (middle); or search for antiques in Sheung Wan (bottom left and right).

celebrate big deals and the very wealthy hold wedding receptions. The speciality, shark's fin, comes in different gradings and prices. The most basic shark's fin soup costs around HK$260 for a single bowl and the glove-wearing waiters will happily take you through the price structure. The restaurant has two branches: (☎ 2882-2899), ground and 1st floors, Sunning Plaza, 1 Sunning Rd, Causeway Bay; and (☎ 2730-0288), shop 63, ground floor, Ocean Galleries, Harbour City, Tsim Sha Tsui.

The *Spring Moon* (☎ 2366-6251) in The Peninsula Hotel (Map 5) is a grand and impressive restaurant. Complementing the high standards of the hotel in which it can be found, the food is excellently prepared, and the ambience is stunning.

It may not win any awards for its name, but *The Chinese Restaurant* (☎ 2311-1234) has a good reputation for its Cantonese dishes. Again seafood is the speciality, but the high ceilings and traditional booth seating make for an unusual dining experience. The design is based on Chinese teahouses of the 1920s. The restaurant is on the 2nd floor, Hyatt Regency (Map 5), 67 Nathan Rd, Tsim Sha Tsui.

On the harbour side of the Regent Hotel (Map 5) in Tsim Sha Tsui, the *Lai Ching Heen* (☎ 2721-1211) has repeatedly won awards for its refined Cantonese cuisine (although the elegant interior and stunning view must have influenced the judges somewhat). The menu changes with each lunar month, and if the selections get confusing, there's always a waiter hovering nearby to act as a guide.

### International

Undeniably the territory's most fantastic restaurant setting, both inside and out, is at *Felix* (☎ 2366-6251), which takes in nearly all of Hong Kong from high atop The Peninsula (Map 5). High ceilings, vast windows and hulking copper-clad columns surround the Art Deco table settings. At either end of the dining room are what look to be giant metal washtubs, within which you will find a bar, a mini disco and a wine-tasting room. Then

there are the bathrooms, which are still the talk of Hong Kong (you can find out why for yourself). Somehow it all fits together, and even if you're not taken with the interior, you'd have to be made of stone to resist the simply stunning views out every corner of every window. The food, if you even notice it, is a fusion of eastern and western cuisines. It is of course quite tasty, but portions are not generous. At least your eyes won't go hungry. Felix is open from 6 pm to 2 am daily.

*Gaddi's* (☎ 2366-6251) still holds onto its reputation as *the* French restaurant in Hong Kong. Also in The Peninsula Hotel (Map 5), this place has boasted virtually the same menu (and some of the same staff) for 30 years. Obviously the system doesn't need fixing. The atmosphere is a bit stuffy, but the food should keep you happy.

Doing its best to unseat Gaddi's is *Petrus* (☎ 2877-3838), sitting near the clouds on the 56th floor of the Island Shangri-La Hotel (Map 6) in Central. On the whole the setting is more relaxing than Gaddi's: even the ever-attentive waiters seem unobtrusive. Many diners opt for the seven-course set dinner (HK$720), probably because this lets them focus on the view and the extensive wine list. Petrus is open for lunch and dinner daily, except Sunday when only dinner is served.

*Sabatini* (☎ 2721-5215) is a direct copy of its namesake in Rome, with designs painted on the walls and ceilings, and a polished tile floor. Even classic Italian heavyweights, like fettuccine carbonara, come across as light but filling, leaving room to sample the exquisite appetisers. The wine list should keep you entertained – if you can't find what you want, you're just not trying. The restaurant is on the 3rd floor, Royal Garden Hotel (Map 5), 69 Mody Rd, Tsim Sha Tsui East.

No one seems to have a bad thing to say about *M at the Fringe* (☎ 2877-4000), which is hidden in the basement of the Fringe Club (Map 6) at 2 Lower Albert Rd, Central. The menus constantly change, keeping gastronomes on their toes. Everything is here: ratatouille, couscous and kohlrabi – the soups are excellent. It's worth saving room for dessert, if you have that kind of self-restraint. Reservations are a must.

Depended upon by fussy Italians for fine food from the mother country, *Nicholini's* (☎ 2521-3838), 8th floor, Conrad International Hotel (Map 6), Hong Kong Island, pays serious attention to authentic Italian dining. The pastas are fabulous, and seafood gets an expert workover.

Over on the south side of the island in Stanley, *Tables 88* (Map 10; ☎ 2813-6262) is housed in what used to be the local police station. Though the building dates from 1854, you wouldn't guess so from the love-it or hate-it decor. The menu is continental, and the food is worth the price. The restaurant is at 88 Stanley Village Rd, diagonally opposite the Stanley bus station.

There is no shortage of top-class Japanese restaurants in Hong Kong. Upon entering *Sui Sha Ya* (☎ 2838-1808) you will be greeted by a character in full Samurai armour. Once

you've calmed down, you can indulge in expensive but superb Japanese food. The restaurant is on the 1st floor, Lockhart House, 440 Jaffe Rd, Causeway Bay.

Over in Tsim Sha Tsui East, in the basement of the Kowloon Shangri-La (Map 5), you'll find the Japanese restaurant *Nadaman* (☎ 2721-2111), whose authentic, traditional setting has won a deserved reputation. The meals are very expensive, although the set menu at lunch time is excellent value. Another branch (☎ 2820-8570) exists in the Island Shangri-La Hotel (Map 6), Admiralty.

Some continental-style hotel restaurants that combine excellent service, food and atmosphere include:

*Mandarin Grill* (☎ 2522-0111), 1st floor, Mandarin Oriental Hotel (Map 6), 5 Connaught Rd, Central
*Panorama* (☎ 2369-4111), 4th floor, New World Hotel (Map 5), 22 Salisbury Rd, Tsim Sha Tsui
*Plume* (☎ 2721-1211), ground floor, Regent Hotel (Map 5), 18 Salisbury Rd, Tsim Sha Tsui

# Entertainment

## CINEMAS

Hong Kong films are in Cantonese, but almost always have English-language subtitles, as well as Chinese characters. The latter is for export markets: Chinese audiences in Taiwan, China and South-East Asia may not understand a word of Cantonese, but they'll be able to read the characters.

Foreign films are mostly screened in their original language. If the film is in a language other than English, there will often be English as well as Chinese subtitles. Some of the more popular foreign films, particularly of the action genre, are dubbed into Cantonese, but generally these are only shown in neighbourhoods where foreigners are few and far between.

Foreign movies tend to arrive in Hong Kong one to three months after being released in their home market. Nearly all the major releases make it here, so if you've been travelling for a while, Hong Kong is a good place to catch up.

Hong Kong Chinese are obsessed with movies and cinemas are often packed, especially on the weekends. Many cinemas have assigned seating. You pick your seats at the ticket window, which explains why the queues move so slowly. Most places offer advance booking at the ticket office. Several places have advance booking by telephone, including the United Artists chain, so you can book tickets with your credit card. There are half price tickets on Tuesday.

For a complete list of cinema phone numbers and addresses, check out *HK Magazine's* 'HK2' section, which also has reviews of current films and where they are showing. The monthly *bc magazine* also has film reviews and a list of cinemas. To see what's playing that day it's best to check one of the local English-language newspapers.

Most theatres only screen the mainstream stuff, and there is unfortunately little interest in Hong Kong for the more intelligent movies. This is a shame, as you quickly find that most of the cinemas are screening the same films. There are a few cinemas, however, that try to break the mould. One good place is *Cine-Art House* (Map 7; ☎ 2827-4778), ground floor, Sun Hung Kai Centre, Wan Chai. Also in Wan Chai, the *Lim Por Yen Theatre* at the Hong Kong Arts Centre (Map 7; ☎ 2582-0200), always has art films showing, and stages film festivals for more cerebral viewers. One example is the annual European Film Festival – take your beret.

The *Space Museum* (Map 5; ☎ 2734-2722) also regularly screens arthouse movies at 10 Salisbury Rd, Tsim Sha Tsui. Events include 'German Film Forum' – not for the popcorn crowd. Other highbrow movies periodically appear at such venues as Sha Tin Town Hall, Tsuen Wan Town Hall and Tuen Mun Town Hall.

The *Alliance Française* (Map 7; ☎ 2527-7825), 2nd floor, 123 Hennessy Rd, Wan Chai, is the place to take in Gallic cinema. The new-fangled *British Council* (Map 6; ☎ 2913-5582), 3 Supreme Court Rd, Admiralty, regularly presents seasons of British 'teabags in the kitchen sink' films to entertain homesick Brits. Check the Cultural Centres section in the Facts for the Visitor chapter for the addresses of other useful organisations that screen foreign movies.

In terms of screen and sound quality and overall standard of service, the United Artists (UA) theatres are the most advanced, though others are now catching up. Some cinemas in Hong Kong show Motion Picture Industry Association advertisements warning against using video cameras to record films in the cinema – pirating for the Chinese market is rampant.

## PERFORMING ARTS

To see what's on and where, check the weekly *HK Magazine's* 'HK2' section which has listings for western music, dance and theatre as well for Chinese traditional music

## Hong Kong Movies

Hong Kong cinema is a law unto itself, marked by extreme violence, magnificent stunts, crass humour, ultra-cheap budgets and amazing weaponry. Worshipped by many in the west, Hong Kong films have an amazing diversity that keeps the B-movie wall of your local video store stocked with fantasy, martial arts, erotica, category III (over 18), action and horror.

However, Hong Kong movies have matured recently, especially with the defection to Hollywood of director John Woo, followed by strongman actor Chow Yun Fat. Woo has turned his hand successfully to Hollywood extravaganzas such as *Broken Arrow*, *Face/Off*; recent classics like *Reservoir Dogs* owe it all to the Hong Kong genre (*City on Fire* is a must-see). Jackie Chan's films continue to improve – the recent *Rumble in the Bronx* was a sign of where he is heading. *Chungking Express* is the film to see if you are considering staying at the Chungking Mansions, or if you just want to see a fantastic movie about Hong Kong life.

Here's a thumbnail introduction to some Hong Kong movie gems:

**Martial Arts/Kung Fu:**
*Drunken Master 2* (1994): one of Jackie Chan's finest moments, a great tribute to classical kung fu.
*Enter the Dragon* (1973): Bruce Lee shows the world his legendary six-pack stomach (watch out for Jackie Chan and Samo Hung in the crowd scenes).
*Prodigal Son* (1981): Samo Hung and Yuen Biao in a spellbinding history of Wing Chun kung fu.

**Action**
*City on Fire* (1987): Chow Yun Fat and Danny Lee in this gruesome inspiration to Quentin Tarantino's *Reservoir Dogs*.
*Hard Boiled* (1992): Chow Yun Fat impossibly dodges bullets in this John Woo number.
*The Killer* (1989): Chow Yun Fat sports a bad moustache while dodging hails of lead.

**Comedies**
*Aces Go Places 1, 2, 3, 4 & 5*: a series of films (many thought No 2 was the best), following the misadventures of undercover police officers Baldie and King Kong.
*God of Gamblers*: another series, in which the hero is a young gambler who cannot lose because of his supernatural powers. No 3 is probably the funniest.
*92 Legendary La Rose Noise* (1992): an irreverent action spoof on older Hong Kong romantic movies.

**Human Dramas**
*Au Revoir Mon Amour* (1991): a classic tragic romance set in Shanghai.
*Cageman* (1992): depicts rich real estate developers pitched against the poor 'cage people', the destitute who live in rented beds cordoned off with wire.
*He's a Woman, She's a Man* (1994): an award-winning romance with a very interesting plot.

**Films to be Avoided**
*All New Human Skin Lanterns* (1993)
*Devil Foetus* (1983)
*Man Behind the Sun 2: Laboratory of the Devil* (1993)
*Raped by an Angel* (1993)

and other performances. The colourful and dependable *bc magazine* reviews everything in town. The Hong Kong Tourist Association (HKTA) has two free handouts that are also helpful: the more comprehensive *Hong Kong Diary*, issued weekly; and the monthly *Official Hong Kong Guide*. All these publications give information on performance venues, times and prices. The local English-language daily papers are also worth checking, though they tend to miss some events.

Most major events are staged at the *Hong Kong Cultural Centre* (Map 5; ☎ 2734-2010) in Tsim Sha Tsui; *City Hall* (Map 6; ☎ 2921-2840) in Central; the *Hong Kong Academy for Performing Arts* (Map 7; ☎ 2584-8514) and the *Hong Kong Arts Centre* (Map 7; ☎ 2582-0200), both in Wan Chai. Sometimes performances also make it to various civic centres and town halls in the New Territories.

Bookings for most high-culture happenings can be made by telephone through

URBTIX (☎ 2734-9009) between 10 am and 8 pm. Tickets can either be reserved with ID card or passport numbers (and picked up within three days of ordering), or paid for in advance by credit card. You can collect tickets at one of the many URBTIX outlets throughout the city. Take your passport for proof of identity. There are URBTIX windows at the City Hall in Central, the Hong Kong Arts Centre in Wan Chai and the Hong Kong Cultural Centre in Tsim Sha Tsui. Some Tom Lee Music stores also have URBTIX facilities. *HK Magazine* also lists all URBTIX outlets.

### Chinese Opera

Among the best times to see Chinese opera are during the annual Hong Kong Arts Festival, held in February/March, or the Festival of Asian Arts, which takes place every other year in October/November. The HKTA has leaflets giving full details of the festivals, and *HK Magazine* and *bc magazine* also give complete listings. The Urban Council also staged the first ever Chinese Opera Festival from October to November 1997 – check with the HKTA for more information.

Cantonese opera can be seen throughout the year at *Sunbeam Theatre* (☎ 2563-2959), 423 King's Rd, North Point. Performances generally run for about a week, and are usually held in the evening, though sometimes there are matinees. Tickets cost anywhere from HK$50 to HK$300. This place does not deal with many foreigners, and very little English is spoken, nor is there usually any English-language summary of the opera being performed. If you can't reach an English speaker at the theatre, call the HKTA hotline (☎ 2807-6177). They usually have an idea of what's playing, and if not they should be willing to help you find out. To get to Sunbeam Theatre, take the MTR to North Point station. The theatre is right above the station, on the north side of King's Rd, near the intersection with Shu Kuk St. Just look for the garish Chinese opera posters.

Chinese opera performances are sometimes held at the *Hong Kong Cultural Centre*

and *City Hall*. Check the HKTA's *Hong Kong Diary* or the local English-language newspapers for details on times and venues.

### Theatre

Local theatre groups mostly perform at the *Hong Kong Arts Centre*, the *Hong Kong Academy for Performing Arts* and the *Hong Kong Cultural Centre*. Performances are mostly in Cantonese, though summaries in English are usually handed out. Tickets cost anywhere between HK$60 and HK$200, depending on the seats and the venue.

Smaller theatre companies occasionally stage plays at the *Fringe Club* (Map 6; ☎ 2521-7251), 2 Lower Albert Rd, Central. Often the themes are local and feature amateur actors but productions with a more universal appeal are also staged.

### Arts Festivals

Hong Kong hosts several of these each year. Exact dates vary, so if you want to time your visit to coincide with any of these events it would be wise to first contact the HKTA overseas office nearest you (see the Tourist Offices section of the Facts for the Visitor chapter). Some of the large events include:

*Hong Kong Arts Festival* – a month of music, the performing arts and exhibitions by hundreds of local and international artists; held in February/March.

*Hong Kong Fringe Festival* – the Fringe Club sponsors three weeks of performances by an eclectic mix of up-and-coming artists and performers from Hong Kong and overseas; held in late January/early February.

*Hong Kong International Film Festival* – brings in hundreds of films from around the world, and is used to showcase new local and regional productions; held in March or April.

*International Arts Carnival* – features mime, puppetry, theatre, dance and children's drama; held in July or August.

*Festival of Asian Arts* – one of Asia's major cultural events, bringing in musicians, dancers, opera singers and other performance groups from all over the region; held every other year in October/November.

*Hong Kong Folk Festival* – the Hong Kong Folk Society brings together well known international acts and local musicians; held in November.

*Hong Kong Youth Arts Festival* – events from visual arts, drama and dance to the literary arts and music; held in October/November/December.

## ART

See the Things to See & Do chapter for information on opening times of the *Hong Kong Museum of Art* (Map 5; ☎ 2734-2167). Apart from the permanent exhibitions, the museum is also the venue for exhibitions of international collections.

With its thriving art market, Hong Kong is also the scene of a diverse number of exhibitions by galleries in the territory. Take the time to visit a few and avail yourself of the opportunity to find out more about not only modern Chinese art, but Vietnamese, Japanese, Korean, Russian and western art as well. Recent exhibitions have included the realist works of Chinese artist Cheng Yuanan at *Galerie du Monde* (Map 6; ☎ 2525-0529), 328 Pacific Place, 88 Queensway. The *Fringe Gallery* at the Fringe Club (Map 6; ☎ 2521-7251) in Central (see Theatre earlier) also has regular exhibitions. Consult *HK Magazine* and *bc magazine* for a comprehensive list of galleries and exhibitions, and see the Arts, Crafts & Antiques section of the Shopping chapter for more inspiration.

## CLASSICAL MUSIC

Hong Kong holds its own in this department. There are performances every week, often featuring foreign ensembles. Less frequent are Chinese classical or folk music concerts. *HK Magazine*, *bc magazine,* the HKTA's *Hong Kong Diary* and the entertainment sections of the English-language newspapers all have details on venues, performance times, ticket prices and booking. Many of these performances are held at the *Hong Kong Cultural Centre* (Map 5; ☎ 2734-2010) in Tsim Sha Tsui, so it might be worth stopping by there to pick up its monthly schedule.

In general, it's cheaper to go to performances by local ensembles like the Hong Kong Philharmonic or the Hong Kong Chinese Orchestra. But the Hong Kong government subsidises the cost of bringing in foreign acts, so prices are sometimes pretty reasonable. Tickets range from as low as HK$50 for a seat at a local performance to HK$300 for something like the English Chamber Orchestra.

In addition to the Hong Kong Cultural Centre, classical concerts are often held at two other venues: *City Hall* (Map 6; ☎ 2921-2840) in Central and the *Hong Kong Academy for Performing Arts* (Map 7; ☎ 2584-8514) in Wan Chai.

## ROCK/JAZZ

The live music scene is improving, with the opening of new concert halls and venues. In previous years, there was a distinct lack of venues. The territory had stadiums, but none large enough to pack in the numbers needed by profit-conscious band managers; there were also problems with noise pollution and complaining neighbours. Misunderstandings between artists and promoters were also not unusual – in 1997, Michael Jackson's lawyer had to write to a Hong Kong concert organiser, threatening to sue if they continued to claim that the pop star was going to play live in the territory. However, an increasing number of bands and solo acts are making it out to Hong Kong. Sting, Primal Scream, Oasis and the Prodigy, among others, have performed in Hong Kong in recent years.

Hong Kong pop stars are another matter of course, and concerts by singer/idols like Andy Lau, Faye Wong, Aron Kwok, Jackie Cheung, Beyond and Li Ming are frequent. Canto-pop is the name for the local pop music, which few westerners take to. If you give it a chance, however, you will find some terrific tunes lurking in there. While not to everyone's taste, some Canto-pop songs are great.

A few bars, most notably the Jazz Club, bring in international artists from time to time. Most are jazz and blues musicians, but other types clamber on stage as well.

The local scene is a bit more lively. There are usually a couple of decent rock bands playing around town, and there are numerous bars with house bands that play dance tunes.

Hong Kong is not really a friendly environment for musicians. The few bars that dare to book original bands are usually small or lack a decent sound system. Things do seem to be picking up though: more bars are presenting live music, and local audiences are increasingly receptive to bands that play something other than pop tunes or classic rock. At the time of writing, one of the most popular local bands were The Bastards, who had built quite a cult following.

To find out what's going on, pick up a copy of *HK Magazine*. The 'HK2' section lists who's playing where in the music section. The monthly *bc magazine* also has a good live music guide.

### Live Venues

A lot of places have on-again, off-again live music, but there are a few spots that have bands most nights of the week.

First to grab the microphone is the *Jazz Club* (☎ 2845-8477), 2nd floor, California Entertainment Building (Map 6), Lan Kwai Fong, Central. This has long been the salvation of true music lovers, and many jazz greats have stood on its stage. But the club also books rock, blues, folk and other kinds of acts, both local and foreign. The club is not very big, so it helps to book tickets well in advance for the bigger names. Drinks are murderously expensive (HK$52 for a bottle of beer), but there's a two-for-one happy

hour from 7 to 9 pm that helps soften the blow. Tickets for local acts are around HK$100, and overseas bands usually cost anywhere from HK$200 to HK$300 (half price for members).

Ashley Rd has its own little time warp in the form of *Ned Kelly's Last Stand* (Map 5; ☎ 2376-0562), 11A Ashley Rd, Tsim Sha Tsui. A tradition continues with Colin Aithison and the Kelly Gang playing Dixieland jazz from Tuesday to Sunday between 9.15 pm and 1.45 am. Ken Bennett and the Kowloon Hongkers play on Monday.

Nearby on Ashley Rd is the *Amoeba Bar* (Map 5; ☎ 2376-0389), which has live music down in the bar's basement; the crowd is nearly all young Cantonese.

For years *The Wanch* (Map 7; ☎ 2861-1621) in Wan Chai was one of the few venues for live bands. There's more competition now, but The Wanch still has live music seven nights a week from 9 pm. The selection centres mainly on rock and folk groups, with the occasional solo singer/guitarist thrown in. Jam night is on Wednesday starting at 10 pm. Prices here are better than most places, and are discounted during their particularly good happy hours, which run from 3 to 9 pm daily and 1 to 4 am on Friday and Saturday nights.

*JJ's* (Map 7; ☎ 2588-1234) at the Grand Hyatt Hotel, 1 Harbour Rd, Wan Chai sees regular appearances from Hawkeye, a funky five-piece from Boston, and other bands. Entry costs HK$100 from Monday to Thursday and HK$200 on Friday and Saturday.

Sunday jazz nights happen at the trendy *bb's* (Map 7; ☎ 2529-7702), 114-120 Lockhart Rd, Wan Chai. Entry is free, and the bar jazzes up at around 8 pm.

Mid-Levels is the site of the *Rickshaw Jazz Room* (Map 6; ☎ 2525-3977), 22 Robinson Rd, a free venue of jazz, blues, country, folk and big-band jazz.

Up and coming local sounds get an airing at *The Warehouse*, Frank White Music Studio, Aberdeen High St. This venue hosts local alternative live bands on Saturday.

Except for the Jazz Club, Lan Kwai Fong doesn't have any other really serious music

**ENTERTAINMENT**

---

### Elvis lives in Lan Kwai Fong, and he's Cantonese

Elvis impersonator Melvis Kwok Lam, 42, has been serenading the yuppies and tourists of Lan Kwai Fong for the past five years. Usually earning HK$20 a song, his best targets are drunk Elvis fans, who instinctively dig deep into their pockets. Often dressed with adhesive sideburns clinging to his face, Melvis has a stunning array of outfits that span the King's career. The best time to track him down is on weekends – just look for the bouffant quiff and thrusting pelvis among all the suits. ■

venues. *F-Stop* (Map 6; ☎ 2868-9607) is a tiny place at 14 Lan Kwai Fong Lane that squeezes bands onto its minuscule stage on Friday and Saturday nights from 10 pm. This place is really for the teenage set; the upstairs section is covered with graffiti and held together with string and sealing wax. You can see its huge neon guitar a mile off.

*Mad Dogs* (Map 6; ☎ 2810-1000), a rollicking British-style pub at 1 D'Aguilar St, has music three or four nights a week, usually in the form of a solo singer/guitarist. The bar has a counterpart in Tsim Sha Tsui, *Mad Dogs Kowloon* (Map 5; ☎ 2301-2222), which also has music occasionally.

Up on Lower Albert Rd, just on the border of Lan Kwai Fong, is the *Dragon's Back Gallery* at the Fringe Club (Map 6; ☎ 2521-7251). This is the venue for a whole medley of trendy sounds from Latin jazz and mainstream jazz to rock, pop, blues, country and folk. Most nights are free.

On the Tsim Sha Tsui side is *Chasers* (Map 5; ☎ 2367-9487), 2-3 Knutsford Terrace, which has live music every night. Most nights the guitars and drumsticks are in the hands of resident band Square Eyes, who have a repertoire of rock based covers and mainstream hits.

For mellow 1940s and 1950s jazz, put on your smoking jacket and sip Cognac at *The Bar* (☎ 2315-3135), the Peninsula (Map 5), Salisbury Rd. The smooth sounds start at 9.30 pm.

There are a number of other bars that have live music on a less regular basis. For more details, see the Pubs/Bars section later in this chapter and check out the music listings in both *HK Magazine* and *bc magazine*.

### Concerts

Concerts are usually held these days either at the *HITEC Rotunda* in Kowloon Bay (☎ 2620-2222) or in the new extension to the Hong Kong Convention and Exhibition Centre in Wan Chai (Map 7). They are not huge venues, hence the alienating prices (around HK$480), but they manage to get in names like the Prodigy, Oasis, The Chemical Brothers and Primal Scream, which probably makes it worth it.

Another venue is the *Hong Kong Coliseum* (Map 5; ☎ 2355-7233), 9 Cheong Wan Rd, Hung Hom. This is a 12,500 seat indoor facility next to Kowloon KCR station. The sound here is abysmal, but this is where some of the big names come when they're in town.

Smaller acts are sometimes booked into the *Ko Shan Theatre* (☎ 2334-2331) on Ko Shan Rd, Hung Hom. This is actually not a bad venue. The sound isn't great, but the back portion of the seating area is open-air, and the theatre is fairly small, so that most seats give you a good view.

Known mainly as the site of the wildly popular Hong Kong Rugby Sevens, the *Hong Kong Stadium* (Map 7; ☎ 2895-7895) at Eastern Hospital Rd, Causeway Bay, is Hong Kong's largest venue for sporting and cultural events, expanded not long ago to seat 40,000. The main reason was to house more rugby fans, but the government also figured it would be a good way to attract big international music acts as well. But the planners didn't take into account the local residents, who after the first few concerts raised a tremendous stink about the noise and crowds. Bureaucrats scrambled to find a solution. At one point someone suggested turning off the stage speakers and issuing audiences with headphones!

The only other big place to see a band is *Queen Elizabeth Stadium* (Map 7; ☎ 2591-1347), 18 Oi Kwan Rd, Wan Chai. This is not bad for sporting events, but it's one lousy place to see a concert: you'd get better acoustics in an aircraft hanger.

### CLUBS/DISCOS

Hong Kong has developed a pretty active club scene, and more and more bars are offering dance and thematic club nights; aided by the arrival of some talented, professional DJs. Most of the club nights take place on Friday and Saturday, but there are some midweek nights as well. Cover charges range from HK$50 to HK$150, but look out for theme nights where you might be allowed in free if you're among the first 50 through the door in 1970s gear (or whatever). As with most bars and clubs in Hong Kong, beer and drinks range from HK$30 up to HK$70 at the really expensive places.

Both *HK Magazine* and *bc magazine* have nightclub listings, and the latter also boasts a regular column called 'Club Scene'. It's a good idea to check these as club nights come and go, and venues fall in and out of fashion. They'll also keep you up to date with forthcoming theme nights.

Serious clubbers who will travel anywhere for *that* night should check out possible schedules in *HK Magazine* and especially *bc magazine* for events in Shenzhen and Guangzhou. At the time of writing, two organisers, SPACE and Ministry of Sound (☎ 2521-2030) had arrived from London, joining forces to venture over the border to Shenzhen and broaden the horizon of clubland. The border closes at 10.45 pm and reopens at 7 am, which fits in just fine with club hours.

There are also plenty of straightforward discos that don't play techno where you can dance until you drop, or until the sun rises, whichever comes first.

### Central & Admiralty (Map 6)
*JP Encounter* (☎ 2521-0309), ground floor, Bank of America Tower, Central Harcourt Rd, Central, is a stylish place with a nifty spiral staircase and tremendous chandeliers; and is also the scene of Blah Blah Blah on Friday and Saturday nights. The DJs are pure skill, and wacky theme nights keep it all fresh. However, the venue is due for an overhaul. Admission: Friday, HK$130 for men (plus two beers), ladies free; Saturday, HK$100 for everyone. Beer is HK$55 a bottle.

*CE Top* (☎ 2541-5524), 9th floor, 37-43 Cochrane St, Central, is a rooftop club hosting a medley of club nights including a mix of funk, jazz, disco, drum n' bass, hip hop and rare groove, plus quite a strong gay leaning (but that's not to say it's not for straights).

*Club Rosa* (☎ 2801-5885) at the Zona Rosa restaurant in Lan Kwai Fong is now in

the hands of DJs, with thumping house music on one floor and cool funk on the other. It starts at 11 pm on Friday and Saturday.

Also in Lan Kwai Fong, *Dillinger's Steak House* (☎ 2521-2202), 38-44 D'Aguilar St, holds a disco on Friday and Saturday from around 11 pm.

There's not much else going on down Lan Kwai Fong way, although a few of the bars have dance floors the size of a telephone box. *California* (☎ 2521-1345) is a bit pretentious, but really packs in the crowds, especially when the tables are cleared off the dance floor. Thursday, Friday and Saturday are free to get in but you'll be stung viciously for a beer (HK$60 a bottle).

### Wan Chai (Map 7)
The other hub of the club galaxy revolves around Wan Chai. This is where the late night crowd settles in for the wee hours. One of the first destinations for naval sailors stopping in Hong Kong for a little R&R, the endless neon of Wan Chai is mainly propped up by seedy bars (with the odd snappy watering hole), ghastly hostess clubs, hole-in-the-wall sandwich parlours and the occasional dance venue.

One Wan Chai institution is the *Neptune Disco* (☎ 2528-3808), basement, Computer Centre, 54 Lockhart Rd. Slightly seedy, decidedly downmarket and completely unpretentious, Neptune gets going when other clubs shut at 3 am. People mainly come to dance, and if you're not dancing you're in the wrong place. Happy hour is from 4 to 8 pm and entry is free.

Over at 98 Jaffe Rd, *Neptune Disco II* (☎ 2865-2238) lacks the character of its progenitor, but is open just as late (until around 7 am). There's a HK$140 cover charge for men that includes one drink. Women need only pay HK$50. In the same league as Neptune is *Big Apple* (☎ 2529-3461), which thumps to club classics on weekends at 20 Luard Rd. Recently elected as Hong Kong's raunchiest nightspot, go there and vote for yourself. Entry is free.

*bb's* (☎ 2529-7702) hasn't put a foot wrong since it opened and has extended its credibility to drum n' bass and acid jazz dance sessions on Saturday at *The Blue Lizard Lounge* upstairs (11 pm till late). Sunday softens up with live jazz from 8 pm. Entry is free.

The hip option has got to be at the *The Viceroy* (☎ 2827-7777), 2nd floor, Sun Hung Kai Centre; the scene of one-off live gigs, the Punchline Comedy Club and salsa nights. Discover salsa dancing and music from 9.45 pm for HK$120. Dance parties at the Viceroy have become the place to be seen.

Looking for something a bit more downmarket? You can't go lower than the *New Makati* (☎ 2866-3928), a sleazy pick-up joint at 100 Lockhart Rd. If you go in and decide to take a seat in one of the dimly lit booths, make sure you don't plop down on top of a groping couple. The cover charge is HK$70 for men, HK$40 for women, and includes one drink.

Voted in as 1997's 'Best Pick-Up Bar' by the readers of *HK Magazine*, *Joe Banana's* (☎ 2529-1811) is a source of contention: some people rave about it, while others blast it as the worst meat market in town. Anyway, the DJ starts moving his elbows at 7 pm. There's a cover charge of HK$100 on Friday and Saturday after 9 pm for men and after 1 am for women. You can get two-for-one cocktails on Wednesday, plus there is a daily happy hour from 11.30 am to 10 pm. You must be over 21 to go here.

*Rick's Café* (☎ 2528-1812), at 78-82 Jaffe Rd, has a branch in Wan Chai that seems just as popular as the original in Tsim Sha Tsui (see the Tsim Sha Tsui section following). Sunday nights feature soul, rhythm and blues and hip hop laced with two-for-one alcoholic beverages while women get a free shot of spirits with every drink. Entry is free.

*Carnegie's* (☎ 2866-6289), 55 Lockhart Rd, lays it on with the rock memorabilia, and it seems a bit Hard Rock Café-esque, but Friday and Saturday see the place thumping from 9 pm. Entry is HK$50 plus one free drink. Bands play here two nights a week (usually Thursday and Sunday).

*Manhattan* (☎ 2824-0380) mainly draws a Cantonese crowd, and is a slightly subdued

version of Catwalk. Strobe lights, smoke machines and techno-pop set the scene. Manhattan is in the New World Harbour View Hotel in Wan Chai. The cover charge is HK$88 from Sunday through to Thursday, HK$140 Friday and Saturday, and includes one drink.

### Tsim Sha Tsui (Map 5)

Tsim Sha Tsui is not a great deal of fun when it comes to dancing. One of the better known clubs is *Rick's Café* (☎ 2367-2939), 4 Hart Ave. The decor is cheesy *Casablanca*, complete with palm trees and Bogie and Bergman photos on the walls; check out the frightful advert on local TV. The dance floor usually features western men and Filipino women. Entry is free from Monday to Thursday; Friday and Saturday costs HK$120. Ladies get free shots on Wednesday nights.

*Bahama Mama's Caribbean Bar* (☎ 2368-2121), 4-5 Knutsford Terrace, is popular. The theme here is (can you guess?) tropical, complete with palm trees and surfboards. It really is a friendly spot, and somehow stands apart from most of the other watering holes. On Friday and Saturday nights there is a DJ spinning tracks to get folks onto the bonsai-sized dance floor. From 5 to 9 pm, the bar slouches back to a reggae beat. There's a HK$100 minimum charge after 11 pm on Friday and Saturday nights. Jazz bands grace the stage after 9 pm on Sunday.

*Catwalk* (☎ 2369-4111), on the 18th floor of the New World Hotel, 22 Salisbury Rd, is the hot spot for Hong Kong's young wealthy. There's live music (usually quite good) in one section, a disco in another and karaoke in several other areas. Mobile phones, designer watches and Cognac are the order of the day. Catwalk also features one of Hong Kong's highest cover charges: HK$200 on Friday and Saturday, although this does include two drinks. The fee falls to HK$120 from Sunday to Thursday for men, and it's free for women.

Nearby in the Regent hotel, the posh *Club Shanghai* (☎ 2721-1211) usually has an American band cranking out dance tunes five or six nights a week. The place is decked out à la 1930s Shanghai, down to opium pipes (not filled) on each table. The cover charge is HK$120 from Sunday to Thursday, and HK$150 on Friday and Saturday (this includes one drink).

Though a miserable venue for big-name gigs, the *Hard Rock Café* (☎ 2377-8118), on Kowloon Park Drive in Tsim Sha Tsui, is not a bad spot to hit the dance floor. All the guitars and rock memorabilia spice up the place a bit, and there is usually a live band playing. Otherwise there's a DJ working the tunes from about 10.30 pm. Entry is HK$80 for men and women get in free.

## PUBS/BARS

Drinking is a larger part of Hong Kong social life than in many other Chinese societies. Though there are still many Chinese who either don't touch or only occasionally sip alcohol, the influence of western culture and Hong Kong's increasing affluence have made alcohol more popular. Bars, though alien to traditional Chinese culture, can be found everywhere in Hong Kong, and are fairly well patronised, especially by younger Chinese men and business executives.

Hong Kong's expats drink with abandon. Hordes of western professionals descend on Lan Kwai Fong, Wan Chai and Tsim Sha Tsui on Friday and Saturday nights to engage in what cynics call Hong Kong's number one form of expatriate recreation. It's not a cheap sport: a beer or standard cocktail will routinely cost HK$30 to HK$50, making it easy to part with HK$500 to HK$600 on a good night. However, the endemic popularity of happy hours has helped soften the blow, although to really get your money's worth you need to kick off in the late afternoon. Most happy hours last from around 5 to 9 pm, but a few places offer breaks for late-nighters as well, usually from 1 to 2 am. Aside from the two-for-one deals, reduced prices for drinks usually range from 20% to 50% off.

There's no way to list all of Hong Kong's bars here, nor any reason to. Many are quite similar, if not in decor, then in atmosphere, as one evening in Lan Kwai Fong will demonstrate. The following are places that many people feel have a little extra to offer. In addition to these, check out the music and dancing venues listed earlier: all of them are bars, and some are quite good.

### Lan Kwai Fong (Map 6)

Central's Lan Kwai Fong has the highest concentration of bars in Hong Kong. Though still in many ways a foreigner's drinking ghetto, there are more and more Chinese heading here for a night on the town as well. Most of the bars are clustered around the four streets that make up the Lan Kwai Fong quadrant, but there are a few, like the aforementioned Fringe Club and Mad Dogs, which sit on the periphery.

Some of the bars around here are pretty pretentious (they're easy to spot). One place that bucks this trend is *Club 64* (☎ 2523-2801), 12 Wing Wah Lane. Apparently named after the Tiananmen Square massacre (64 being the name of the event in Chinese – *luk sei* in Cantonese, or *liu si* in Mandarin, the fourth of the sixth month – 4 June), this is still a pretty funky place to chill out. Members of the militant April 5th Action Group drink here – you can see them at other times on the front page of the papers, trying to get into the Legislative Council or being dragged off by police from a demonstration. A sign of the times if ever there was one is that the graffiti (in English and Chinese) that used to cover the walls has been white-washed over. Despite the new political hegemony, this is still one of the best bars in town for non-poseurs, angry young men and those who want simple, unpretentious fun. Club 64 also has one of Hong Kong's better happy hours: from 10 am to 8 pm when pints of draught beer are HK$21, bottles HK$18.

More upmarket and featuring an open verandah seating area is *Le Jardin Club* (☎ 2526-2717) at 10 Wing Wah Lane. This is a great bar, with loads of atmosphere and plenty of people enjoying themselves. If you come out of Club 64 and turn right, you will see some stairs heading up in the corner of Wing Wah Lane; they lead to Le Jardin.

If you're a fan of German beer, both *Schnurrbart* (☎ 2523-7436) and *Bit Point*

(☎ 2523-4700) take the time and effort to draw a beer the right way. Most of the draught beers are pilseners, but both have a fine selection of bottled beers too. Schnurrbart also has a dizzying choice of German and Austrian schnapps – ask for the special menu. Bit Point occasionally serves beer in a huge glass boot for those who like to have half of their beer down their shirt.

Across the street in California Tower, *Sherman's Bar and Restaurant* (☎ 2801-4946) has had a refit and emerged as a cool exemplary of aluminium chic, bathed in cold, opaque lighting. Surgeons and architects will find it fascinating.

If your aim is to slam down a lot of drinks in as little time as possible, you'll be in good company in either Hardy's or Yelts Inn. With frequent live (and occasionally talented) music acts, *Hardy's* (☎ 2522-4448) suits rowdy beer swillers. *Yelts Inn* (☎ 2524-7790), with its moody colours, pictures of prominent communists and blaring tunes, is a place for downing shots, which you'll see plenty of people doing here.

*La Dolce Vita* (☎ 2810-8098) is as sweet as life gets. This is where the gorgeous young things come to watch each other and be watched. Come here to check out the fashions and get a blast of a hundred different perfumes and aftershave lotions.

*Oscar's* (☎ 2804-6561), the place with the surging mob out front, is as trendy as they come, and proud of it.

Just around the corner from Oscar's at 26 D'Aguilat St is the cunningly titled *D'Aguilar 26* (☎ 2877-1610).

Up the hill, just outside Lan Kwai Fong proper, on Wyndham St, is *La Bodega* (☎ 2877-5472). Though also a fully fledged restaurant, this place has nice tapas and a wine bar in the basement.

### Central, Soho & Admiralty (Map 6)

Outside of Lan Kwai Fong, the bars are a bit uniform and unexciting. One area that will no doubt see some innovation is Soho, the new restaurant ghetto around Staunton and Elgin Sts. Already home to a few bars and a queue of eateries, this part of town will (much to the horror of locals) probably continue in its pursuit of fun. Voted by readers of *HK Magazine* as the best new bar in Hong Kong in 1997, *Staunton's Bar & Café* (☎ 2973-6611) is swish, cool and on the ball. The only problem is that they have a conditional alcohol licence, conditional on not serving any of the demon stuff after 11 pm, so get your last few pints in at 10.59 pm, or tuck into some muesli and milk (HK$35). The situation may have changed by the time you read this; you can find Staunton's at 10-12 Staunton St.

Also located on Staunton St is *Club 1911* (☎ 2810-6681), an elegant bar steeped in colonial nostalgia.

Not far from the Mid-Levels escalator at 39 Hollywood Rd is *The Globe Café & Bar* (☎ 2543-1941), hugely popular and packed with expats.

Hotel bars are where you want to go if you want a more sedate experience and better service. Try the *Captain's Bar* (☎ 2522-0111), on the ground floor of the Mandarin Oriental Hotel. After 5 pm you can't enter wearing either jeans or a collarless shirt, and truth be told, you'd be more appropriate wearing a suit. But if you've got the right attire (and plenty of money) it's worth coming here just to drink from one of the Mandarin's chilled silver mugs.

For the view, you can't beat the *Harlequin Bar* (☎ 2522-0111) on the Mandarin Oriental Hotel's 24th floor, especially at night. See Victoria Harbour in all its glory while sipping your HK$65 drink. Still, the money buys not only the drink and the view but some outstanding service as well. This is a good place to go when you feel like being pampered.

At the other end of the scale, in Hutchison House lies the *Bull and Bear Pub* (☎ 2525-7436) probably the closest thing to a real British pub in Hong Kong, fitted out with mock Tudor oak beams. English licensing laws do not apply, however, so you can go on drinking after 11 pm. All the standard pub fare (bangers and mash, mushy peas, meat pies) are available, along with a decent selection of bitters and lagers.

*Pomeroy's* (☎ 2523-4772) is a popular spot on level 3 of the Pacific Place shopping mall in Central.

If you want to go really top-end in more ways than one, *Cyrano* (☎ 2877-3838) on the 56th floor of the Island Shangri-La Hotel can oblige with fantastic views and equally impressive prices. The bartenders do their best to make up any type of drink you require, and their skills are often put to the test by the demanding upper crust types who frequent this spot.

### Wan Chai (Map 7)

Most of the bars are in a cluster along Jaffe and Lockhart Rds at the western end of Wan Chai. Most of these can serve up decent pub grub and continental food, often with quite a deal of choice; some are mixed bars/clubs/restaurants. Like Lan Kwai Fong, on Friday and Saturday night this area is crawling with party-goers and the lonely searching for a place to drink or dance, or both. It's also fairly busy during the week.

Knowledgeable beer drinkers should like *BB's* (☎ 2529-7702), which has several beers on tap custom-brewed for it by Hong Kong's biggest microbrewery, the South China Brewing Co. The beer is outstanding, and in addition BB's has an enviable collection of bottled imports from around the world. This bar has become a trendy focus of the Wan Chai bar world, especially with the introduction of The Blue Lizard Lounge upstairs which regularly moves and grooves (see the Clubs/Discos section earlier). The bar is at 114 Lockhart Rd.

Also serving up memorable draught beer is *Delaney's* (☎ 2804-2880), an authentic Irish pub incongruously on the 2nd floor of the shiny One Capital Place building, 18 Luard Rd. This place is immensely popular, so you'll probably have to battle crowds, deafening noise and a fog of cigarette smoke to get to the bar. But it's worth the effort, because here you can order a draught Guinness stout poured with the care and expertise it deserves (which also makes it expensive). The food is also good: they get through 400kg of potatoes a week. They also have

their own house brew, Delaney's Own Real Ale, made by the South China Brewing Co.

Packed at weekends, choked with cigarette smoke and rocking to live bands, *The Wanch* (☎ 2861-1621) celebrated 10 years in the business in 1997, without any let-up in its reputation. This is not the place for a quiet, intimate chat. Follow the smell of Capstan filterless cigarettes to 54 Jaffe Rd. *Joe Banana's* (☎ 2529-1811) at 23 Luard Rd, is also a trendy focal point of the Wan Chai bar scene, and hosts the odd Miss Wet T-shirt and Mr Wet Boxer Shorts competition.

The bar/restaurant/nightclub *The Viceroy* (☎ 2827-7777), 2nd floor, Sun Hung Kai Centre, 30 Harbour Rd, is a place to be seen. Also the scene of the Punchline Comedy Club and live bands, the Wan Chai bar scene has seen a shake-up since its arrival.

Pool players can get chalking cues at the nearby *Flying Pig* (☎ 2865-3730), 2nd floor, 81-85 Lockhart Rd, an entertaining little place decked out in aviation memorabilia, including airline seats. The pool table gets shunted aside for dancing at weekends. Downstairs from the Flying Pig is *Ridgways* (☎ 2866-6608), which also has a pool table.

Scattered around the area are several Tudor-style pubs with names like the *Horse & Groom, Royal Arms, Horse & Carriage*. They certainly don't feel English, but they're good enough for a (relatively) cheap beer and perhaps a plate of greasy chips.

The *Old China Hand* is usually filled with, yes, old China hands, who seem to spend most of their time here. Interesting, but not a lively scene.

For those who came to see the Wan Chai of Suzie Wong, there are a few strip clubs feeding off the nostalgia and tourists. Most are littered along Lockhart Rd, where the proprietors will pounce and march you into a tacky world of pink neon and extortionate prices. Only for the terminally sad. The most popular of the lot is probably *Country Club 88* (☎ 2861-1009) which seems to fill every stool around its circular bar.

Finally, if you want to spend lots of money, head over to the *Champagne Bar* (☎ 2588-1234) at the Grand Hyatt Hotel. You really

ENTERTAINMENT

should only come here if you've a reason to celebrate, or if someone else is buying. How else can you justify spending HK$120 to HK$400 for a glass of champagne?

## Causeway Bay (Map 7)

Things start to thin out around here, but there are still some bars that do a thriving business, helped in part by people who are sick of hanging out in Lan Kwai Fong or Wan Chai.

*The Jump* (☎ 2832-9007) is a neat and spacious American-style bar/restaurant with funky high seats. Also on hand is a big menu of burgers, Cajun flavours and Mexican dishes. Usually hopping at weekends, there is a HK$100 cover charge on Friday and Saturday nights after 11 pm, which includes one drink. It's on the 7th floor, Causeway Bay Plaza 2, 463 Lockhart Rd.

There are a few bars in the Times Square shopping complex that also seem able to draw a steady crowd. *Roy's* at the new China Max (☎ 2506-2282), on the 11th floor, works hard to keep its customers entertained and often has live music. In Times Square, *La Placita* (☎ 2506-3308) is also big on entertainment, with an eight-piece band and more unique offerings like Brazilian dance shows. There's another branch of *Oscar's* (☎ 2861-1511) packed with suits at Podium 3, World Trade Centre, 280 Gloucester Rd.

Considerably more subdued, but also draw a fairly unusual, is the very small *Brechts* (☎ 2577-9636), 123 Leighton Rd, an arty kind of place given more to intimate, cerebral conversation than serious raging. The decor is pseudo-German, and includes oversized portraits of Mao and Hitler.

Back to the mainstream now with the *King's Arms* (☎ 2895-6557). Squeezed in between two glass and steel office blocks at Sunning Plaza, this indoor-outdoor place is an old favourite. The service can be frosty, but it's still easy to stay here for a few hours.

Another favourite expat den, for some reason, is the *Dicken's Bar* (☎ 2894-8888), in the basement of the Excelsior Hotel. This is a hearty, sporty establishment for those on expense accounts, and some nights there's live music.

Just in case you missed the Tudor-style pubs in Wan Chai, there are two more tucked away on Cannon St: *Royal's Pub* and *Shakespeare Pub*. These are mainly the domain of Hong Kong Chinese, but foreigners are made to feel welcome. *Piccadilly Tavern* (☎ 2882-8912), 8 Sunning Rd, is typical of this genre of pub.

Further out in Quarry Bay is a beer-lover's must in the form of the *East End Brewery* (☎ 2811-1907) at 23-27 Tong Chong St. Choose from 30 microbrewed and speciality beers from around the world, including Taikoo Brew and Aldrich Bay Pale Ale.

## Stanley (Map 10)

There are a number of gwailo pubs that get raging in the late afternoon and continue until after midnight. A large share of this market belong to *Smuggler's Inn* (☎ 2811-1907), 90A Main St.

*Lord Stanley's Bar & Bistro* (☎ 2813-1876), 92A Main St, offers a similar mix of loud music and good food.

## Tsim Sha Tsui (Map 5)

Bars are more spread out in Tsim Sha Tsui, but there are three basic clusters: along Ashley Rd; within the triangle formed by Hanoi, Prat and Chatham Rds; and up by Knutsford Terrace. In addition to the bars listed here, see the Clubs/Discos section and under Live Venues in the Rock/Jazz section. There are other nondescript watering holes scattered about. Should you decide to go exploring, bear in mind that a few of the smaller places are more for Hong Kong Chinese than foreigners. If you're treated to a chilly welcome just continue on to another bar: there are plenty of options.

If you want to see one of Hong Kong's more humorous local bars, check out *Jouster II* (☎ 2723-0022), 19 Hart Ave. Made up to look like a medieval castle, down to a knight in armour and a miniature drawbridge, it's a pretty amusing place. The crowd is mostly Chinese, and the volume can get deafening when several tables all start drinking games.

Up on Prat Ave is the Kowloon branch of *Delaney's* (☎ 2301-3980). This one seems even more authentically Irish than the original in Wan Chai: lots of dark wood, green felt and a long bar that you can settle into for the long haul. Just up the street is *Schnurrbart* (☎ 2366-2986), which is smaller and somewhat more restrained than its counterpart in Lan Kwai Fong. The beer is just as good though. Hordes of Germans descend on *Biergarten* (☎ 2721-2302), 8 Hanoi Rd, for porknuckle and sauerkraut and several excellent beers on tap. In addition to night crawling, any of these places would make for a fine afternoon breather from shopping or sightseeing.

*MC2 Media Café* (☎ 2369-9997) in the Mirimar Hotel arcade, 1-23 Kimberley Rd, has a decent selection of microbrewery beers and at the time of writing was staging a beer buffet where you could drink all you want for HK$55.

The *Watering Hole* (☎ 2312-2288), basement, 1A Mody Rd, is a salt-of-the-earth spot where locals and expats sometimes congregate for a swilling session.

Sitting up at the northern end of Ashley Rd is the infamous *Kangaroo Pub* (☎ 2376-0083), the bane of those Australian expats struggling to prove that not all their countrymen are lager louts. This place gets pretty lively, and there are some decent Aussie beers like Cooper's and VB.

Finally, for James Bond fans, there's *Bottoms Up* (☎ 2367-5696), basement, 14 Hankow Rd. Duty brought 007 here on one of his Asian sojourns, and the club is still milking it for all its worth. Just because Mr Bond made it here doesn't mean you have to, however; this place is a true sleaze pit. Park your Aston-Martin elsewhere.

### Gay Bars

The gay scene in Hong Kong used to be on life-support but a small revolution has taken place in the last few years. A cluster of bars and clubs have opened up around Glenealy and Wyndham Sts, giving the male gay community a focus. Furthermore, now that Hong Kong realises that the PLA are not (yet) targeting gay venues, coming out for Hong Kong Chinese seems less fraught with worry.

Add to that the growing awareness of businessmen of the value of the 'pink dollar', and you can see that big changes are afoot.

Two new bars on Glenealy St, Central, *Zip* (☎ 2523-3595) at 2 Glenealy St and *Flex* (☎ 2525-4328), 7 Glenealy St, take in most of the action. Flex is really stylish, decked out in purple and decorated with sculptures and is absolutely packed out at weekends; Zip goes overboard with an outdoor waterfall and is equally crowded. These two bars make up an aperitif to the evening which usually moves on to clubland with *Propaganda* (Map 6; ☎ 2868-1316), 1 Hollywood Rd. As Propaganda's ads are proud to proclaim, this is Hong Kong's premier gay meeting place. Cover charges get steeper as the week goes on: entry is free from Monday to Wednesday, HK$80 on Thursday, HK$110 on Friday and HK$150 on Saturday. This is a newer and larger version of its old premises in Wyndham St.

*CE Top* (☎ 2541-5524) is not exclusively gay, but it's definitely part of the gay map of Hong Kong. You can find it on the 9th floor, 37-43 Cochrane St, Central.

Considerably more subdued is *Petticoat Lane* (☎ 2973-0642), at 2 Tun Wo Lane in Central (where the Mid-Levels escalator cuts between Lyndhurst Terrace and Hollywood Rd). It's a small place with French decor, and is more suited to chatting than bopping. It was voted as Hong Kong's best gay bar by readers of *HK Magazine* in 1997, despite attracting a lot of straight customers as well.

*Club 97* (Map 6; ☎ 2586-1103/2810-9333), at 9 Lan Kwai Fong Lane, has a happy hour on Friday nights, with half price drinks and shows. Unfortunately, it is a members only club, although members are allowed to take along one person.

The lesbian scene in Hong Kong is *very* low profile, and still lacks either an organisation or a focal point.

### HOSTESS CLUBS

At least in terms of expense, this is the peak of Hong Kong nightlife. The territory boasts some of the world's largest and most elaborate hostess clubs, where you pay through the nose to have young women in revealing outfits sit, talk and dance with you. Whether things go further than that probably depends on the club. Even at the lower-end hostess clubs a restrained evening can easily cost US$500. At some of the top spots the bill rises into the thousands. The ritziest places are mostly in Tsim Sha Tsui East; somewhat less exorbitant options are in Wan Chai.

*Club Bboss* (Map 5; ☎ 2369-2883), New Mandarin Plaza, 14 Science Museum Rd, Tsim Sha Tsui East, bills itself as a 'Japanese-style nightclub'. Certainly the prices are Japanese-style. With more than 1000 hostesses of various nationalities, it's a good place to practice your Thai or Tagalog, if you don't mind paying HK$1000 for lessons.

## SPECTATOR SPORT

There's not much variety to spectator sports in Hong Kong. This may change after 1997, when Hong Kongers may gradually be infected with the sports mania that has long gripped a large part of the Chinese population. Some of the mainstream sports that people in Hong Kong watch are listed here. For sports you can play yourself, see the Activities section of the Things to See & Do chapter.

### Horse-Racing

Hong Kong's racing season lasts from mid-September to early June and there are usually 65 meetings per season. Normally, races at the *Sha Tin* track in the New Territories are held on Saturday from 1 to 6 pm. At *Happy Valley,* on Hong Kong Island, races are normally on Wednesday evenings from about 7 to 11 pm, though some races are also held on Saturday. The HKTA can provide you with a schedule for the season. You can also check the sports sections of the English-language newspapers.

Some admission charges include: in-field enclosure HK$2; public enclosure HK$10; pavilion stand HK$30; tourist and member's guest tickets HK$50. The tourist ticket entitles you to a visitor's badge and a seat in the members' box. These badges can be purchased at the gate on race day, or up to two

days in advance at any of the Hong Kong Jockey Club's off-track betting centres, which are everywhere. For visitors, two of the most conveniently located ones are at 39-41 Hankow Rd in Tsim Sha Tsui and 64 Connaught Rd in Central. You'll need your passport to prove you are only visiting.

During race meetings, extra buses and trams serve Happy Valley Racecourse from all over Hong Kong Island. Alternatively you can take the MTR to Causeway Bay station, exit through Times Square and walk about 15 minutes to get there. The KCR has special trains that go directly to the Sha Tin track on race days.

Another option is to sign up for the HKTA's 'Come Horseracing Tour'. It costs HK$490 per person for transportation to and from the track, a seat in the members' box, lunch or dinner before the meeting, guide service and ample information on betting procedures. For more information call the HKTA tour operations (☎ 2807-6390).

### Rugby Sevens

The only other sporting event that sparks the same kind of enthusiasm is the Seven-A-Side rugby tournament, popularly known as the Rugby Sevens. Teams from all over the world come together in Hong Kong every March (or early April) for three days of 15-minute matches. Even people who aren't rugby fans scramble to get the scarce tickets, for in addition to the sport, there's a lot of action in the stands. For many, the Rugby Sevens is a giant three-day party.

Getting tickets is the hard part, as many are reserved for members of overseas rugby clubs. Hong Kong companies, public relations firms and society's upper crust also get sizeable allocations, leaving few for ordinary fans. Information on ticket sales can be found in the local newspapers, usually sometime in mid-February.

For details on the tournament and buying tickets, you can contact the Hong Kong Rugby Football Union (☎ 2504-8300), Room 2004, Sports House, 1 Stadium Path, So Kon Po, Causeway Bay. The HKTA's overseas offices may also be able to provide you with information as well.

## Cricket

The Hong Kong International Cricket Series is held in late September/early October every year. This two-day event at the Hong Kong Stadium hosts teams from Australia, New Zealand, England, the West Indies, India and Pakistan battling it out in a speedy six-a-side version of the limited overs game.

## Football (Soccer)

Hong Kong has a fairly lively amateur football league. Games are played on the pitches inside the Happy Valley Racecourse and at Mong Kok Stadium. The sports sections of the English-language papers carry information on when and where matches are held. Alternatively you can contact the Hong Kong Football Association (☎ 2712-9122), 55 Fat Kwong St, Ho Man Tin, Kowloon.

## Tennis

There are several international tennis tournaments held annually in Hong Kong. The largest are the Salem Open, held in April, and the Marlboro Championship, which takes place usually in October. The tournaments are held in Victoria Park in Causeway Bay. Check the local English-language newspapers for information on times and ticket availability.

# Shopping

Hong Kong still rides on its reputation as one of the world's top shopping spots – but times have changed. Skyrocketing rents have sent prices soaring across the board, even for basic items. Moreover, many of the goods that people used to come to Hong Kong for, such as electronics and garments, are now available in many other places, often for less money. New York, for example, is a much better place to buy a camera, computer or camcorder, Bangkok has cheaper clothing and silks, and Chinese souvenirs and some antiques cost far less just across the border in Guangdong.

What hasn't changed is the variety. If anything, Hong Kong has a wider array of things to buy than ever before. If you've come here to shop, you'll find plenty to keep you occupied, but to find the real bargains you're probably going to have to pound a lot of pavement.

Sitting adjacent to China's vast labour pool, Hong Kong offers some good deals on clothing, footwear, luggage and other items that require little technology to produce. Even here, however, prices are on the rise.

There are no hard and fast shopping hours in Hong Kong, but shops in the major districts generally are open as follows: Central and Western from 10 am to 6 or 7 pm; Causeway Bay and Wan Chai from 10 am to 10 or 11 pm; Tsim Sha Tsui, Yau Ma Tei and Mong Kok from 10 am to 9 pm; and Tsim Sha Tsui East from 10 am to 7.30 pm. Causeway Bay is the best part of town for late-night shopping.

Most shops are open seven days a week, but on Sunday and holidays many open only from 1 to 5 pm. Street markets are open all day and well into the night. Almost everything closes for two or three days during the Chinese New Year period. However, the period just prior to the Chinese New Year is the best time to go on a spree – everything goes on sale because the stores want to clear out old stock.

## SHOPPING TIPS

Hong Kong has more than its fair share of unscrupulous stores and shopkeepers. Even in the honest places there is often little concept of after-sale service. Of course, not every place is out to get you, and there's a good chance you'll never come across dishonesty. But a little preparation can avoid a lot of misery, so here are some tips to keep in mind before you start spending your hard-earned cash.

### Guarantees

When buying things like cameras or electronic goods, it's best to get something that comes with an international warranty: a local one won't do you much good once you get home. Every guarantee should carry a complete description of the item (including model and serial number), as well as the date of purchase, the name and address of the shop it was purchased from, the shop's official stamp and the name of the sole agent in Hong Kong responsible for the product. If the shop won't give you a warranty, chances are you're dealing with grey market equipment (ie, imported by somebody other than the official local agent) which usually either comes with no guarantee at all, or one which is only valid in the country of manufacture. The Hong Kong Tourist Association's (HKTA) *Official Shopping Guide* has the addresses and phone numbers of most of Hong Kong's sole agents and distributors.

### Refunds & Exchanges

Many shops will exchange goods if they are defective or, in the case of clothing, if the garment simply doesn't fit. Be sure to keep receipts (see below) and go back to the store as soon as possible.

Refunds are almost never given in Hong Kong, but most stores will give you credit towards another purchase. Usually there is no need to put a deposit on anything unless it is being custom-made, like a tailored suit or a pair of glasses. Some shops might ask for a deposit if you're ordering something that they normally wouldn't stock, but this isn't all that common.

### Receipts

Receipts can often just be a scrap of paper with an illegible Chinese scrawl, but it is in your interest for it to be printed and legible. This will pay off if you need to exchange the item later, if customs questions you on the price of goods purchased abroad, or for insurance purposes upon your return home. Insist on getting an itemised receipt, and avoid handing over the cash until you have the goods in hand and they've written a receipt.

### Rip-Offs

While most shops are honest, there are also some pretty shady stores in Hong Kong, most of which prey solely on tourists. The HKTA recommends that you shop only in stores which display the HKTA membership sign, a red Chinese junk sailing against a white background. This sounds like great advice except that a lot of good stores are not HKTA members. Furthermore, many of the dubious camera and video shops in Tsim Sha Tsui are HKTA members, so this may not be any guarantee.

The most common way to cheat tourists is simply to overcharge. In the tourist shopping district of Tsim Sha Tsui, you'll rarely find price tags on anything. Checking prices in several stores therefore becomes essential. However, shopkeepers know that tourists compare prices in several locations before buying, so they will often quote a reasonable or ridiculously low price on a big ticket item, and get the money back by overcharging on small items or accessories. You may be quoted a reasonable price on a camera, only to be gouged on the lens cap, neck strap, case, batteries and flash.

Some dishonest shopkeepers may remove components that should have been included free (like the connecting cords for the speakers on a stereo system) and demand more money when you return to the shop. The

---

**Fake Goods**

Watch out for counterfeit brand goods. Fake labels on clothes are the most obvious example, but there are fake Rolex and Dunhill watches, CDs, tapes, Gucci leather bags, jade, jewellery, ceramics and even fake herbal medicines. Hong Kong's customs agents have been cracking down hard on fake electronics and cameras, so this is not as big a problem as it once was.

However, counterfeit watches are everywhere. Some fakes are obvious, but others are more skilfully made – most of the Rolexes sold by pesky hawkers on Nathan Rd are abysmal copies, but other outlets come up with reasonably expensive imitations that are convincing. If you discover that you've been sold a fake brand name watch when you thought you were buying the genuine article, it would be worthwhile to contact the police or customs as this is definitely illegal. Also beware of factory rejects. ■

---

truly vicious ones may even take your purchase into the back room to 'box it up', and then remove essential items that you've already paid for. Another tactic is to replace some of the good components with cheap or defective ones. Also be alert for signs of wear and tear – the equipment could be second-hand.

Needless to say, go for brand names. One of the big retail scams of 1997 was the sale of dodgy Guangdong-made speakers for HK$10,000 a pair, advertised as a top of the range model from the USA. The speakers were worth about HK$250 at the most. This sort of thing happens on a regular basis. If you haven't heard of the brand, and the goods are pricey, don't buy.

### Getting Help

There isn't much you can do if a shop simply overcharges. However, if you discover that the goods are defective or something is missing, return to the shop immediately with the goods and receipt. Sometimes it really is an honest mistake and the problem will be cleared up at once. Honest shopkeepers will exchange defective goods or replace missing

SHOPPING

components. On the other hand, if the shop intentionally cheated you, expect a bitter argument.

If you feel that you were defrauded, there are a few agencies that might be able to help you. The first place to try is the HKTA (☎ 2807-6177); if the shop is a member of the HKTA can lean on the owners, but don't expect miracles. If not, the HKTA can at least advise you on who to contact for more help.

Another place to try is the Hong Kong Consumer Council's complaints and advice line (☎ 9229-2222). The council has advice centres you could pop into if you wish to speak to someone. There are two centres: one (☎ 9221-6228) on the ground floor, Harbour Building (Map 6), 38 Pier Rd, Central; and the other (☎ 9226-4011) on the ground floor, Morning Joy Building, 141-143 Kau Pui Lung Rd, To Kwa Wan, Kowloon.

### Shipping Goods

Goods can be sent home by post, and some stores will package and post the goods for you (especially if it is a large item), but you may want to check before you go and buy that antique couch. Also find out whether you will have to clear the goods at the country of destination or whether they will go directly to your door. If the goods are fragile, it is sensible to buy insurance in case of damage during transit. Make sure you keep all receipts.

Sometimes doing it yourself can save some money, although it may not be worth the hassle. Smaller items can be shipped from the post office or United Parcel Service (☎ 2735-3535), which offers services from Hong Kong to 40 countries. It ships by air and accepts parcels weighing up to 30kg.

If you want to ship heavier goods by air, many air cargo companies have offices at Chek Lap Kok airport. Among the better known companies is DHL (☎ 2765-8111). Check the *Yellow Pages for Consumers* for more listings.

### WHERE TO SHOP

The three major shopping districts are Causeway Bay, Tsim Sha Tsui and Mong Kok. Each one has something different to offer, although one thing they all have in common is constant, dense crowds.

**Causeway Bay** (Map 7) has perhaps the broadest spectrum in terms of price, and the most monumental crowds at weekends. The luxury end of the market is well represented by numerous designer clothing shops and a cluster of Japanese department stores (Sogo, Mitsukoshi, Daimaru and Matzusakaya). Times Square is a vast shopping experience. There are also plenty of places selling medium-priced clothing, electronics, sporting goods and household items; you can also stumble upon lively street markets in the area. Tower Records and HMV both can be found in Causeway Bay. Jardine's Bazaar and the area behind it are home to stalls and shops peddling cheap clothing, luggage and footwear.

**Tsim Sha Tsui** (Map 5) is a curious mix of tackiness and sophistication. Nathan Rd itself is a huge avenue of camera shops, watch shops, electronics shops and leather and silk emporiums. Despite being the worst part of town for bargain hunters, it is strong in luxury and quality goods; a large number of designer shops congregate in the area. Some of these lie along Nathan Rd, but the bulk are to be found in Harbour City (see the Shopping Malls section following for more details), a huge labyrinth of a shopping complex that stretches nearly 1km from the Star Ferry Terminal north along Canton Rd. For middle and low-priced clothing you can try the back streets east of Nathan Rd. Tsim Sha Tsui East has a string of mostly upscale shopping malls, the biggest being the Tsim Sha Tsui Centre at 66 Mody Rd.

**Mong Kok** (Map 4) caters mostly to local shoppers, and there are some good prices to be found here on clothing, sporting goods, camping gear, footwear and daily necessities. There's nothing very exotic, but for everyday items it's a popular spot.

Of course, there is plenty to shopping outside these areas as well. Hong Kong's finest luxury offerings are mostly found in the glittering shopping malls in Central and Admiralty (Map 6). The Landmark, Galleria and Pacific Place malls, among others, have branches of most international luxury retailers, as well as some home-grown varieties. Some of Hong Kong's top jewellery and accessory shops are also in these districts.

For antiques, head to Hollywood Rd in **Sheung Wan** (Map 6), where there is a long string of shops selling Chinese and Asian items. Some of the really good spots have genuine treasures, but be on your guard.

**Wan Chai** (Map 7) is another good spot for medium and low-priced clothing, sporting goods and footwear, but like Mong Kok, the area caters mainly for locals. Wan Chai has no glamour, but it's well worth searching for bargains. For basic items, it may be worth also checking out the shopping malls on eastern Hong Kong Island, northern Kowloon or even the New Territories. Being further from the main business districts, these malls charge retailers lower rents, which can translate into lower prices for

consumers; and during the week they're less crowded than the central districts. One of the biggest of these is Cityplaza, an enormous shopping complex in Quarry Bay at Tai Koo MTR station to the east of Central. Up in the New Territories, the Sha Tin New Town Plaza is another mammoth mall, and can be easily reached by taking the KCR to Sha Tin station.

If you're targeting the budget end, there's no better place to start than one of Hong Kong's street markets. Hong Kong's biggest market is the night market held on **Temple St** (Map 4), which basically runs parallel to Nathan Rd in Yau Ma Tei. If it's cheap (and in many cases shoddy), it will be on sale at this cornucopia of surprises: clothes, cassettes, fake designer goods, watches, leather goods, pens, alarm clocks, radios, knives, cheap jewellery, pirate CDs and tapes, illegal porn, potions, lotions and hundreds of other downmarket items. Alongside the market are

RICHARD I'ANSON

Hong Kong's street markets, such as the Temple St and Tung Choi St markets in Kowloon, are a great place to go hunting for bargains – but you get what you pay for.

SHOPPING

numerous noodle and seafood restaurants and stalls where you can grab a bite in between purchases (for more details see the Yau Ma Tei section of the Things to See & Do chapter). The market runs roughly from 6 pm to midnight.

Not far away, the **Tung Choi St** market (Map 4), two blocks east of Mong Kok MTR station, mainly sells cheap clothes. People start setting up their stalls as early as noon, but it's better to get here between 6 and 10 pm, when there's a lot more on offer. Another bustling market is the one on Apliu St (noon to 9 pm) in Sham Shui Po, one block west of Sham Shui Po MTR station. If you're looking strictly for clothing, you can also try **Jardine's Bazaar** (Map 7) in Causeway Bay. The majority is women's clothing, but there are some male garments toward the back. A bit more upscale and fun is the Stanley market, in the village of **Stanley** (Map 10) on southern Hong Kong Island. Here you'll find brand name clothing, sports shoes, lower grade jewellery and art, souvenirs and lots of little trinkets (see the Stanley section of the Things to See & Do chapter for more details).

At any of these markets, it's good to check out the shops on the sides of the street, hidden behind all the street stalls. Often the real bargains (if there are any) can be found here, and staff are generally a bit less pushy as well.

Another bargain option is to go to one of Hong Kong's factory outlets. Most of these deal in ready-to-wear garments, but there are a few that also sell carpets, shoes, leather goods, jewellery and imitation antique pieces. Often the prices aren't that much less than in retail shops though. It's important to check purchases carefully, since at most outlets all sales are final and many items are factory seconds and imperfect. If you decide to go factory-outlet hopping, it's advisable to invest HK$69 in *The Complete Guide to Hong Kong Factory Bargains* by Dana Goetz & Caroline Radin, sold in most bookshops. This gives a thorough rundown on what to expect and could save you a lot of time. The book is regularly updated, as factory outlets come and go. The HKTA also has a useful handout on factory outlets.

Shopping is still one of Hong Kong's biggest tourist draws, and the HKTA's *Official Shopping Guide* has brief rundowns on various consumer goods with addresses and phone numbers of HKTA member stores that sell them. The HKTA also publishes a number of free special-interest pamphlets such as the *Shopping Guide to Consumer Electronics* and the *Shopping Guide to Jewellery*. A useful book for the devoted shopper in Hong Kong is Fiona Campbell's *The Guide to Shopping in Hong Kong*, which exhaustively covers the maze of retail outlets in the city.

### Shopping Malls

Malls make for convenient shopping, and the scale of Hong Kong's malls means that you can find most of what you want all in one place. They are generally open seven days. Listed here are the largest of Hong Kong's shopping malls.

*Citiplaza,* 111 King's Rd, Tai Koo, Quarry Bay – the largest shopping centre in eastern Hong Kong and directly linked up to the MTR

*New World Centre* (Map 5), 20 Salisbury Rd, Tsim Sha Tsui – one of Kowloon's major malls

*Ocean Terminal/Harbour City* (Map 5), 5 Canton Rd, Tsim Sha Tsui – a vast conglomeration of malls fused into one

*Prince's Building* (Map 6), Chater Rd, Central – a quieter and more civilised shopping experience bursting with all you could need

*The Galleria* (Map 6), 9 Queen's Rd, Central – a classy enclave of top-end shopping

*The Landmark* (Map 6), 16 Des Voeux Rd, Central – classy designer labels all under one roof

*The Mall* (Map 6), Pacific Place, 8 Queensway, Admiralty – easily reached by MTR, this mall has the lot, including a UA cinema complex; packed at weekends

### WHAT TO BUY
### Arts, Crafts & Antiques

Hong Kong has a rich and colourful array in this category – treasures await both the serious and not-so-serious collector. Serious collectors of art and antiques (including ceramics) will probably restrict themselves to the reputable names among the antique shops and auction houses, while more amateur collectors can content themselves with the glut of choice that remains.

Caution is the by-word for this game, for Hong Kong is the receptacle of a lot of expert forgeries and reproductions. However, among the ersatz crowd shine some real gems that have made their way to Hong Kong from China and South-East Asia – genuine Ming and Qing furniture, Tibetan carvings, Korean and Japanese treasures, traditional Chinese landscape paintings, calligraphic scrolls and snuff bottles all wait to be discovered. Just remember that most of the really good pieces are in private collections and are often sold through Christie's or Sotheby's.

Most of Hong Kong's antique shops are bunched along Hollywood Rd in Sheung Wan (Map 6). The shops make for a fascinating stroll – religious statues and carvings lean against each other among a jumble of antique furniture, screens and wall-hangings. The shops at the western end of Hollywood Rd tend to be less expensive and carry more dubious antiques. However, they also stock a wide range of old books and magazines, propaganda posters, badges from the Cultural Revolution and all sorts of bric-a-brac from China and Hong Kong that makes for interesting browsing.

The more reputable places should have tags on all their items stating the price as well as the antique's name, age and whether any restoration work has been done. If you are interested in a piece, ask if the vendor can supply a certificate of authenticity. By all means haggle the price down and ask for trade terms if you're in the business yourself.

If you're hunting for quality items, try one of the following: Zitan (☎ 2523-7584) at 43-55 Wyndham St in Central has a superb range of antique Chinese furniture; if you are hunting for Tibetan religious art and artefacts, The Tibetan Gallery (☎ 2530-4863) at 55 Wyndham St has a rich selection; also in Wyndham St is Tai Sing Company (☎ 2525-9365), known for quality Chinese antiques; Schoeni Fine Oriental Art (☎ 2542-3143) at 27 Hollywood Rd has a dizzying range of traditional Chinese collectables. Some more well known places include: Hobbs & Bishop Fine Art (☎ 2537-9838), 28 Hollywood Rd and Luen Chai Curios Store (☎ 2540-4772) at 142 Hollywood Rd.

Don't overlook the opportunity to visit the auctions at Sotheby's Hong Kong (☎ 2524-8121), Tower Two, 18th floor, Lipo Chun Chambers, 189 Des Voeux Rd, Central, and Christie's (☎ 2521-5396), 28th floor, Alexandra House, 16-20 Chater Rd. Auctions are usually held twice a year in April and November. The pre-auction preview (usually held at the Furama Kempinski Hotel for Sotheby's and the JW Marriot Hotel for Christie's) presents you with the opportunity to examine items coming up for sale and rub shoulders with the big buyers from the international art market. Both auction houses have regular sales in ceramics, jewellery, jade, stamps, snuff bottles, artworks, traditional and contemporary Chinese paintings, and calligraphy.

For Chinese arts and crafts, the main places to go are the large Chinese-run department stores scattered throughout Hong Kong. You can get all sorts of hand-carved wooden pieces, ceramics, paintings, enamel, calligraphy, jade, silk garments and even bolts of silk. Many pieces are modern, garish and are only really souvenir items. It's much cheaper to pick this stuff up in China, where most of it is made.

One of the biggest chains is Chinese Arts & Crafts, which is also the most upmarket of these type of stores: you can actually find some pretty valuable pieces at these places. Branches include: Admiralty (☎ 2523-3933), Unit 230, Pacific Place (Map 6), 88 Queensway; Central (☎ 2845-0092), ground floor, Prince's Building (Map 6), 3 Des Voeux Rd Central; Tsim Sha Tsui (☎ 2735-4061), Star House (Map 5), 3 Salisbury Rd; Wan Chai (☎ 2827-6667), ground floor, lower block, China Resources Building, 26 Harbour Rd.

A bit more pedestrian are the Yue Hwa Chinese Products Emporium stores, where in addition to art and crafts you can also buy clothing, appliances, books, etc. This is a great place to pick up little gifts for friends back home. The largest branch (Map 5; ☎ 2384-0084) is at 301-309 Nathan Rd, Yau Ma Tei. Others are in the Mirador Hotel arcade (Map 5), 54 Nathan Rd, and Park Lane Shopper's Boulevard, 143 Nathan Rd (near Kowloon Park).

Similar in quality and selection are CRC department stores. There are three branches on Hong Kong Island: 92 Queen's Rd Central, Central (☎ 2524-1051); 488 Hennessy Rd (☎ 2577-0222) and the Lok Sing Centre (☎ 2890-8321), 31 Yee Wo St – both are in Causeway Bay.

For folk crafts, one of the nicest stores in town is Mountain Folkcraft (Map 6; ☎ 2523-2817), 12 Wo On Lane, Central, near Lan Kwai Fong. This place has batiks, clothing, wood carvings and lacquerware made by ethnic minorities in China and other Asian countries. The shop attendants are friendly, and prices, while not cheap, are not outrageous either.

There are also a few antique shops in the Ocean Terminal/Harbour City (Map 5) complex in Tsim Sha Tsui, but getting a good price there is said to be difficult. They are mainly concentrated in a corridor of shops called The Silk Road; here you can find cloisonné, bronzes, jade, lacquer, ceramics, rosewood furniture and screens. Art Orient at Room 342 in the Ocean Terminal has a fine selection of Buddhist and Tibetan artefacts.

If you're serious about your antique shopping, you may want to pick up *Hong Kong Antique, Fine Art and Carpet Galleries* by Barbara Anderson. Available at most bookstores, it has become a bit dated but is still a comprehensive pocket guide that should prove useful.

Hong Kong is also an excellent place to pick up fine art. The city's galleries display a rich and varied selection of Chinese modern and traditional art, regional and South-East Asian art, as well as artworks from other places. Art galleries provide a perfect opportunity to escape the bustle of Hong Kong and enter a different cultural milieu, and they also provide a unique learning experience. Following is just a small selection of what is on offer.

Alisan Fine Art (☎ 2526-1091) in Room 315, Prince's Building (Map 6), 10 Chater Rd, Central, has regular exhibitions of contemporary mainland Chinese and expatriate Chinese artists. Contemporary Russian, Chinese and European works can be found at Schoeni Art Gallery (☎ 2869-8802) on 18th floor, Coda Plaza 51, Garden Rd, Central. Schoeni frequently represents major mainland Chinese artists such as Wang Yidong and Liu Dahong.

If you want to pick up modern European works, try the Row Gallery (☎ 2801-5766; Web site www.thepress.com/3d/rgallery/home.htm.) at Room 401, Pacific House (Map 6), Queen's Rd, Central, which, although small, usually has a collection of lithographs by Picasso, Matisse, Salvador Dali and other 20th century masters.

For fun modern art and sculpture, check out Vincent Lee Fine Arts (Map 6; ☎ 2801-6788; email hkvlfa@hk.linkage.net) which can be found in G/3 at the Ritz Carlton Hotel in Central.

## Bookshops & Stationery

Hong Kong has a reasonable if unimaginative selection of bookstores, though they're almost always far too pricey. The service tends to be reluctant and ill-informed. Too often stocked to the hilt with stale hardbacks (usually business or law books), my advice is to bring your own books. If you want to order a book you can't find, this will inevitably be expensive and require a long wait. Bookshops in Hong Kong are generally very dated in their approach to bookselling – it's infuriating to go into shop after shop and find all the books (and magazines) sealed in plastic film, which sabotages the art of browsing. Stationery can generally be found in bookstores such as Bookazine, Jumbo Grade and Times.

One of the larger bookshops is Swindon Books (Map 5; ☎ 2366-8001), 13 Lock Rd, Tsim Sha Tsui. There are also branches in Tsim Sha Tsui (Map 5; ☎ 2735-9881) at shop 346, 3rd floor, Ocean Terminal and at the Star Ferry Terminal (Map 5). The Hong Kong Book Centre (Map 6) at 25 Des Voeux Rd,

Central is a basement bookstore with a vast selection of books and magazines.

Times bookshops are dotted around Hong Kong and have an average range of books and stationery. Branches include: (☎ 2367-4340) basement, Golden Crown Court, 66-70 Nathan Rd, Tsim Sha Tsui; (☎ 2525-8797) ground floor, Hong Kong Club Building, 3 Jackson Rd, Central; shop P315-316, 3rd floor, World Trade Centre, 280 Gloucester Rd, Causeway Bay. Bookazine is somewhat similar, and has branches on the 2nd floor of Prince's Building (Map 6; ☎ 2522-1785), the basement of Jardine House (Map 6; ☎ 2523-1747) and other locations.

There is a *South China Morning Post* bookshop (☎ 2801-4423) at the Star Ferry Terminal (Map 6) in Central. There is another in Times Square (Map 7), Matheson St, Causeway Bay. Jumbo Grade has a number of branches including: (☎ 2526-3873) shop 144, Pacific Place (Map 6), Queensway; and (☎ 2521-5509) shop 134-135, Prince's Building (Map 6), Central.

Joint Publishing Company (☎ 2525-0105), 9 Queen Victoria St (opposite the Central Market) in Central, is an outstanding store to find books about China or books and cassette tapes for studying Chinese languages. Another good shop for Chinese-related works is Cosmos Books (Map 7; ☎ 2528-3605), 30 Johnston Rd, Wan Chai.

A very good specialist range of business, legal and professional titles can be found in The Professional Bookshop (☎ 2526-5387) at 104A Alexandra House, Chater Rd, Central.

Books relating to the arts can be found at the Performing Arts Shop (☎ 2734-2091) in the Hong Kong Cultural Centre in Tsim Sha Tsui (Map 5). The Tai Yip Company (☎ 2732-2088/9) has an excellent and extensive range of art books and cards in their shop on the 1st floor of the Hong Kong Museum of Art in Tsim Sha Tsui (Map 5).

New age books can be found at Age of Aquarius (☎ 2577-4944), 1st floor, 2-6 Foo Ming St, Causeway Bay. Here you can find literature on UFOs, tarot, astrology, meditation and alternative therapies.

The Government Publications Office (☎ 2537-1910), in the Government Offices (Map 6), 88 Queensway, Admiralty, is open from 9 am to 4 pm daily and from 9 am to 1 pm on Saturday.

Hong Kong has very few second-hand book outlets, but occasionally a stall goes up with cheap paperbacks – there is usually one selling second-hand fiction at Central's Star Ferry Terminal (Map 6). Some of the junk shops at the western end of Hollywood Rd, just south of Sheung Wan, also stock old paperbacks.

### Cameras & Film

Stanley St in Central (Map 6) is one of the best spots in Hong Kong for buying photographic equipment – there are several camera shops and competition is keen. Everything carries price tags, though some low-level bargaining might be possible.

Photo Scientific (Map 6; ☎ 2522-1903), 6 Stanley St, is the favourite of Hong Kong's professional photographers. You might find equipment elsewhere for less, but this place has a rock-solid reputation – labelled prices, no bargaining, no arguing and no cheating. Photo Scientific stocks everything from tripods, darkroom supplies, and photographer's jackets with hundreds of pockets to every type of film. Almost next door is Color Six (Map 6; ☎ 2526-0123), 18A Stanley St, which probably does the best photo processing in town. Colour slides can be processed in three hours. Many special types of film are on sale here which can be bought nowhere else in Hong Kong, and all professional film is kept refrigerated. Prices aren't the lowest in town (developing costs are HK$1.10 per exposure plus HK$12 per roll) but the quality is excellent. There are also plenty of swift developing places all over the city including the Fotomax chain, which can develop your film in one hour for HK$75 (36 exposures).

Other reputable photographic supplies outlets include Hing Lee Camera Company (Map 6; ☎ 2544-7593) on the ground floor, 25 Lyndhurst Terrace, Central, and Everbest

SHOPPING

Photo Supplies (☎ 2522-1985), which can be found at 28B Stanley St, Central.

Despite the endless number of shops selling cameras, Tsim Sha Tsui is probably the worst place to buy a camera. Many shops blatantly overcharge tourists. This particularly applies to Nathan Rd. No shops here put price tags on equipment and charging double or more is standard.

### Camping & Travel Gear

There are a number of stores in Mong Kok (Map 4) where you can buy all sorts of useful items for travelling or camping, such as backpacks, sleeping bags, water bottles, Swiss Army knives etc. Some stores worth checking out include: Chamonix Alpine Equipment (Map 4; ☎ 2388-3626), 395 Shanghai St; Well Mount Sports (Map 4; ☎ 2391-9256), 56 Tung Choi St; and Wise Mount Sports (Map 4; ☎ 2787-3011), 75 Sai Yee St. Li Yuen Sts East and West in Central (Map 6) have stalls selling very cheap rucksacks made over the border in Guangdong, which are actually reasonably durable.

For travel garments, there is an outstanding group of stores called Pro Cam-Fis. It's a local outfit that designs and manufactures items like travel vests, Gore-Tex raingear, hiking shirts and pants which unzip to become shorts. These items are definitely more upmarket than what you'll find in Mong Kok, but they are also high quality and durable. Pro Cam-Fis locations include: shop 265 (☎ 2736-9866), Ocean Centre (Map 5), Tsim Sha Tsui; shop 61 (☎ 2302-0000), Park Lane Shopper's Boulevard, Nathan Rd, Tsim Sha Tsui; and shop 611 (☎ 2506-2211) at Times Square (Map 7), Causeway Bay.

### Carpets & Rugs

These are not really that cheap in Hong Kong, but there is a good selection of silk, wool, new and antique carpets. Imported carpets from China, Pakistan, India, Iran, Afghanistan, Tibet and Turkey are widely available. The best carpets have a higher number of knots per square inch (more than 550) and are richer in detail and colour than cheaper carpets. Silk carpets are generally hung on the wall rather than used on the floor. Older carpets use natural dyes.

The bulk of Hong Kong's carpet and rug shops are clustered on Wyndham St in Central. There are also a few places in Ocean Terminal (Map 5), Tsim Sha Tsui like the Chinese Carpet Centre (☎ 2735-1030), with a huge selection of new carpets and rugs. You can custom order from Hong Kong's own Tai Ping Carpets, which has a showroom (☎ 2522-7138) on the ground floor of Wing On Plaza (Map 5), 62 Mody Rd, Tsim Sha Tsui. Other noted shops include Mir Oriental Carpets (☎ 2521-5641), 52 Wyndham St, Central, which has thousands of carpets in stock from around the world. Al Shahzadi Persian Carpet Gallery (☎ 2834-8298), 265 Queen's Rd East, Admiralty, has carpets from Afghanistan, Iran, Russia and other countries.

### Clothes & Shoes

This is what the vast majority of Hong Kong's stores sell. It seems impossible that so many clothing and fashion shops could survive. But Hong Kong Chinese are a trendy bunch who spend a sizeable amount of their earnings on clothes. The emphasis in Hong Kong is on slick and neat fashion, the chic rather than the radical, and the result is a very well-dressed and stylish city.

For bargain basement clothes shopping, one of the best places is Granville Rd in Tsim Sha Tsui (Map 5). The eastern end is not much more than a row of downmarket shops with bins and racks of discount clothing, including a fair amount of factory rejects. Clothes are definitely cheap, but the selection from store to store isn't great, and you need to check carefully for any flaws. In general the stores with permanent signs carry better stock, and this is where you'll have a better chance of getting something that is really good value for money. Also take the effort to check the upstairs shops; some of these places have good deals on silk garments. There are also some cheap places on Nathan Rd in Tsim Sha Tsui, but veteran Hong Kong shoppers avoid them. Most of the brand name items are fakes, and even fall apart after several washes.

On Hong Kong Island, Jardine's Bazaar in Causeway Bay (Map 7) has stall after stall of low-cost garments, though it may take some hunting to find anything decent. If you can't, try Lee Garden Rd, where there are several sample shops and some places to pick up cheap jeans. The street markets at Temple St (Yau Ma Tei), Tung Choi St (Mong Kok) and Apliu St (Sham Shui Po) have some of the cheapest clothes anywhere, both in terms of price and quality. Tung Choi St and adjacent Sai Yeung Choi St South are also good places to hunt for sports shoes and hiking boots.

For mid-priced items, Causeway Bay and Tsim Sha Tsui, particularly east of Nathan Rd, are good hunting grounds. Take the time to pop into one of the dozens of Bossini, Baleno, Giordano, U2 or Esprit clothing chain stores. They all specialise in mainstream fashionable items that are well made and affordable, similar to The Gap, Next or River Island. Quality at these places is good, and prices are very reasonable. All these places tend to stock fairly similar items, but it's worth checking a few of them: most have frequent sales, and if stock is sold out at one shop you may find it at another. Marks & Spencer also has a number of branches in Hong Kong, including: (☎ 2923-7925) unit 313-418, 3rd floor, Times Square (Map 7), Causeway Bay; (☎ 2921-8303) 1st floor, Central Building (Map 6), Queen's Rd Central; (☎ 2921-8897) Shop B12, Landmark shopping centre (Map 6), Central.

The section of Lockhart Rd near the Sogo department store in Causeway Bay (Map 7) is a good place to look for footwear: there are a lot of shops around here, and the competition makes for pretty good value. Check around though, as some places have considerably better prices than others for the same product. It's also worth taking a stroll down Johnston Rd in Wan Chai, which has lots of mid-priced and budget clothing outlets.

For upmarket clothes, head to the shopping malls in Central and Tsim Sha Tsui and the Japanese department stores in Causeway Bay. Most of the top international designers are represented in Hong Kong, and there are also some interesting local fashions.

In Central (Map 6), the best places to shop for top-end garments, accessories and footwear are the Landmark shopping centre, the Galleria shopping centre, the Prince's Building and the Pedder Building. In Admiralty the Pacific Place shopping mall has an impressive array of top-end shops, as well as some good mid-range offerings. In Tsim Sha Tsui (Map 5) the Ocean Terminal/Harbour City complex has so many clothing and shoe stores, it would probably take a year to go through them all. Locals say that in general the shops in Central, while expensive, generally give better value for money than those in Ocean Terminal/Harbour City.

In Central, you might want to duck into Shanghai Tang (☎ 2525-7333), on the ground floor of the Pedder Building (Map 6). Started up by David Tang, a flamboyant Hong Kong businessman, this store sparked something of a fashion wave in Hong Kong with its updated versions of traditional Chinese garments. A renewed interest and appreciation of traditional Chinese lines in fashion surfaced in 1997. What's on offer isn't cheap, but the designs are unique and generally tasteful. Tailoring is available. Other places to try for traditional Chinese jackets and designs are Blanc De Chine (☎ 2524-7875) in Room 201, Pedder Building (Map 6), Central; China Team, 36 Nathan Rd, Tsim Sha Tsui; Sunrise Co, 39a Mody Rd, Tsim Sha Tsui.

Although people still flock to Hong Kong's tailors, getting a suit or dress made here is not the great bargain it used to be. For a quality piece of work you'll probably pay close to what you would in New York or London. An exception might be some of the Indian tailors who flag you down on the streets of Tsim Sha Tsui, but just remember that you usually get what you pay for. Some of these places offer same-day suits. The material is often decent, it's just the way it's all put together. Bear in mind that most tailors will require a 50% nonrefundable deposit. And the more fittings you go to, the more comfortable the clothes will feel. For men's suits, the Pacific Custom Tailors (☎ 2845-5466) in the Pacific Place shopping mall (Map 6) do an outstanding job, though prices are fairly high.

Hong Kong is a haven for international names of quality, a smattering of which include: Alfred Dunhill (☎ 2524-4767), shop G14A, ground floor, Prince's Building (Map 6), Central; (☎ 2530-0464) shop 315-316, Level 3, The Mall, Pacific Place shopping mall (Map 6), 88 Queensway, Central; (☎ 2893-1026) ground floor, Sogo department store (Map 7), 555 Hennessy Rd, Causeway Bay; branches also exist in The Peninsula hotel (Map 5) and the Hyatt Regency Hotel (Map 5) in Kowloon.

There are several classy shops in Central: Giorgio Armani (☎ 2530-1998), shop 18-20A, Alexandra House (Map 6), 16-20 Chater Rd, Central; Hermes Boutique (☎ 2525-5900), G08/09, Galleria Shopping Centre (Map 6), 9 Queen's Rd, Central; (☎ 2522- 6229) level 3, Pacific Place shopping mall (Map 6), 88 Queensway, Central. There is also a branch (☎ 2315-3262) at shop BE 7-9, basement, The Peninsula (Map 5), Salisbury Rd, Tsim Sha Tsui.

Other quality shops include: Salvatore Ferragamo (☎ 2831-8457), shop 111, The Regent (Map 5), Salisbury Rd, Tsim Sha Tsui; unit 1 and 2, ground floor, Mandarin Oriental Hotel (Map 6), 5 Connaught Rd, Central; Nina Ricci Boutique (☎ 2721-4869), room 149, lobby floor, The Regent (Map 5), 18 Salisbury Rd, Tsim Sha Tsui; (☎ 2311-5922) shop BE 13 and 15, the basement, The Peninsula (Map 5), Salisbury Rd, Tsim Sha Tsui; Yves Saint-Laurent (Map 6), Shop M9, Mandarin Oriental (Map 6), 5 Connaught Rd, Central; Lane Crawford, Times Square (Map 7), 1 Matheson St, Causeway Bay.

**Children's Clothes** For children, Mothercare is at (☎ 2523-5704) shop 338-340, 3rd floor, Prince's Building (Map 6), Central; (☎ 2735-5738) shop 137, Ocean Terminal, Harbour City (Map 5), Canton Rd, Tsim Sha Tsui. Chicco (☎ 2377-3369), at shop 023a, Marina Deck, Ocean Terminal (Map 5), Tsim

Sha Tsui, is top-end shopping for kiddies clothing. On the toys front, Toys 'R' Us (☎ 2730-9462) has a branch at shop 032, Ocean Terminal, Harbour City (Map 5), 5 Canton Rd.

### Cigars

For some, cigar smoking is an almost unparalleled exotic delight. Rest assured, Hong Kong comes up with a few cigar parlours that can furnish the needy with a Monte Cristo to round off that excellent meal. Tabaqueria Filipina (☎ 2523-8752), 30-32 Wyndham St, Central, is a short dash from many a restaurant in the area. Davidoff (☎ 2724-8984), at shop EL3 in The Peninsula hotel (Map 5), Tsim Sha Tsui, has an excellent range for those who find cigars indispensable.

### Computers

Hong Kong is not a bad place to buy computers, unless you're coming from the USA, in which case shop at home. As every other businessperson seems to be carrying a laptop, Hong Kong is clearly well situated computer wise, and prices are not bad, at least for Asia. The biggest mark-ups are on smaller items like floppy disks and printer cartridges.

One of better places to go is Star Computer City, on the 2nd floor in Star House (map 5), Tsim Sha Tsui. There are around 20 stores up here, so you can probably find what you need. Though it's less conveniently located, you may be able to get better deals at Mong Kok Computer Centre (Map 4), at the intersection of Nelson and Fa Yuen Sts in Mong Kok. It's mostly patronised by locals, but there are dozens of small shops and you can usually find someone who speaks English. Another vast emporium is the East Asia Computer Plaza in the basement of the Silvercord Building (Map 5), at 30 Canton Rd, Kowloon.

The Golden Shopping Centre, basement and 1st floor, 146-152 Fuk Wah St, Sham Shui Po, has the cheapest collection of desktop computers, accessories and components in Hong Kong. The speciality here is generic computers – machines assembled from various components by the shops themselves. To get there, take the MTR to Sham Shui Po station and follow the signs.

Most people buy computers in Kowloon, for the variety and lower prices. But Hong Kong Island does have one reasonable computer arcade (Computer 88), in Windsor House (Map 7), Causeway Bay.

Computers are prone to breakdowns, so when choosing a shop don't go by price alone: evaluate the service and the kind of warranty offered. Before leaving Hong Kong it's also a good idea to run the computer continuously for several days to make sure it is free of defects. One shop with a good reputation is Reptron Computers (☎ 2506- 3812), shop nos 705 and 728, Times Square (Map 7), 1 Matheson St, Causeway Bay.

### Electronics

Sham Shui Po in Kowloon is a good neighbourhood to search for electronic items. You can even buy (and sell) second-hand goods here. If you take any of the west exits from the MTR at Sham Shui Po station, you'll find yourself on Apliu St. This is one of the best areas in Hong Kong to go find the numerous permutations of plug adapters you'll need if you plan to use your purchase in Hong Kong, or if you are heading for China.

Mong Kok is another good neighbourhood to look for electronic gadgetry. Starting from Argyle St and heading south, explore the streets parallel to Nathan Rd, such as Canton Rd and Tung Choi, Sai Yeung Choi, Portland, Shanghai and Reclamation Sts.

There are also quite a few electronics shops in Causeway Bay, with windows stuffed full of camcorders, CD players and other goodies. Locals generally avoid these places: apparently many of them are under the same ownership, ensuring that prices are kept high across the various stores in the area. Also, it's probably best to avoid the shops in Tsim Sha Tsui, many of which are skilled at fleecing foreign shoppers.

Though the selection isn't as good, the Fortress group of stores is quite reliable, and will always give you a warranty with your

---

### Ivory

Ivory jewellery, chopsticks and ornaments used to be big sellers in Hong Kong, fuelling the demand for elephant tusks and contributing to the slaughter of Africa's already depleted elephant population. In 1989, the Hong Kong government signed the CITES (Convention on International Trade in Endangered Species) treaty, which effectively bans the import of raw ivory.

In the meantime, the only carved ivory products being sold in Hong Kong are those which were supposedly manufactured before the ban went into effect. There are also items made of hippopotamus teeth and walrus tusk, and even pieces made from the tusks of long-dead Siberian woolly mammoths! Any ivory retailer needs to have all sorts of documentation proving where and when the goods were made. Many countries now ban the importation of ivory altogether, no matter how it was manufactured, or from what animal it was taken. ∎

---

purchase. There are branches all over Hong Kong, including Central, Causeway Bay, Sheung Wan, Tsim Sha Tsui and Wan Chai.

Remember that most electrical appliances in Hong Kong are designed to work with 220V. Some manufacturers now equip their computers, stereos and video machines with a device that senses the voltage and adapts to it – others have a little switch for 110/220V operation. Be sure you have the correct plug for wherever you plan to use your purchase.

### Jade

The Chinese attribute various spiritual qualities to jade, including the power to prevent ageing (look out for old Hong Kong Chinese wearing jade bracelets) and keep evil spirits away. It's very popular in Hong Kong and commands a high price, which may be an incentive to think about buying it somewhere else. The other problem is a high number of shifty jade dealers who delight at the thought of skimming extra profits off tourists.

There are two different minerals which can be called jade: jadeite from Myanmar (Burma); and nephrite, commonly from

Canada, China, New Zealand and Taiwan. While the colour green is usually associated with jade, the milk-white shade is also highly prized. There are also shades of pink, red, yellow, brown, mauve and turquoise. Most so-called Chinese jade sold in Hong Kong actually comes from elsewhere.

Jade usually comes in the form of jewellery (earrings, bracelets, pendants, necklaces and rings) or carvings. Large jade carvings are often crisscrossed with cracks that run through the stone – these are natural flaws.

Unfortunately Hong Kong also does a thriving trade in fake jade. The deep green colour associated with some jade pieces can be achieved with dye, as can the white, green, red, lavender and brown of other pieces. Green soapstone and plastic can be passed off as jade too. One trick is to sell a supposedly solid piece of jade jewellery which is actually a thin slice of jade backed by green glue and quartz.

If you're interested in looking at and possibly purchasing some jade, head on up to the jade market (Map 5) in Yau Ma Tei, about a 10 minute walk from Yau Ma Tei MTR station. Unless you're knowledgeable about jade, to limit yourself to modest purchases. The jade market is open daily from 10 am to 3.30 pm. For details, see the Yau Ma Tei section of the Things to See & Do chapter.

Serious buyers stick with reputable dealers, and the Sotheby's and Christie's auctions. Their jade sales have some spectacular pieces. The advantage of buying through auction is that you can easily research the history of the piece (through auction catalogues and certificates of authenticity) and the auctions attract international dealers, which means that word generally gets around if there is a fake or a piece of doubtful authenticity for sale.

### Jewellery

Jewellery stores do an amazingly brisk trade in Hong Kong, aided by the traditional Chinese desire for gold and other tangible investments. Remember that the gold used in Hong Kong is generally very pure, which lends a dark tinge to the metal. Care should

be taken when visiting these shops, since visitors are targets for less reputable retailers.

King Fook and Tse Sui Luen are two chains which guarantee to buy back any jewellery they sell to you at its current wholesale price. Of course, be sure you keep the receipt. One of the most fantastic-looking branches is King Fook (☎ 2822-8573) at 30 Des Voeux Rd, Central, worth checking out for its sheer garishness. Other branches include: (☎ 2845-6766) shop 216, Pacific Place shopping mall (Map 6), Admiralty; (☎ 2576-1032) ground floor, Hong Kong Mansion, 1 Yee Wo St, Causeway Bay; and (☎ 2313-2768) Miramar Hotel shopping arcade (Map 5), 118-130 Nathan Rd, Tsim Sha Tsui. Tse Sui Luen shops can be found at: (☎ 2921-8800) Commercial House, 35 Queen's Rd, Central; (☎ 2893-2981) 141 Johnston Rd, Wan Chai; (☎ 2838-6737) 467 Hennessy Rd, Causeway Bay; and (☎ 2332-4618) 315 Nathan Rd, Tsim Sha Tsui. There is also a factory outlet (☎ 2878-2618) at ground floor, Wah Ming Building, 34 Wong Chuk Hang Rd, Aberdeen.

### Music

Hong Kong is pretty much on the ball when it comes to tunes. HMV is here in force (inquiries ☎ 2377-9797) and is constantly flinging its doors open to larger and larger music supermarkets. The Central Building (Map 6) branch is massive, and it's open seven days from 10 am to 10 pm. HMV goes in wholesale for listening points where you can listen to a whole range of CDs before forking out – this means it's easy to spend the whole day here wearing headphones and staring at the carpet. CDs are quite cheap – with discs selling for around HK$110. They also do a large range of video CDs, DVDs and music/film magazines. Don't expect to find cassette tapes anywhere though – it's CDs, CDs and CDs only. HMV can be found in the Central Building, Pedder St, Central; Swire House, Central; Windsor House, Causeway Bay; Sands Building, Peking Rd, Tsim Sha Tsui and New Town Plaza, Sha Tin. It also has a great range of music magazines, but they are expensive.

Tower Records (☎ 2506-0811) is also in town, and can be found in Shop 701, 7th floor, Times Square (Map 7), 1 Matheson St, Causeway Bay. Also worth looking out for are the KPS video rental shops, some of which also have a pretty good range of CDs for sale. The best one is in the Silvercord Shopping Centre (Map 5) on Canton Rd in Tsim Sha Tsui; the branch on Jaffe Rd in Wan Chai (Map 7) isn't bad either; they also have a branch on the 3rd floor of Prince's Building in Central. You can also buy CDs at the street markets on Temple St, Yau Ma Tei, and Tung Choi St, Mong Kok, but these are usually pirated and the sound quality can be poor.

Unless you really have to, don't bother buying any musical instruments in Hong Kong. There's not a great selection, and prices are truly outrageous. If you absolutely need something, your best bet is Tom Lee music stores, with branches in Causeway Bay, Tsim Sha Tsui and Wan Chai.

If you're looking to buy Chinese instruments, again Hong Kong is not a great place. There are a few shops along Wan Chai Rd between Johnston and Morrison Hill Rds in Wan Chai, but what they offer is generally not good value for money. It might even be cheaper to buy a train ticket up to Guangzhou in neighbouring Guangdong Province and buy something there.

## Wine

If you're looking for fine wines, Rémy has a string of branches in Hong Kong. Branches include: (Map 6; ☎ 2523-5904) 117 Swire House, Central; (Map 6; ☎ 2845-5995) 311, the Mall, Pacific Place; (☎ 2967-9091) 202 Citiplaza 2, Tai Koo Shing, Quarry Bay; 013 Harbour City, Canton Rd, Tsim Sha Tsui. La Cave (☎ 2537-7288) keeps the wine flowing in Central at 24 Wyndham St. The deli Vino & Olio (Map 6; ☎ 2523-4483) serves wine to the accompaniment of mozzarella, pesto, grappa, olive oil, cheeses, fresh herbs, pasta and other Italian essentials; you can find it at 54 D'Aguilar St, Lan Kwai Fong. Oliver's Fine Foods (Map 6) in the Prince's Building also offers a wide range of wines.

If you're dining in the Lan Kwai Fong area and the restaurant doesn't have a liquor licence, pop around to Hop Hing Vintners (Map 6; ☎ 2523-7628), where you can purchase a bottle and return armed to your table. Hop Hing is on the corner of Graham and Staunton Sts.

If you are going to go to Macau, wine collectors should know that there is a vintner's at the Jetfoil Pier in Macau that has a duty-free (but still costly) selection of famous and rare wines. The selection is absolutely magnificent, and includes some very expensive specimens.

SHOPPING

# Excursions

If you have the time, it's definitely worth taking a day to explore 'the other Hong Kong' of the New Territories and Outlying Islands. A trip to one or two of the islands or an afternoon romp in the New Territories will show you a side to Hong Kong that is rarely advertised. Life in the more rural parts of Hong Kong is so relaxed it's hard to believe that the frantic urban sprawl is only a bus or boat ride away. Some of the views can be stupendous and sublime, and the walks are often an adventure.

Wedged between China and urban Hong Kong, the New Territories has lost a lot of its rural character, especially in the western half, where the bulk of the New Towns are situated. But the eastern section, especially around the Sai Kung peninsula and Clear Water Bay, has some of Hong Kong's most beautiful scenery and hiking trails.

If you only have one day to get out and about, it would probably best be spent checking out one of the Outlying Islands. Get up early, jump on a ferry, sit out on the back deck and enjoy the sun and the stunning views. The islands are where Hong Kong's roots as a society of farmers and fishers can still be seen. Try and avoid the weekends when half of Hong Kong makes the weary pilgrimage away from skyscrapers and exhaust fumes to these oases of calm. The bars of Lamma Island are full of expats, heads in hands, moaning at their beers 'if only I'd known Lamma was so beautiful, I would never have lived in Kennedy Town for two years.' Make a date to go there and see just how atmospheric and exotic it is.

The other option is to make the journey over to Macau, the historic Portuguese enclave 65km to the west. Dating back to the 1500s, Macau is a different world completely. Although nearly as crowded, it moves at a much slower, more relaxed pace. The pace is Mediterranean – Vespas buzz past, brightly coloured Minis zip down narrow side streets and everyone lets their hair down. Macau is a splendid enclave of churches and European textures fused by a languid Latin temperament; Hong Kong is slick, metallic and modern, Macau is historic, romantic and lazy. Ancient churches sit next to Chinese temples, cobbled streets lead off from busy thoroughfares, and flavours waft on the sea breeze from neighbouring Chinese and Portuguese restaurants. It's worth coming just for the Portuguese food and wine. The whole experience is one of romantic European decay, a crumbling edifice of Portugal in China.

Macau is only about one hour away by jetfoil or jet boat, although immigration at both ends adds another 40 minutes or so to the journey. Still, it's easy to do the trip in one day, though there are plenty of places to stay if you want to do some more exploring and fit in a few more meals.

## NEW TERRITORIES (Map 2)
### Tai Mo Shan
At 957m Tai Mo Shan is Hong Kong's highest mountain, and also one of the closest to the urban area. There is a road leading up most of the way but unless you have your own car you will have to walk from the bus stop, a hike of about 4km. Views from the top are quite impressive if the weather is clear, and there are numerous hiking trails in and around the peak. There is no food or water available, so bring some along.

**Getting There & Away** Take the MTR to the Tsuen Wan terminus, and from there catch the No 51 bus. The bus stop is on the overpass above the station. The bus heads up Route Twisk. The bus stop for Tai Mo Shan is at the top of the pass: just tell the bus driver 'Tai Mo Shan' and he'll let you off there. If you're starting off from Central you can also take the hoverferry to Tsuen Wan from Pier 6 at the Outlying Islands ferry piers (Map 6), then catch bus No 51 from the Tsuen Wan Ferry Pier.

EXCURSIONS

Top: Scenes from the peaceful rural retreat of Lamma Island, popular with expatriates.
Middle: Only an hour from Central are the quiet beaches of the Outlying Islands.
Bottom Left: Scenes from the Bun Festival, held annually on Cheung Chau.
Bottom Right: More colour and glitter from a Chinese festival in Central.

TONY WHEELER

GLENN BEANLAND

RICHARD I'ANSON

RICHARD I'ANSON

Top: Po Lin Monastery on Lantau Island is recognisable from many martial arts films.
Middle Right: Dragons are believed to dwell in mountains in Chinese mythology.
Bottom Left: Ten Thousand Buddhas Monastery, Sha Tin, actually home to 12,800 Buddhas.
Bottom Right: Incense coils are burnt by worshippers at Sheung Wan's Man Mo Temple.

## Kam Tin

This small town contains the walled village of Kat Hing Wai, where the Tang Clan settled in the 10th century after migrating from what is now Guangdong Province. The village that stands today was built in the 16th century and is still home to several hundred descendants of the Tang, which was the first of the Cantonese 'Five Great Clans' to make the move down to what would become Hong Kong. Inside, the village has many trappings of 20th century Hong Kong, but the 6m walls still stand, surrounded by a moat. Inside, there is a small main street with a series of little alleys. The main street is packed with souvenir stands, so don't go here expecting to be transported back to ancient China. Visitors are expected to make a 'donation' of HK$5 when entering the village.

**Getting There & Away** Take the MTR to the Tsuen Wan terminus, and then catch the No 51 bus, which also passes by Tai Mo Shan. Kam Tim is the last stop on the route. You can also take a hoverferry from Central to Tsuen Wan and catch the No 51 bus there (see Getting There & Away under Tai Mo Shan earlier in this chapter).

## Clear Water Bay Peninsula

Being part of the eastern New Territories, the Clear Water Bay Peninsula is characterised by wonderfully untamed and rough contours, a wild backdrop to the modernity of urban Hong Kong. The most south-eastern nob of the New Territories is the Clear Water Bay Peninsula, wedged in by Junk Bay (Tseung Kwan O) to the west and Clear Water Bay (Tsing Sui Wan) to the east; Joss House Bay (Tai Miu Wan) nestles to the south. Junk Bay is now the sight of vast land reclamation and housing development, but the eastern coastline is still unscarred and offers exceptional walks, some fine beaches and the oldest Tin Hau temple on the coast of Guangdong.

At **Tai Au Mun** you will find yourself in the heartland of the **Clear Water Bay Country Park**. Trails head off in various directions; you can either bound down the

path to the north, towel in hand, to the beach of **Lung Ha Wan** (literally 'Lobster Bay') or take the road south (Tai Au Mun Lu) to two more beaches. The sandy shores of **Clear Water Bay Beach No 1** and **Clear Water Bay Beach No 2** are lapped by clean water, but try and go midweek during summer as this is a popular destination.

A 30-minute walk away from the crabs and seashells to the south, the road winds down past Tin Ha Shan (273m) to the venerably ancient **Tin Hau** temple, perched on the tip of the peninsula, overlooking **Joss House Bay**. The place offers a seagull's view out over the waves to the island of **Tung Long Chau** to the south. This temple is one of the oldest nodes of spiritual power in Hong Kong and is dedicated to the protector of fisher folk, the Queen of Heaven, Tin Hau. Although the site dates back to 1266, the building is of later construction (1878) and it suffered heavily during the passage of Typhoon Wanda in 1962, warranting further renovation. To the east of the temple is the **Clear Water Bay Golf Course** and the charming village of **Poi To O**.

From the temple, hiking trails lead back to Tai Au Mun, or hikers can take the trail up Tin Ha Shan and then continue on the trail to **High Junk Peak** (Tiu Yu Yung) and then cross down to Tai Au Mun.

**Getting There & Away** Take the MTR to Choi Hung and jump on bus No 91, outside the station. The bus passes Silverstrand Beach (Ngan Sin Wan); you can get off here and go for a dip, before heading on to Tai Au Mun to the south. If you want to go to Lung Ha Wan, get off the bus at Tai Au Mun proper, but if you want to see the beaches in Clear Water Bay, continue on the bus which stops at the terminus just above them.

## Sai Kung Peninsula

This is arguably the most unspoiled part of the New Territories, though the area around Sai Kung Town is quite urbanised. But north of the town are terrific hiking trails and some of the territory's best beaches, though the latter are unfortunately no longer the pristine

EXCURSIONS

stretches of white sand that greeted hikers a few years ago.

**Sai Kung Town** was originally a fishing village, and though it's now more of a suburb, some of the original port feel remains. Fishing boats still put in an occasional appearance, and on the waterfront there is a string of seafood restaurants that draw patrons from all around the territory, despite their high prices. Sai Kung Town is an excellent spot to launch an expedition into the surrounding region and to return for excellent food in the evening.

A short journey to one of the islands off Sai Kung Town is worth doing. Hidden away are some excellent beaches that are worth reaching on a *kaido* (small ferry). Kaidos bounce over the waves from the promenade down by the sea; most head over to **Sharp Island** (Kiu Tsui Chau) about 1.5km away. Hap Mun Bay, a sandy beach in the south of the island is served by kaidos as is Kiu Tsui Bay on the western shore. The other islands of Pak Sha Chau (White Sand Islet) and Cham Tau Chau (Pillow Islet) are also visited by kaidos, although the service is far more irregular.

Also reached by kaido from Sai Kung Town is the small island of **Yim Tin Tsai** (Little Salt Field), where you can find a Christian church in the form of St Joseph's chapel, the focus of the island's devote Catholic population. Yim Tin Tsai is connected to the much larger **Kau Sai Chau** by a narrow spit that becomes submerged at high tide.

North of the town lies the sprawling **Sai Kung Country Park**. From the Park Visitor Centre at Pak Tam Chung there are trails out to High Island Reservoir and the beautiful beaches at Tai Long Wan. These hiking paths form part of the 100km-long **MacLehose Trail** that stretches from east to west across the New Territories. Getting to either the reservoir or the beaches and back will take up most of the day, although sometimes you can hitch a ride on park service trucks that will take you part of the way. If you're in the mood for something less strenuous, the **Sheung Yiu Folk Museum**, a restored 200-year-old Hakka home, is just a 30 minute walk from the Park Visitor Centre at Pak Tam Chung. To get to Pak Tam Chung, take the No 94 bus, which leaves hourly from Sai Kung Town.

After reaching Pak Tam Chung the bus continues on and terminates at the Wong Shek boat pier. It's possible to get off at Pak Tam Au, access stage two of the MacLehose Trail and take it down to the beaches at **Tai Long Wan**. (Tell the driver you want to go to Chek Keng, which is a little village midway between the road and the beaches.) It's a good two hour hike, but the views en route are great and there are little restaurants at the beaches where you can reward yourself with a beer and a plate of fried noodles. Don't forget to leave the beaches early enough to catch a bus back. The last bus leaves Wong Shek pier at 7.35 pm, passing by the trail head about eight to 10 minutes later. There is also a ferry that leaves Chek Keng for Wong Shek around 4 to 5 pm.

Tai Long Wan is a rewarding hike, but the logistics are a bit tricky. It's best to first buy one of the countryside series maps of the Sai Kung Country Park area from the Government Publications Office or the *Sai Kung & Clear Water Bay* map, published by Universal Publications (see Maps in the Facts for the Visitor chapter). For more information, you can contact the Country Parks Division of the Agriculture & Fisheries Department (☎ 2733-2132).

**Places to Eat** Of the seafood restaurants in Sai Kung, *Tung Kee* (☎ 2792-7453), 96-102 Man Nin St, has the best reputation. You pick your own fish or shellfish from the tanks and the cooks take it back into the kitchen to work their magic with it. This place is often packed, and it's not cheap either, but it's worth it.

If it's Italian food that you crave, try *Pepperoni's* (☎ 2792-2083) on Po Tung Rd, just off Hiram's Highway, the main road leading through town. This little indoor-outdoor place serves up surprisingly good pasta and pizza, made from famously fresh ingredients. Also on Po Tung Rd, at No 183 is *Al Fresco's* (☎ 2792-6388) which does a decent line in international food. *Black Sheep* (☎ 2792-6662) and *Jaspa's* (☎ 2792-6388) can both be found on Sha Tsui Path, at No 9 and 13 respectively; both serve decent international cuisine.

There are also a bunch of noodle shops and a few Chinese and western restaurants in the heart of Sai Kung Town. It's small enough that you should be able to size up all your options by walking around the town centre for 20 minutes or so.

**Getting There & Away** Take the MTR to Choi Hung station, and exit where the sign says 'Clear Water Bay Road North'. Here you can catch either the No 92 bus or the more frequent No 1 green minibus. The bus takes around 35 minutes while the minibus takes around 20 minutes.

## CHEUNG CHAU (Map 13)

At one time a refuge for pirates, and later an exclusive island retreat for British colonials, Cheung Chau is now the most crowded of the Outlying Islands. Some 22,000 people, many of them commuters, are crammed onto Cheung Chau's 2.5 sq km; hardly any *gwailos* (foreigners, usually of European descent) live on Cheung Chau. There is also a sizeable fishing community here, part of which resides on the junks and sampans anchored in the typhoon shelter surrounding the ferry pier.

Cheung Chau Village has become quite urbanised, but is still fun to explore, with narrow alleys, old creaking homes and shops, burning incense and drying fish. There are also some gorgeous walks around the northern and southern ends of the island. Cheung Chau, along with Lamma Island, has no motorised transport (except for a few small tractors), which adds to the casual atmosphere. However, on weekends the island is crawling with thousands of city dwellers who come out to feast on seafood or play at the beach. Many of them rent vacation homes overnight and there's even a hotel, the massive Warwick. Prices are quite high during the weekend. Like all the Outlying Islands, Cheung Chau can very easily be done as a day trip so there's no need to stay overnight here unless you really like the place.

### Beaches

The main beach is **Tung Wan**, about 10 minutes walk from the ferry pier, straight across the narrow isthmus of the island. There are lots of little restaurants and shops around here, and you can also rent windsurfing equipment. A quieter spot is **Tai Kwai Wan**, a small sandy beach on the north-west part of the island. On the north-east side is **Tung Wan Tsai**, which is smaller still and also a bit rocky.

**Kwun Yam Wan Beach** is just south of Tung Wan, and is named after a temple dedicated to the Goddess of Mercy (Kwun Yam, also known as Kuan Yin) at the top of a hill near the end of the beach. You can also continue up the footpath to Fa Peng Knoll and walk along Don Bosco Rd to get to **Nam Tam Wan**. This beach is a bit rocky, but the scenery along the way here makes for a nice walk.

Finally if you take Peak Rd, a wonderful walk which leads through trees past the island's cemetery, you'll come to **Pak Tso Wan**, an isolated sandy beach which offers good swimming. Peak Rd continues onto Sai Wan (West Bay), from where you can either walk or catch a sampan back to Cheung Chau Village.

### Temples & Other Sights

Probably the most interesting of these is the colourful **Pak Tai Temple**, built in 1783 to honour a Taoist deity who vanquished the Demon King and his allies, the tortoise and the serpent. Pak Tai has become the patron god of Cheung Chau, and is the leading deity in the annual Cheung Chau Bun Festival (see the Festivals section in the Facts for the Visitor chapter). Inside the temple is a sword said to date from the Song Dynasty (960-1279) – recovered from the sea by fishermen more than 100 years ago – and a 100-year-old sedan chair used to carry Pak Tai's image around in festival processions. Note that all the statues of Pak Tai have a defeated serpent

**EXCURSIONS**

## Cheung Chau Walking Tour

If you've had it with urban Hong Kong and want a rural escape, then why not catch a ferry to Cheung Chau and embark on this charming walk – it will take you past flotillas of junks, restaurants, mahjong parlours, temples, magical trees, beaches and some wonderful vistas of the sea and gorgeous countryside. The walk takes about two and a half hours and the trail is not really strenuous. The latter part of the walk is truly lovely, and best done towards the end of the day in good weather for the best light conditions. Don't go on a weekend, as everyone else will be there as well, go on a weekday and have the walk to yourself. Take your camera!

After leaving the ferry, turn left down **Praya St**, where a street of restaurants gaze out to sea. Many of these are seafood restaurants, and a few western eateries also exist – this is the place to come to eat at the end of the walk, which makes a full circle. Continue along Praya St, which eventually becomes **Pak She Praya Rd**. Here you will see rows and rows of **junks** moored in the harbour. Many of these boats are the refuge of houseboat people, who make their living and their homes upon the waves. Along the side of the road you will also see a few bicycle rental shops where you can rent out bikes – in fact it's far more fun and leisurely just to stroll.

Just past Pak She Fourth Lane is a playing ground, and to the right is the **Pak Tai Temple**, a beautifully coloured temple built in the Qing Dynasty and one of the most important historical monuments of Cheung Chau. This is the site of the Bun Festival held every year in May. Leaving the temple behind you and heading back south down Pak She St (which eventually connects to San Hing St), you will pass a **traditional Chinese building**, the third house on the left. The building is guarded by two stone lions and behind them hang two posters of the door gods whose job it is to expel evil spirits. Pak She St is also the site of a number of **traditional Chinese medicine** stores which are worth a browse; two small **bakeries** sell small Chinese cakes at Nos 46 and 56.

Continuing south, you will pass a small shrine to the **Earth God** on the left at the intersection of Pak She St and Kwok Man Rd. The islanders on Cheung Chau leave offerings to the earth god who lives in objects of nature. San Hing St is a street of different flavours: **herbalist shops** display their wares in large glass jars while at No 30 a shop sells **paper money** and incense (*heung*); paper money is traditionally burned in memory of the deceased or at the new year. Another incense shop is located at No 68 (incense is burned in temples as a way of communicating with the gods). Other shops to look out for are those selling bamboo hats which are worn by the fishing community in Cheung Chau. Further up is a **mahjong gambling den** which is usually an explosion of sound as the counters are shuffled on the table. Mahjong is not encouraged by the authorities in Hong Kong, as the only legal form of gambling is horse-racing; mahjong is a 'covert' form of gambling.

under one foot and a beaten tortoise under the other.

There are several temples dedicated to **Tin Hau**, the patron goddess of fisher folk. There is one just north of the Pak Tai Temple, and another at the southern end of Cheung Chau Village, along the waterfront. The third is at Sai Wan, at the southern tip of the island. You can either walk or take a sampan marked 'Sai Wan' from the main ferry pier. The five minute ride costs around HK$2 and takes you through the fishing junks moored in the harbour. Near the temple is **Cheung Po Tsai Cave**, said to have been a hiding place for a ruthless, bloodthirsty 19th-century pirate.

At the foot of Peak Rd is a temple dedicated to Kwan Tai and lastly there's the **Kwun Yam Temple**, which sits on a hill overlooking Kwun Yam Wan Beach.

### Places to Eat

Because Cheung Chau is not a gwailo ghetto like Yung Shue Wan on Lamma, restaurants are limited. However, there are lots of little sidewalk restaurants along the waterfront where you can choose your own seafood. On Tung Wan Rd there is the *East Lake* restaurant, which is quite popular with locals and expats, especially in the evening when there are often outdoor tables set up. The *Garden Café* (☎ 2981-4610) is a pleasant western-style pub and restaurant where you can find such timeless classics as baked beans on toast (HK$18), eggs on toast (HK$18), fresh mushrooms on toast (HK$30), chicken and mushroom pie, chips and mushy peas (seriously!) (HK$58) and they can even grill up a rainbow trout. Next to Kwun Yam Wan Beach is the *Windsurfer Bar* and on the other

As you turn the corner at the end of San Hing St and enter Tung Wan Rd, you will see a **sacred tree** on the right. This ancient banyan is believed to be inhabited by earth spirits, which explains the small shrine at its foot. Tung Wan Rd leads up to **Tung Wan** beach, the most popular beach on the island where windsurfing competitions are held.

Walk along the beach towards the huge Warwick Hotel and take the road to the rear which will lead you up the steep Cheung Chau Sports Rd; when you see a pavilion ahead, turn right onto Kwun Yum Wan Rd (named after the goddess of compassion, the name means Kwun Yum Bay Rd) and pass the sports ground. The **Kwan Kung Pavilion**, a temple dedicated to Kwan Tai, the god of war and righteousness, is a few minutes ahead; the deity is also the symbol of power and loyalty. As you come out of the temple, turning left will put you on Peak Rd. Walking along here will take you past a series of attractive residential properties.

This walk along Peak Rd all the way to Sai Wan is truly beautiful, quiet and calm. This was one of the most relaxing and enjoyable walks I have ever done; it is worth timing this walk to coincide with dusk as the light conditions are very special. The walk takes you past pavilions, sleeping cemeteries, wonderful views out to sea and woods, all the way to Sai Wan where you can get a kaido back to Cheung Chau village.

On the walk you will pass the **Cheung Chau Meteorological Station** which offers splendid views of the island and the sea. Further on is the **Yee Pavilion**, dedicated to the Chinese poet Zhang Renshi. The rocks surrounding the temple are inscribed with eulogies from fellow poets.

Further ahead and through the trees is the **cemetery**, affording a quiet and solemn view over the South China Sea. Below is a crematorium. Soon you will come to a forked road which leads off to Pak Tso Wan to the left – take the fork to the right and head down to Sai Wan. You will pass through the **Care village**, a small settlement set up in 1968 with money from an American/Canadian charity.

Further on is another fork in the road: you can either turn right for the 'Kaido Service Ferry Pier', where you can get a boat back to Cheung Chau village; or you can turn left and visit the **Cheung Po Tsai Cave** and the **Tin Hau Temple**. The cave is supposed to have been where the Qing Dynasty pirate Cheung Po Tsai stored his booty, after his exploits on the South China Sea. At one time, the pirate had unchallenged dominion over the coast of Guangdong Province. You can get into the cave and torches are provided at the entrance. Backtracking will take you to the Tin Hau temple, which is dedicated to the Queen of Heaven and Goddess of the Sea.

At the **ferry pier**, you can take a boat back to Cheung Chau village for HK$2 (they often ask for more, but HK$2 is the correct price). Boats leave every few minutes and take you back to Praya St.

**Damian Harper**

side not far from the ferry pier at 1-2 Kin Sun Lane is *Coffee or Tea*, where you can get, you guessed it, coffee and tea. *McDonald's* has extended its frontier to the plot of land opposite the ferry pier; *Park N' Shop* and *Welcome* are also on Pak She Praya Rd, so you can stock up on food and drink if you are going hiking.

**Getting There & Away**
The ferries to Cheung Chau leave every hour between 6.25 and 12.30 am from Pier 7 at the Outlying Islands ferry piers in Central (Map 6). The last boat back to Central leaves Cheung Chau at 11.30 pm.

The ride takes about one hour, and the adult one-way fare is HK$9.20 from Monday to Saturday morning, and HK$12.50 on Saturday afternoon, Sunday and public holidays.

Children 12 and under and seniors pay half price. Fares for deluxe class, which lets you sit on the open-air deck on the stern, are HK$17 and HK$32 respectively. On weekdays there are also several hoverferries in the morning and afternoon. The fare is HK$24. Tea, coffee, soft drinks, beer and some basic snacks are available.

**LAMMA ISLAND (Map 11)**
Known mainly for its seafood restaurants but deserving more press for its lush scenery, Lamma Island also has excellent beaches, beautiful hikes and some superb pubs. The third-largest island, after Lantau and Hong Kong, Lamma is home to Chinese fishers, farmers and commuters, and the hills above the main village, Yung Shue Wan, are littered with small homes and apartment blocks.

EXCURSIONS

Lamma Island is also the focal point of the Hong Kong gwailo slacker community. These people can be seen disembarking the Lamma ferry with guitar slung over back, barked at by the village dogs. In fact, Lamma is the haven of a wide spectrum of expatriate society: editors, journalists, businesspeople, doctors, poets and the incurably romantic. The fact is that Lamma is quite beautiful and really the only place to live, if you haven't got a house on the Peak. Flat rental prices are rock bottom, and where else can you get an overgrown wilderness of banana trees and plants with 1.2m-wide leaves in your back garden? OK, so the spiders are pretty monstrous, but at least they are colourful (you can see them slung out on massive webs bigger than tennis rackets between the trees). If you're walking around at night, watch out for the armies of frogs that jump across paths underfoot. The rustling sounds in the bushes at night are generally innocuous amphibians, but don't go anywhere near the Lamma Island centipede, whose bite can apparently kill a small cat. If you do get bitten, Lamma's only ambulance will probably come and pick you up.

**Yung Shue Wan** itself is a haphazard cluster of old homes, restaurants, bars and tiny shops spreading out from the narrow main street (there is also a Hongkong Bank ATM). The name 'Lamma' is an approximation of the Cantonese words for 'southern Y' which describes both the island's shape, a Y, and its location south of Hong Kong.

The second largest village is **Sok Kwu Wan**, which lies midway down the island on the eastern shore. Its livelihood is derived from a nearby quarry and a string of extremely popular seafood restaurants that cater to a steady stream of mainlanders. Ferries serve both villages, though boats to Sok Kwu Wan are fairly infrequent. There are no cars on Lamma, as everything is within walking distance.

One very popular pastime in Hong Kong is to hire a junk and cruise out to either Yung Shue Wan or Sok Kwu Wan for a seafood lunch or dinner. On the weekends, junks can also be seen moored off the beaches on Lamma's western shore. Aside from the wide selection of restaurants, Lamma is popular because of its proximity to Hong Kong Island. By ferry it's only a 45 minute journey, by junk around two hours. Unless there are a lot of you it's not very economical to come by junk, as the rental rate for eight hours is from HK$2500 to HK$2800. For details on junk rental, see the Activities section of the Things to See & Do chapter.

Even the longest hikes on Lamma can easily be done in one day. Should you decide to make a few days of it, there is accommodation in Yung Shue Wan in the form of several basic hotels and vacation guesthouses; check the notice board on the wall just after you disembark from the ferry as rooms are often advertised for makeshift guesthouses. There is also a fairly expensive hotel at Hung Shing Ye Beach.

Like the other islands, it's best to avoid Lamma on the weekends, when it gets overrun with city visitors.

### Beaches

The easiest beach to access is the one at **Hung Shing Ye**, about 25 minutes walk from the Yung Shue Wan ferry pier. This is also the most popular beach on Lamma (it has a shark net), and there's usually a fair number of people down there. But if you get there early in the morning you will find it deserted. There are a few restaurants and drink stands nearby, as well as the *Concerto Inn* (☎ 2982-1668), a hotel that also serves hot and cold drinks, as well as some mediocre western food. The only fly in the ointment is the massive power station opposite, which occasionally loudly vents steam. The reason why the power station is so big is that it provides all of Hong Kong Island's electricity, which runs through vast cables buried under a road that runs across Lamma.

The nicest beach on Lamma is at **Lo So Shing**, about halfway down the island on the western shore. The beach is not that big, but it's charming and has a nice cover of shady trees, which come in handy at the height of summer. During the April to October swimming season there is a small snack stand and lifeguard/first aid stations in operation here. From Sok Kwu Wan, turn right from the ferry pier and follow signs initially for the Lamma Youth Camp before turning left for the beach. Walking time is about 30 minutes. From Yung Shue Wan it takes around 1½ hours following the Yung Shue Wan-Sok Kwu Wan pathway and then veering right for the beach.

About a 20 minute walk east of Sok Kwu Wan is a fairly isolated beach at **Mo Tat Wan**, behind which lies a village that dates back 400 years, one of the oldest in Hong Kong. Turn left from the ferry pier at Sok Kwu Wan and keep walking. Occasionally sampans will take you there before continuing on to Aberdeen, but these are infrequent.

If you want to spend the night in these parts, the *Tung O Bay Homestay* (☎ 2982-8461) has spacious dorms (HK$100 per bed) and double rooms (HK$300), meals, hot tubs and a sandy beach. It also has a sauna on the beach heated with driftwood.

If you want to get even more remote, continue past Mo Tat Wan to the south-east tip of the island, where there are beaches at **Shek Pai Wan** and **Sham Wan**.

### Hikes

A popular hike on Lamma is to walk from **Yung Shue Wan** to **Sok Kwu Wan**, or vice-versa. It takes about 1½ hours and affords some good views of the ocean, Lamma's barren, rocky hillsides and Hong Kong Island. If you start off from Yung Shue Wan it's best to first check the Sok Kwu Wan ferry schedule to avoid a long wait at the other end. From the Yung Shue Wan ferry pier take the main road through town, out past Hung Shing Ye Beach and keep following the signs. It's a concrete path and there's little chance of getting lost.

A shorter but equally scenic walk is out to **Pak Kok**, at the north-east tip of the island. From the Yung Shue Wan ferry pier, take the steep set of stairs on the right, near the Man Lai Wah Hotel, and follow the signs. Some ferries from Yung Shue Wan to Kennedy Town and Central go via Pak Kok; see the Getting Around chapter for more details.

If you're feeling really ambitious you can tackle **Mt Stenhouse**, a 353m peak that dominates the southern end of the island. From Sok Kwu Wan the hike to the top and back takes around two hours. It's a steep climb and the trails are often not well defined, so allow for some extra time. If you start from Yung Shue Wan, the entire trip will probably take around five hours.

Lamma is crisscrossed with little hiking trails that make for great exploring. If you're interested it would be wise to first buy one of the countryside series maps for Lamma Island, which are available at the Government Publications Office.

### Places to Eat

Both Yung Shue Wan and Sok Kwu Wan have rows of seafood restaurants, and you can't really go wrong at any of them. In Yung Shue Wan one of the most popular seafood places is the *Lancombe* (☎ 2982-0881), 47 Main St. It has some nice outside tables at the back, and though service is often quite slow, it gives you a chance to relax and enjoy the scenery. The deep-fried salt-and-pepper squid is excellent, as are the steamed prawns. Prices are also very reasonable.

On the way into town from the ferry pier you'll pass the *Man Fung Seafood Restaurant* (☎ 2982-1112) and the *Sampan Seafood Restaurant* (☎ 2982-2388). The latter is popular with locals and expats, boasting an excellent view of the sea.

There are several western restaurants: the *Deli Lamma* (☎ 2982-1538), serves continental fare with a Mediterranean influence, but it's pretty expensive for what you get. *Toochka's* (☎ 2982-0159) has outdoor tables and is popular for its Indian dishes, although it also offers a continental spread.

Down near where the main street makes a sharp left is the *Waterfront* (☎ 2982-0914), Lamma's most refined eatery. There are sea views from nearly every table on its three levels, and the ambience is quite inviting. The menu includes everything from British pub grub to Thai curries and Italian pasta. It's a bit expensive, but the overall effect is very pleasant.

Health conscious eaters can curl up with a good book at the *Bookworm Café* (☎ 2982-4838) on Yung Shue Wan Main St. Very much for the muesli and lentil set, here you can tuck into a vegetarian burger and peruse the second-hand book selection.

If you want to eat all the things the doctor didn't order – like thick chips soaked in gravy and pies; you can get them at *Dino's* if you can get your order through the wall of Lamma regulars at the bar. They were about to expand upstairs at the time of writing.

Across the road is the *Aroy Thai* where you get friendly service and good value Thai food; the food is nothing special but the vegetable curry is a bargain. *Pizza Milano* is the token Italian eating place in the locality.

On the drinks front, the *Fountain Head Bar* is the best of the bunch, and not too expensive (and they dish out free salted peanuts) although it's a bit pricier than Dino's.

If you feel like a stroll, walk down to the *Han Lok Yuen Pigeon Restaurant* (☎ 2982-0680) which sits on a hillside looking down over Hung Shing Ye Beach. In addition to the succulent roast pigeon, this place also serves up excellent seafood. It's well worth the walk. Other tempting dishes worth the hike are the minced quail and the deep-fried squid. The views are good too, and most seating is outdoors. The restaurant is closed on Monday, is open only until 7 pm on Sunday.

In Sok Kwu Wan, the *Rainbow Seafood Restaurant* (☎ 2982-8100) and the *Genuine Lamma Hilton* (☎ 2982-8220; no connection with the hotel group) are both quite good. Both these and all the other restaurants are right along the waterfront on either side of the ferry pier. Prices aren't much cheaper than in Hong Kong, so be prepared.

In Sok Kwu Wan remember to carefully check the bill at the end of your meal, as some of the restaurants have been known to overcharge. This doesn't always mean they're trying to rip you off: it may be an honest mix-up as there are usually a lot of tables all simultaneously clamouring for service.

If you want to get away from the bright lights and crowds at Sok Kwu Wan, you can hike around 20 minutes east to the *Coral Seafood Restaurant* (☎ 2982-8328) in Mo Tat Wan. The menu is pretty much the same as those in Sok Kwu Wan, but the setting is quieter and prices a bit lower.

### Getting There & Away
Ferries to Lamma leave regularly, but it's best to pick up a copy of the latest ferry schedule from the information centre of the Hong Kong & Yaumatei Ferry Co (HYF) near the Outlying Islands ferry piers in Central (Map 6). Ferries leave from Pier 6.

Ferries to Yung Shue Wan leave approximately every hour from 6.45 to 12.30 am, but a few intervals last almost two hours. The last boat to Central from Yung Shue Wan leaves at 10.35 pm. There are seven sailings a day to Sok Kwu Wan between 8 am and 11 pm. The last boat from Sok Kwu Wan back to Central sails at 10 pm.

The adult fare is HK$9.20 from Monday to Saturday morning, and HK$12.50 on Saturday afternoon, Sunday and public holidays. Deluxe class fares are HK$17 and HK$32 respectively, but unless it's a big boat with an open-air back deck, it's not really worth the money. Tea, coffee, soft drinks and beer can be bought on board, along with snacks. An irregular service is also provided by Polly Ferries during peak hours in the morning and late afternoon. Intrepid caterers sell coffee to the hordes of expats that flow onto the morning sailings from Yung Shue Wan – the coffee on board is dreadful.

### LANTAU ISLAND (Map 12)
With more than 140 sq km of peaks, valleys, beaches and fields, Lantau is pretty much the most pristine chunk of Hong Kong. There are several good mountain hikes, some interesting villages and a few monasteries, the largest of which is the Po Lin Monastery, site of a 26m-high Buddha statue.

This is a particularly good place to get away from the city. Spend the day hiking Sunset or Lantau Peak: even though urban Hong Kong can be clearly seen from the top, you'll feel like the city is in another world. You can head down to the fishing village of Tai O and check out street scenes that have changed little from 50 years ago.

More than half the island has been designated country parkland, and there are more than 70km of walking and hiking trails, as well as camping and barbecue sites. Despite its size Lantau doesn't have too many beaches, and getting to most of them requires some hiking.

The main village is **Mui Wo**, also known as Silvermine Bay because of the old silver mines in the vicinity. This is where the ferries land from Central dock, and where you can catch buses to other parts of the island. The back streets of the town, about 300m inland from the ferry pier, are mildly interesting to walk around. There is a small beach here, but the water is usually quite foul, so it's not much good for swimming. There are also a few run-down hotels and holiday homes, but there's no need to stay overnight on Lantau unless the mood strikes you.

Lantau is also home to a modern residential community called **Discovery Bay**, on the north-east end of the island. There is no road between Disco Bay (as it's locally known) and the rest of Lantau, and it generally functions apart, having its own ferry service to Central. Unless you have friends to visit, there's really no reason to visit Discovery Bay.

Lantau is served by eight bus routes and a small fleet of taxis. Buses leave the Mui Wo ferry pier about 10 to 15 minutes after ferries arrive, so if you want to hang around the town for a while you'll have to wait about an hour before you can catch another bus. Taxis come and go sporadically. Like Cheung Chau and Lamma, Lantau is swamped on the weekends with urbanites, and buses and taxis are in high demand. It's far better to come here during the week when there are no crowds, except at the Po Lin Monastery.

### Po Lin Monastery

Sitting atop the 520m-high Ngong Ping plateau, this monastery and its enormous bronze Buddha statue are Lantau's main tourist draw. Established in 1928, Po Lin (Precious Lotus) has become the largest Buddhist monastery in Hong Kong. The main temple hall has undergone numerous renovations over the years, and the older buildings are now mostly hidden behind newer structures.

On a hill above the monastery sits the **Buddha statue**, forged in China and funded through charity. Tourist literature notes that it is 'the world's largest, seated, outdoor bronze Buddha'. There are bigger Buddhas out there (notably the 71m-high Grand Buddha in Leshan, China), but apparently they're not sitting, outdoors, or made of bronze. Even if it's not the biggest, Po Lin's Buddha is certainly impressive, and it's worth hiking up the steps to get a closer look, as well as the surrounding scenery. The steps up to the statue are open from 10 am to 6 pm.

Near the monastery are the **Lantau Tea Gardens**. These are not much more than a tourist attraction, as the weary-looking shrubs don't produce much tea any more. The best part is the little tea house, where you can enjoy a cup of the home-grown blend.

The statue of Buddha at the Po Lin Monastery may not be the biggest, but it is impressive.

Just east of the of the tea gardens is the trail head for **Lantau Peak**, which at 934m is the second highest in Hong Kong. This approach is quite steep. For more information, see under Hikes later in this section.

**Places to Stay & Eat** The *Lantau Tea Gardens* (☎ 2985-5161) has a few tiny (really grotty) rooms starting at HK$170 for a single during the week and HK$200/300 for a single/double at weekends. About 10 minutes walk east of the tea gardens is the *SG Davis Youth Hostel* (☎ 2985-5610), which has dormitory beds and several camp sites. Beds are HK$25 per night, camp sites cost HK$15, and you must be a YHA member to stay here.

There is a vegetarian restaurant in the monastery complex that lets you sample what the monks eat. A plate of spring rolls, vegetables and rice costs around HK$40.

**Getting There & Away** The No 2 bus connects Mui Wo with the Po Lin Monastery (via Pui O). Departures are approximately hourly from 8.20 am to 6.35 pm. The last bus back to Mui Wo leaves Po Lin at 7.30 pm. The fare is HK$9.50 from Monday to Saturday and HK$16 on Sunday and public holidays. Air-con buses are HK$14.50 and HK$23 respectively. The ride takes around 45 minutes. Bus No 21 connects the Po Lin Monastery with Tai O. There is also a taxi rank at the Po Lin Monastery, although it is often empty.

### Tai O

One hundred years ago this village used to be an important trading and fishing port, exporting salt and fish to China. The export trade has all but died, and residents now make their living from farming, fishing and processing shrimp paste and dried fish, which gives the town a rather pungent air. Tai O is built half on Lantau and half on an island just offshore – a bridge connects the two. While there are plenty of modern conveniences around, in many ways life goes on as it has for decades. It's a great place to spend a few hours just walking around. Stilt houses connected by precarious wooden walkways line the shore, and everywhere there are intriguing little alley ways. There are also a few good seafood restaurants in town, most of which have no name. Try your luck!

**Getting There & Away** The No 1 bus connects Mui Wo with Tai O. Departures are approximately half-hourly from 6 to 1.30 am. The last bus back to Mui Wo leaves Tai O at 10.15 pm. The fare is HK$7.50 from Monday to Saturday and HK$12 on Sunday and public holidays. Air-con buses are more expensive.

### Beaches

The only decent beach that's easily accessible is **Cheung Sha**, which stretches along the southern part of the island. There are changing and first aid facilities and basic snacks and drinks available during the April to October swimming season. Bus No 1, 2, 4 and 5 all pass by here.

One of Lantau's nicest beaches is at **Fan Lau**, a tiny hamlet at the western tip of the island. However, getting here requires an 8km hike (see the following Hikes section). Both Cheung Sha and Fan Lau generally have clean water, although sometimes rubbish from the nearby shipping channels washes up on shore (this is still Hong Kong, remember).

### Hikes

One of the nicest hikes on the island is up to **Sunset Peak** (869m). Starting from Mui Wo the ascent is gradual, and brings you up through rolling hills and meadows. You can also catch a bus from Mui Wo and get off at the trail head at Nam Shan, about 2km up the road. Any bus will do but No 7, bound for Pui O, is the cheapest. From the trail head, the hike is about 6.5km and at a leisurely pace takes around three hours. The trail will take you down to the road leading to Tung Chung. From here you can either wait for an infrequent bus, or walk down to the main road and Cheung Sha beach, where buses come by more often.

**Greening Hong Kong**
If you're hiking through what you hoped was an untouched area and the sight of rubbish everywhere drives you into a fit of environmental pique, don't despair. There are organisations in Hong Kong which concern themselves with the environment in the territory, and the animals who share it. Below is a list of the most prominent green groups active in Hong Kong:

*Earthcare* (☎ 2578-0522): focuses on animal welfare, ecology and education

*Environment Front* (email envfront@rocket mail.com): environmental protection in suburban Hong Kong

*Friends of the Earth* (☎ 2528-5588): all aspects relating to the protection and improvement of the living environment of Hong Kong

*Green Island Society* (email ronald@falcon. cc.ukans.edu): protection of Hong Kong wildlife and its natural habitats

*Green Lantau Association* (☎ 2985-5099): concerned with environmental issues which affect Lantau Island

*Green Power* (email greenpow@hk.linkage. net): promotes awareness of green issues in Hong Kong

*Greenpeace China* (☎ 2854-8300): technically more involved in ecological problems of a more global scale, but has an office in Hong Kong

*Hong Kong Dolphinwatch* (☎ 2984-1414): raises awareness of the plight of Hong Kong's pink dolphins; organises cruises for tourists to view dolphins

*Produce Green* (☎ 2674-1190): aims to develop green concepts

*World Wide Fund for Nature* (WWF) (☎ 2526-1011): environmental protection through the use of conservation and educational measures

If you're in good shape and feeling ambitious, you might consider continuing on to **Lantau Peak**. Although it's only about 4km from the Tung Chung road to the Po Lin Monastery on the other side of the peak, it's pretty steep going, and there are some concrete steps along the way that pound the soles of your feet. For your efforts you will be rewarded with great views from the summit. Unfortunately, many Hong Kongers are still careless with waste disposal, and the summit is awash with plastic and paper wrappers, styrofoam containers and drink cans. From the Po Lin Monastery there are frequent buses back to Mui Wo. You can also do this hike in reverse, starting from Po Lin, though it's even steeper uphill going this way.

The trails across Sunset and Lantau Peaks form part of the 70km **Lantau Trail**, which starts at Mui Wo, cuts across the island to Tai O and then loops back along the southern shore. Any of the 12 sections will take you through beautiful scenery. One particularly good combination is section No 7 and 8, from Shek Pik Reservoir, around the western tip of the island through the hamlet of Fan Lau and on up the coast to Tai O. It's a long one at 16km, but most of the going is flat and on a weekday you may not see another person on the trail.

The HKTA may be able to supply you with some government pamphlets on Lantau's country parks and the Lantau Trail. If not, you can contact the Country Parks Division of the Agriculture & Fisheries Department (☎ 2733-2132) in Tsim Sha Tsui. Maps of both Lantau and the Lantau Trail are also available at the Government Publications Office.

### Getting There & Away
Ferries to Mui Wo leave approximately hourly between 7 and 12.20 am from Pier 7 at the Outlying Islands ferry piers in Central (Map 6). The journey time is around 50 minutes, but some ferries stop at the nearby island of Peng Chau, which stretches the trip out by 20 minutes. The last boat from Mui Wo to Central leaves at 11.10 pm.

The adult one-way fare is HK$9.70 from Monday to Saturday morning, and HK$17 on Saturday afternoon, Sunday and public holidays. Children under 13 and seniors pay half price. Fares for deluxe class, which gives you access to the open-air back deck, are HK$16 and HK$30 respectively.

During the week there are also several hoverferry sailings each day. Departures from Pier 6 at the Central ferry terminal (Map 6) are at 9.40 am, 11.20 am, 2.25 pm and 4.25 pm. From Mui Wo hoverferries leave at 10.20 am, 12.10 pm, 3.10 pm and 5.10 pm. The hoverferry takes 30 minutes, and a one-way trip costs HK$24 (children and seniors pay half price). As with other HYF ferries, hot and cold drinks, beer and snacks are available.

## MACAU (Map 15)

Although there's plenty to see in Hong Kong, just a short hop across the water lies Macau, the oldest surviving European settlement in Asia. Just an hour away is a world so different from Hong Kong with its alleys and cobbled roads, colourful and cheery street scenes, replete with churches crumbling into a long, romantic decline. The colonial stamp on Macau is far deeper than on Hong Kong, where the colonial past survives in a few austere churches and the odd bureaucratic edifice, while in Macau the colourful Catholic churches are gems, surrounded on all sides by roads studded with buildings making up the fabric of Macau's history. This pervasive sense of another era steeps Macau and makes it fun and an adventure to explore.

The Latin temperament found a good home here. Instead of the order and efficiency so evident in Hong Kong, one finds here a relaxed, almost hands-off attitude to administration. Portuguese and Chinese societies have mixed here in a way that was never possible in the class-conscious British colony. Although making money is carried on with similar zeal, residents of Macau know when enough is enough and relax with good food and drink; a languorous passivity and unconcern seems to be a tradition imported wholesale from their Portuguese colonists; it all creates a wonderful world of effortless charm. Coming from Hong Kong to Macau is like journeying from London to Lisbon.

For the time being, anyway, Macau still has that precious mystique that Hong Kong has now lost. Until 20 December 1999, Macau will be administered by Portugal and then returned to China (unlike British Hong Kong, sovereignty still belongs ultimately to China). Macau borders the city of Zhuhai in China, and you can still stroll across the border (with a visa) and feel that borderland frisson.

Unlike the uncertainty and panic that preceded the return of Hong Kong to China, Macau has approached the period of transition with little trepidation. Macau has largely managed to avoid the prickly issues that crawled under the skin of the Hong Kong handover negotiations.

The Portuguese enclave has had a number of members of its legislature elected for about 20 years, and the Portuguese didn't rush in proposals to widen the franchise or speed up democratisation at the last minute. The current legislature will continue to serve throughout the handover, unlike what happened in Hong Kong, and Macau already has a local supreme court, side-stepping one area that became a feature of the Hong Kong disputes.

Another important difference lies in Macau's status not as a colony, but as a territory under the temporary administration of Portugal. This means a different sort of relationship exists between Portugal and China, and not one forged from mistrust and suspicion. Macau has always had to take its cues from China in matters regarding the administration of the territory while Hong Kong has existed as a separate realm, administered according to an independent, colonial law. On top of that, while British trading companies in Hong Kong still have a lot of clout, Portuguese business interests in Macau take a back seat. Residents were also chuffed that Portugal gave everyone born in Macau a Portuguese passport, allowing them the right to live anywhere in the European Union, while the UK baulked at the issue. Furthermore, Macau is geographically and culturally much closer to China than Hong Kong is; bordering Zhuhai, Macau sees a daily traffic of workers and shoppers crossing the border both ways, which creates the sense of one community.

But before we get too upbeat, it's important to realise that not everyone is happy about this arm-in-arm camaraderie. Despite

Macau having its own Basic Law (similar to that inaugurated in Hong Kong), many are upset at the lack of resilience to China and the apparent timidity when it comes to fighting for human rights and democracy.

And let's not forget that 1997 was a bad year for Macau's tourist industry. A rising number of gangland killings gave tourists an unexpected attraction they could have done without. One hotel was raked with AK47 gunfire, due to some bad marksmanship in the killing of a young Triad member. Tourist arrivals were down some 36% in August compared to the same month the year before, and despite the Macau Tourist Office's chirpy mantra 'We are among the eight million visitors who shop with confidence in Macau' there was no avoiding the fact that coping with flying bullets and explosions needs the sort of confidence that only a Triad upbringing could foster.

Most of the killings revolved around Macau's No 1 industry (gambling) and the way the profits are carved up among the Triads. Gambling yields 40% of government revenue and is the backbone of the local economy; with so much money at stake, it is hardly surprising that the Triads are heavily involved. The gangland warfare occurred at a time when Macau's economy was experiencing a downturn. It appears that shrinking revenue seems to have sparked a fight for disappearing capital.

A lucrative market exists in chaperoning wealthy gamblers from mainland China who bring in money big-time – about two-thirds of all casino revenue. It was the struggle for that market that led to a number of the deaths. Macau trembled on the edge of Triad civil war when the leader of the 14K gang was shot dead. By the year's end, 29 people had died. It is assumed that the hired hands responsible for the killings were recruited from former members of the PLA on the mainland. After the killings, they just slip back over the border and vanish into the enormity of China.

This all presents a huge problem for China, set to inherit Macau, lock, stock and gun-barrel on 20 December 1999. Beijing

will want to hang on to the lucrative gambling industry while crushing the Triads. Macau's manufacturing base has upped and left to exploit the cheaper labour that south China offers, leaving gambling, prostitution and drug dealing to prosper. Prostitution is particularly endemic in the territory, and far more obvious than in Hong Kong. Many of the prostitutes that line the streets around the sleazy hotels in the west of the peninsula are Mandarin-speakers from the mainland, especially from the northern provinces. The bright lights of Zhuhai and Macau are beacons to this migrant workforce.

Things have calmed down since 1997, but it is too early to say whether the Triads are gearing up for another showdown. Keep an eye on the papers if you want to visit Macau to revel in its wonderfully eclectic mix of European and Chinese styles, without the added backdrop of gunfire.

Another time when Macau is not relaxed is during the weekend, when the population seems to double with Hong Kongers over for a weekend of gambling and dining. Do everything you can to come here during the week. On the weekend, ferry tickets are difficult to buy, hotel rates go up and catching a taxi becomes nearly impossible. The other time is at the Chinese New Year, when the city rocks to fireworks and the streets are mayhem. Getting a hotel room at this time is tough and you'll probably either end up in a five-star suite or in a damp, dingy *pensione* (hotel).

The following information should get you through a day or two in Macau. Lonely Planet's *Hong Kong, Macau & Guangzhou* takes a much more detailed look at the enclave.

## History
In the early 16th century Portugal embarked on an aggressive campaign to cash in on Asia's lucrative trade routes. After forcefully securing colonial footholds in Goa (India) and Malacca (Malaysia), the Portuguese set their sights on China. In typical fashion, the Chinese imperial court brushed off the entreaties of these western barbarians. But

Portuguese persistence won out, and in the mid-1550s they were allowed to rent a small peninsula on the southern coast, possibly in exchange for wiping out a band of local pirates. This area, known variously as Aomen, Amagao or Macau, was quickly developed, despite that fact that China never formally ceded it to Portugal.

Macau became a key link in Portugal's major Asian trade routes, and Portuguese merchants became export agents for the Chinese, who were forbidden to go abroad on pain of death. This gave Portugal a near monopoly on all large-scale commerce with China. Macau also served as the staging point for Jesuit missionaries charged with spreading the word of God in the 'Middle Kingdom'.

Macau successfully fought off encroachment by the Dutch in the early 17th century, but Portugal's subsequent decline as a world power weighed heavily on the enclave. It still managed to struggle on as an outpost for Europeans trading with China. The British annexation of Hong Kong in 1841 changed that, and Macau gradually became a backwater. The problem of keeping the place financially viable, however, was solved by Governor Isidoro Francisco Guimaraes (who ruled from 1851 to 1863) who introduced legalised gambling, which is still the enclave's main source of revenue.

Although Portugal was actually ready to give Macau up in the mid-1970s, the Chinese apparently were content to maintain the status quo. It wasn't until 1987 – after Hong Kong's return to China had been decided – that a Sino-Portuguese pact was signed, handing Macau back to China on 20 December 1999. It will then become, like Hong Kong, a 'Special Administrative Region' and enjoy a 'high degree of autonomy' in all matters except defence and foreign affairs.

Even today China's relationship with Macau is quite close, and thousands of people cross the border daily going to and from work on the other side. One gets the feeling that Macau won't change much after 1999, except for the flags flying over the government offices.

## Information

**Tourist Offices** The Macau Government Tourist Office (☎ 315-566) has a branch on the 2nd floor of the ferry terminal, on the right side as you exit immigration. You can get all you need here. Free maps, walking tours, introductions to the history of Macau, pamphlets on temples, churches, gardens, forts, hotels and outlying islands are all here. There is also an office in Hong Kong (☎ 2857-2287), 336 Shun Tak Centre, 200 Connaught Rd, Sheung Wan. Chek Lap Kok airport should also have a representative counter, so keep an eye out after you fly into Hong Kong. In Hong Kong you can call ☎ 9220-3022 for an update on tourist information concerning Macau.

**Money** Macau has its own currency, the pataca, written as M$. However, its value is only a few cents less than that of the Hong Kong dollar, which circulates freely in Macau, so there really is no need to change money. Sometimes taxi drivers, restaurants and smaller stores may give you change in patacas, but all accept the Hong Kong currency and the bigger places give change in it as well.

## Things to See & Do

Macau is much smaller than Hong Kong in both population (500,000, of whom 95% are Chinese) and size (23.5 sq km). This means it's possible to walk to most of the sights, except for those on the islands of Taipa and Coloane, which can be easily reached by bus or taxi.

**Peninsular Macau** A good number of the sights on the peninsula are near Centro, the central business and government area. The main street running through here is Avenida de Almeida Ribeiro which, along with Avenida do Infante D'Henrique, cuts across the width of the peninsula.

Midway along Avenida de Almeida Ribeiro is the **Leal Senado**, which houses the municipal government offices. It's a classical structure that looks out over a public square and a large fountain. This whole area was recently renovated, and looks like a page from a guidebook to Portugal. The sense of colour and grandiose colonial excess will have you happily camera snapping. Behind the Leal Senado stands **St Augustine's Church**, which has foundations dating back to 1586, although the present church was built in 1814.

Wind your way up the path at the north end of the Leal Senado public square and you will come across **St Dominic's Church**, a beautiful 17th-century baroque cathedral. It is only open in the afternoon.

Continuing up the cobbled main street will take you to Macau's most famous landmark, the **Façade of St Paul's Cathedral**. This magnificent façade, along with the steps leading up to it and the mosaic floor behind it, are the only remains of what was once considered the finest church in Asia. Built by Jesuits in 1602, the church caught fire during a major typhoon in 1835. The façade has been described as a 'sermon in stone', recording some of Christianity's major events in its beautiful stone carvings. If you come here at night, after a meal, the whole edifice is lit up making for a wonderful spectacle. During the spring festival, the locals actually shoot fireworks at the façade, which is bizarre.

On the hill overlooking St Paul's is **Monte Fort**, which was built by the Jesuits around the same time. In 1622 the fort's cannons (which are still there) destroyed a Dutch warship, helping to dissuade the Dutch from further attempts to take over Macau. From on top of the fort there are sweeping views of Macau and, across the river, China.

A few blocks north, near the modern Church of St Anthony, stands the **Luis de Camoes Museum**. Once the headquarters of the British East India Co, this building now houses early Chinese terracotta, enamel ware and pottery, paintings, old weapons and paintings and sketches of old Macau and Guangzhou (formerly Canton). The museum is open daily from 11 am to 5 pm except Wednesday and public holidays. Admission is M$1.

Just behind the museum is the **Camoes Grotto & Gardens**, which house a memorial to the 16th-century Portuguese poet Luis de Camoes. There is some dispute as to whether Camoes ever made it to Macau, but the gardens are quite pleasant and are popular with the local Chinese, some of whom you might see playing checkers. Not far from the museum is the **Old Protestant Cemetery**, resting place of the many non-Portuguese who ended up in Macau.

North of Centro, on Ferreira de Almeida, are the restful **Lou Lim Ieoc Gardens**. The gardens and the ornate mansion adjacent (which is now a school) once belonged to the wealthy Chinese Lou family. The gardens are a mixture of European and Chinese plants, with huge shady trees, lotus ponds, pavilions, bamboo groves, grottoes and strangely-shaped doorways. The twisting pathways are said to be modelled after the famous gardens of Suzhou in eastern China.

Around the corner from the Lou Lim Ieoc Gardens, at the junction of Avenida da Sidonio Pais and Rua de Silva Mendes, is the **Sun Yatsen Memorial Home**, dedicated to the revolutionary who inspired China after the fall of the Qing Dynasty. Sun practised medicine in Macau before turning to revolution. The house was built as a memorial to Sun, and replaced the original, which blew up when it was being used as an explosives store. Inside there are flags, photos and other relics of Sun's life. The museum is open every day from 10 am to 1 pm and from 2.30 to 5 pm, except Tuesday.

Sitting on the highest point on the peninsula is the **Guía Lighthouse**, which was first lit in 1865. The complex is still used as a meteorological station, and offers terrific views.

It's a bit out of the way, lying up on Avenida do Coronel Mesquita, but if you like temples, the **Kun Lam Temple** complex is of interest. The Kun Lam (the Goddess of Mercy) Temple dates back 400 years, though the original temple on the site was probably built more than 600 years ago. It's also where the first treaty of trade and friendship between the USA and China was signed, in

1844. This area is a popular spot for fortune-tellers.

At the southern tip of the peninsula is the **A-Ma Temple**, which dates back to the 17th century. A-Ma (more commonly known by her Hong Kong pseudonym Tin Hau) became A-Ma-Gao to the Portuguese, and they named their colony after it. The temple consists of several shrines from the Ming Dynasty. Come here during the spring festival and you will be rewarded with a chaotic display of worshippers and deafening bundles of crackers exploding.

Opposite the A-Ma Temple is the outstanding **Maritime Museum**, which has a rich collection of boats and other artefacts related to Macau's seafaring past. It's open from 10 am to 5.30 pm daily except Tuesday. Entrance is M$8 (half price Sunday).

Moving up along the east side of the peninsula is **Rua da Praia Grande**, one of the most scenic streets in the city. Here you find the pink **Governor's Residence**, which you may only admire from outside. On the hill behind it is **Penha Church**, a cathedral that enjoys great views of the surrounding area.

Further to the north is the mildewed **St Lawrence's Church** on Rua de Sao Lourenço, surrounded by palms. Originally built of wood in the 1560s, it was later reconstructed in stone. One of the church's twin cream and white towers once served as an ecclesiastical prison. The interior is exceptional and worth seeing for its wooden ceiling. The church is open from 10 am to 4 pm during the week and from 10 am to 1 pm on Sunday.

Gambling is the main activity on Macau; but even if you're not interested in casinos, it's worth checking out the kitsch architecture of the **Lisboa Hotel**. It's just above the large traffic junction on the airport road, near the Bank of China.

The biggest event of the year is the **Macau Grand Prix**. As in Monaco, the streets of the town make up the track. The 6km circuit starts not far from the Lisboa Hotel and follows the shoreline along Avenida da Amizade, going around the reservoir and back through the city. The Grand Prix consists of two major races, one for cars and the other for motorcycles. Pedicab races are included as a novelty event. The race is a two day event held on the third weekend in November. More than 50,000 people flock to see it and accommodation becomes very scarce. Certain areas in Macau are designated as viewing areas. Streets and alleys along the track are blocked off, so it's unlikely you'll be able to get a good view without paying

**Taipa & Coloane** There are two outlying islands in Macau: Taipa and Coloane. The former has been overrun by amazingly ugly high-rise apartments, and there's not a whole lot to see here. **Taipa Village** has managed to resist being totally remade, and its narrow streets are fairly interesting to scout around. In the village, the **Taipa House Museum** is a good example of what life looked like at the beginning of this century. It's open every day except Monday from 9.30 am to 1 pm and from 3 to 5.30 pm.

**Coloane** is larger and boasts a few nice beaches, something Taipa lacks. In fact because of the island's many coves, inlets and caves, it was regularly used by pirates as a base. The northern sides of both islands have been carved away to make room for a power plant and Macau's new airport and deep-water port complex. But the southern side of Coloane is still fairly peaceful, and even has a few nice hiking trails.

**Seac Pai Van Park** is about 1km south of the causeway leading to Taipa. Its 20 hectares contain a fountain, some nice gardens and an aviary. The park is open from 8 am to 6 pm daily (closed Monday) and admission is M$5. The aviary costs another M$5. Behind the park are two hiking trails. The **Coloane Trail** makes an 8.6km loop around the island, while the **North-East Coloane Trail** takes in the north-east section only and stretches for 6.2km. You can get to the park from Macau Peninsula by taking Bus No 21A and 25 which leave from Hotel Lisboa.

**Coloane Village** is a picturesque hamlet with a few temples, some nice restaurants and a lazy, relaxed atmosphere. The main

Top Left: Monte Fort, Macau, built by Jesuit missionaries In about 1600.
Top Right: Portuguese architecture in Macau, a legacy of almost 450 years as a colony.
Bottom Left: Macau is smaller than Hong Kong and can easily be toured on foot or bicycle.
Bottom Right: Monte Fort's cannons were fired only once in anger – with deadly effect.

A walking tour of Macau highlights its dynamic features: street scenes from Largo do Senado (top left, right and middle); St Paul's Cathedral, which was destroyed by fire during a typhoon in 1835, leaving only the monumental façade (bottom left); and the Catholic institution of the Santa Casa do Misericordia building in Largo do Senado (bottom right).

attraction here is the **Chapel of St Francis Xavier**, built in 1928, which contains a piece of the right arm bone from the missionary of the same name, who died on nearby Shang Ch'an Island in 1552. At the southern end of town there is a **Tin Hau temple**.

On the south side of the island is Coloane's claim to fame, **Hac Sa Beach**. Hac Sa means 'black sand', and the sand here does have a grey to black colour. This can make the water look very polluted, but actually it's perfectly clean and fine for swimming. The area is beautiful, with lots of pine trees to provide shade, and on weekends people swarm here. On a really clear day you can see the mountains on Hong Kong's Lantau Island. Hac Sa is also the site of the incredible Fernando's restaurant (see Places to Eat later in the Macau section).

### Places to Stay

Macau is full of hotels, giving you plenty of options should you decide to stay overnight. However, nearly all of them are booked up on Friday and Saturday, so it's best to come during the week. Rates for Friday and Saturday are around 40% higher as well. Chinese New Year is another time to avoid, although the mark-up on the hotels is a small price to pay for the fireworks, fun and mayhem on the streets. This partial list will give you an idea of what's available. The Macau Government Tourist Office at the ferry terminal can provide you with complete details for all price levels of accommodation in Macau.

Booking into a number of hotels in Macau, if you are a single man, is an invitation for the concierge to tempt you with forbidden fruits. Prostitution is endemic in Macau, and far more open than in Hong Kong. Be blunt with the concierge if you don't want constant phone calls. Prostitutes linger in droves at the western end of Avenida de Almeida Ribeiro and the surrounding area.

Most people from Hong Kong book their hotels in advance, often at the booking offices in the Shun Tak Centre in Sheung Wan, where the ferries to Macau leave. Doing this saves a considerable amount off the walk-in rate. Here it is a simple matter to book your Turbo Cat ticket over to Macau and get a special deal on a hotel. Any of the countless outlets at the ferry terminal in the Shun Tak Centre can do this for you. This saves time and effort and is a lot cheaper. If you haven't booked a place already, many of the mid to top-range hotels have counters at the Macau terminal. Weigh them all up and book your room here as you will get a hefty discount (up to 50%). Some touts may also approach you offering discounts for hotels. Don't worry: they're usually reliable and are just trying to drum up business during the slow midweek period.

If you've booked a mid to top-range hotel room, follow the crowds out to the front of the terminal where nearly all the hotels operate a shuttle bus for their guests. Even if you just want to check out the hotel, jump on board. This saves a lot of time and effort.

If you're going for the more downmarket accommodation, bargain hard. The tourist business has been hit in Macau and prices fluctuate quite wildly, depending on conditions. Don't necessarily think the prices quoted here are the lowest – bargain hard and say *peng di la* ('make it cheaper').

Macau's true budget accommodation is not far from the centre of town. They generally form a cluster to the south-west of the Leal Senado square, around the area off Rua da Caldeira and Rua das Lorchas, a lively area of narrow lanes, food stalls and coloured shutters. Despite being pretty grotty, there are a few cosy retreats that won't cost too much; plus you're within striking distance of all the major sights.

The cheapest is the *Vong Hong Hospedaria* (☎ 573-016), 45 Rua das Lorchas. For IYHF card-holding spartans only, this place has midget singles for M$30 and small doubles for M$40. The walls are paper-thin and the whole place is quite grim, but what can you expect at these prices? Another real cheapie which is actually far better than a lot of the others on offer is the *San Va Hospedaria* (☎ 573-701) at 67 Rua de Felicidade; the stairs leading up are bright and cheery, even though the rooms are little more than partitioned closets – even so, some are better than others so take a peek. The only problem is that the walls are very thin, but things appear to be quite safe as the friendly concierge is always around. Singles start at M$60. Rua de Felicidade is chock-a-block with hole-in-the-wall restaurants, so take your pick.

Also in the area is the *Pensao Tai Fat*, 41-45 Rua da Caldeira, where they can almost speak English and have damp singles/doubles for M$180/200. Not so pleasant. There are many others in the area, so look around and try your luck and remember to bargain at all costs.

Costing a bit more but well worth it is the *East Asia Hotel* (☎ 922-433), 1A Rua da Madeira. The hotel is housed in a classic colonial-style building, and though it's been remodelled it has lost none of its charm. Spacious singles/doubles with private bath start at M$340/400. There's a fine restaurant on the 2nd floor that serves dim sum for extremely reasonable prices.

Also near the centre of town, is *Hotel Sintra* (☎ 710-111), Avenida Dom Joao IV. This is a standard mid-range Macau hotel, with standard rates: M$550 (weekdays) and M$782 (weekends) per night for a double. It's nothing special, but is comfortable enough. Book your room either in Hong Kong at the ferry terminal or at the Macau ferry terminal for a much cheaper price. The hotel has a shuttle bus to and from the ferry terminal. Another centrally located place is the *Metropole Hotel* (☎ 388-166), 62 Rua da Praia Grande. Doubles here are around M$396 if booking at the Macau ferry terminal. A decent and clean hotel where you can get a good deal is the *Sun Sun Hotel* (☎ 939-393), Praca Ponte e Horta 14-16; you can get a good deal (M$280 a double) if you book it through one of the agents in Hong Kong at the Macau ferry terminal.

For the top of the range hotels, there are really only a few places worth considering. *Bela Vista Hotel* (☎ 965-333) is a colonial hotel in the south of the Macau Peninsula that was going to seed until it was bought by Hong Kong's Mandarin Oriental Hotel Group not long ago. It has been painstakingly restored and has regained all of its

former elegance. There are only eight rooms and suites, ranging from M$2100 to M$4000 per night during the week. The most expensive room at the Bela Vista has a glorious view from the balcony and includes a sitting room. It may be expensive at M$4000 (at the weekend it goes up to M$5500), but if you want to indulge in colonial luxury, there's no better place than this. The hotel is on Rua Comendador Kou Ho Neng.

The *Mandarin Oriental Hotel* is not as grand as its Hong Kong cousin, but is still a superb five star hotel. Doubles are M$910 from Sunday to Thursday, M$1040 on Friday and M$1300 on Saturday. The Mandarin runs a shuttle bus from the Macau ferry terminal – look for the assistants in red coats.

Built into the remains of an old fortress, the *Pousada de Sao Tiago* (☎ 378-111) is right up there with the Bela Vista in terms of character, if not quite as luxurious. Sitting above Avenida de Republica, the hotel commands a splendid view of the harbour, and the interior decor, with its flagstones and wooden raftered ceilings, is just as enjoyable. Even if you don't stay here, it's worth stopping by for a drink on the terrace. Doubles range from M$1380 to M$1680. The honeymoon suite is M$1850 and the most expensive suite costs M$3500.

Perched on the southern shore of Coloane Island is the massive *Westin Resort* (☎ 871-111), Estrada de Hac Sa. Though not quite as elegant, it has all the amenities one expects of a five star hotel, and the setting is fantastic. All rooms have large, private balconies where you can sip your coffee or wine and contemplate the South China Sea. There is a beautiful outdoor swimming pool, a golf course and a full suite of indoor recreational facilities. Doubles range from M$2000 to M$2150. Again, booking it in Hong Kong (☎ 2803-2003) is much cheaper than turning up at reception.

### Places to Eat

This topic deserves its own separate volume, and this book doesn't pretend to do it justice. Suffice to say that if you exhaust these few places there are a lot of other great options out there. Don't overlook wandering the streets in search of stalls selling stir-fried food and *yuk gon*, dried sweet strips of pork and other meats that are very popular in Macau.

Macau's Chinese food is quite good, but it's the Portuguese food that makes coming here such a culinary delight. One place not to be missed is the legendary *Fernando's* (☎ 882-531), 9 Hac Sa Beach, Coloane. The original part of the restaurant, a graffiti-filled hole in the wall, doesn't look like much, but head out the back to the main brick dining hall and prepare yourself for a slice of heaven. Must-order dishes include roast chicken, clams, fried shrimp and the simple but outstanding salad. This place is always crowded, and you can't make reservations, but there's a bar area where you can sip cappuccino or sangria while you wait for a table. Prices are quite reasonable. Credit cards are not accepted. It's at the far end of the Hac Sa Beach car park. Look for a little wooden sign that says 'Fernando'.

One of Macau's most authentic Portuguese places is also on Coloane, this one in Coloane Village, at 8 Rua das Gaivotas. *Cacorola* (☎ 882-226) looks like a piece of Portugal was beamed over to Macau, customers and all. It serves up a fabulous variety of nouvelle cuisine, Portuguese-style. Specialities include tuna and black bean salad, beef steak with garlic and rabbit stew. This friendly restaurant is closed on Monday. It's just off the main square.

If you like really hot food and want something Chinese, you can't go wrong with the *Honggei Chuenchoi* (☎ 577-895), a very small Sichuan restaurant just off Avenida de Almeida Ribeiro at 188 Gatzai Gai. The food here is fabulous and blistering and much better than any of the 'Sichuan' food in Hong Kong. A full meal won't set you back more than HK$80.

*Comida A Portuguesa Carlos* (☎ 300-315) has some of the warmest service in town, as well as outstanding food: it's the kind of place where the owner comes over and chats with you over a glass of wine. It's at 28 Rua Bispo Medeiros, near the Lou Lim Ieoc Gardens. Credit cards are not accepted. Another highly recommended place is *A Lorcha Restaurant* (☎ 313-193), 289 Rua do Almirante Sergio, near the A-Ma Temple and the Maritime Museum at the southern tip of the peninsula.

Not far away is *Oporto Interior* (☎ 967-770) at 259B Rua do Almirante Sergio, a popular restaurant with a cosy atmosphere. The seafood is tasty and the service decent. Almost next door, in the same neighbourhood in the south of the peninsula, is the *Restaurante Litoral* (☎ 967-878), a very popular restaurant that attracts a big crowd.

Right next to the ferry terminal is an outstanding Italian restaurant. *Pizzeria Toscana* (☎ 726-637) does everything right, from pizza to pasta to cappuccino. It's also a good place to pick up some snacks for the ferry ride back to Hong Kong. It's down at the end of the spectacularly ugly long building across from the ferry terminal. Look for sign a depicting the 'leaning tower of Pizza'.

### Getting There & Away

Macau and Hong Kong are linked by an interesting selection of jet-powered ferries, which make it possible to do the 65km trip in around one hour. Departures in Hong Kong are from the Macau ferry terminal, near the Shun Tak Centre, 200 Connaught Rd, Sheung Wan (Map 6). The terminal is connected by underground walkway to Sheung Wan MTR station. The Hongkong & Yaumati Ferry Co also has ferries to Macau from the China Hong Kong City terminal in Tsim Sha Tsui (Map 5).

There are several different ferry services. The fastest and most stable are the Far East Jetfoils, twin-decked hydrofoils powered by Boeing jet engines. These make the trip in around 50 minutes, and are by far the most popular. The service runs 24 hours a day, catering to the late-night gamblers and partiers. Sailings are every 15 to 30 minutes during the day, but the frequency drops to hourly from around 1 am to 6 am. There are economy and 1st class sections, but the difference is minimal: 1st class gives you a slightly better view. Ticket prices during the week are HK$123 for economy and HK$136 for 1st class. On weekends the price goes up to HK$134 and HK$146 respectively. Late-night sailings cost HK$152 and HK$166.

Far East Jetfoils recently introduced a larger vessel called the Foilcat, which is a bit roomier and slightly faster. Ticket prices are HK$10 higher than those quoted above. Jetfoil tickets can be purchased up to 28 days in advance in Hong Kong at the Shun Tak Centre or booked by phone (☎ 2859-6956) if you have a credit card. Pick them up at the advance ticket window on the 1st floor of the Shun Tak Centre.

The next most popular option is the Turbo Cat, a more spacious and luxurious jet-powered catamaran that makes the journey in about 70 minutes. The interior is more pleasant than the jetfoils, but because it rides on the surface of the water, not above it, the Turbo Cat tends to jump around a lot more. If you're prone to seasickness, take the jetfoil. The Turbo Cat service runs approximately half-hourly from 7.30 am to 8 pm, and then hourly from 9 until 11 pm. Weekday ticket prices are HK$137 for economy and HK$239 for 1st class. Weekend prices are HK$148 and HK$254 respectively. You can book by credit card (☎ 2921-6688); after booking you can pop your credit card into a ticket machine at Shun Tak Centre for your ticket. Turn up 45 minutes before departure.

HYF's service from the China Hong Kong City terminal in Tsim Sha Tsui uses the same kind of boats as the Turbo Cat. Sailings are hourly from 8.30 am to 8 pm and ticket prices are similar to those for Turbo Cat.

If you're interested in the 'slow boat' to Macau, there's always the ironically named High-Speed Ferries. These look like scaled-down cruise ships, and make the trip in about one hour and 40 minutes, which is actually fairly quick. The best thing about these is the back deck, which is an enjoyable place to sit if the weather is good. The price is also appealing: from HK$61 to HK$97 (1st class) weekdays and HK$84 to HK$121 on week-ends. Sailings from Hong Kong are at 9.30 am and 3 and 8 pm. From Macau, departures are 12.15, 5.30 and 10.30 pm.

Unless you are going during the weekend there's little need to buy a round-trip ticket. With all the ferry departures, it's fairly easy to get a ticket in Macau.

For those who can afford HK$1200 for a one-way flight, there is a helicopter service between Hong Kong and Macau. The flight takes just 20 minutes, but immigration at both ends adds up so that you only save around 40 minutes compared with taking a jetfoil. However, you can't beat the view. There are 10 to 12 flights daily in each direction. For more information call East Asia Airlines (☎ 2859-3359) at the Shun Tak Centre.

Macau is served by an airport, with direct flights from a number of cities including Lisbon, Seoul, Singapore, Taipei, Bangkok and a number of cities in China.

You will be required to go through immigration formalities in both Hong Kong and Macau, so bring your passport.

### Getting Around

Macau is well served by buses. Fares are from M$2 to M$4 and you pay on board. The most important routes for visitors are as follows:

No 3 – runs from the Jetfoil (ferry) pier past Hotel Lisboa onto Avenida Almeida Ribeiro in the Centro district

No 3A – runs from Jetfoil pier down to Avenida de Almeida Ribeiro over to wharf and floating casino

No 25 – runs from Barrier Gate through Centro on Avenida do Infante D'Henrique, over to Taipa and on to Hac Sa Beach in Coloane

No 28C – runs from Jetfoil pier past Hotel Lisboa, then north to Lou Lim Ieoc Gardens, Kun Iam Temple and ends at Barrier Gate (border with China)

Taxis are pretty easy to find except on week-ends, when Macau is swarming with visitors from Hong Kong. Flagfall is M$8 and each additional 0.25km costs M$1. There are sur-charges of M$5 and M$10 for rides to Taipa and Coloane islands, respectively. Don't board one of the ubiquitous pedicabs unless you want to be ripped off as they are about the same price as taxis.

# Language

Hong Kong's official language is Cantonese, a southern Chinese dialect that originated in neighbouring Guangdong Province.

While Cantonese is used in everyday life, English still dominates commerce, banking and international trade. However in the lead-up to and after 1997, many noticed a sharp decline in the level of English-speaking proficiency. In fact, the level of spoken English in Hong Kong is nowhere near as good as that spoken in Singapore (where many grow up bilingual). Those Hong Kong Chinese who speak English well are usually wealthy and educated, and thus can emigrate more easily.

Many Hong Kongers have begun studying Mandarin, the national language of the PRC, and the most widely spoken Chinese dialect. There's been a fair number of Mandarin speakers in Hong Kong since the 1950s, when many refugees fled there from China. Until recently, however, the younger generation has generally not bothered studying Mandarin, preferring English as their second language. Mandarin is also vital to doing business with China, as many business executives will attest – few mainlanders will bother to learn Cantonese, which is viewed by many view as a barbarous southern dialect.

Short-term visitors can get by in Hong Kong without knowing a word of Cantonese. There are still plenty of English speakers, especially in the tourist zones, although fluency varies considerably. All signs on streets and public transport are bilingual, so there's no problem getting around. About the only time you'll have a real problem is when visiting budget noodle shops, many of which don't have English menus. Here you'll probably have to resort to the international language – pointing at what others are eating.

## SPOKEN CHINESE

Cantonese differs from Mandarin as much as French does from Spanish. Speakers of both dialects can read Chinese characters, but they pronounce many words differently. For example, when Mr Ng from Hong Kong goes to Beijing, Mandarin speakers will read his name as Mr Wu.

Chinese has a fairly limited number of consonant-vowel combinations, thus many words appear to have the same pronunciation. The Cantonese word for 'silk' sounds just like the words for 'lion', 'private', 'master' and 'affair'. What distinguishes each word is its tone. If you get your tones mixed, you risk saying something entirely different from what you intended. This is particularly true of Cantonese, which is said to have seven tones, compared with only four for Mandarin.

## WRITTEN CHINESE

Officially, written Chinese has about 50,000 pictographs or characters which symbolise objects or actions. Most of these have become archaic, but about 6000 remain in common use, and there are around 2000 basic characters you'd need to know to read a newspaper.

The written language allows Chinese people from around the country to overcome the barrier posed by more than 200 different dialects. Both Cantonese and Mandarin speakers can understand the same newspaper but if they read it aloud it would sound like two different tongues. Hong Kong also has 150 of its own Chinese characters which are used solely to represent colloquial Cantonese words. These are not understood by speakers of other dialects, or even some Cantonese speakers from the mainland.

Hong Kong, like Taiwan, uses the original 'complex' character set, as opposed to the system of simplified characters adopted by China in the 1950s in a bid to increase literacy. The result is that many of the characters you'll see in Hong Kong look quite different from their counterparts in China. In Hong Kong, Chinese characters can be read from

LANGUAGE

## Mandarin versus Cantonese

The character below means 'to go', and is displayed with its pronunciation in Mandarin (on the left) and Cantonese (on the right).

qù 去  hui 去

Chinese dialects have a host of differences, yet share close affinities as well – Cantonese (the dialect spoken in Guangdong, including Hong Kong, and parts of Guangxi) is probably as different from Mandarin (a northern dialect that has become the common language of China) as French is from Italian. This means that mutual intelligibility is not possible unless a lot of guesswork and patience (or alcohol) is called into play; however, many southern Chinese speakers of Cantonese are at least familiar with Mandarin and have little problem with it, while many Mandarin speakers just switch off when they hear Cantonese. In the balance, Mandarin is a more useful dialect to learn than Cantonese.

Mandarin speakers who turn to the colossal task of learning Cantonese have to contend with different tones (seven if you're keen, six if you're not), different pronunciation and a busload of slang that Mandarin doesn't have. The tones of Cantonese are in a far wider range than those of Mandarin, and that's what gives the dialect its sing-song quality; Mandarin only has four tones which are tightly bunched together. The sounds of Cantonese are sometimes similar to those of Mandarin, and sometimes wildly different, so guessing doesn't always work, although guessing is done wholesale leading to much puzzlement and laughter all round. Cantonese slang is a rich part of the dialect, and is constantly evolving, especially in Hong Kong. In its pure form, and because it has to act as the lowest common denominator of communication, Mandarin finds itself almost devoid of an evolving slang vocabulary.

On the plus side, most of the grammar is the same (apart from a few anomalies) so cross-dialect learners can at least hit the ground running on that front. Many of the proverbs, idioms and phrases are the same, even though some basic expressions differ (the differences are easily learned). And of course, the written form is the same. Cantonese does insist on a few of its own non-standard characters, but for the most part it is the same language. Written Chinese in Hong Kong is composed of traditional characters, while simplified characters are used on the mainland, but problems of intelligibility are not huge. There are also strong indications that a war is being waged between simplified characters and traditional characters on the mainland.

Last but not least, there exists a tonal relationship between Mandarin and Cantonese which can lead to reasonably accurate guesswork as to how the tone will translate. For example, the rising tone of Mandarin almost exclusively becomes its opposite, the low falling tone of Cantonese. With a little study, the relationship between the tones of the two dialects can be learned. ■

left to right, right to left, or top to bottom. In China the government has been trying to get everyone to read and write from left to right.

## CANTONESE PRONUNCIATION

Cantonese pronunciation is not an easy affair. The following guide is designed to help you pronounce the Cantonese words and phrases in this book with as little difficulty as possible. As such it glosses over some aspects of pronunciation that you would need to know if you planned to study the language in depth. Note that the examples given reflect British pronunciation.

**a**   as in 'father'
**ai**  as the 'i' in 'find', but shorter

**au**  as the 'ou' in 'bout'
**e**   as in 'let'
**ei**  as the 'a' in 'say'
**eu**  as the 'ur' in 'urn' (with pursed lips)
**i**   as the 'ee' in 'see'
**iu**  similar to the word 'you'
**o**   as in 'go' when word final; as in 'go' elsewhere
**oi**  as the 'oy' in 'boy'
**oo**  as in 'soon'
**ou**  as the 'ow' in 'sow'
**u**   as in 'put'
**ue**  as in 'Sue'
**ui**  as 'oo' + 'ee'

Consonants are generally pronounced as in English, with the following exceptions:

| **j** | as the 'dz'in 'adze' |
| **ch** | as the 'ts' in 'tsar' |
| **ng** | as in 'sing' |

## CANTONESE TONES

The best way to learn tones is by ear, ideally from a teacher who takes the time to distinguish each one clearly. The system we use to show tones in this language guide is based on the Yale romanisation system. It's designed to make pronunciation of Cantonese tones as simple as possible and may not necessarily reflect what you come across where official transliteration systems are used.

In the Yale system six basic tones are represented: three which do not noticeably rise or fall in pitch (high, middle and low) and three which either rise or fall in pitch (high rising, low rising and low falling). Remember that it doesn't matter whether you have a high or low voice when speaking Cantonese as long as your intonation reflects relative changes in pitch. The following examples show the six basic tones – note how important they can be to your intended meaning:

- **high tone:** represented by a macron above a vowel, eg *fōo*, 'husband'
- **middle tone:** represented by an unaccented vowel, eg *foo*, 'wealthy'
- **low tone:** represented by the letter 'h' after a vowel, eg *fooh*, 'owe'; note that when 'h' appears at the beginning of a word it is still pronounced, elsewhere it signifies a low tone
- **middle tone rising:** represented by an acute accent, eg *fóo*, 'tiger'
- **low tone falling:** represented by a grave accent followed by the low tone letter 'h', eg *fòoh*, 'to lean'
- **low tone rising:** represented by an acute accent and the low tone letter 'h', eg *fóoh*, 'woman'

For a more in-depth guide to Cantonese pronunciation and a more comprehensive phrase list, get hold of Lonely Planet's *Cantonese phrasebook*.

## PHRASE LIST

Although English speakers can get by in Hong Kong without knowing any Cantonese, knowing a few simple phrases will be greatly appreciated by many of the people you meet there. See the special 'Hong Kong's Chinese Cuisine' section in the Places to Eat chapter for a list of Chinese dishes.

### Pronouns

I
| *ngóh* | 我 |

you
| *néhìh* | 你 |

he/she/it
| *kúhìh* | 佢 |

we/us
| *ngóh dēìh* | 我哋 |

you (pl)
| *néhìh dēìh* | 你哋 |

they/them
| *kúhìh dēìh* | 佢哋 |

### Greetings & Civilities

Hello, how are you?
| *néhìh hó ma?* | 你好嗎？ |

Fine.
| *géìh hó* | 幾好 |

Fine, and you?
| *géìh hó, néhìh nē?* | 幾好，你呢？ |

So so.
| *màh má déìh* | 麻麻地 |

Good morning.
| *jó sàhn* | 早晨 |

Goodbye.
| *bāàhìh baàhìh, joìh gin* | 拜拜/再見 |

See you tomorrow.
| *tìng yahìh joìh gin* | 聽日再見 |

### Requests, Thanks & Apologies

Please wait a moment.
| *chéng dáng yāt jahn* | 請等一陣 |

Excuse me. (calling someone's attention)
| *m gōìh* | 唔該 |

Please hurry up.
| *m gōìh faàhìh dì* | 唔該快啲 |

Please slow down.
| *m gōìh mahàhn dì* | 唔該慢啲 |

## GLOSSARY OF PLACE NAMES

| | | | |
|---|---|---|---|
| Aberdeen | 香港仔 | Hong Kong Cultural Centre | 香港文化中心 |
| Admiralty | 金鐘 | Hong Kong Convention | |
| Admiralty Centre | 金鐘廊 | & Exhibition Centre | 香港會議展覽中心 |
| Alexandra House | 亞歷山大大廈 | Hong Kong Island | 香港島 |
| | | Hong Kong Park | 香港公園 |
| Bank of China | 中國銀行 | Hung Hom | 紅磡 |
| Causeway Bay | 銅鑼灣 | | |
| Central | 中環 | Ice House St | 雪廠街 |
| Central Building | 中建大廈 | | |
| Chai Wan | 柴灣 | Jade Market | 玉器市場 |
| Chater Rd | 遮打道 | Jardine House | 怡和大廈 |
| Chek Lap Kok Airport | 赤鱲角機場 | Jardine's Bazaar | 渣甸街 |
| Cheung Chau | 長洲 | | |
| Chungking Mansions | 重慶大廈 | Kai Tak Airport | 香港啓德國際機場 |
| Connaught Rd | 干諾道中 | KCR (Kowloon Canton Railway) | 九廣鐵路 |
| D'Aguilar St | 德忌笠街 | Kowloon | 九龍 |
| Des Voeux Rd | 德輔道 | | |
| Discovery Bay | 愉景灣 | Ladder St | 樓梯街 |
| | | Lai Chi Kok | 荔枝角 |
| Exchange Square | 交易廣場 | Lamma Island | 南丫島 |
| | | Lan Kwai Fong | 蘭桂坊 |
| Fanling | 粉嶺 | | |
| | | Lantau Island | 大嶼山 |
| Happy Valley | 跑馬地 | Lippo Centre | 力寶中心 |
| Hollywood Rd | 荷利活道 | | |
| Hongkong and Shanghai Bank | 匯豐銀行 | Macau Ferry Terminal | 港澳碼頭 |
| | | Mid-Levels | 半山區 |
| Hong Kong Arts Centre | 藝術中心 | Mong Kok | 旺角 |

Thank you very much.
  *dōh jē saàhìh, m gōìh saàhìh*
  多謝哂/唔該哂
Thanks. (for a gift or special favour)
  *dōh jē*      多謝
Thanks. (making a request or purchase)
  *m gōìh*      唔該
You're welcome.
  *m sáih haàhk hēìh*   唔駛客氣
Excuse me. (after bumping into someone)
  *duìh m juhèh*    對唔住
I'm sorry.
  *m hó yi si*     唔好意思
Don't worry about it.
  *m gán yiùh*     唔緊要
Can you please help me take a photo?
  *hóh m hóh yíh bōng ngóh yíng jēùhng séùhng a?*
  可唔可以幫我影張相呀？

Is it OK to take a photo?
  *hóh m hóh yíh yíng séùhng a?*
  可唔可以影相呀？

**Small Talk**
Do you speak English?
  *néhìh sìk m sìk góng yìng mán a?*
  你識唔識講英文呀？
Do you understand?
  *néhìh mìhng m mìhng a?*
  你明唔明？
I understand.
  *ngóh mìhng*     我明
I don't understand.
  *ngóh m mìhng*    我唔明
Can you repeat that please?
  *chéng joìh góng yat chi?*
  請再講一次？

## GLOSSARY OF PLACE NAMES

| | | | |
|---|---|---|---|
| MTR (Mass Transit Railway) | 地下鐵路 | Star Ferry | 天星 |
| | | St George's Building | 聖佐治大廈 |
| Nathan Rd | 彌敦道 | Swire House | 太古大廈 |
| New Territories | 新界 | | |
| Noon Day Gun | 午炮 | Tai O | 大澳 |
| | | Tai Po | 大埔 |
| Ocean Park | 海洋公園 | Temple St Night Market | 廟街夜市 |
| Pacific Place | 太古廣場 | Tiger Balm Gardens | 胡文虎花園 |
| Peak Tram | 山頂纜車 | The Landmark | 置地廣場 |
| Pedder St | 畢打街 | Tsim Sha Tsui | 尖沙咀 |
| Prince's Building | 太子行 | Tsuen Wan | 荃灣 |
| Quarry Bay | 鰂魚涌 | Victoria Park | 維多利亞公園 |
| Queen's Rd, Central | 皇后大道中 | Victoria Peak | 山頂 |
| Repulse Bay | 淺水灣 | Wan Chai | 灣仔 |
| Sai Kung | 西貢 | Wellington St | 威靈頓街 |
| Sai Kung Peninsula | 西貢半島 | Worldwide Plaza | 環球大廈 |
| Sha Tin | 沙田 | Wyndham St | 雲咸街 |
| Shek O | 石澳 | | |
| Sheung Shui | 上水 | Yau Ma Tei | 油麻地 |
| Sheung Wan | 上環 | Yuen Long | 元朗 |
| Shun Tak Centre | 信德中心 | Yuen Po St Bird Garden | 園圃街雀鳥公園 |
| Silvermine Bay | 梅窩 | | |
| Standard Chartered Bank | 渣打銀行 | Zoological & Botanical Gardens | 香港動植物公園 |
| Stanley | 赤柱 | | |

What is this called?
*nì goh giùh māt yéh a?*
呢個叫乜嘢呀？

My name is ...
*ngóh giùh ...*
我叫 ...

What is your surname? (polite )
*chéng mahn gwaih sing?*
請問貴姓？

My surname is ...
*síùh sing ...*
小姓 ...

This is Mr/Mrs/Ms (Lee).
*nì wáih hahìh (léhìh) sìn sāàhng/ taàhìh táàhìh/síùh jé*
呢位係（李）先生/太太/小姐

Glad to meet you.
*hó gō hing yihng sìk néhìh*
好高興認識你

### Getting Around

bus stop
*bā sí jahàhm*  巴士站

airport
*gēih chèhùhng*  機場

subway station
*dēih tit jahàhm*  地鐵站

pier
*máh tàhùh*  碼頭

north
*bāk*  北

east
*dūng*  東

south
*nàhàhm*  南

west
*sāih*  西

I'd like to go to ...
*ngóh séùhng huìh ...*  我想去 ...

Where is the ...?
*... háih bìn doh a?*　... 喺邊度呀？
Does this (bus, train etc) go to ...?
*huih m huih ... a?*　去唔去 ... 呀？
How much is the fare?
*géih dōh chín a?*　幾多錢呀？
I want to get off at ...
*ngóh séuhng háih ... lohk chē*
我想喺 ... 落車
Stop here please. (taxi, minibus)
*m gōih, nì doh yáhùh lohk*
唔該，呢度有落？
How far is it to walk?
*hààhng loh yiùh géih nohìh a?*
行路要幾耐呀？
Where is this address please?
*m gōih, nì goh dēih jí háih bìn doh a?*
唔該，呢個地址喺邊度呀？
Please write down the address for me.
*m gōih sé goh dēih jí béih ngóh*
唔該寫個地址俾我

### Accommodation
Do you have any rooms available?
*yáhùh mó fóng a?*　有冇房呀？
I'd like a (single/double) room.
*ngóh séùhng yiùh yāt gāàhn*
*(dāàhn yàhn/sēùhng yàhn) fóng*
我想要一間（單人/雙人）房
I'd like a quiet room.
*ngóh séùhng yiùh yāt gāàhn*
*jihng dì gē fóng*
我想要一間啲嘅房
How much per night?
*géih dōh chín yāt máhàhn a?*
幾多錢一晚呀？
Can I get a discount if I stay longer?
*juhèh nohìh dī yáhùh mó jit kaùh a?*
住耐啲有冇折扣呀？

### Food
Do you have an English menu?
*yáhùh mó yīng mán chāàhn páàhìh a?*
有冇英文餐牌呀？
Can you recommend any dishes?
*yáhùh māt yéh hó gaàhìh siùh a?*
有乜嘢好介紹呀？
I'm a vegetarian.
*ngóh sihk jāàhìh*
我食齊

I'd like the set menu please.
*ngóh yiùh goh to chāàhn*
我要個套餐
Please bring me a knife and fork.
*m gōìh béih ngóh yāt foòh dō chā*
唔該俾我一副刀叉
Please bring the bill.
*m gōìh, màahìh dāàhn*　唔該，埋單

### Shopping
How much is this?
*nī goh géih dōh chín a?*
呢個幾多錢呀？
That's very expensive.
*hó gwaìh*　好貴
Can you reduce the price?
*pèhng dī dāk m dāk a?*
平啲得唔得呀？
I'm just looking.
*ngóh sīn táìh yāt táìh*　我先睇一睇

### Numbers

| | | |
|---|---|---|
| 0 | *lìhng* | 零 |
| 1 | *yāt* | 一 |
| 2 | *yih (léhùhng)* | 二（兩） |
| 3 | *sāàhm* | 三 |
| 4 | *sēìh* | 四 |
| 5 | *ng* | 五 |
| 6 | *luhk* | 六 |
| 7 | *chāt* | 七 |
| 8 | *baàht* | 八 |
| 9 | *gáùh* | 九 |
| 10 | *sahp* | 十 |
| 11 | *sahp yāt* | 十一 |
| 12 | *sahp yih* | 十二 |
| 20 | *yih sahp* | 二十 |
| 21 | *yih sahp yāt* | 二十一 |
| 30 | *sāàhm sahp* | 三十 |
| 100 | *yāt baàhk* | 一百 |
| 101 | *yāt baàhk lìhng yāt* | 一百零一 |
| 110 | *yāt baàhk yāt sahp* | 一百一十 |
| 112 | *yāt baàhk yāt sahp yih* | 一百一十二 |
| 120 | *yāt baàhk yih sahp* | 一百二十 |
| 200 | *yih baàhk* | 二百 |
| 1000 | *yāt chīn* | 一千 |
| 10,000 | *yāt mahàhn* | 一萬 |
| 100,000 | *sahp mahàhn* | 十萬 |
| 1,000,000 | *yāt baàhk mahàhn* | 一百萬 |

## Health

I'm sick.
  *ngóh yáhùh bēng*        我有病
I need a doctor.
  *ngóh yiùh táih yī sāng*   我要睇醫生
It hurts here.
  *nī doh m sùeh fuhk*       呢度唔舒服
I have asthma.
  *ngóh hāàhùh chúèhn*      我哮喘
I have diarrhoea.
  *ngóh tó ngōh*            我肚痾
I'm allergic to (antibiotics/penicillin).
  *ngóh duìh (kong sāng so/*
  *pòòhn nèhìh sāìh làhm) gwoh mán*
  我對（抗生素/盤尼西林）過敏
My friend is sick.
  *ngóh pàhng yáhùh yáhùh bēng*
  我朋友有病

I'd like to see a female doctor.
  *ngóh yiùh wán yāt wáìh núhìh yī sāng*
  我要搵一位女醫生

## Emergencies

Help!
  *gaùh mēng a!*        救命呀！
Watch out!
  *síùh sām!*           小心！
Thief!
  *chéùhng yéh a!*      搶嘢呀！
Call the police!
  *giùh gíng chaàht!*   叫警察！
Call an ambulance!
  *giùh gaùh sēùhng chē!*  叫救傷車！

# Glossary

GLOSSARY

**amah** – a servant, usually a woman, who cleans houses and looks after the children. Older Chinese women from the countryside used to find work as amahs, but in Hong Kong now the job is mostly done by Filipinas and other South-East Asian migrant workers.

**cheong sam** – originating in Shanghai, a fashionable, tight-fitting Chinese dress with a slit up the side. Often worn on special occasions, it's also the favoured gown for a bride departing on her honeymoon.
**CMB** – China Motor Bus

**dai pong dong** – open-air street stalls; great places to enjoy some tasty dishes from a sidewalk folding table, especially at night.

**fung shui** – literally meaning 'wind-water', the Chinese art of geomancy which aims to balance the elements of nature.

**godown** – a warehouse, usually located on or near the waterfront.
**gongfu** – a form of Chinese martial arts, usually called kung fu in the west; see also *taijiquan*.
**gwailo** – a foreigner, particularly a westerner. In Cantonese the term means 'ghost person' or 'foreign devil' and stems from the 19th century when westerners began to come to China in force. Hong Kongers claim the term no longer has any negative connotation, though some foreigners are less than fond of the name.
**gwaipo** – a female foreigner, particularly a westerner. *'Gwai'* means 'devil' or 'ghost', *'po'* is Cantonese for woman.

**Hakka** – a Chinese ethnic group who speak a different dialect from Cantonese; some Hakka people still lead traditional lives as farmers in the New Territories.
**HKTA** – Hong Kong Tourist Association
**hong** – a company, usually engaged in trade. Often used to refer to Hong Kong's original trading houses, such as Jardine Matheson or Swire, which have grown to become major conglomerates.

**II** – Illegal Immigrant; the name generally given to the mainland Chinese immigrants that slip across the border into Hong Kong from China.

**junk** – originally referred to Chinese fishing and war vessels with square sails. Now applies to the diesel-powered, wooden pleasure yachts which can be frequently seen on Hong Kong's harbour.

**kaido** – small to medium-sized ferry which makes short runs on the open sea, usually used for non-scheduled service between small islands and fishing villages.
**karaoke** – a system that allows you to sing along to the recorded melody of popular songs. A popular social activity among the Chinese, it takes place in bars, specialised 'karaoke lounges' and private homes. The word 'karaoke' (meaning 'empty music') was borrowed from Japan, which bears responsibility for its invention.
**KCR** – Kowloon-Canton Railway
**KMB** – Kowloon Motor Bus

**LRT** – Light Rail Transit

**mahjong** – popular Chinese-style 'card game' played among four with tiles engraved with Chinese characters.
**MTR** – Mass Transit Railway

**PLA** – People's Liberation Army
**PRC** – People's Republic of China

**sampan** – a type of motorised wooden launch capable of only carrying a few people, used mostly for inter-harbour tranport.
**SAR** – Special Administrative Region. Hong Kong is now known as Hong Kong SAR, a

region of China that is under special administration.

**shroff** – an Anglo-Indian word meaning 'cashier'.

**taijiquan** – slow-motion shadow boxing, a form of exercise; commonly shortened to *taiji* ('tai chi' in the west).

**taipan** – the 'big boss', usually of a large company.

**Tanka** – a Chinese ethnic group who traditionally live on boats. Somewhat looked down upon by other Chinese groups, they are among Hong Kong's original inhabitants.

**Triad** – Chinese secret society. Originally founded to protect Chinese culture from the influence of usurping Manchurians, but their modern-day members are little more than secretive gangsters. Hong Kong's Triads are mainly involved in drug-running, prostitution and protection rackets.

**URBTIX** – Urban Ticketing System

# Index

Colour map references are in **bold** type.

# LONELY PLANET PHRASEBOOKS

**Nepali**
phrasebook

**Ethiopian**
Amharic
phrasebook

**Latin American**
**Spanish**
phrasebook

**Ukrainian**
phrasebook

**Greek**
phrasebook

**Vietnamese**
phrasebook

*Building bridges,*
*Breaking barriers,*
*Beyond babble-on*

*Listen for the gems*

*Speak your own words*

*Ask your own*
*questions*

*Master of*
*your*
*own*
*image*

- handy pocket-sized books
- easy to understand Pronunciation chapter
- clear and comprehensive Grammar chapter
- romanisation alongside script to allow ease of pronunciation
- script throughout so users can point to phrases
- extensive vocabulary sections, words and phrases for every situation
- full of cultural information and tips for the traveller

*'...vital for a real DIY spirit and attitude in language learning'* – Backpacker

*'the phrasebooks have good cultural backgrounders and offer solid advice for challenging situations in remote locations'* – San Francisco Examiner

*'...they are unbeatable for their coverage of the world's more obscure languages'* – The Geographical Magazine

---

Arabic (Egyptian)
Arabic (Moroccan)
Australia
 *Australian English, Aboriginal and Torres Strait languages*
Baltic States
 *Estonian, Latvian, Lithuanian*
Bengali
Brazilian
Burmese
Cantonese
Central Asia
Central Europe
 *Czech, French, German, Hungarian, Italian and Slovak*
Eastern Europe
 *Bulgarian, Czech, Hungarian, Polish, Romanian and Slovak*
Ethiopian (Amharic)
Fijian
French
German
Greek

Hindi/Urdu
Indonesian
Italian
Japanese
Korean
Lao
Latin American Spanish
Malay
Mandarin
Mediterranean Europe
 *Albanian, Croatian, Greek, Italian, Macedonian, Maltese, Serbian and Slovene*
Mongolian
Nepali
Papua New Guinea
Pilipino (Tagalog)
Quechua
Russian
Scandinavian Europe
 *Danish, Finnish, Icelandic, Norwegian and Swedish*

South-East Asia
 *Burmese, Indonesian, Khmer, Lao, Malay, Tagalog (Pilipino), Thai and Vietnamese*
Spanish (Castilian)
 *Basque, Catalan and Galician*
Sri Lanka
Swahili
Thai
Thai Hill Tribes
Tibetan
Turkish
Ukrainian
USA
 *US English, Vernacular, Native American languages and Hawaiian*
Vietnamese
Western Europe
 *Basque, Catalan, Dutch, French, German, Irish, Italian, Portuguese, Scottish Gaelic, Spanish (Castilian) and Welsh*

---

# LONELY PLANET TRAVEL ATLASES

Lonely Planet has long been famous for the number and quality of its guidebook maps. Now we've gone one step further and produced a handy companion series: Lonely Planet travel atlases – maps of a country produced in book form.

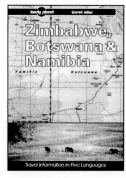

Unlike other maps, which look good but lead travellers astray, our travel atlases have been researched on the road by Lonely Planet's experienced team of writers. All details are carefully checked to ensure the atlas corresponds with the equivalent Lonely Planet guidebook.

The handy atlas format means no holes, wrinkles, torn sections or constant folding and unfolding. These atlases can survive long periods on the road, unlike cumbersome fold-out maps. The comprehensive index ensures easy reference.

- full-colour throughout
- maps researched and checked by Lonely Planet authors
- place names correspond with Lonely Planet guidebooks
  – no confusing spelling differences
- legend and travelling information in English, French, German, Japanese and Spanish
- size: 230 x 160 mm

***Available now:***
Chile & Easter Island • Egypt • India & Bangladesh • Israel & the Palestinian Territories •Jordan, Syria & Lebanon • Kenya • Laos • Portugal • South Africa, Lesotho & Swaziland • Thailand • Turkey • Vietnam • Zimbabwe, Botswana & Namibia

---

# LONELY PLANET TV SERIES & VIDEOS

Lonely Planet travel guides have been brought to life on television screens around the world. Like our guides, the programmes are based on the joy of independent travel, and look honestly at some of the most exciting, picturesque and frustrating places in the world. Each show is presented by one of three travellers from Australia, England or the USA and combines an innovative mixture of video, Super-8 film, atmospheric soundscapes and original music.

Videos of each episode – containing additional footage not shown on television – are available from good book and video shops, but the availability of individual videos varies with regional screening schedules.

***Video destinations include:*** Alaska • American Rockies • Australia – The South-East • Baja California & the Copper Canyon • Brazil • Central Asia • Chile & Easter Island • Corsica, Sicily & Sardinia – The Mediterranean Islands • East Africa (Tanzania & Zanzibar) • Ecuador & the Galapagos Islands • Greenland & Iceland • Indonesia • Israel & the Sinai Desert • Jamaica • Japan • La Ruta Maya • Morocco • New York • North India • Pacific Islands (Fiji, Solomon Islands & Vanuatu) • South India • South West China • Turkey • Vietnam • West Africa • Zimbabwe, Botswana & Namibia

*The Lonely Planet TV series is produced by:*
**Pilot Productions**
The Old Studio
18 Middle Row
London W10 5AT  UK

**For video availability and ordering information contact your nearest Lonely Planet office.**

***Music from the TV series is available on CD & cassette.***

# PLANET TALK

## *Lonely Planet's FREE quarterly newsletter*

We love hearing from you and think you'd like to hear from us.

**When...**is the right time to see reindeer in Finland?
**Where...**can you hear the best palm-wine music in Ghana?
**How...**do you get from Asunción to Areguá by steam train?
**What...**is the best way to see India?

**For the answer to these and many other questions read PLANET TALK.**

Every issue is packed with up-to-date travel news and advice including:

* a letter from Lonely Planet co-founders Tony and Maureen Wheeler
* go behind the scenes on the road with a Lonely Planet author
* feature article on an important and topical travel issue
* a selection of recent letters from travellers
* details on forthcoming Lonely Planet promotions
* complete list of Lonely Planet products

*To join our mailing list contact any Lonely Planet office.*

**Also available: Lonely Planet T-shirts. 100% heavyweight cotton.**

---

# LONELY PLANET ONLINE

## *Get the latest travel information before you leave or while you're on the road*

Whether you've just begun planning your next trip, or you're chasing down specific info on currency regulations or visa requirements, check out Lonely Planet Online for up-to-the minute travel information.

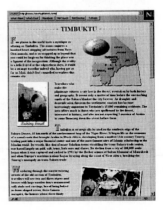

As well as travel profiles of your favourite destinations (including maps and photos), you'll find current reports from our researchers and other travellers, updates on health and visas, travel advisories, and discussion of the ecological and political issues you need to be aware of as you travel.

There's also an online travellers' forum where you can share your experience of life on the road, meet travel companions and ask other travellers for their recommendations and advice. We also have plenty of links to other online sites useful to independent travellers.

And of course we have a complete and up-to-date list of all Lonely Planet travel products including guides, phrasebooks, atlases, Journeys and videos and a simple online ordering facility if you can't find the book you want elsewhere.

*www.lonelyplanet.com*
*or*
*AOL keyword: lp*

# LONELY PLANET PRODUCTS

Lonely Planet is known worldwide for publishing practical, reliable and no-nonsense travel information in our guides and on our web site. The Lonely Planet list covers just about every accessible part of the world. Currently there are nine series: *travel guides, shoestring guides, walking guides, city guides, phrasebooks, audio packs, travel atlases, Journeys – a unique collection of travel writing and Pisces Books - diving and snorkeling guides.*

## EUROPE

Amsterdam • Andalucia • Austria • Baltic States phrasebook • Berlin • Britain • Canary Islands• Central Europe on a shoestring • Central Europe phrasebook • Czech & Slovak Republics • Denmark • Dublin • Eastern Europe on a shoestring • Eastern Europe phrasebook • Estonia, Latvia & Lithuania • Europe • Finland • France • French phrasebook • Germany • German phrasebook • Greece • Greek phrasebook • Hungary • Iceland, Greenland & the Faroe Islands • Ireland • Italian phrasebook • Italy • Lisbon • London • Mediterranean Europe on a shoestring • Mediterranean Europe phrasebook • Paris • Poland • Portugal • Portugal travel atlas • Prague • Romania & Moldova • Russia, Ukraine & Belarus • Russian phrasebook • Scandinavian & Baltic Europe on a shoestring • Scandinavian Europe phrasebook • Slovenia • Spain • Spanish phrasebook • St Petersburg • Switzerland •Trekking in Spain • Ukrainian phrasebook • Vienna • Walking in Britain • Walking in Italy • Walking in Switzerland • Western Europe on a shoestring • Western Europe phrasebook

***Travel Literature:*** The Olive Grove: Travels in Greece

## NORTH AMERICA

Alaska • Backpacking in Alaska • Baja California • California & Nevada • Canada • Chicago • Deep South• Florida • Hawaii • Honolulu • Los Angeles • Mexico • Mexico City • Miami • New England • New Orleans • New York City • New York, New Jersey & Pennsylvania • Pacific Northwest USA • Rocky Mountain States • San Francisco • Seattle • Southwest USA • USA phrasebook • Washington, DC & the Capital Region

***Travel Literature:*** Drive thru America

## CENTRAL AMERICA & THE CARIBBEAN

• Bahamas and Turks & Caicos • Bermuda • Central America on a shoestring • Costa Rica • Cuba • Eastern Caribbean • Guatemala, Belize & Yucatán: La Ruta Maya • Jamaica • Panama

***Travel Literature*** Green Dreams: Travels in Central America

## SOUTH AMERICA

Argentina, Uruguay & Paraguay • Bolivia • Brazil • Brazilian phrasebook • Buenos Aires • Chile & Easter Island • Chile & Easter Island travel atlas • Colombia  Ecuador & the Galápagos Islands • Latin American Spanish phrasebook • Peru • Quechua phrasebook • Rio de Janeiro • South America on a shoestring • Trekking in the Patagonian Andes • Venezuela

***Travel Literature:*** Full Circle: A South American Journey

## ISLANDS OF THE INDIAN OCEAN

Madagascar & Comoros • Maldives • Mauritius, Réunion & Seychelles

## AFRICA

Africa - the South • Africa on a shoestring • Arabic (Moroccan) phrasebook • Cairo • Cape Town • Central Africa • East Africa • Egypt • Egypt travel atlas• Ethiopian (Amharic) phrasebook • The Gambia & Senegal • Kenya • Kenya travel atlas • Malawi, Mozambique & Zambia • Morocco • North Africa • South Africa, Lesotho & Swaziland • South Africa, Lesotho & Swaziland travel atlas • Swahili phrasebook • Tunisia • Trekking in East Africa • West Africa • Zimbabwe, Botswana & Namibia • Zimbabwe, Botswana & Namibia travel atlas

***Travel Literature:*** Mali Blues • The Rainbird: A Central African Journey • Songs to an African Sunset: A Zimbabwean Story

# MAIL ORDER

Lonely Planet products are distributed worldwide. They are also available by mail order from Lonely Planet, so if you have difficulty finding a title please write to us. North American and South American residents should write to 150 Linden St, Oakland CA 94607, USA; European and African residents should write to 10a Spring Place, London NW5 3BH; and residents of other countries to PO Box 617, Hawthorn, Victoria 3122, Australia.

## NORTH-EAST ASIA

Beijing • Bhutan • Cantonese phrasebook • China • Hong Kong • Hong Kong, Macau & Guangzhou • Japan • Japanese phrasebook • Japanese audio pack • Korea • Korean phrasebook • Kyoto • Mandarin phrasebook • Mongolia • Mongolian phrasebook • North-East Asia on a shoestring • Seoul • South-West China • Taiwan • Tibet • Tibet phrasebook • Tokyo

*Travel Literature*: Lost Japan

## MIDDLE EAST & CENTRAL ASIA

Arab Gulf States • Arabic (Egyptian) phrasebook • Central Asia • Central Asia phrasebook • Iran • Israel & the Palestinian Territories • Israel & the Palestinian Territories travel atlas • Istanbul • Jerusalem • Jordan & Syria • Jordan, Syria & Lebanon travel atlas • Lebanon • Middle East • Turkey • Turkish phrasebook • Turkey travel atlas • Yemen

*Travel Literature:* The Gates of Damascus • Kingdom of the Film Stars: Journey into Jordan

## ALSO AVAILABLE:

Brief Encounters • Travel with Children • Traveller's Tales• Not the Only Planet

## INDIAN SUBCONTINENT

Bangladesh • Bengali phrasebook • Bhutan • Delhi • Goa • Hindi/Urdu phrasebook • India • India & Bangladesh travel atlas • Indian Himalaya • Karakoram Highway • Nepal • Nepali phrasebook • Pakistan • Rajasthan • South India • Sri Lanka • Sri Lanka phrasebook • Trekking in the Indian Himalaya • Trekking in the Karakoram & Hindukush • Trekking in the Nepal Himalaya

*Travel Literature:* In Rajasthan • Shopping for Buddhas

## SOUTH-EAST ASIA

Bali & Lombok • Bangkok • Burmese phrasebook • Cambodia • Ho Chi Minh City • Indonesia • Indonesian phrasebook • Indonesian audio pack • Indonesia's Eastern Islands • Jakarta • Java • Laos • Lao phrasebook • Laos travel atlas • Malay phrasebook • Malaysia, Singapore & Brunei • Myanmar (Burma) • Philippines • Pilipino phrasebook • Singapore • South-East Asia on a shoestring • South-East Asia phrasebook • South-West China • Thailand • Thailand's Islands & Beaches • Thailand travel atlas • Thai phrasebook • Thai audio pack • Thai Hill Tribes phrasebook • Vietnam • Vietnamese phrasebook • Vietnam travel atlas

## AUSTRALIA & THE PACIFIC

Australia • Australian phrasebook • Bushwalking in Australia • Bushwalking in Papua New Guinea • Fiji • Fijian phrasebook • Islands of Australia's Great Barrier Reef • Melbourne • Micronesia • New Caledonia • New South Wales • New Zealand • Northern Territory • Outback Australia • Papua New Guinea • Papua New Guinea phrasebook • Queensland • Rarotonga & the Cook Islands • Samoa • Solomon Islands • South Australia • Sydney • Tahiti & French Polynesia • Tasmania • Tonga • Tramping in New Zealand • Vanuatu • Victoria • Western Australia

*Travel Literature:* Islands in the Clouds • Sean & David's Long Drive

## ANTARCTICA

Antarctica

# THE LONELY PLANET STORY

Lonely Planet published its first book in 1973 in response to the numerous 'How did you do it?' questions Maureen and Tony Wheeler were asked after driving, busing, hitching, sailing and railing their way from England to Australia.

Written at a kitchen table and hand collated, trimmed and stapled, *Across Asia on the Cheap* became an instant local bestseller, inspiring thoughts of another book.

Eighteen months in South-East Asia resulted in their second guide, *South-East Asia on a shoestring*, which they put together in a backstreet Chinese hotel in Singapore in 1975. The 'yellow bible', as it quickly became known to backpackers around the world, soon became *the* guide to the region. It has sold well over half a million copies and is now in its 9th edition, still retaining its familiar yellow cover.

Today there are over 350 titles, including travel guides, walking guides, language kits & phrasebooks, travel atlases and travel literature. The company is the largest independent travel publisher in the world. Although Lonely Planet initially specialised in guides to Asia, today there are few corners of the globe that have not been covered.

The emphasis continues to be on travel for independent travellers. Tony and Maureen still travel for several months of each year and play an active part in the writing, updating and quality control of Lonely Planet's guides.

They have been joined by over 80 authors and 200 staff at our offices in Melbourne (Australia), Oakland (USA), London (UK) and Paris (France). Travellers themselves also make a valuable contribution to the guides through the feedback we receive in thousands of letters each year and on our web site.

The people at Lonely Planet strongly believe that travellers can make a positive contribution to the countries they visit, both through their appreciation of the countries' culture, wildlife and natural features, and through the money they spend. In addition, the company makes a direct contribution to the countries and regions it covers. Since 1986 a percentage of the income from each book has been donated to ventures such as famine relief in Africa; aid projects in India; agricultural projects in Central America; Greenpeace's efforts to halt French nuclear testing in the Pacific; and Amnesty International.

*'I hope we send people out with the right attitude about travel. You realise when you travel that there are so many different perspectives about the world, so we hope these books will make people more interested in what they see. Guidebooks can't really guide people. All you can do is point them in the right direction.'*

– Tony Wheeler

## LONELY PLANET PUBLICATIONS

**Australia**
PO Box 617, Hawthorn 3122, Victoria
tel: (03) 9819 1877  fax: (03) 9819 6459
e-mail: talk2us@lonelyplanet.com.au

**USA**
150 Linden St
Oakland, CA 94607
tel: (510) 893 8555 TOLL FREE: 800 275-8555
fax: (510) 893 8572
e-mail: info@lonelyplanet.com

**UK**
10a Spring Place,
London NW5 3BH
tel: (0171) 428 4800  fax: (0171) 428 4828
e-mail: go@lonelyplanet.co.uk

**France:**
1 rue du Dahomey, 75011 Paris
tel: 01 55 25 33 00  fax: 01 55 25 33 01
e-mail: bip@lonelyplanet.fr

**World Wide Web: http://www.lonelyplanet.com
or *AOL keyword: lp***

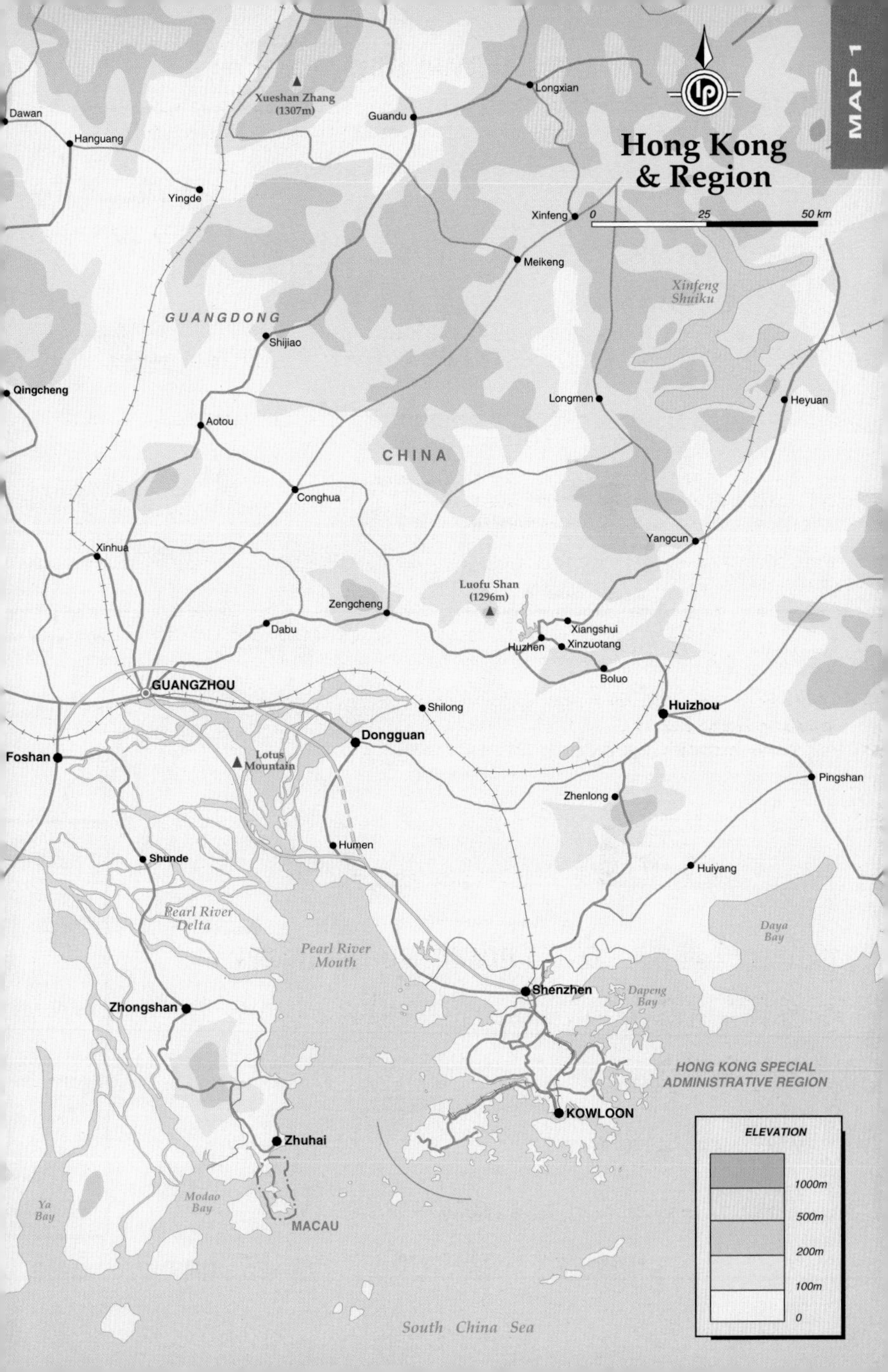

MAP 1

# Hong Kong
# & Region

Dawan

Hanguang

Yingde

Xueshan Zhang
(1307m)

Guandu

Longxian

Xinfeng

Meikeng

*Xinfeng
Shuiku*

*G U A N G D O N G*

Shijiao

Qingcheng

Aotou

Longmen

Heyuan

*C H I N A*

Conghua

Xinhua

Yangcun

Zengcheng

Luofu Shan
(1296m)

Dabu

Xiangshui
Xinzuotang
Huzhen

Boluo

GUANGZHOU

Shilong

Huizhou

Foshan

Dongguan

*Lotus
Mountain*

Zhenlong

Pingshan

Shunde

Humen

Huiyang

*Pearl River
Delta*

*Pearl River
Mouth*

*Daya
Bay*

Zhongshan

Shenzhen

*Dapeng
Bay*

*HONG KONG SPECIAL
ADMINISTRATIVE REGION*

KOWLOON

Zhuhai

*Ya
Bay*

*Modao Bay*

MACAU

*South China Sea*

0    25    50 km

| ELEVATION | |
|---|---|
| | 1000m |
| | 500m |
| | 200m |
| | 100m |
| | 0 |

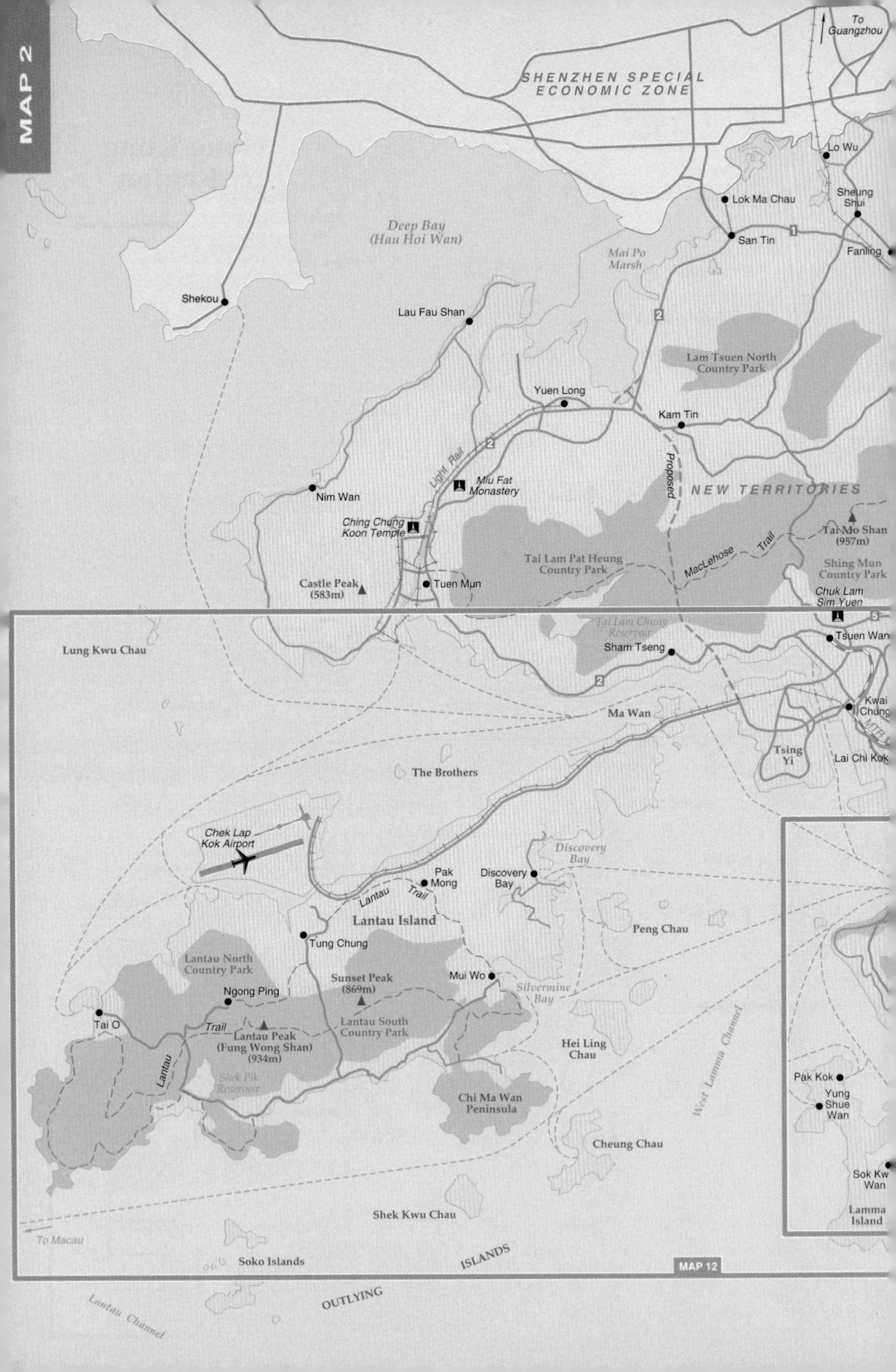

MAP 2

To Guangzhou

SHENZHEN SPECIAL
ECONOMIC ZONE

Lo Wu

Lok Ma Chau

Sheung
Shui

Deep Bay
(Hau Hoi Wan)

Mai Po
Marsh

San Tin

Fanling

Shekou

Lau Fau Shan

Lam Tsuen North
Country Park

Yuen Long

Kam Tin

2

Nim Wan

Light Rail

Miu Fat
Monastery

NEW TERRITORIES

Tai Mo Shan
(957m)

Ching Chung
Koon Temple

Proposed

MacLehose

Trail

Shing Mun
Country Park

Castle Peak
(583m)

Tai Lam Pat Heung
Country Park

Chuk Lam
Sim Yuen

Tuen Mun

Tai Lam Chung
Reservoir

Tsuen Wan

Lung Kwu Chau

Sham Tseng

2

Kwai
Chung

Ma Wan

Tsing
Yi

Lai Chi Kok

The Brothers

Chek Lap
Kok Airport

Discovery
Bay

Lantau
Trail

Pak
Mong

Discovery
Bay

Peng Chau

Lantau Island

Lantau North
Country Park

Tung Chung

Sunset Peak
(869m)

Mui Wo

Silvermine
Bay

Ngong Ping

West Lamma Channel

Tai O

Trail

Lantau Peak
(Fung Wong Shan)
(934m)

Lantau

Lantau South
Country Park

Hei Ling
Chau

Pak Kok

Yung
Shue
Wan

Slick Pit
Reservoir

Chi Ma Wan
Peninsula

Cheung Chau

Sok Kw
Wan

Shek Kwu Chau

Lamma
Island

To Macau

Soko Islands

ISLANDS

OUTLYING

Lantau Channel

MAP 12

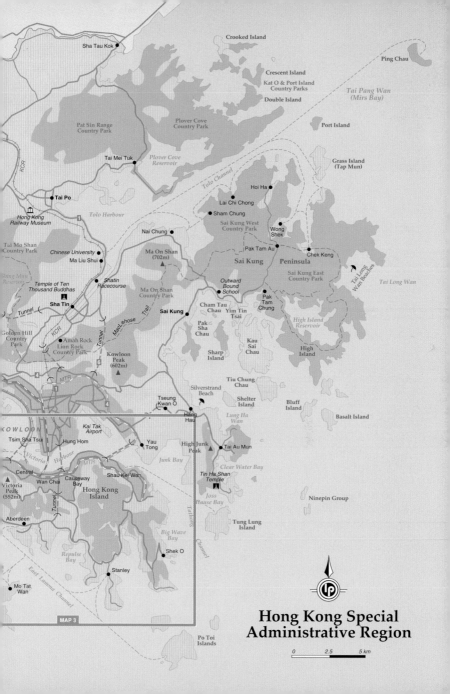

# Hong Kong Special Administrative Region

0    2.5    5 km

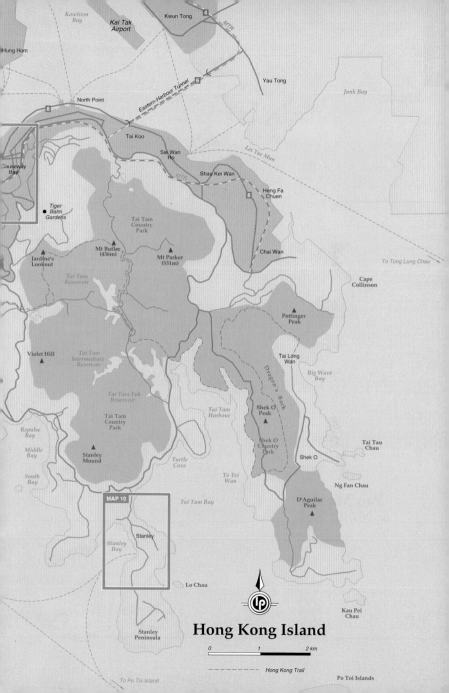

Kowloon Bay

Kai Tak Airport

Kwun Tong

Hung Hom

North Point

Eastern-Harbour Tunnel

MTR

Yau Tong

Junk Bay

Tai Koo

Lei Yue Mun

Sai Wan Ho

Causeway Bay

Shau Kei Wan

MTR

Heng Fa Chuen

Tiger Balm Gardens

Tai Tam Country Park

Chai Wan

To Tung Lung Chau

Mt Butler (436m)

Mt Parker (531m)

Jardine's Lookout

Cape Collinson

Tai Tam Reservoir

Pottinger Peak

Violet Hill

Tai Tam Intermediate Reservoir

Tai Long Wan

Big Wave Bay

Tai Tam Tuk Reservoir

Dragon's Back

Tai Tam Harbour

Shek O Peak

Repulse Bay

Tai Tam Country Park

Shek O Country Park

Tai Tau Chau

Middle Bay

Stanley Mound

Turtle Cove

Shek O

South Bay

To Tei Wan

Ng Fan Chau

MAP 10

Tai Tam Bay

D'Aguilar Peak

Stanley

Stanley Bay

Lo Chau

Kau Pei Chau

Stanley Peninsula

**Hong Kong Island**

0        1        2 km

To Po Toi Island

Hong Kong Trail

Po Toi Islands

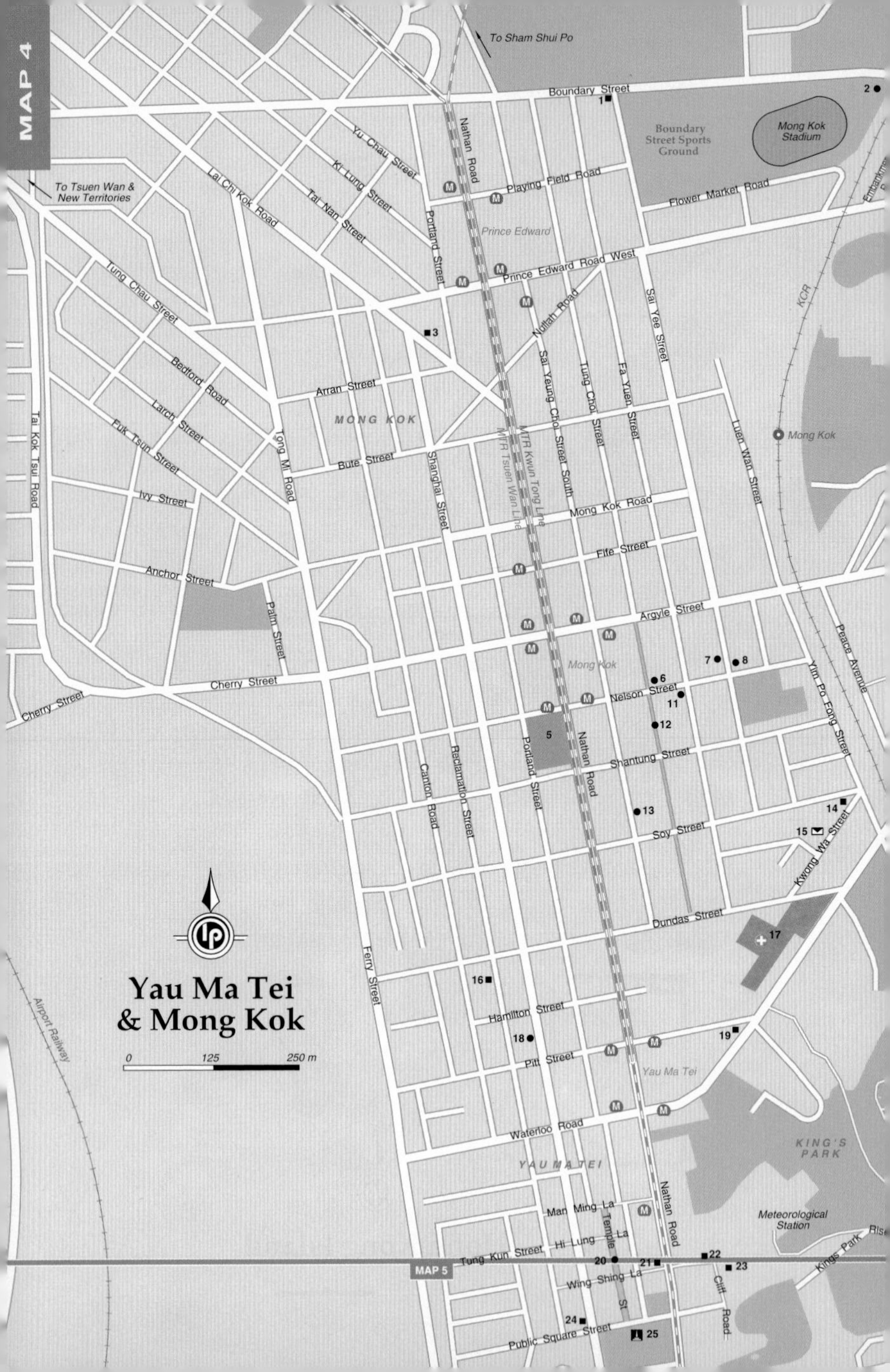

MAP 4

To Sham Shui Po

Boundary Street

2 ●

Boundary
Street Sports
Ground

Mong Kok
Stadium

Playing Field Road

Yu Chau Street

Ki Lung Street

Tai Nan Street

Nathan Road

Portland Street

Flower Market Road

To Tsuen Wan &
New Territories

Lai Chi Kok Road

Prince Edward

Ⓜ

Ⓜ

Prince Edward Road West

Sai Yeung Choi Street South

Nathan Road

Tung Choi Street

Fa Yuen Street

Sai Yee Street

KCR

Tung Chau Street

Bedford Road

Larch Street

Fuk Tsun Street

Tong Mi Road

Shanghai Street

Arran Street

■ 3

MONG KOK

Bute Street

Tai Kok Tsui Road

Ivy Street

Anchor Street

Reclamation Street

Mong Kok Road

MTR Kwun Tong Line

MTR Tsuen Wan Line

Tuen Wan Street

Ⓜ Mong Kok

Cherry Street

Cherry Street

Palm Street

Fife Street

Ⓜ

Argyle Street

Ⓜ

Ⓜ

Mong Kok

7 ● ● 8

Canton Road

Portland Street

Nathan Road

Nelson Street

● 6

5

● 11

● 12

Shantung Street

● 13

Soy Street

Yim Po Fong Street

Palace Avenue

14 ■

15 ✉

Kwong Wa Street

**Yau Ma Tei
& Mong Kok**

Ferry Street

Dundas Street

✚ 17

16 ■

Hamilton Street

18 ●

Pitt Street

Ⓜ

Ⓜ

19 ■

0    125    250 m

Yau Ma Tei

Ⓜ

Waterloo Road

KING'S
PARK

YAU MA TEI

Airport Railway

Man Ming La

Hi Lung La

Temple La

Meteorological
Station

Tung Kun Street

20 ●

21 ■

■ 22

23 ■

Wing Shing La

Ching Road

King's Park Rise

MAP 5

24 ■

Public Square Street

🏛 25

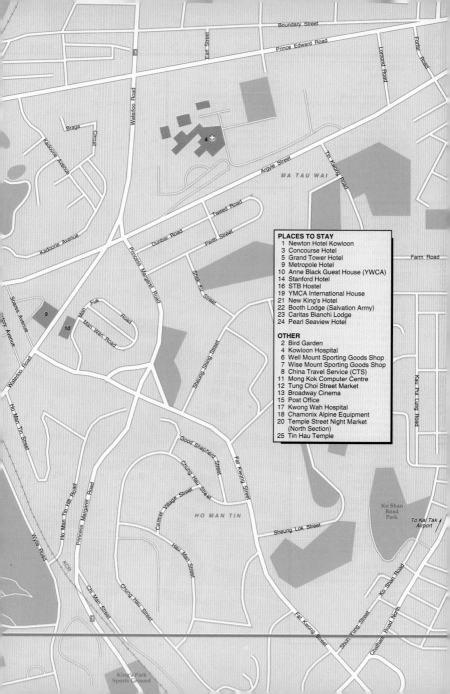

**PLACES TO STAY**
1 Newton Hotel Kowloon
3 Concourse Hotel
5 Grand Tower Hotel
9 Metropole Hotel
10 Anne Black Guest House (YWCA)
14 Stanford Hotel
16 STB Hostel
19 YMCA International House
21 New King's Hotel
22 Booth Lodge (Salvation Army)
23 Caritas Bianchi Lodge
24 Pearl Seaview Hotel

**OTHER**
2 Bird Garden
4 Kowloon Hospital
6 Well Mount Sporting Goods Shop
7 Wise Mount Sporting Goods Shop
8 China Travel Service (CTS)
11 Mong Kok Computer Centre
12 Tung Choi Street Market
13 Broadway Cinema
15 Post Office
17 Kwong Wah Hospital
18 Chamonix Alpine Equipment
20 Temple Street Night Market
   (North Section)
25 Tin Hau Temple

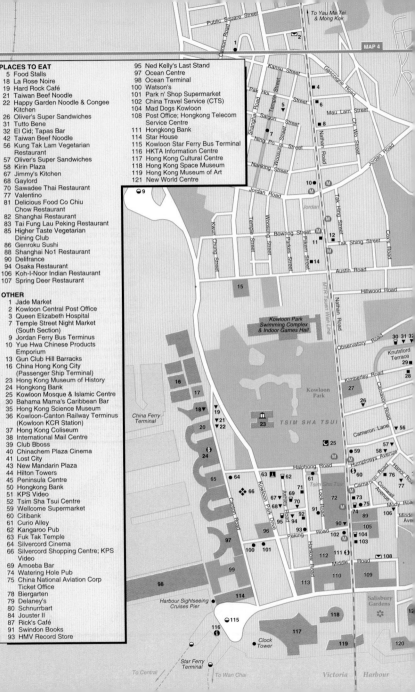

MAP 5

MAP 4

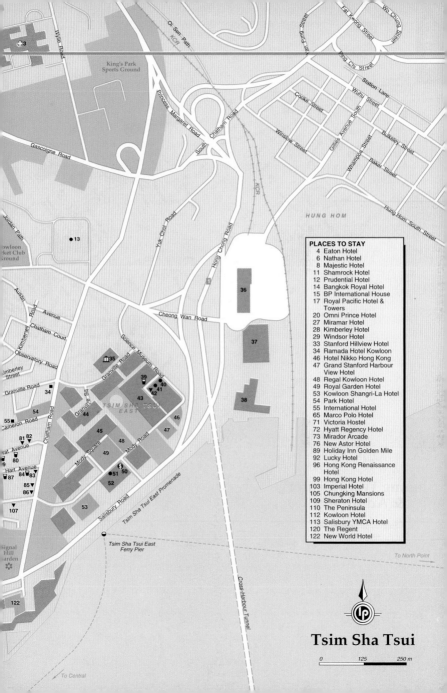

## PLACES TO STAY

4 Eaton Hotel
6 Nathan Hotel
8 Majestic Hotel
11 Shamrock Hotel
12 Prudential Hotel
14 Bangkok Royal Hotel
15 BP International House
17 Royal Pacific Hotel &
  Towers
20 Omni Prince Hotel
27 Miramar Hotel
28 Kimberley Hotel
29 Windsor Hotel
33 Stanford Hillview Hotel
34 Ramada Hotel Kowloon
46 Hotel Nikko Hong Kong
47 Grand Stanford Harbour
  View Hotel
48 Regal Kowloon Hotel
49 Royal Garden Hotel
53 Kowloon Shangri-La Hotel
54 Park Hotel
55 International Hostel
65 Marco Polo Hotel
71 Victoria Hostel
72 Hyatt Regency Hotel
73 Mirador Arcade
76 New Astor Hotel
89 Holiday Inn Golden Mile
92 Lucky Hotel
96 Hong Kong Renaissance
  Hotel
99 Hong Kong Hotel
103 Imperial Hotel
105 Chungking Mansions
109 Sheraton Hotel
110 The Peninsula
112 Kowloon Hotel
113 Salisbury YMCA Hotel
120 The Regent
122 New World Hotel

# Tsim Sha Tsui

0    125    250 m

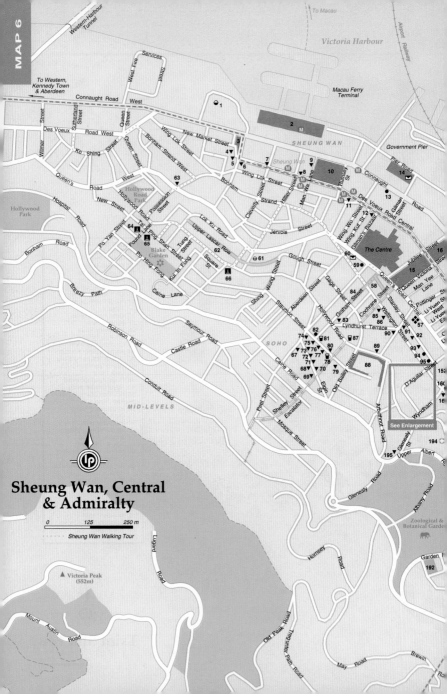

MAP 6

To Macau

Victoria Harbour

Airport Railway

Western-Harbour Tunnel

West Fire Services Street

Macau Ferry Terminal

To Western, Kennedy Town & Aberdeen

Connaught Road West

Government Pier

Pier Road

Des Voeux Road West

Queen's Road West

New Market Street

Wing Lok Street

Bonham Strand West

SHEUNG WAN

Connaught

Des Voeux Road Central

Hollywood Road Park

Possession Street

Wing Lok Street

Cleverly Strand

Hillier St

Man Wa Lane

Hospital Road

Hollywood Park

New Street

Queen's Road West

Bonham Strand

Jervois Street

Gilman's Bazaar

The Centre

Jubilee St

Pottinger St

Po Yan Street

Pound Lane

Tai Ping Shan Street

Lok Ku Road

Upper Lascar Row

Square St

Gough Street

Queen's Road Central

Stanley Street

Man Yee Lane

Li Yuen St West

Li Yuen St

Blake Garden

Kut Hing Fong

Caine Lane

Shing Wong Street

Aberdeen Street

Gage Street

Graham Street

Cochrane Street

Wellington Street

D'Aguilar Street

Wyndham

See Enlargement

Breezy Path

Staunton Street

Hollywood Road

Lyndhurst Terrace

Seymour Road

SOHO

Caine Road

Elgin Street

Old Bailey St

Robinson Road

Castle Road

Arbuthnot Road

Gleneally Road

Conduit Road

Shelley Street

Escalator

Mosque Street

Upper Albert

MID-LEVELS

Peel Street

Graham Street

Gleneally Road

Hornsey Road

Glenealy

Zoological & Botanical Garden

# Sheung Wan, Central & Admiralty

0    125    250 m

········· Sheung Wan Walking Tour

▲ Victoria Peak (552m)

Lugard Road

Old Peak Road

Tramway Path Road

May Road

Garden F

192

Brewin

Mount Austin Road

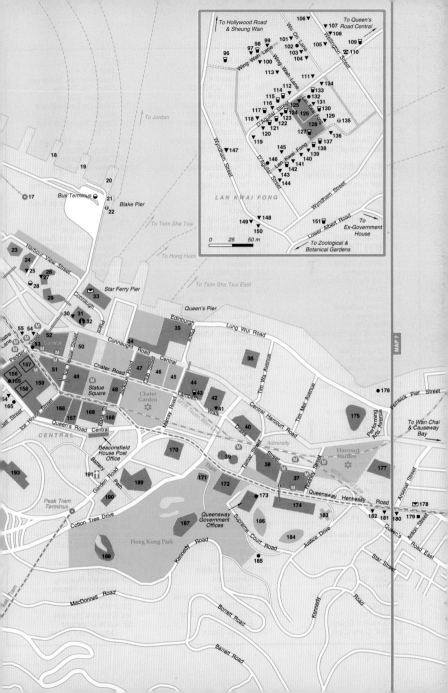

## PLACES TO STAY
45 Furama Kempinski Hotel
46 Ritz-Carlton Hotel
50 Mandarin Oriental Hotel
179 Wesley Hotel
183 JW Marriot Hotel
184 Conrad International Hotel
186 Island Shangri-La Hotel
192 YWCA Garden View International House

## PLACES TO EAT
4 Golden Snow Garden Restaurant
5 Hsin Kuang Restaurant
6 Delifrance
7 Ho Choi Seafood Restaurant
8 Korea Garden
9 Korea House Restaurant
11 Oliver's Super Sandwiches
12 Law Fu Kee Noodle Shop
25 Fauchon
27 Oliver's Super Sandwiches
30 Pier One
41 Secret Garden Korean Restaurant
54 Haagen-Dazs
55 Delifrance
58 Night Market (food stalls)
63 Kaffa Kaldi Coffee
67 Casa Lisboa
68 2 Sardines
69 Club Casa Nova
70 The Bayou
71 Desert Sky
72 Caramba!
73 Red Star Bar & Café
74 La Comida
75 Café au Lac
76 Club Scandinavia
77 Nepal
78 Stauntons Bar and Café
79 Le Fauchon
80 Sherpa
83 Miyoshiya Ramen Shop
85 Jim Chai Kee Noodle Shop
86 Fat Heung Lam Vegetarian Restaurant
89 Club Sri Lanka
90 TW Café
91 Jim Chai Kee Noodle Shop
92 Luk Yu
93 Genroku Sushi
97 The Curry Club

99 Bon Appetit Vietnamese Restaurant
100 Good Luck Thai Restaurant
101 Papillon Restaurant
103 Trio's Restaurant
104 Pearl Vietnamese Restaurant
105 Yung Kee Restaurant
106 Greenlands India Club
107 Fukuki Japanese Restaurant
108 Tai Woo Seafood Restaurant
111 Kiyotaki
112 Beirut
113 Chop Chop Café
116 Tutto Meglio
118 Al's Diner
119 Supatra's
120 Dillinger's Steak House
123 McDonald's
125 California Coffee
126 California Tower (Indochine 1929; Thai Lemongrass; Uncle Russ; Tony Roma's; California Bar)
127 Café des Artistes
128 California Entertainment Building (American Pie, Hanagushi; Il Mercato; Koh-I-Noor; Jazz Club)
129 Midnight Express
131 Zona Rosa
134 Haagen-Dazs
136 Yorohachi Japanese Restaurant
139 Post 97
140 Tutta Luna
141 Little Italy
143 Tokio Joe's
144 Va Bene
145 HK Baguette
147 Ashoka
148 La Bodega
149 Wyndham Street Thai
150 Wyndham Street Deli
152 Jimmy's Kitchen
161 City Café
162 Aujourd'hui
163 Tandoor Indian Restaurant
164 Delifrance
180 Yoshinoya Beef Bowl
181 Bacchus
182 Cosmic Noodle Bar & Café
195 Mozart Stub'n

## OTHER
1 Macau Ferry Terminal Bus Terminus
2 Shun Tak Centre
3 Western Market
10 Wing On Department Store
13 China Travel Service (CTS)
14 Government Offices & Post Office
15 Central Market
16 Hang Seng Bank Building
17 Airport Railway Central Station
18 Pier 5 - Ferries to Tuen Mun & Tai O
19 Pier 6 - Ferries to Lamma Island; Hoverferries to Tuen Mun, Tsuen Wan & Tsing Yi
20 Pier 7 - Ferries to Lantau Island, Peng Chau & Cheung Chau
21 Ferries to Jordan Road Pier
22 Public Toilets
23 Tower Three, Exchange Square
24 Forum Shopping Mall
26 Tower Two, Exchange Square
28 Exchange Square Bus Terminus (Ground Level)
29 Tower One, Exchange Square
31 Jardine House
32 HKTA Information Centre
33 General Post Office
34 City Hall (Upper Block); Public Library
35 City Hall (Lower Block)
36 Prince of Wales Building
37 United Centre
38 Queensway Plaza
39 Lippo Centre
40 Far East Finance Centre
42 Bank of America Tower
43 Bull & Bear Pub
44 Hutchison House
47 Hong Kong Club Building
48 Legislative Council Building
49 Prince's Building
51 Alexandra House
52 Swire House
53 HMV
56 Queen's Theatre
57 Lane Crawford Department Store

RICHARD I'ANSON

The familiar sight of a Star Ferry departing Kowloon Pier, Tsim Sha Tsui, for Hong Kong Island.

MAP 7

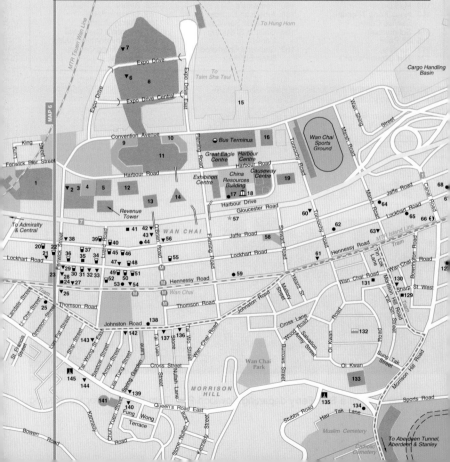

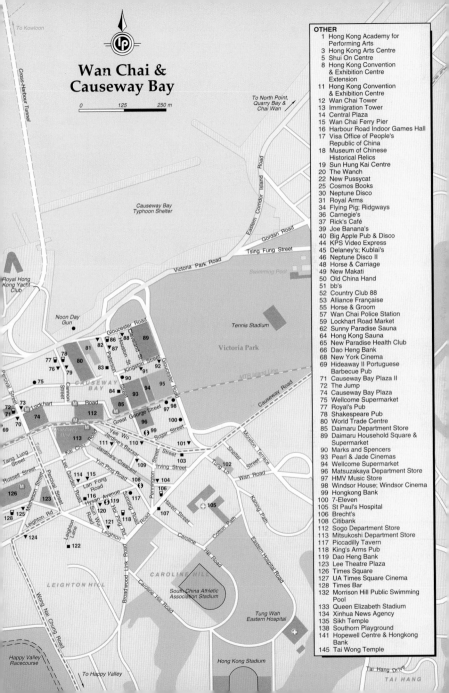

# Wan Chai & Causeway Bay

0    125    250 m

**OTHER**

1 Hong Kong Academy for
  Performing Arts
3 Hong Kong Arts Centre
5 Shui On Centre
8 Hong Kong Convention
  & Exhibition Centre
  Extension
11 Hong Kong Convention
  & Exhibition Centre
12 Wan Chai Tower
13 Immigration Tower
14 Central Plaza
15 Wan Chai Ferry Pier
16 Harbour Road Indoor Games Hall
17 Visa Office of People's
  Republic of China
18 Museum of Chinese
  Historical Relics
19 Sun Hung Kai Centre
20 The Wanch
22 New Pussycat
25 Cosmos Books
30 Neptune Disco
31 Royal Arms
34 Flying Pig; Ridgways
36 Carnegie's
37 Rick's Café
39 Joe Banana's
40 Big Apple Pub & Disco
44 KPS Video Express
45 Delaney's; Kublai's
46 Neptune Disco II
48 Horse & Carriage
49 New Makati
50 Old China Hand
51 bb's
52 Country Club 88
53 Alliance Française
55 Horse & Groom
57 Wan Chai Police Station
59 Lockhart Road Market
62 Sunny Paradise Sauna
64 Hong Kong Sauna
65 New Paradise Health Club
66 Dao Heng Bank
68 New York Cinema
69 Hideaway II Portuguese
  Barbecue Pub
71 Causeway Bay Plaza II
72 The Jump
74 Causeway Bay Plaza
75 Wellcome Supermarket
77 Royal's Pub
78 Shakespeare Pub
80 World Trade Centre
85 Daimaru Department Store
89 Daimaru Household Square &
  Supermarket
90 Marks and Spencers
93 Pearl & Jade Cinemas
94 Wellcome Supermarket
96 Matsuzakaya Department Store
97 HMV Music Store
98 Windsor House; Windsor Cinema
99 Hongkong Bank
100 7-Eleven
105 St Paul's Hospital
106 Brecht's
108 Citibank
112 Sogo Department Store
113 Mitsukoshi Department Store
117 Piccadilly Tavern
118 King's Arms Pub
119 Dao Heng Bank
123 Lee Theatre Plaza
126 Times Square
127 UA Times Square Cinema
128 Times Bar
132 Morrison Hill Public Swimming
  Pool
133 Queen Elizabeth Stadium
134 Xinhua News Agency
135 Sikh Temple
138 Southorn Playground
141 Hopewell Centre & Hongkong
  Bank
145 Tai Wong Temple

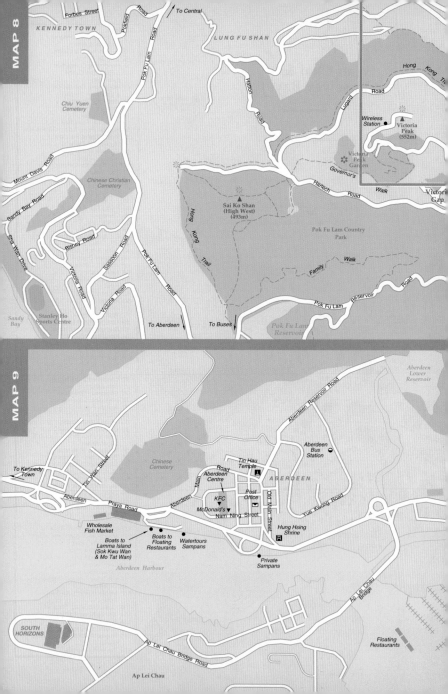

MAP 8

Forbes Street

KENNEDY TOWN

Pokfield Road

Pok Fu Lam Road

To Central

LUNG FU SHAN

Chiu Yuen
Cemetery

Hatton Road

Lugard Road

Hong Kong Trail

Road

Wireless
Station

Victoria
Peak
(552m)

Victoria
Peak
Garden

Governor's

Walk

Victoria
Gap

Mount Davis Road

Chinese Christian
Cemetery

Sai Ko Shan
(High West)
(493m)

Hong Kong Trail

Pok Fu Lam Country
Park

Hartech Road

Sandy Bay Road

Bisney Road

Seasoon Road

Pok Fu Lam Road

Victoria Road

Sha Wan Drive

Victoria Road

Family

Walk

Road

Sandy
Bay

Stanley Ho
Sports Centre

To Aberdeen

To Buses

Pok Fu Lam Reservoir

Reservoir

Pok Fu Lam
Reservoir

MAP 9

Aberdeen Reservoir Road

Aberdeen
Lower
Reservoir

To Kennedy
Town

Chinese
Cemetery

Ha Wan Street

Aberdeen Praya Road

Aberdeen Main Road

Tin Hau
Temple

Road
Aberdeen
Centre

KFC

McDonald's

Nam Ning Street

Post
Office

Old Main Street

ABERDEEN

Aberdeen
Bus
Station

Yue Kwong Road

Hung Hsing
Shrine

Wholesale
Fish Market

Boats to
Lamma Island
(Sok Kwu Wan
& Mo Tat Wan)

Boats to
Floating
Restaurants

Watertours
Sampans

Private
Sampans

Aberdeen Harbour

Ap Lei Chau
Bridge

SOUTH
HORIZONS

Ap Lei Chau Bridge Road

Floating
Restaurants

Ap Lei Chau

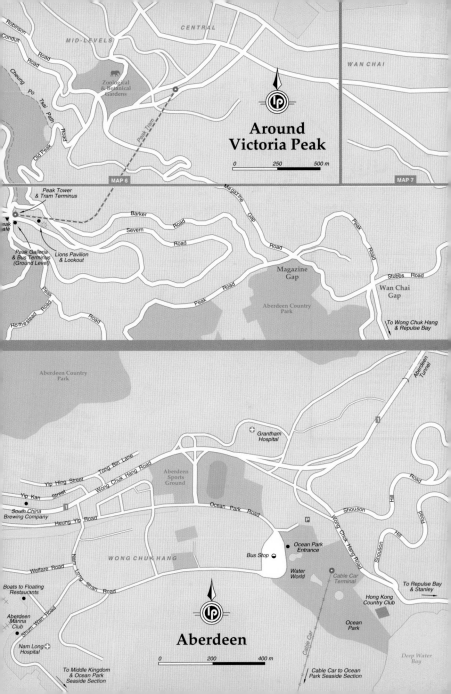

# Around Victoria Peak

0    250    500 m

MAP 6

MAP 7

Robinson Road
Conduit Road
Cheung Po Tsai Path
MID-LEVELS
CENTRAL
WAN CHAI
Zoological & Botanical Gardens
Peak Tram
Old Peak Road

Peak Tower & Tram Terminus
Peak Cafe
Peak Galleria & Bus Terminus (Ground Level)
Lions Pavilion & Lookout
Barker Road
Severn Road
Magazine Gap Road
Peak Road
Peak Road
Homestead Road
Peak Road
Peak Road
Magazine Gap
Aberdeen Country Park
Stubbs Road
Wan Chai Gap
To Wong Chuk Hang & Repulse Bay

Aberdeen Country Park
Aberdeen Tunnel
Grantham Hospital
Tong Bin Lane
Yip Hing Street
Wong Chuk Hang Road
Aberdeen Sports Ground
Yip Kan Street
South China Brewing Company
Heung Yip Road
Ocean Park Road
Shouson Hill Road
Shouson Hill Road
Welfare Road
Nam Long Shan Road
WONG CHUK HANG
Ocean Park Entrance
Bus Stop
Water World
Wong Chuk Hang Road
Cable Car Terminal
To Repulse Bay & Stanley
Hong Kong Country Club
Boats to Floating Restaurants
Aberdeen Marina Club
Shum Wan Road
Nam Long Hospital
Ocean Park
Deep Water Bay

# Aberdeen

0    200    400 m

To Middle Kingdom & Ocean Park Seaside Section
Cable Car to Ocean Park Seaside Section
Cable Car

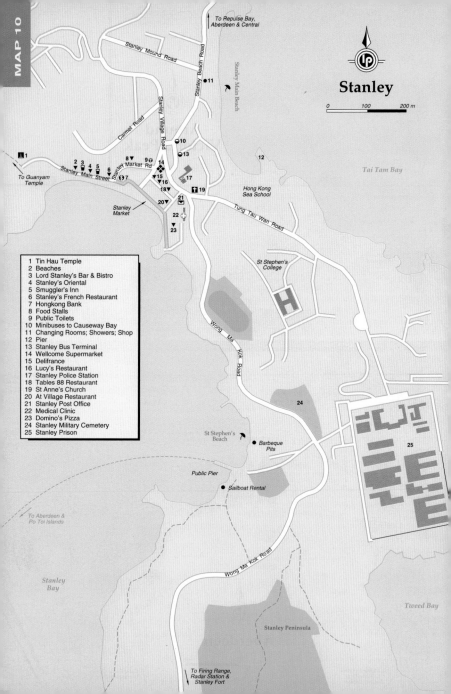

MAP 10

# Stanley

0    100    200 m

To Repulse Bay,
Aberdeen & Central

Stanley Mound Road

Stanley Beach Road

Stanley Main Beach

Stanley Village Road

Carmel Road

● 11

Tai Tam Bay

● 10

1

Stanley Market Rd

2 3    4    5    6

Stanley Main Street

8 ▼    9 ⊙

⊙ 7

● 13

14

15 ▼
16 ▼
18 ▼

17

19

21

12

Hong Kong
Sea School

Tung Tau Wan Road

20 ▼

22

23

Stanley
Market

St Stephen's
College

Wong Ma Kok Road

24

25

St Stephen's
Beach

● Barbeque
Pits

Public Pier

● Sailboat Rental

To Aberdeen &
Po Toi Islands

To Guanyam
Temple

Wong Ma Kok Road

Stanley
Bay

Tweed Bay

Stanley Peninsula

To Firing Range,
Radar Station &
Stanley Fort

1   Tin Hau Temple
2   Beaches
3   Lord Stanley's Bar & Bistro
4   Stanley's Oriental
5   Smuggler's Inn
6   Stanley's French Restaurant
7   Hongkong Bank
8   Food Stalls
9   Public Toilets
10  Minibuses to Causeway Bay
11  Changing Rooms; Showers; Shop
12  Pier
13  Stanley Bus Terminal
14  Wellcome Supermarket
15  Delifrance
16  Lucy's Restaurant
17  Stanley Police Station
18  Tables 88 Restaurant
19  St Anne's Church
20  At Village Restaurant
21  Stanley Post Office
22  Medical Clinic
23  Domino's Pizza
24  Stanley Military Cemetery
25  Stanley Prison

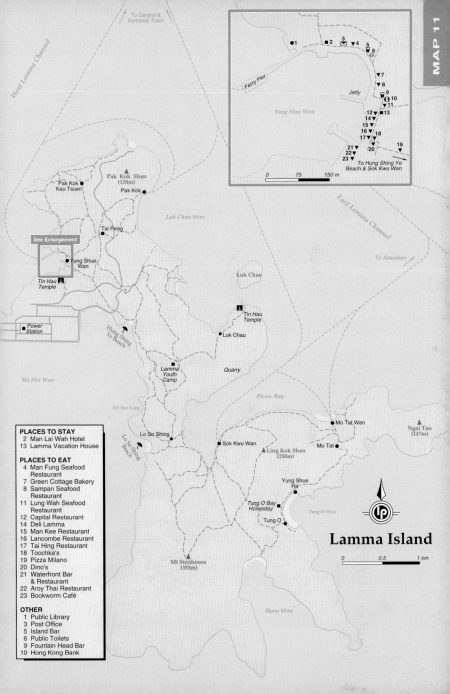

MAP 11

To Central &
Kennedy Town

West Lamma Channel

To Aberdeen

East Lamma Channel

**Inset map (top right):**

1
2
3
4
5 6
9
7
8
9
10
11
12  13
14
15
16  18
17
21
22
23  20
19

Ferry Pier

Yung Shue Wan

Jetty

To Hung Shing Ye
Beach & Sok Kwu Wan

0        75        150 m

**Main map:**

Pak Kok
Kau Tsuen

Pak Kok Shan
(138m)

Pak Kok

Tai Peng

See Enlargement

Yung Shue
Wan

Tin Hau
Temple

Power
Station

Hung Shing Ye Beach

Luk Chau Wan

Luk Chau

Tin Hau
Temple

Luk Chau

Quarry

Ha Mei Wan

Lamma
Youth
Camp

Tit Sha Lung

Picnic Bay

Lo So Shing Beach

Lo So Shing

Sok Kwu Wan

Ling Kok Shan
(250m)

Mo Tat Wan

Mo Tat

Ngai Tau
(147m)

Yung Shue
Ha

Tung O Bay
Homestay

Tung O

Tung O Wan

Mt Stenhouse
(353m)

Sham Wan

**Lamma Island**

0        0.5        1 km

## PLACES TO STAY
2   Man Lai Wah Hotel
13  Lamma Vacation House

## PLACES TO EAT
4   Man Fung Seafood
    Restaurant
7   Green Cottage Bakery
8   Sampan Seafood
    Restaurant
11  Lung Wah Seafood
    Restaurant
12  Capital Restaurant
14  Deli Lamma
15  Man Kee Restaurant
16  Lancombe Restaurant
17  Tai Hing Restaurant
18  Toochka's
19  Pizza Milano
20  Dino's
21  Waterfront Bar
    & Restaurant
22  Aroy Thai Restaurant
23  Bookworm Café

## OTHER
1   Public Library
3   Post Office
5   Island Bar
6   Public Toilets
9   Fountain Head Bar
10  Hong Kong Bank

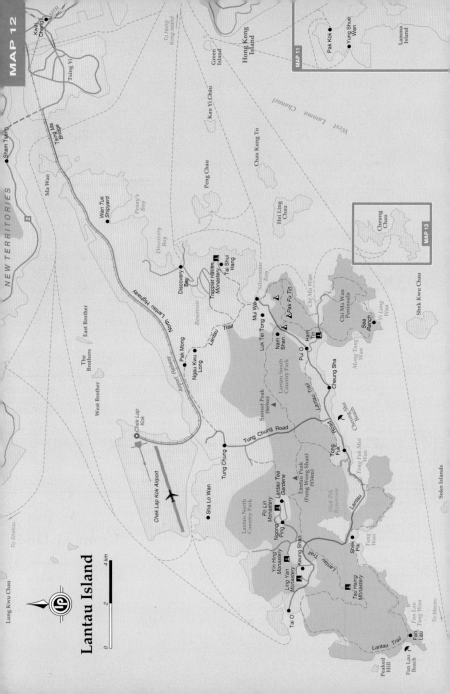

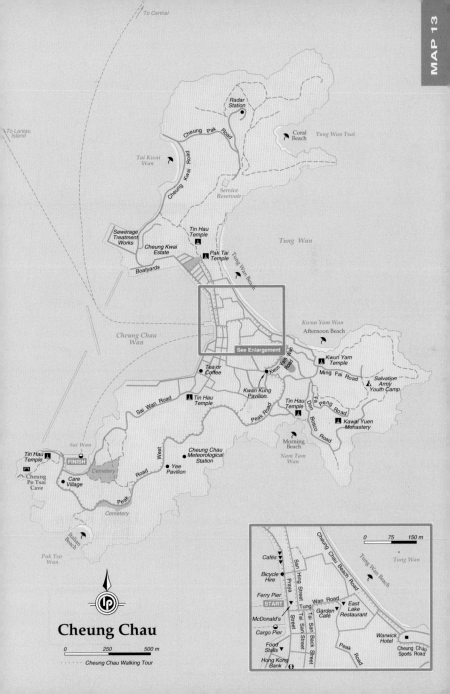

MAP 13

To Central

Radar
Station

Cheung    Pak    Road

Coral
Beach          Tung Wan Tsai

Tai Kwai
Wan

To Lantau
Island

Cheung Kwai Road

Service
Reservoir

Sewerage
Treatment
Works

Tin Hau
Temple

Cheung Kwai
Estate

Pak Tai
Temple

Tung Wan

Tung Wan Beach

Boatyards

Cheung Chau
Wan

Kwun Yam Wan

Afternoon Beach

See Enlargement

Tea or
Coffee

Kwun Yam Road

Kwun Yam
Temple

Ming Fai Road

Salvation
Army
Youth Camp

Kwan Kung
Pavilion

Sai Wan Road

Tin Hau
Temple

Peak Road

Tin Hau
Temple

Fa Peng Road

Don Bosco Road

Kawai Yuen
Monastery

West

Cheung Chau
Meteorological
Station

Yee
Pavilion

Morning
Beach

Nam Tam
Wan

Sai Wan

Tin Hau
Temple

FINISH

Cemetery

Care
Village

Cheung
Po Tsai
Cave

Peak    Road

Cemetery

Italian
Beach

Pak Tso
Wan

Cheung Chau

0        250        500 m

····· Cheung Chau Walking Tour

### Enlargement

Cafés

Bicycle
Hire

Ferry Pier

START

McDonald's

Cargo Pier

Food
Stalls

Hong Kong
Bank

San Hing Street

Praya

Tung Wan Road

Tai San Street

Tai San Back Street

Cheung Chau Beach Road

Tung Wan

Tung Wan Beach

East
Lake
Restaurant

Garden
Café

Warwick
Hotel

Peak    Road

Cheung Chau
Sports Road

0        75        150 m

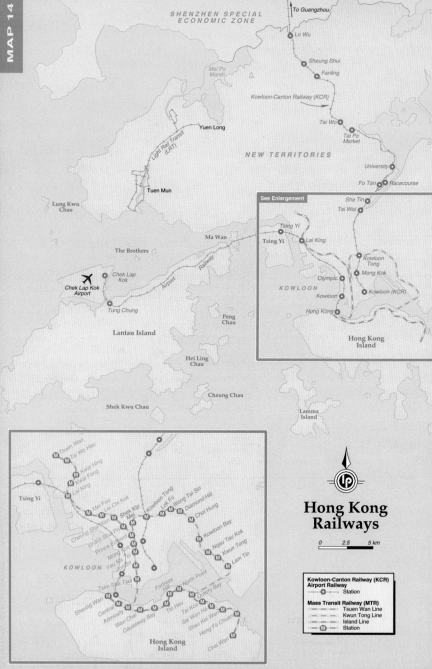

MAP 14

SHENZHEN SPECIAL
ECONOMIC ZONE

To Guangzhou

Lo Wu

Sheung Shui

Fanling

Mai Po
Marsh

Kowloon-Canton Railway (KCR)

Yuen Long

Tai Wo

Tai Po
Market

NEW TERRITORIES

Light Rail Transit
(LRT)

University

Fo Tan    Racecourse

Tuen Mun

See Enlargement

Sha Tin

Tai Wai

Tsing Yi

Lung Kwu
Chau

Tsing Yi    Lai King

Ma Wan

Kowloon
Tong

The Brothers

Railway

Olympic    Mong Kok

KOWLOON

Kowloon (KCR)

Chek Lap
Kok

Airport

Kowloon

Chek Lap Kok
Airport

Hong Kong

Tung Chung

Peng
Chau

Hong Kong
Island

Lantau Island

Hei Ling
Chau

Cheung Chau

Shek Kwu Chau

Lamma
Island

Tsuen Wan
Tai Wo Hau

Kwai Hing

Kwai Fong

Lai King

Tsing Yi

Mei Foo    Lai Chi Kok

Kowloon Tong
Lok Fu    Wong Tai Sin
Shek Kip
Mei    Diamond Hill

Choi Hung

Cheung Sha Wan
Sham Shui Po
Prince Edward

Kowloon Bay

Ngau Tau Kok

Mong Kok

Kwun Tong

Yau Ma Tei
Jordan

Lam Tin

KOWLOON

Tsim Sha Tsui

Fortress
Hill    North Point

Sheung Wan

Quarry Bay

Central

Tin Hau    Tai Koo
Sai Wan Ho

Admiralty

Wan Chai

Shau Kei Wan

Causeway Bay

Heng Fa Chuen

Chai Wan

Hong Kong
Island

## Hong Kong
## Railways

0    2.5    5 km

MAP 15

## Macau

0  250  500 m

Route of Macau Grand Prix Circuit

### PLACES TO STAY

14 Fu Hua Hotel
53 Hotel Sintra
55 Sintra Hotel
62 Pousada Ritz Hotel
63 Bela Vista Hotel
68 Pousada de Sao Tiago
21 Mondial Hotel
27 Nam Yue Hotel
29 Guia Hotel
30 Royal Hotel
31 Estoril Hotel
34 Holiday Hotel
38 East Asia Hotel
41 Grandeur Hotel
42 Kingsway Hotel
43 Mandarin Oriental Hotel
44 Pensão Tai Fat
45 Vong Hong Hospedaria
46 Sun Sun Hotel
47 San Va Hospedaria
51 Metropole Hotel

### PLACES TO EAT

13 McDonald's
25 Yaohan Department Store;
    McDonald's
32 Restaurante Violeta
48 Honggei Chuenchoi
    Sichuan Restaurant
57 Oporto Interior
58 Restaurante Litoral
59 A Lorcha Restaurant
64 Ali Curry House

### OTHER

1 Barrier Gate
2 CTM Telephone Company
3 Lin Fung Miu (Lotus Temple)
4 Canidrome
5 Mong-Ha Fortress
6 Talker Pub
7 Kun Lam Temple
8 Our Lady of Piety Cemetery
9 Montanha Russa Garden
10 Macau-Seac Tin Hau Temple
11 Pak Val Plaza
12 CTM Telephone Company
15 Luís de Camoes Museum
16 Camoes Grotto & Gardens
17 Old Protestant Cemetery
18 Kiang Wu Hospital
19 Lou Lim Ieoc Gardens
20 Flora Garden
22 Sun Yatsen Memorial Home
23 Grand Prix Control Tower; Stands
24 Hong Kong-Macau Ferry Terminal;
    Tourist Office
26 Jai Alai Casino
28 Guia Lighthouse
31 St Michael's Cemetery
33 St Michael's Cemetery
35 Façade of St Paul's Cathedral
36 Monte Fort
37 Macau-Guangzhou Ferry Terminal
39 St Dominic's Church
40 Macau Forum
49 St Augustine's Church
50 Leal Senado
52 Hong Kong Bank
54 Bank of China
56 St Lawrence's Church
60 A-Ma Temple
61 Penha Church
65 Governor's Residence
66 Maritime Museum
67 Barra Hill

To Hong Kong

To Taipa, Airport & Coloane

To Guangzhou

CHINA

Sun Yat-sen Memorial Park

Ilha Verde

Inner Harbour

Reservoir

Outer Harbour

Jetfoil Pier

Baía da Praia Grande

Nam Van Lakes

# Map Legend

Note: not all symbols displayed above appear in this book

## BOUNDARIES

International Boundary
Provincial Boundary

## ROUTES

Freeway, with Route Number
Major Road, with Tunnel
Minor Road
City Road, with steps
City Street
City Lane
Train Route, with Station
Tram Route
Metro, Tsuen Wan Line
Metro, Kwun Tong Line
Metro, Island Line
Cable Car or Chairlift
Ferry Route
Walking Track/Tour

## AREA FEATURES

Building
Beach
Christian Cemetery
Non-Christian Cemetery
Hotel
Market
Park, Gardens
Pedestrian Mall
Urban Area

## HYDROGRAPHIC FEATURES

Canal
Coastline
Creek, River
Lake, Intermittent Lake
Rapids, Waterfalls
Salt Lake
Swamp

## SYMBOLS

| | National Capital | CAPITAL |
| | Provincial Capital | CAPITAL |
| | City | CITY |
| | Town | Town |
| | Village | Village |

Place to Stay
Camping Ground
Hut/Chalet
Place to Eat
Pub or Bar

Airport
Bank
Castle or Fort
Cathedral, Church
Cliff or Escarpment
Hospital
Lighthouse
Lookout
Metro Entrance/Exit
Monument
Mosque
Mountain
Museum
One Way Street

Parking
Picnic Area
Police Station
Post Office
Shopping Centre
Shrine
Stately Home
Swimming Pool
Telephone
Temple, Monastery
Toilet
Tourist Information
Transport
Zoo